The Sophists in Plato's Dialogues

The Sophists in Plato's Dialogues

David D. Corey

SUNY PRESS

Published by State University of New York Press, Albany

Printed in the United States of America

For information, contact State University of New York Press, Albany, NY
www.sunypress.edu

Production, Jenn Bennett
Marketing, Michael Campochiaro

Library of Congress Cataloging-in-Publication Data

Corey, David D.
The sophists in Plato's Dialogues / David D. Corey.
pages cm
Includes bibliographical references and index.
ISBN 978-1-4384-5617-1 (hc : alk. paper)
ISBN 978-1-4384-5618-8 (pb : alk. paper)
ISBN 978-1-4384-5619-5 (ebook)
1. Plato. Dialogues. 2. Sophists (Greek philosophy) I. Title.
B395.C654 2015
184—dc23

2014022078

10 9 8 7 6 5 4 3 2 1

To my teachers of Greek
Matthew Christ, Nate Greenberg, Jim Helm, and Tom VanNortwick
And to Cecil Eubanks

CONTENTS

ACKNOWLEDGMENTS

This book was made possible in part by a generous research leave from Baylor University and through the expert assistance of numerous graduate students at Baylor, especially Matt Dinan, Patrick Cain, Josh King, and Corrine Peters. Several friends and colleagues commented on parts of the manuscript along the way. Rob Miner, Jake Howland, Mary Nichols, Catherine Zuckert, and Cary Nederman were especially helpful. Avi Mintz at the University of Tulsa deserves special thanks for reading the entire manuscript, offering detailed comments, and tirelessly pressing me to get this book in print.

Above all, I thank my wife, Elizabeth Corey, who has read the entire book multiple times and been an unwavering source of support and inspiration.

Earlier versions of Chapters 4 and 5 appeared respectively in *History of Political Thought* 29, no. 1 (2008): 1–26; and in Christopher A. Dustin and Denise Schaeffer, eds., *Socratic Philosophy and Its Others* (Lanham: Lexington Press, 2013), 91–114. They appear here with the kind permission of these presses.

David D. Corey
Waco, Texas
May 2014

ABBREVIATIONS

Abbreviated Titles for Works of Plato

Ap.	*Apology*
Charm.	*Charmides*
Crat.	*Cratylus*
Cri.	*Crito*
Euthyd.	*Euthydemus*
Euthphr.	*Euthyphro*
Gorg.	*Gorgias*
Hipp. Maj.	*Hippias Major*
Hipp. Min.	*Hippias Minor*
Lach.	*Laches*
Men.	*Meno*
Phd.	*Phaedo*
Phdr.	*Phaedrus*
Prm.	*Parmenides*
Prt.	*Protagoras*
Rep.	*Republic*
Symp.	*Symposium*
Soph.	*Sophist*
Tht.	*Theaetetus*

OTHER ABBREVIATIONS

DK	Diels and Kranz, *Die Fragmente der Vorsokratiker*
DL	Diogenes Laertius, *Lives of Eminent Philosophers*
EN	Aristotle, *Nicomachean Ethics*
Il.	Homer, *Iliad*
Mem.	Xenophon, *Memorabilia*
Nem.	Pindar, *Nemean Ode*
Od.	Homer, *Odyssey*
Th.	Hesiod, *Theogony*
TLG	*Thesaurus Linguae Graecae*
WD	Hesiod, *Works and Days*

ONE

INTRODUCTION

Tradition ascribes thirty-five dialogues to Plato, and more than half of them (21) touch on the theme of sophistry in one way or another.[1] In some dialogues, Plato casts the sophists as leading interlocutors of Socrates; in others they are mentioned for their intellectual tendencies and pedagogical practices. Frequently Plato exposes readers to hearsay about the sophists—sometimes friendly, sometimes hostile. At times he has Socrates defend them, but not always. And, constantly, he hints at the many ways in which Socrates seems both like and unlike the sophists. The richness and frequency of Plato's handling of the sophists gives rise naturally to certain questions: What was Plato's purpose in presenting these controversial figures? What was his view of them? And how did he expect readers to understand their relationship to Socrates?

This book springs from the suspicion that such questions have not been adequately answered. The dominant and indeed almost universally held view is that Plato was the sophists' implacable foe, that he presented them in his dialogues in order to discredit them, and that his campaign against them was motivated by a deep desire to separate what he regarded as the sham wisdom of the sophists from the genuine wisdom of his teacher, Socrates.[2] This view no doubt has its attractions, not least of which is that it captures something of a dramatic, almost epochal struggle for the soul of Athens and the integrity of philosophy in Plato's handling of the sophists. But how well does it ultimately line up with evidence from the dialogues?

In his dialogue, *The Sophist*, Plato has a silent Socrates look on while a stranger from Elea investigates the nature of sophistry with a pupil, Theaetetus. The dialogue ends when, after prodigious effort, the interlocutors finally agree on a definition of sophistry. The definition is intensely negative,[3] but it is also tendentious—or so readers of this dialogue should understand. For it fails to accommodate the full range of sophistic traits that Theaetetus and the stranger had outlined over the dialogue's labyrinthine course. Moreover, and just as importantly, around the midpoint of the dialogue, Theaetetus and the stranger hesitatingly agree that Socrates (or some group of figures indistinguishable from Socrates) should be classed among the sophists for attempting to educate the young by means of a purgative art of refutation (231a–c). One thus wonders: Why would Plato's chief dialogue on the sophists (if the *Sophist* can be described that way) dismiss these figures on obviously tendentious grounds and, at the same time, allow Socrates to appear vexingly intermingled with them, if his purpose were indeed to distinguish Socrates and the sophists once and for all?

Plato's handling of sophistry in the *Meno* raises similar questions. When Socrates there suggests to Anytus that people who want to learn virtue or excellence (*aretē*) might do well to consult the sophists, Anytus reacts with horror: the sophists are "plainly the ruin and corruption of those who associate with them!"[4] But Plato does not leave it there. He rather has Socrates interrogate Anytus: Is it really credible to suppose that a great sophist like Protagoras has been corrupting all of Greece for forty years while receiving pay and gratitude in the process? The question goes unanswered, so Socrates continues: "Has one of the sophists done you some injustice, Anytus? Or why are you so harsh toward them?"[5] Anytus responds notoriously that he has in fact never had any experience of the sophists at all. To which Socrates reasonably retorts that Anytus must be some kind of prophet; for how else could he know whether there is something good or bad in a matter of which he has no experience? Thus is Anytus revealed to be a thoughtless proponent of a mere prejudice against the sophists. But, again, why would Plato have Socrates stand up for the sophists in this way if his goal were to discredit them?

Or consider Plato's fascinating presentation of the sophist, Prodicus. Though there is no dialogue called the *Prodicus*, this sophist is treated in more than a dozen different places in the Platonic corpus, once as a character in the *Protagoras* and often as the originator of certain useful ideas or skills that Socrates wants to consider.[6] In multiple dialogues, Socrates claims to have studied with Prodicus, and he frequently goes on to employ one of this sophist's best known skills (an art of making careful distinctions, called *diairesis*) in order to dispel intellectual confusion and expose fallacies. But why would Plato portray this sophist so sympathetically and indeed go so far as to stress his role as Socrates' teacher if his purpose were to dissociate Socrates from the sophists and tarnish their reputation?

Further examples could easily be cited to suggest that Plato's handling of the sophists is more varied and complex than frequently assumed. But rather than pile example on example, I set out a summary of the argument that emerges gradually over the chapters that follow. The argument of this book is that Plato did not cast the sophists merely to criticize them, much less to villainize them or attack them as the enemies of philosophy.[7] Rather he treated them with remarkable care as teachers engaged in an enterprise similar in many ways to that of Socrates. He used them, moreover, to illuminate what was most distinctive about Socratic philosophy while at the same time supplying readers with necessary propaedeutic experiences to begin to engage in it.

On a more particular level, my thesis involves three basic claims. First, I argue that Plato made crucial and sometimes fundamental distinctions among the various figures we today call sophists. Plato's sophists were neither a school nor a movement. Specific figures differed from each other in manifest ways—in what they studied, how and what they taught, how they stood in relation to conventional civic norms and, most importantly, how they related to Socrates. Moreover the sophists, on Plato's account, were categorically different from another important group of intellectuals, the "rhetoricians," even though both groups taught rhetoric.[8] In Plato the sophists are defined with remarkable consistency as professional teachers of aretē (human excellence or virtue) while the rhetoricians made no claim to teach aretē and in fact tended to denounce its conventional forms. Based on this important distinction, I claim that Plato treats only five major sophists in the dialogues. These are Protagoras, Prodicus, Hippias, and the brothers Euthydemus and Dionysodorus. Contrary to the modern tradition of classifying the sophists, Plato does not typically present such figures as Gorgias, Thrasymachus, Callicles, Polus, Antiphon or Critias as sophists in the precise sense of the word.[9]

Second, I argue that Plato intentionally discloses deep affinities between Socrates and the sophists, affinities that approach the very heart of what it means to philosophize in the Socratic manner. One affinity is their shared interested in aretē. At a time when most intellectuals focused primarily on questions of cosmology, religion, and natural science, Socrates and the sophists focused squarely on human excellence. It was Socrates who would become famous for pulling philosophy "down from the heavens," implanting it in the cities of men, and compelling it to attend to questions of virtue and vice.[10] But the truth is that the sophists also pulled philosophy down from the heavens. The so-called Socratic turn was anticipated by Protagoras, the oldest of the sophists, who maintained that the gods were too obscure to admit of knowledge and that man was, at any rate, the "measure of all things."

Another affinity between Socrates and the sophists relates to certain shared techniques. Scholars have long noted that Socrates' practice of *elenchus* (refutation) bears a strong resemblance to the method of eristic (verbal combat) developed by Protagoras, Euthydemus, and Dionysodorus. Both Socrates and the sophists crafted speeches that made "weaker arguments appear stronger." But this is not all. Plato's Socrates also candidly acknowledged a methodological debt to Prodicus in the dialogues. And he likewise shared with other sophists a broad range of rhetorical tactics, some aimed at pedagogical effectiveness, others at minimizing the potential friction that could sometimes arise between intellectuals and the city.

A final affinity between Socrates and the sophists lies in their mutual recognition of a basic epistemological insight. With the exception of Hippias, who appears to have been an outlier in this regard, all the sophists as well as Socrates recognized that appearances (*phainomena*) both physical and intellectual were vexingly unstable. Such things as justice, beauty, piety, and nobility seemed susceptible of radical change depending on the angle from which they were viewed; and Socrates as well as the sophists were interested in the implications of this for human life. Socrates tried to respond to this problem by seeking some plane on which ideas might ultimately stand still, the plane of the "forms" as he calls it in some of Plato's accounts. This differed markedly from the various ways in which the sophists responded to the experience of instability. But that Socrates and the sophists both recognized and reacted to this problem put them in a class of their own and often brought them into fascinating conflict with traditionalists of various stripes.

The third and final part of my argument addresses the reasons why Plato might have wanted to emphasize these manifold similarities between Socrates and the sophists. This is something that cannot be explained (or not easily) on the assumption that Plato was the sophists' inveterate enemy. Again, why would someone who ostensibly wished to dissociate Socrates from the sophists once and for all allow readers to see so many deep affinities? I argue that Plato casts the relationship between Socrates and the sophists in such complex terms for two reasons. One is propaedeutic. If Socratic philosophy is understood as an effort to respond to the instability of appearances, then it can *only* be engaged in by individuals who sense that instability. Yet human beings typically attempt to suppress such uncomfortable experiences, failing to acknowledge that, for instance, their understanding of justice does not account for what they themselves deem just in every instance. People have multiple, competing understandings of important moral concepts vying for primacy in their minds, but they do not realize their inconsistency. And here the sophists have a valuable role to play. In Plato's account, Socrates *uses* the sophists and sometimes plays the role of sophist himself in order to awaken interlocutors and readers from their dogmatic slumber. He uses them to reveal the inconstant nature of appearances. This generates wonder (*thaumas*), which, according to Socrates, is nothing else than the beginning (*archē*) of philosophy (*Theaetetus*, 155d).

The second reason Plato casts the relationship between Socrates and the sophists in such complex terms can be described as *protreptic*—not simply preparing students for philosophy, but positively leading them to practice it. What is philosophy? This question is hardly exhausted by saying it is Socrates' unique way of searching out something above and beyond the realm of vacillating appearances. Certainly it is that. But it is, beyond that, a whole way of life, a commitment to honesty and integrity in the face of the unknown, a disposition to seek lovingly and patiently for the source of our being, a dissatisfaction with partial answers and false prophets, and above all an understanding of what, given the conditions in which we find ourselves, it means to live a life of excellence or virtue (aretē). The love of wisdom (*philosophia*) as such is essentially related to aretē, and yet wisdom and aretē are *themselves* among those problematic appearances that admit of instability. What wisdom and aretē finally mean looks different depending on the angle from which they are viewed.

Plato did not try to suppress this fact. He did not compose dialogues that uniformly celebrate Socrates as a philosopher with sound answers about wisdom and virtue; nor did he orchestrate a blanket dismissal of the sophists as impostors. Rather, he wrote dialogues in which Socrates and particular sophists (among other interlocutors) appear vexingly interrelated. Indeed, as a rule, the closer one looks at Plato's treatments of Socrates and the sophists, the more do apparent differences give way to similarities. This pattern can be appreciated in every dialogue relating to the sophists. Plato has made them difficult to distinguish. But why would he do that? My argument is that he does so because he sees in the relationship between Socrates and the sophists a possible entry point to the practice of philosophy itself. He sees that readers who honestly admit that their first impressions on the matter of Socrates and the sophists are inadequate may well be fit to seek the truth about philosophy and in so seeking actually to engage in it. This is what I mean when I say that Plato uses the problem of Socrates and the sophists as a protreptic.

Connection to Recent Scholarship

How does this book's argument relate to recent work on the sophists and their presentation in Plato? Studies of Greek sophistry have been bountiful in recent decades, and to a certain extent all such studies necessarily touch on Plato, for he is one of the most valuable sources of information we have on the sophists.[11] But the primary aim of almost all recent scholarship has been not so much to deepen our understanding of Plato's rich portraits or his goals in presenting the sophists, but rather to uncover facts about the "historical" sophists, washed clean of any distortions that may have been wrought by the biases of Plato or other conveyers of information. Scholars have thus been engaged in a subtle and challenging sifting operation—poring over sources such as Plato's dialogues for "fragments" of information, which, once sifted, might be reassembled into an unbiased account.[12]

Moreover, and more significantly given the aims of the present study, scholars engaged in the effort to uncover the historical sophists have tended to rely heavily on the common view that Plato was the sophists' enemy as a starting point for analysis. Thus Eric Havelock expressed his method of reconstructing the sophists as follows: "the historian, even as he discounts Plato's judgmental evaluation of sophistic, can find in Plato's hostility a valuable guide, a signpost, to what precisely sophist doctrine was. *It was everything that Platonism was not.*"[13] Similarly, G.B. Kerferd began his study by lamenting that "for much of our information we are dependent upon Plato's profoundly hostile treatment of [the sophists], presented with all the power of his literary genius and driven home with a philosophical impact that is little short of overwhelming."[14] And John Dillon and Tania Gergel begin their more recent study by announcing that "Plato is, of course, a declared foe of the sophists and all that they stand for, so that we cannot expect from him a sympathetic portrayal," even if Plato does (according to them) occasionally allow one or two sophists to speak briefly in their own voices.[15]

Against this backdrop I want to stress that this book is not primarily an effort to understand the historical sophists, but rather a work of Plato scholarship. I am interested first and foremost in what Plato thought about the sophists and what his purposes were in casting them in the dialogues. I write on the assumption that Plato's views were complex and his purposes not always transparent; and I write, moreover, under the conviction that to strive to understand what Plato thought about the sophists is an activity worthwhile per se. After all, save for Socrates, who wrote nothing, Plato is perhaps the most informed commentator on the sophists we have. And he is not merely a commentator but also a penetrating philosophical interpreter of the first rank. To learn, therefore, what Plato thought—not just on the surface but in depth—about figures as alluring and controversial as the sophists should be fascinating in its own right.

That having been said, it may indeed be an incidental benefit of this study to challenge and perhaps change the way historians of the sophists assess some of the fragments within the sophistic corpus, especially those from Plato's dialogues. For if it turns out that Plato's relationship to the sophists cannot be simply characterized in terms of opposition, then scholars may be led to reconsider any fragments that have been interpreted on that basis.

This study owes a great deal to the work of diverse specialists who have written on Plato's handling of particular sophists,[16] and it contributes to an interdisciplinary current in Plato scholarship that has become more and more visible over the past fifty years. I now say a few words about this approach to reading Plato as a way of foreshadowing the method that is employed here.

The Literary-Philosophic Approach to Plato

The past century has witnessed some astonishing advances in the way we read Plato. The change has been frequently remarked and turns chiefly on recognizing the philosophical importance of the "literary and dramatic aspects" of the dialogues.[17] With some wit and lightheartedness, Malcolm Schofield has described the seismic shift as follows:

> In the bad old days questions about the literary properties of the Platonic dialogues were not much canvassed by philosophical readers—unless they happened to be Straussians or (in even older days) Neo-Platonists. [But now] . . . the relation of form to content has become a prime subject of philosophical interest, sometimes handled gushingly or flat-footedly, but at best with tact and sophistication. . . .[18]

The bad old days to which Schofield alludes are in truth not so far behind us; and many scholars still continue to trudge along as if nothing has changed. But something has changed. The old way of interpreting the dialogues was chiefly doctrinal and didactic. That is to say, scholars treated the dialogues as tantamount to philosophical treatises designed to teach Plato's doctrines straightforwardly to readers. That the dialogues were not in fact treatises, but rich literary creations with carefully constructed characters, settings, conflicts, resolutions, reversals, and so on, was regarded as unimportant. Perhaps such literary aspects would make the philosophical doctrines more pleasant to consider, but they were not thought to have serious bearing on Plato's doctrinal articulation. Form and content were thus viewed as largely unrelated.

Along with this way of interpreting Plato came the "mouthpiece" assumption and a deep interest in compositional chronology. The mouthpiece assumption was the pervasive but problematic belief that Plato's own views were more or less identical to those of the lead character in any given dialogue (usually but not always Socrates). The lead character thus spoke as Plato's mouthpiece. This view has come under devastating criticism in recent years not only because it is difficult to see how such radically diverse characters as Socrates, Parmenides, the Eleatic Stranger, and the Athenian Stranger could serve as so many mouthpieces for one and the same man, but also because it approximates a "fallacy" to assume that the views and arguments of literary characters are the same as those of their author. We do not make this assumption when reading Shakespeare; why should we make it when reading Plato?[19]

The chief problem with the mouthpiece assumption is that the views of Plato's imagined spokesmen often change from dialogue to dialogue and sometimes entail outright contradictions. Even the views of Socrates alone, as Plato presents him, appear inconsistent across the dialogues. It was primarily as a way of responding to this problem that the interest in compositional chronology arose. If the dialogues seemed to contain changes of position, then perhaps this could be explained in terms of the "development of Plato's thought" over the course of his career.[20] If so, then knowledge of the dates of the dialogues would be crucial for explaining inconsistencies in the corpus. The project of Platonic chronology thus took off, and various accounts of Plato's intellectual trajectory were offered in light of rival schemes of dating and grouping of the dialogues.[21]

But the interest in compositional chronology has likewise come under criticism in recent decades and is today regarded by many interpreters of Plato as relatively unimportant compared to other interpretive approaches and problems.[22] Following in the footsteps of Joseph Cropsey, Catherine Zuckert has at length demonstrated the fruitfulness of arranging the dialogues according to Socrates' biography (i.e., the dramatic dates of the dialogues) rather than the date of composition.[23] Similarly scholars of the Tübingen School, believing the purpose of the dialogues to lie elsewhere than in Plato's communication of serious doctrine, have loosened the grip of the chronological orientation in parts of Germany and Italy.[24] And a widely eclectic group of scholars in the United States with backgrounds in philosophy, literature, and political philosophy have made huge strides in showing the ways in which certain literary and dramatic features of the dialogues intermingle with philosophical arguments to shape the meaning of a dialogue as a whole.[25]

Taking stock of the massive shift away from reading the dialogues as Platonic treatises toward reading them as literary and dramatic works of philosophy, Gerald Press has remarked that the "most broadly shared conviction" among the new generation of Plato scholars is that "thought and art, philosophy and literature, ideas and their expression, form and content are not to be distinguished from each other, but rather are marked in their interpenetration." Indeed the question now according to Press "is no longer *whether* literary and dramatic matters are important for understanding the dialogues, but *how*."[26]

This is precisely what numerous studies over the past fifty years have begun to address. Though this is not the place for a lengthy "how to" treatment of various hermeneutic techniques, it will be useful nevertheless to list a few of the most important insights made by scholars attentive to the literary dimension of the dialogues. Here are just a few guiding principles.

1. Most characters in the Platonic dialogues are carefully drawn psychological "types," and the arguments made by Socrates (in the dialogues in which he takes the lead) are more often than not designed specifically with that type in mind. This does not necessarily mean the dialogues contain no generalizable doctrine; but it does mean that to decipher whatever teachings may be available, one must look beyond the context-dependent remarks of Socrates to a particular character; one must transpose from the particular to the general.
2. Plato often undercuts or otherwise qualifies the surface "doctrine" of a dialogue by confronting readers with various obstacles. These include contradictions (blatant or subtle) as the argument unfolds, fallacies in the proofs, and friction between words and deeds—which is to say between the teachings on offer and the actual behavior of the one offering them. Careful study of such obstacles often reveals deeper insights into a dialogue's meaning.
3. Plato leads the way toward deeper interpretations of his dialogues also through his use of various literary cues. These include cues deriving from the formal structure of the dialogue; from allusions to (and alteration of) myths, dramas, epics and historical events; from emphases placed at nodal

> points such as openings, endings, and centers; and from word play such as metaphor, ambiguity, double entendre, and the like.

One could go on to discuss the importance of irony on multiple levels of the dialogues, the importance of rhetoric in general, as well as Plato's tendency to bury crucial information in the middle of apparent digressions from the main argument. But the best place to treat such techniques of writing and interpretation is in the chapters ahead, where they can be presented and evaluated in practice. The present list of hermeneutic considerations is only meant to be indicative.

Such has been the shift in Platonic interpretation over the past century. My own attitude toward this shift is largely enthusiastic. Certainly the "mouthpiece" approach to interpreting Plato needed to be revised, and the belief that the meaning of any given dialogue is exhausted by its arguments on the surface has been shown to be grossly inadequate. Moreover the new insights and hermeneutic techniques that have resulted from taking the literary dimensions of the dialogues seriously have been nothing short of revolutionary. Still, I would stress that the greatest scholarship from the "bad old days" of Platonic interpretation has remained extremely valuable as I have set about the task of understanding Plato's treatment of the sophists. I therefore repair often to Plato scholars from generations past in the chapters ahead and have found engaging them quite fruitful.

But returning now to the matter of the sophists, the larger point must be stressed. With few exceptions, the revolution in Platonic interpretation that has occurred gradually over the past century and enriched our understanding of Plato's thinking and his purposes has not made its way to the banks of sophistic scholarship.[27] Even the latest studies touching on Plato's attitude toward the sophists continue to treat the dialogues as communicating Plato's "doctrine" more or less transparently on the surface, and most continue to employ the "mouthpiece" assumption.[28] The work that lies ahead is thus to reexamine the question of Plato's attitude toward the sophists through the lens of the more refined hermeneutics now at our disposal.

To do this, I begin in Chapter 2 by reconsidering the various definitions and characterizations of the sophists in Plato's dialogues, paying careful attention to the characters who are speaking, the dramatic situations in which the speeches occur, and the overarching purposes of the dialogues in which they occur. This method yields a relatively clear and startling result, which is that Plato used the word "sophist" in its most precise sense to refer to figures with two traits in common: the claim to teach virtue (aretē), and the practice of charging a fee. I thus define the Platonic sophists as "paid teachers of aretē," and draw a line between the sophists (Protagoras, Prodicus, Hippias, Euthydemus, and Dionysodorus) and the rhetoricians (Thrasymachus, Gorgias, Polus, and Callicles). Again, even though all or most sophists taught rhetoric, they did so as part of a broader curriculum in *aretē*. The rhetoricians by contrast did not claim to teach aretē. Failure to mark this distinction has been the chief cause of false generalizations about the nature and role of the sophists in Plato's dialogues. Moreover, as teachers of aretē the sophists were engaged in an activity that overlapped significantly with that of Socrates. Even though Socrates did not accept fees and claimed not to know what aretē was (much less whether it could be taught), his fundamental interest in aretē as an intellectual problem for himself and for his students brought him inevitably into contact with the sophists. But what was the precise relationship between the sophistic and Socratic approach to aretē? And what was Plato doing in general with the sophists in the dialogues—that is, what should readers take away from Plato's handling of them? These questions arise naturally once the definitional spadework has been done, and the aim of my subsequent chapters is to consider each sophist with such questions in mind.

To this end, Chapter 3 offers fresh examination of the so-called Great Speech in Plato's *Protagoras* and reveals something of the depth of Plato's respect for this sophist. Often the Great Speech is treated as Protagoras' attempt to demonstrate that virtue can be taught. But it entails much more. The challenge Socrates puts to Protagoras has a rhetorical and political dimension that scholars have not yet fully explored. And in meeting Socrates' challenge, Protagoras reveals himself not only to be a thinker and teacher of the first order, but also to have much in common with Socrates. Both, for instance, use myth in similar ways as a pedagogical tool; and both engage in forms of veiled speech in order to communicate different messages concomitantly to different audiences. Moreover, recognition of these similarities facilitates a richer and deeper account of what separates Protagoras and Socrates. In this chapter, the differences between them center on Socrates' abiding search for a "saving knowledge" that goes beyond

Protagoras's conventional moral orientation and which leads him (Socrates) to take a more circumspect view of such key Protagorean concepts as "virtue" and "prudence."

Chapter 4 studies the figure of Prodicus as he is treated across numerous dialogues, most importantly in the *Protagoras* and *Theaetetus*. Prodicus is described on multiple occasions as Socrates' teacher, and I argue that these reports are true. I then show what Socrates likely learned from Prodicus, as well as the ways in which Socrates' own philosophical and pedagogical enterprise went beyond what his teacher could offer.

Chapter 5 is an analysis of Plato's treatment of Hippias in the *Hippias Minor*. Hippias is in many ways the most roughly handled of Plato's sophists, at least on the surface. However, by focusing on the chief literary theme that courses through the dialogue—the theme of *polytropia*, or "versatility," as it is sometimes translated—I show how Hippias supplies a valuable touchstone for evaluating Socrates' own polytropic tendencies. Nowhere does Socrates appear more sophistic than in this short dialogue, and yet through this very portrait readers can see some precise ways in which Socrates differs from the sophists, particularly in his self-awareness of his polytropic tendencies and his ability to marshal them in the service of philosophy.

Whereas Chapters 3, 4, and 5 focus chiefly on the fascinating similarities and differences between Socrates and specific sophists, Chapters 6 and 7 turn also to the question of Plato's intention in incorporating the sophists into the dialogues. In these chapters my argument about Plato's propaedeutic and protreptic purposes comes to the fore. Chapter 6 analyzes Plato's *Euthydemus* and shows how Socrates' practice of protreptic on a pupil named Clinias is also designed as a protreptic for Socrates' auditor, Crito, and even more for us, Plato's readers. Throughout the chapter Socrates and the sophists are compared and contrasted, and this is revealed in the end to be a necessary part of philosophic education. In Chapter 7, I return to the figure of Protagoras, this time as he is portrayed posthumously in Plato's *Theaetetus*, and show again how Plato's Socrates carefully orchestrates an encounter with Protagorean sophistry as a means of advancing his pedagogical and philosophical goals.

The final chapter of the book, Chapter 8, turns to the passages most frequently cited in support of Plato's supposed critique of the sophists, passages from the *Meno, Gorgias, Republic*, and *Sophist*. Using the same dramatic, literary, and philosophical methods of interpretation employed throughout this study, I show how unconvincing these passages are as evidence for Plato's ill will toward the sophists and how they instead support the basic arguments developed here: that the sophists and rhetoricians are distinct groups that Plato handled quite differently, that Socrates and the sophists have more in common than first meets the eye, and that Plato uses the sophists in the dialogues for chiefly propaedeutic and protreptic purposes.

TWO

DEFINING THE PLATONIC SOPHISTS

> We had better, I think, begin by studying the sophist and try to bring his nature to light in a clear formula. At present, you see, all that you and I possess in common is the name. The thing to which each of us gives that name we may perhaps have privately before our minds, but it is always desirable to have reached an agreement about the thing itself by means of explicit statements, rather than be content to use the same word without formulating what it means. It is not so easy to comprehend this group we intend to examine or to say what it means to be a sophist.
>
> —The Eleatic Stranger in Plato's *Sophist* 218b–c, trans. Cornford

This chapter addresses three closely related questions: first, who were the sophists in Plato's dialogues? In other words, which figures (e.g., Protagoras, Gorgias, Thrasymachus) does Plato present as sophists? Next, what is a sophist according to Plato—what definitional criteria underlie his use of the term? And, finally, how should we understand the significance of the sophists for Plato? This last question cannot be fully answered here and is treated over the course of the book. But the first two questions can be answered. They are, indeed, the necessary foundation for approaching the third question correctly. If one errs in determining who and what the sophists were according to

Plato, then one will almost certainly formulate false conclusions about their significance.

Popular responses to all three questions often miss the mark. A prevalent view, for example, is that the sophists were figures like Thrasymachus in the *Republic* or Callicles in the *Gorgias*. Prevalent, too, is the view that "sophist" for Plato was perfectly synonymous with "teacher of immorality," or "teacher of rhetoric," or "bad logician." And almost universal is the view that the significance of the sophists for Plato lay in their role as enemies of the Socratic-Platonic philosophical endeavor and of well-ordered civic life. This is why Plato is supposed to have attacked them. But does Plato really attack the sophists as enemies of philosophy and the state? Is this really the nature of his engagement with them?[1]

In this chapter, I show that Plato used the word *sophist* in a most precise sense to refer to figures who had two traits in common: they (1) professed to teach virtue (*aretē*) and (2) charged a fee. I thus define the Platonic sophists as "paid teachers of aretē."[2] Next, I explore two important implications of this definition. One is that for Plato the sophists and rhetoricians were distinct groups, even though all or most of the sophists also taught rhetoric. In other words, Gorgias, Thrasymachus, and Callicles were not sophists according to Plato insofar as they did not promise to teach aretē. Failure to appreciate this fact has, perhaps more than anything else, led modern scholars to make false claims about the moral character and significance of the Platonic sophists. A second implication is that Socrates was both like and unlike the sophists in fascinating ways.[3] Like the sophists, he taught students to concern themselves first and foremost with aretē and to do so by means of reason, not merely by the dictates of convention. But unlike the sophists, he did not accept fees, and he claimed not to know what aretē was or whether it could be taught. Both the similarities and the differences are striking and lead naturally to further questions. How did Socrates' discussions of aretē compare to those of the sophists? Why did Socrates claim not to know what aretē was?

The more one thinks about it, the more Plato seems intentionally to invite readers to reflect on Socrates' character *in terms of* the sophists, and this is precisely what I shall do in subsequent chapters.[4] But for the present, we see what the word *sophist* meant for Plato when he used it in his most precise way. To supply some context for this, we also consider the broader meanings of the word that were common prior to Plato's time.

Sophists before the "Sophists"

The word, sophist (*sophistēs*, plr. *sophistai*), derives from *sophos*—"wise," "wise one"—and means literally someone who practices wisdom.[5] From the beginning of the fifth century it was used to designate at least three different kinds of wise men: poets, pre-Socratics (as we would now call them), and practical experts. In all three cases it appears to have been a term of respect.

Consider, for example, how Pindar uses the word in its earliest known appearance in Greek literature (roughly 475 BC). "Heroes," writes Pindar, "supply a theme for sophists," who "celebrate [them] with lyres and flutes in full-voiced harmonies."[6] The meaning of the term is here equivalent to "poet" or "musician," and there is no hint of criticism. The great poets Homer, Hesiod, and Simonides were all called sophists by fifth-century authors; and the famous musicians, Agothocles and Pythocleides, could be dubbed sophists, too, without stretching the meaning of the term.[7]

That the figures we now label "pre-Socratics" were also called sophists is evident in Herodotus, for example, where Pythagoras is described as such (IV.95.10), and also in Xenophon, where those who "speculate about the cosmos" are called sophists (*Memorabilia* I.i.11). The passage from Xenophon does not mention names, but speculation about the cosmos was the characteristic activity of the pre-Socratics.[8] And according to the later testimony of Isocrates, it was not at all unusual to hear Parmenides, Empedocles, and Anaxagoras described as sophists.[9] That the term could be used not only of poets and musicians but also of pre-Socratics shows something of its initial range. As G.B. Kerferd has noted, "sophist" was not quite as far-ranging as *sophos* (wise one), which could be used of all sorts of experts, but it was at least far-ranging enough to encompass multiple types of individuals functioning in one way or another as "exponents of knowledge in early communities."[10]

The third intellectual type attracting the name *sophist* was the man of practical wisdom. Hence the seven sages (*hepta sophoi*) were sometimes called sophists (*hepta sophistai*).[11] Solon especially was described in this way and was apparently the first Athenian to receive the title.[12] That the seven sages were called sophists may perhaps seem unsurprising, because the term was used already of poets. The sages' pithy maxims were indeed masterpieces of poetic utterance: "nothing in excess," "know thyself," "forethought in all things." But the practical bent of their maxims must also have contributed to the title. Xenophon

(*Cyropaedia* III.1.14 and 38) tells a story of an ancient *sophistēs* whose wisdom was much admired by an Armenian prince, Tigranes. Tigranes would take the sophist on hunting trips in order to hear his insights. Before long, the prince's father had the sophist put to death in the belief that he was a corrupting influence. But this belief was evidently mistaken. At his execution, the sophist delivered these lines to the prince: "Be not angry with your father, Tigranes, for putting me to death; for he does it not from any spirit of malice, but from ignorance, and when men do wrong from ignorance, I believe they do it quite against their will." Here is a case of a "sophist" who was neither a poet nor, evidently, a student of the cosmos, but an imparter of sage moral advice. It was perhaps for this kind of wisdom, too, that the seven sages earned their titles.

By the middle of the fifth century, the word *sophistēs* plainly had multiple meanings and there is evidence that at about this time it began to acquire yet another. The title of a mid-fifth-century work (now lost) by a certain Damastes of Sigeum was, *Concerning Poets and Sophists*. This suggests that poets and sophists were for Damastes something distinct.[13] And in a similar vein, Xenophon (*Memorabilia* IV. 2.1; IV.2.8) describes a famous library of his day as containing "the written works of the most celebrated poets *and sophists*" (my italics). It has been conjectured that what we see in such cases is the use of *sophistēs* to designate prose writers.[14] Isocrates seems to have this meaning in mind, too, when he writes the following advice in his discourse *To Nicocles* (13): "Do not imagine that you can afford to be ignorant of any one either of the famous poets or of the sophists; rather you should listen to the poets and learn from the sophists."[15] And Isocrates' contemporary Alcidamas similarly associates sophists—or at least some of them—with writers of texts.[16] In all these cases, "poets" and "sophists" seem to stand as distinct categories of writer.

Because the word *sophist* seems to have conveyed feelings of respect early on, we are led naturally to wonder about the unflattering or pejorative connotations of the term. When, for example, did "sophist" begin to imply a "corruptor of youth" or a "master of verbal wrangling"? Unfortunately, this question does not permit a precise answer. Yet one can say with absolute certainty that the change did not occur with Plato. This is important to point out, because the idea that Plato single-handedly twisted a term of respect into one of abuse has been (and remains) quite prevalent.[17] My own view is that Plato was not nearly as critical of the sophists as commentators frequently assume. But, however that may be, he cannot have invented the negative connotations of the term. And this should be obvious, for the *Clouds* of Aristophanes satirized the sophists as unscrupulous teachers of false speech and vain subtleties well before Plato did so.[18] In 423 when the *Clouds* was first produced, Plato was only a child. Moreover, Plato's own *Apology* makes clear that Aristophanes' *Clouds* contributed significantly to negative public sentiment concerning the sophists, especially to sentiment concerning Socrates, whom Aristophanes presented as the sophist *par excellence*.[19]

Was it Aristophanes, then, who created the negative connotations of the term? No doubt, he played a role, but he was likely not alone. The surviving fragments of Athenian comic plays contemporary with Aristophanes' *Clouds* suggest that the sophists were routinely brought in for ridicule.[20] In Eupolis' play *Spongers* of 421, for instance, Protagoras was ridiculed as one who "goes on and on about celestial matters and devours things on earth" (fr. 157). Another fragment of Eupolis reads: "Sophist, teach him to chatter" (fr. 388).[21] And a play called *Konnos*, produced by Ameipsias in 423 included a chorus of *phrontistai* (thinkers) and seems to have mocked the sophists much as Aristophanes *Clouds* did, though no fragment mentions them by name. In general, there is not a wealth of extant evidence, but just enough to show that Aristophanes was not the only comedian to take aim at the sophists. The use of *sophistēs* to denote a "social nuisance," seems to have originated primarily on the Athenian comic stage.[22] In the tragedians, one finds the term employed in less-than-flattering ways, but never with quite the sting it acquires in comedy.[23]

If, then, by the 420s, Athenian comedians could employ the word *sophistēs* in a pejorative way and expect to be understood, the question still remains, what accounts for this change? Older uses of the term still survived, but why did the term *sophist* take such a negative turn? One factor may have been the sudden appearance on the scene of a greater number of sophists or sophist-like figures in Athens. Indeed, evidence suggests that Athens was simply overrun with them.[24] Moreover, the traits of these new arrivals must have seemed so easy to mock. By and large they were foreigners, *arrivistes*, champing at the bit to find an audience and a body of students. They were full of strange notions in ethics, religion, and natural science. And whether they were wealthy and foppish like Hippias of Elis or poor and threadbare like Socrates (in Aristophanes' *Clouds*), they were certainly not the sort of men Athenians traditionally admired. Any or all of these qualities could have contributed to a poor reception.

Another factor may have been the Peloponnesian War (431–404). In the charged political atmosphere of war, tolerance of foreigners often runs thin, and the sophists may well have appeared as a group of outsiders teaching potentially subversive ideas to Athenian youths at the worst possible time. It is useful to recall in this context that Aristophanes' *Clouds* was a wartime play, stressing the burdens of war from the opening scene. Plato too attests to a connection between war and suspicion of sophists. In his *Protagoras* (set in or around 432/1, when the war was just breaking out), Plato has the sophist, Protagoras, allude to the intense envy, ill-will and hostile plots that arise when a foreigner like himself "goes into great cities and there persuades the best of the young to forsake the company of others . . . and to associate with him" (316c–d, trans. Bartlett).

Here, then, are some of the likely reasons why the word *sophistēs*, initially a term of respect, might have become also a term of abuse in the years prior to Plato's writings. Sophists were proliferating. Their traits seemed strange. And their ideas in religion and ethics seemed out of joint with conventional Athenian values. Especially during wartime might these facts have begun to add up.

The survey I have just presented is important for two reasons. First, it helps to correct some prominent misunderstandings—(1) that the term sophist was always a term of abuse, never a term of respect; and (2) that Plato invented the negative connotations of the term in order to defame the sophists. Neither view is correct. In fact the term *sophist* was from early on a term of praise, and certain negative connotations also attached early on, well before Plato began to write dialogues. Second and most importantly, the historical survey allows us to reconsider and reformulate the questions we put to Plato's dialogues concerning the sophists. If we are ultimately interested in understanding the significance of the sophists in Plato's dialogues, then we would do well to consider how Plato uses the term and how he treats these figures overall. We shall find passages in which the sophists are ridiculed in the dialogues. But we must ask whether, or to what extent, such passages convey Plato's own view or represent his ultimate purpose. I suggest here that by defining the sophists quite consistently as "paid professors of aretē," Plato bestows a high philosophical significance on them.

He establishes that they were engaged in an enterprise similar to that of Socrates and he invites readers to take up the challenging task of drawing comparisons.

Plato's Use of *Sophistēs*

The word *sophist* appears 135 times in the dialogues of Plato;[25] and I know of no better way to study Plato's use of the term than to consider the instances with care. Table 2.1 is designed to assist. It is not an exhaustive list of instances (many of which turn out to be repetitive or trivial), but it captures the crucial divisions in Plato's use of the term.

Table 2.1. Sophist References in Plato's Dialogues

Category 1: Generic Sophists	**Category 2: Alleged Sophists**	**Category 3: Self-Professed Sophists**
Cratylus 391b, 398d *Theaetetus* 154e *Sophist* 216d, 218c, 221d, 223a, 224c, 224e, 225e, 231a, 231d–e, 233a, 233c, 234e, 240c, 254a, 260d, 264c, 268c *Statesman* 286b, 291c, 299b, 303c *Phaedrus* 248e *Laches* 186c *Protagoras* 312a, 312b, 312c, 313c, 316d, 342b *Gorgias* 463b, 465c, 519c, 520a, 520b *Meno* 85b, 91b–92e, 95b–c, 96b *Republic*, 492a, 493a, 596d *Timaeus* 19e *Laws* 908d	Protagoras *Cratylus* 391c *Hippias Major* 282d *Sophist* 232d *Meno* 91d Prodicus *Euthydemus* 277e *Hippias Major* 282c *Symposium* 177b *Laches* 197d Hippias *Hippias Major* 281e Euthydemus & Dionysodorus *Euthydemus* 271c *Euthydemus* 277e Gorgias *Hippias Major* 282b *Cf. Apology* 19d–20a Evanus *Apology* 20 b–c Miccus *Lysis* 204a Socrates *Protagoras* 314d *Gorgias* 497a	Protagoras *Protagoras* 316c ff., 319, 349a Prodicus No dialogue, but his presence in the *Protagoras* seems more than sufficient, cf. *Ap.* 19d–20a Hippias *Hippias Major* 281d *Protagoras* 319d–e Euthydemus & Dionysodorus *Euthydemus* 288b

In most cases (Category 1), the word *sophist* is used in a general way with no specific individuals named. In other cases (Category 2), specific figures are named but not when they are present to confirm or deny the traits being ascribed to them. And in a final set of cases (Category 3), specific individuals call *themselves* sophists or seem to accept the appellation when it is associated with them. This last category supplies the most reliable information, I argue, about the sophists' identity.[26] But all three categories reveal essential information.

Category 1

Much of the confusion surrounding Plato's view of the sophists stems from ambiguities in Category 1. Here, various speakers with radically different degrees of knowledge and experience of the sophists offer their apparently definitive opinions without mentioning concrete names and examples. We thus find extreme diversity in Category 1, both in terms of (a) moral tone and (b) beliefs about what the sophists actually teach. As an example of the diversity in tone, compare what Anytus says about the sophists in the *Meno* to what Socrates says there and elsewhere. For Anytus (one of the eventual accusers of Socrates) the sophists are unambiguously wicked: "May no one of my household or friends . . . be mad enough to go to these people and be harmed by them, for they clearly cause the ruin and corruption of their followers" (91c, trans., Grube). A few lines later, Anytus confesses that he is "altogether without any experience" of the sophists, so his credibility is cast into considerable doubt. For Socrates, by contrast, the sophists are teachers worthy of consideration, even if they may prove finally incapable of teaching all they profess to teach (*Meno* 95b–c, 96b). Certainly they are no more corruptors of youth than are Athenian parents and teachers (*Republic* 492a), and they appear to have something invaluable to offer (see e.g., *Meno* 91c–92a, *Apology* 19d–20a). Thus we should not be surprised when in the *Cratylus* (403d–404a), for example, Socrates likens the god Hades to a "perfect sophist" as well as a "philosopher." For Hades loves virtue and uses beautiful words to benefit those with whom he associates. We have occasion in later chapters to reflect on the complex relationship between sophists and philosophers and to consider some criticisms of the sophists more carefully. But for now I simply note the diversity of tone. Plato does not present readers with a simply critical view.

And what do the sophists teach? The diversity of answers to this question seems to stem both from ignorance on the part of some of Plato's characters, as well as from a genuine variety of sophistic types. In the *Protagoras*, Socrates asks Hippocrates, a young admirer of the sophists, what he supposes they teach. Hippocrates answers that they teach students to become "clever at speaking" (312d). But when Socrates follows up with another question—On what subject do sophists make you clever at speaking?—the young man is unable to answer (312e). Here is a case of ignorance. But the question is also difficult in its own right, as a glance at Socrates' statements across the dialogues makes clear. In the *Cratylus* (391b), Socrates presents the sophists generically as experts in the "correctness of names" (i.e., philologists of a sort). In the *Theaetetus* (154e) he presents them as expert debaters. In the *Laches* (186c) and elsewhere he presents them as teachers of virtue. And this is only a small selection of the ways in which they are cast. The difficulty, as we learn from the *Protagoras* and the *Sophist*, where the matter of sophistic diversity becomes thematic, is that the sophists were *not* a homogeneous group. They in fact varied widely in terms of their specialties, personal characteristics, and pedagogical approaches.

Close consideration of Category 1 helps us to understand why Plato's readers might sometimes assume that Plato's own view of the sophists was antagonistic. When Plato's characters criticize the sophists in generic terms without mentioning specific names, it becomes all too easy for readers to mistake a partial view (partial both in the sense of incomplete and in the sense of biased) for Plato's final word. Moreover, without paying careful attention to the speaker's level of knowledge, his immediate audience, and his possible motives, we are likely to ascribe to Plato what is in fact merely the passing expression of one of his characters.[27] This is not to say that the generic descriptions of the sophists are useless from a scholarly point of view. They in fact reveal a great deal about the way these figures were perceived and the various activities for which they were known. But such descriptions must be analyzed with their partiality in mind.

Category 2

More helpful, though still imperfect, are the references in Category 2. Here specific individuals are deemed sophists and valuable information is conveyed about them, but the figures themselves are not present to confirm or deny what is said. Plato thus exposes us to "hearsay" about specific sophists, and all the limitations just mentioned remain crucial: possible biases, the speaker's level of knowledge, his audience, and so on. What is perhaps most immediately striking about the list of alleged sophists in Category 2 is how short it is. At most, nine individuals are deemed sophists in Plato's dialogues: Protagoras, Prodicus, Hippias, Euthydemus, Dionysodorus, Gorgias, Evanus, Miccus, and Socrates.[28] And, again, some of these may be deemed sophists in error. We now consider a few interesting aspects of the list.

One thing to notice is that Thrasymachus is not present. Neither are Callicles and Polus, Socrates' interlocutors for the bulk of the *Gorgias*. This is because these figures are simply never referred to as sophists in Plato's dialogues. In the *Republic*, Thrasymachus is described as clever (*deinos*), wise (*sophos*), and even most wise (*sophōtate*); but he is never labeled a *sophistēs*.[29] Nor is he called a sophist (interestingly enough) by other contemporary authors.[30] This omission is not accidental, as I argue below, but stems from an important line of demarcation between sophists and rhetoricians, the same line that is operative in the case of Polus and Callicles, who consistently voice their admiration for rhetoric and rhetoricians while expressing their vociferous contempt for the sophists (see, e.g., *Gorgias* 520a, 497a). But this gives rise to a question. If a line of demarcation separates rhetoricians and sophists, then why does Gorgias, one of the fathers of rhetoric, appear on the list of sophists in Category 2? The short and simple answer is that Gorgias is called a sophist explicitly in the *Hippias Major* (282b) and implicitly in the *Apology* (19e). But there is more to say about Gorgias, and I shall return to his status below.

The case of Socrates is similarly complex. Socrates is referred to as a sophist by an ill-informed servant in the *Protagoras* (314d); and in the *Gorgias*, his arguments are dubbed "sophisms" by Callicles (497a). Moreover, certain less direct passages are worth considering. In the *Sophist*, Plato has Socrates sit idly by while a conversation unfolds about sophistry, a conversation, which at many points seems to implicate Socrates himself, though he is never explicitly labeled.[31] Similarly in the *Apology*, though Socrates is never called a sophist outright, the charges brought against him (corrupting the young, not believing in the city's gods) make him sound like a sophist. This is, no doubt, why Socrates takes such pains in the *Apology* to differentiate himself from the sophists (19d–20c). And finally, in the *Hippias Minor* we see just how sophistic Socrates really was. For in that dialogue Socrates propounds a series of fallacious and morally dangerous arguments which, in effect, "out-sophist" one of the major fifth-century sophists, Hippias of Elis.[32] In all these cases, Socrates is actually present to confirm or deny whether he is a sophist. Thus I slightly stretch the conditions of Category 2 to include him. But the inclusion seems justified by the strange fact that Socrates does not always cast off the appearance of being a sophist. The *Hippias Minor* and the *Sophist* are perhaps most remarkable in this regard. Plato seems intent on showing readers the remarkable affinity between Socrates and the sophists, and he leaves it to his readers to differentiate them.

The least problematic figures in Category 2 are Protagoras, Prodicus, Hippias, and the brother sophists, Euthydemus and Dionysodorus. All these figures seem actively to embrace the title of sophist (hence their appearance in Category 3), and all but Prodicus have a dialogue devoted entirely to them. Plato thus leaves no room for doubt that he regards these figures as important sophists.

What about Miccus and Evanus? Miccus is dubbed a "serious person and a competent sophist" by Socrates in the *Lysis* (204a), but scholars have long suspected that the term there is not used in its most precise sense.[33] Though Miccus was an admirer of Socrates and a lover of philosophical conversation, he was a wrestling instructor for a living. Socrates seems simply to acknowledge his skill as a teacher in calling him a competent sophist.[34] Evanus of Paros, by contrast, was apparently a genuine sophist. Socrates describes him in the *Apology* (20b–c) as someone whom Callias (a great benefactor of the sophists) had contracted to educate his son in aretē. Evanus was thus a professed teacher of virtue and charged a relatively modest fee of five minas. Unfortunately, little more is known of Evanus, so I do not consider him further in this study.[35]

Category 3

When it comes to identifying and defining the genuine sophists in Plato's dialogues, the references in Category 3 are the most revealing. These are passages in which specific individuals are presented as sophists and appear to *embrace* the title. Moreover, I argue that an important correlation occurs here: All figures in Plato's dialogues who embrace the title of sophist do so on the grounds that they teach aretē for a fee. Thus, to teach virtue and be paid for it is perfectly synonymous with sophistry. Recognition of this fact helps tremendously in thinking through those difficult cases of Category 2: Gorgias and Socrates. But before I consider these cases afresh, I defend the correlation in detail. It seems to me that three basic facts need to be demonstrated: (a) that the figures in Category 3 do indeed embrace the title of sophist; (b) that they are all paid teachers of aretē; and (c) that this correlation is not merely accidental but reflects the very definition of the Platonic sophists. I examine (a) and (b) together and then turn to a separate consideration of (c).

Protagoras is the easiest case to treat, because we have him on record in the *Protagoras* explicitly accepting the term, sophist. "I admit that I am a sophist," he proclaims early on in that dialogue (317b). And he admits, too, that he is a teacher of aretē, for he accepts the fundamental challenge that Socrates poses in the *Protagoras*—to demonstrate that aretē can be taught. Later on in that dialogue, Socrates offers (and Protagoras accepts) the following characterization of his enterprise:

> I think you are the best qualified to investigate the sort of things that decent and respectable individuals ought to examine, and virtue (*aretē*) especially. Who else but you? Not only do you consider yourself to be noble and good but, unlike others who are themselves decent and respectable individuals yet unable to make others so, you are not only good yourself but able to make others good as well, and you have so much self-confidence that . . . you advertise it openly to the whole Greek world, calling yourself a sophist, highlighting yourself as a teacher of virtue (*aretē*), the first ever to have deemed it appropriate to charge a fee for this. (*Prt.* 348d–349a, trans., Stanley Lombardo and Karen Bell)

This description is extremely helpful, for it tells us not only that Protagoras regarded himself as a sophist and a teacher of virtue, but also that he pioneered this new use of the term. Before Protagoras, the word sophist was used in many ways, as we have seen, but it was never used self-referentially to announce oneself as a professional teacher of aretē (at least not in any of the sources that have come down to us).[36] Moreover, and perhaps more fundamentally, prior to Protagoras, there *were* no professional teachers of aretē, which may account in part for this sophist's massive success. Though we have evidence of paid teachers in other areas of life (for example, flute teachers),[37] and evidence of unpaid teachers of aretē,[38] we have no evidence that anyone prior to Protagoras collected a fee for attempting to impart virtue. Protagoras, then, not only fulfills the conditions of (a) and (b) earlier, he appears to have pioneered them.

If Protagoras invented the practice of teaching aretē for a fee, then Hippias and Prodicus must have quickly followed suit. These sophists were a generation younger than Protagoras, but their careers overlapped with his. We even find them together in the same house in Plato's *Protagoras*. Like Protagoras, Hippias and Prodicus both embraced the term *sophist*. Hippias does so explicitly in the *Hippias Major* (281d); while Prodicus does so implicitly by his presence and manner in the *Protagoras* (see esp. 315d–316a).[39] That they both taught aretē is likewise clear. In the *Republic* (600c), Socrates compares Prodicus favorably to Homer for his ability to impart aretē to his students; and we know, too, from many ancient sources that this sophist was famous for a moral lecture he delivered from town to town celebrating the choice of virtue over vice.[40] Hippias, for his part affirms that he teaches aretē when Socrates asks him about this in the *Hippias Major* (283c). Socrates: "Isn't your wisdom the sort that makes those who associate with it and learn it better in regard to *aretē*?" Hippias: "Very much so, Socrates."[41]

Euthydemus and Dionysodorus evidently took up the business of teaching virtue rather late in their careers. Prior to this, they were teachers of military arts and of courtroom oratory. But when Socrates inquires of their occupation in the *Euthydemus* they make clear that they have left their former pursuits behind for something much more alluring: "*Aretē*, Socrates, is what it is; and we think we can impart it better than anyone else and more quickly" (273d, trans. mine). To announce that they have become teachers of aretē is to announce that they have become sophists, as the character, Crito, had suspected from the start (271b–c). This is why Euthydemus and Dionysodorus do not protest when Socrates (in their presence) characterizes their antics as "sophistic mysteries" (277e). These are the newest of the sophists represented in Plato's dialogues. We have occasion later to reflect on the degenerating trend that sophistry takes over time. But what is important here is to see the way that sophistry, whatever its particular forms or inflections, correlates with that essential promise of teaching aretē for a fee.[42]

Now I turn to the question (c) whether this correlation could be accidental. The difficulty is that while we can observe the correlation at work in Category 3, we are dealing there with only five cases (or four, if we count Euthydemus and Dionysodorus as a unit, as Plato humorously does). To draw inferences from such a small number of cases seems hazardous. So, is there any further evidence to support the argument that, for Plato, "sophist" was synonymous with "paid teacher of aretē"? The answer is, yes. If we look back at Category 1, we can now see that the equation of "the sophists" in general with "teachers of aretē" courses through the dialogues, especially when the most discerning observers are speaking (for example, Socrates and the Eleatic Stranger). Thus in the *Laches* (185e–186c), the *Meno* (91a, 91d, 95b–c), the *Gorgias* (519c, 519e, 520d–e), the *Republic* (492a ff.),[43] the *Theaetetus* (167a–b), the *Protagoras* (357e), and the *Sophist* (223a, 224c–d, 224d–e, 225c, 267c [cf. *Euthydemus* 273d]), sophistry is presented as a matter of teaching aretē for pay.[44] The correlation is not perfect in Category 1 due to variations in speaker and context. But the frequency with which it does occur and the trustworthiness of the speakers in question, corroborates what we find in Category 3. To my mind, this evidence is overwhelming. Again, not only does every self-professed "sophist" in Plato's dialogues present himself as a teacher of aretē, but this way of understanding the essence of sophistic education is echoed by the most reliable speakers in the vast majority of dialogues in which the sophists in general are mentioned. This is to say nothing (yet) about the ability of specific sophists to make good on their promise. Plato gives us ample reason to question whether the sophists could really teach aretē as well as they thought. Nor is this yet to remark on the staggering diversity among the sophists regarding the nature of aretē and the best ways to impart it. The point here is only that as a matter of definition, the sophists in Plato's dialogues were figures who claimed to be able to impart aretē for a fee.

But what is at stake here? Why does this definition matter? The answer is that it helps us understand why Plato would have been so interested in the sophists in the first place: He was interested in them because they were engaged in an intellectual enterprise, which in many ways overlapped with that of Socratic philosophy. Next, it helps us pursue the question of Socrates' relationship to the sophists more concretely and profitably. And, finally, it helps us clarify the line of demarcation between the sophists and rhetoricians that we noted earlier. Each of these points is worth considering in greater depth. I treat them now in reverse order.

GORGIAS AND THE RHETORICIANS

In Plato's dialogues, the line of demarcation between sophists and rhetoricians is frequently visible.[45] But what is the basis of the distinction? Its basis, I argue, is precisely that Gorgias and others like him (the rhetoricians) were loath to put themselves forward as teachers of aretē. In fact, they mocked the teachers of aretē and in most cases mocked aretē itself, at least in its conventional forms. Some of the major rhetoricians in the dialogues include Gorgias, Thrasymachus, Polus, and Callicles. And if we consider their outlook, as well as how Plato handles them, we see that the distinction is far from trivial. Indeed, failure to observe this distinction has been a major source of scholarly confusion about Plato's evaluation of the sophists.

Of the figures just named, the only one who should be controversial is Gorgias, for he is the only one who is grouped (if only twice) with the sophists in Plato's dialogues. This happens most clearly in the *Hippias Major* (282b), where Socrates refers in passing to Gorgias as a "well-known sophist" and likens him to Prodicus and Protagoras. The focus of the comparison is the ability of all three to combine public and private enterprises: they all traveled on official business as ambassadors or political advisors while, in a private capacity, teaching the young for a fee. It is noteworthy that Socrates does not consider the *substance* of Gorgias' instruction in this passage of the *Hippias Major*, only his fee.[46] The second passage occurs in the *Apology* (19d–20a), where Socrates again groups Gorgias with certain sophists (this time Prodicus and Hippias) as prominent teachers who charge a fee. Here Socrates does not label Gorgias a sophist, but neither does he distinguish him from them as we would expect. These are the passages that account for Gorgias' appearance in Category 2 above.

But more important by far than what Socrates says or implies in passing about Gorgias is what Socrates uncovers when he speaks to him in person in the dialogue that bears his name. Here all ambiguity is removed:

> Soc: "Gorgias, you tell us yourself what one must call you, as a knower of what art?"
> Gorg: "Of rhetoric [*rhētorikē*] Socrates."
> Soc: "Then one must call you a rhetorician [*rhētora*]?"
> Gorg: "And a good one, Socrates, if you wish to call me what I boast that I am. . . ."
> Soc: "But I do wish."
> Gorg: "Then call me so."
> Soc: "So then should we assert that you are able to make others rhetoricians too?"
> Gorg: "This is indeed what I advertise [epangellomai], not only here but elsewhere too."
> (Gorgias 449a–449b, trans. mine.)

In the *Gorgias*, then, Gorgias makes clear that he views himself as a rhetorician, not (evidently) as a sophist;[47] and he claims that he is quite consistent in presenting himself as such. But why does he do this? Why eschew the name, sophist? The most likely answer comes by way of another dialogue, the *Meno*, where, in the midst of a conversation about other matters, Socrates asks Meno (a former student of Gorgias) a question about the sophists: Does Meno believe that "the sophists, who alone profess to be teachers of *aretē*, really are so"? And Meno replies: "I admire this most in Gorgias, Socrates, that you would never hear him promising this. Indeed, he ridicules [*katagelaō*] the others when he hears them making this claim. He thinks one should make people clever speakers" (95b–c, trans., Grube). Gorgias, in other words, appears to have eschewed the name sophist, because he recognized the basic fact that to be a sophist was to be a teacher of aretē and he did not want to present himself as a teacher of aretē.[48]

This leads to the next question: Why not? What exactly was the basis of Gorgias' reluctance to present himself as a teacher of aretē? The dialogues supply no direct answer to this question, but they are suggestive, and we can certainly venture a guess. In the *Meno*, Socrates and Meno agree that the problem with the sophists in general is that the whole business of teaching aretē is so murky. Who can really tell if aretē has been successfully imparted, or whether it can be imparted at all? Moreover, teachers of aretē find themselves in an awkward (and sometimes even dangerous) position if and when one of their students turns out to be vicious. Since the sophists promise to teach virtue, should not the sophist himself be held responsible for any immoral deeds committed by his students? That Gorgias was worried about this possibility is evident from a remark he makes in the *Gorgias*:

> I think that if someone has become a rhetorician and then does injustice with this power and art, one must not hate the teacher and expel him from the cities. For the teacher imparted it [rhetoric] for just use, and the other used it in the opposite way. It is just, then, to hate, expel, and kill the one who uses it improperly, but not the one who taught it. (457b–c, trans. mine)

By teaching rhetoric alone, divorcing this from the more challenging business of imparting aretē, Gorgias seems to have hoped to avoid the problem of being blamed for his students' misdeeds. His students' moral qualities were, for the most part, their own business, not his.[49] He assumed that his students were good. But if they were not, this could not be saddled on him.

And no wonder Gorgias was worried about this. If we now consider as a group those figures who appear as rhetoricians or students of rhetoric in the dialogues we find that they include some unscrupulous characters indeed. Gorgias himself (let us call a spade a spade) appears to be simply obsessed with power (*dynamis*). At least he advertises his art in these terms: "with this power you will have the doctor as your slave, and the trainer as your slave; and that moneymaker of yours will be plainly revealed to be making money for another and not himself, but for *you* who can speak and persuade multitudes" (*Gorgias* 452e, cf. 456a ff.). And yet Gorgias appears to have been the most decent of the rhetoricians. Plato has Gorgias' student, Polus, confess to Socrates that his interest in rhetoric stems from a deep envy of the powerful, especially tyrants who can kill or exile whomever they wish and confiscate whatever possessions they wish, whether justly or not (466b–c, 468e). Next, Callicles maintains that what is "just by nature" (*dikaios kata phusin*) is for the stronger to carry off by violence the weaker men's things (488b). And Thrasymachus in the *Republic* takes much the same view, that "justice is nothing other than the advantage of the stronger" (*Republic* 338c ff.). The rhetoricians in Plato's dialogues thus tend toward a natural morality of power. They view conventional morality as base and its proponents as naive. This explains why Callicles in the

Gorgias (520a) describes the sophists as "worthless." He would not do so if he were himself a sophist or if he regarded his idol, Gorgias, as one.

From this vantage point, we can now see more clearly what separates the sophists and rhetoricians in Plato's dialogues. The sophists, for their part, put themselves forward as teachers of aretē (human skill and excellence along with moral goodness), and they were, for the most part, morally upstanding characters.[50] The rhetoricians by contrast refused to put themselves forth as teachers of aretē, not merely because they were reluctant to advertise something they could not deliver or because they feared the possibility of a public backlash if one of their students should become a civic nuisance. They refused also because they were in many cases opposed to aretē itself as this was conventionally understood.[51] Thus the rhetoricians distinguished themselves from sophists and even ridiculed them.

That the line of demarcation between sophists and rhetoricians has not always been noticed requires, perhaps, some explanation. The line is not hard to see once it has been pointed out; yet there are good reasons for failing to observe it. One is that the ancients themselves did not always mark the line as carefully as Plato did.[52] The word *sophist* must have seemed more than adequate for many ancient observers to capture the whole lot of intellectuals, whatever their differences. Second, the activities of the sophists and rhetoricians did, in fact, overlap considerably. I illustrate this by listing three potentially confusing facts.

1. Both rhetoricians *and* sophists taught rhetoric. Rhetoric was not the special domain of rhetoricians alone.[53]
2. In a certain (narrow) sense, rhetoric was aretē, even though the rhetoricians did not stress this. Since Homeric times, expertise in rhetoric was regarded as a major component of human excellence.[54]
3. Rhetoricians frequently delivered speeches on moral subjects, exhorting audiences to praise or blame certain things, and they even delivered speeches on virtue itself. Rhetoric could therefore touch upon the topic of aretē.[55]

Such considerations make it easy to see why the sophists and rhetoricians might be grouped together, and yet they were essentially different.[56] Again, the crucial consideration is a moral one. Where the rhetoricians promised to turn students into expert speakers, the sophists promised something categorically different. They promised to effect a moral transformation in the pupil himself, to make him "better," to render him *kalos kai agathos*, noble and good.

Socrates

Once we realize that the sophists in Plato's dialogues were, by definition, paid teachers of aretē, we are in a better position to consider Socrates. Though Socrates shared many traits with the sophists, he differed from them precisely along the lines I have been discussing: he did not accept fees and did not claim to teach virtue. Striking, indeed, is the consistency with which Plato uses these definitional criteria to differentiate Socrates from the sophists. For example, in the *Apology*, Plato has Socrates pose the question directly: "Who is knowledgeable in such aretē, that of the human being and citizen?" And Socrates continues: "As for me, I would be pluming and priding myself on it if I had knowledge of these things. But I do not have knowledge of them, men of Athens" (20b–c, my trans.). And similarly with fees: "if you've heard from anyone that I undertake to teach people and charge a fee for it, that is not true either" (Ap. 19d–e, my trans.). Why, we wonder, did Socrates not accept fees? And why were the sophists ridiculed for accepting them? Since I have addressed these questions at length in a separate study, I shall not take them up here.[57] The point I want to stress here is more basic. That when Plato wants to suggest a difference between Socrates and the sophists, he does so on the basis of *these* definitional criteria. *Because* Socrates did not accept fees or claim to teach virtue, he was not a sophist.[58]

But this gives rise to an interesting question, which I think needs to be taken quite seriously. Could Plato have, perhaps, designed the definition of sophistry we have been considering precisely *in order* to separate Socrates once and for all from the sophists?[59] Because the definition functions so perfectly in this regard the possibility needs to be considered. No doubt, Plato realized that his teacher's death was caused in part by the Athenians' perception that he was a dangerous sophist. Perhaps Plato wanted to vindicate his teacher. And because Plato intended to erect a school on the foundation of Socratic philosophy, he must have felt the need to address the historical record, to show unambiguously that Socrates was not a sophist. In order to do so, he turned his creative genius to the awesome task of manipulating the meaning of a word, of ascribing strict criteria to the word *sophistēs*, which had never attached to it before and which, in effect, excluded Socrates perfectly from its domain. So the argument would run. For purposes of exposition, I call this the "manipulation thesis." Is it plausible?

I offer three considerations to suggest that it is not. First, the definition of sophistry that we have been studying does not appear *ex nihilo* in the dialogues, as if Plato simply changed the meaning of a word. Rather, it appears along with a detailed account of when and with whom the change originated. Its author, according to Plato, was Protagoras, who is made to say in the dialogue that bears his name, that he was indeed the first person to call *himself* a sophist, to present himself openly as a teacher of aretē, and to charge a fee (316c–317c, 328b–c). Protagoras' originality is reiterated later in the same dialogue (348d–349a), and referred to elsewhere as well (*Hippias Major* 282d, 282e). The reports are thus multiple and consistent. Now this does not decide the issue. Plato could have redefined the word *sophist* while at the same time covering his tracks so artfully as to pin that change on Protagoras. But this begins to seem like a stretch and bit too conspiratorial.

Moreover (and secondly), the idea that the sophists were, by definition, paid teachers of aretē appears outside the Platonic corpus, which would be hard to explain if it were merely a Platonic manipulation.[60] The anonymous author of the *Dissoi Logoi*, for example, offers the following one-line argument as a proof that virtue can be taught (DK 90.VI.7): "whatever else do the sophists teach except wisdom and *aretē*?" The line reads as if it were simply common knowledge that the sophists presented themselves as teachers of aretē. And the *Dissoi Logoi* was a text from the sophistic, not the Platonic, tradition. So it is highly unlikely that it would have been affected by Platonic manipulation.[61]

Finally, and most importantly, we must reconsider the very premise of the manipulation thesis—namely, that Plato wished to vindicate Socrates by separating him once and for all from the sophists. That this premise is at best a half truth should be evident to anyone who reads widely and deeply in the dialogues. The fact is that in many places Plato seems to bend over backwards to show how sophistic Socrates could be. One thinks of the *Hippias Minor* in this connection, but also the first book of the *Republic* or that lengthy passage of the *Protagoras* in which Socrates offers a bogus interpretation of the poetry of Simonides. Many such passages could be cited. But none of these would make sense if Plato were intent on separating Socrates from the sophists. Plato appears rather deliberately to illustrate their complex entanglement. Moreover, in several dialogues, Plato shows that Socrates owed a significant debt to the sophists, that he imitated their techniques and incorporated their methods into his own philosophical practice. Protagoras, Prodicus, Hippias, and Euthydemus are all presented as sophists from whom Socrates could (and in some cases did) learn something. Therefore, again, Plato cannot have wished simply to erase the connection between Socrates and the sophists.

A more plausible thesis would be that Plato approached the question of Socrates and the sophists on two levels. On the one hand, he used the definition of sophistry to show in a rough-and-ready way that Socrates was not simply a sophist. Perhaps this would give pause to those Athenians who were inclined, all-too-facilely, to run Socrates and the sophists together. But at the same time, Plato invited a deeper reengagement of the question on a philosophical plane. And here, too, the definition of sophistry proved useful. For it is one thing to say that Socrates did not teach virtue and something else to say *why* he did not: What were his reservations? Whatever did he teach if he did not teach virtue? What *is* virtue? Can virtue be taught? The philosophical questions seem to emerge almost naturally from the definitional criteria. And so too with the matter of pay: *Why* did Socrates not take fees? What were his criticisms of the practice? What is wrong with teaching virtue for pay? Plato's two-level treatment of Socrates' relationship to the sophists turns out to be—as so many aspects of the Platonic dialogues are—an invitation to philosophy. It points toward the fundamental philosophical questions concerning human aretē.

Plato's Purposes

All of which brings us to the final question of this chapter: Why was Plato so interested in the sophists? This question is not one that can be answered with absolute certainty. Plato never tells us in his own voice why he was interested in the sophists. And yet by observing what he did with them—how he defined them, presented them, and made use of them—we can reasonably conjecture. It is not my view that Plato was interested in the sophists only to villainize them. Though he certainly mocked their excesses as well as their philosophical limits, Plato's purposes were never strictly comic or *ad hominem*. What, then, were his purposes? One must begin (to restate the obvious) by seeing who the sophists were, separating them out from the rhetoricians, as Plato himself did. And once it becomes clear that the sophists in Plato's dialogues were paid teachers of aretē, we are in an excellent position to begin. I offer two explanations here, by way of introduction to the subsequent chapters, for Plato's abiding interest in the sophists.

The first is that the sophists supplied a perfect backdrop or canvas on which to present Socrates, because the sophistic and Socratic enterprises were so closely related without being identical. Like the sophists, Socrates was fundamentally interested in human aretē.[62] He wanted to know, first and foremost, how a person ought to live. Like the sophists, he took up aretē in an intellectual way, attempting to rationalize it and order it. Like the sophists, he recognized and exposed inconsistencies, weaknesses, in the conventional view of aretē. And like the sophists, he had followers whom he instructed. Yet despite these striking similarities, Socrates was different from the sophists, because, in the final analysis, the sophists were committed to conventional aretē in ways that Socrates was not. Qua "experts," the sophists were expected to teach, and they were *paid* to teach. Thus even though they may have spent a significant portion of time engaged in criticism of conventional aretē, they needed ultimately to incorporate such activities into the broader fabric of a practical pedagogy or else finally set them aside. And, in any event, the sophists were themselves fundamentally committed to conventional moral goods. They prized honor, wealth and fame, and assumed that their students would too. The sophists were thus bifurcated on the matter of aretē, inclined on the one hand to ask critical questions, but forced on the other to commit to conventional views and assumptions.[63] Not so with Socrates. By eschewing all pretense of expertise and refusing to accept pay, Socrates gained the freedom which philosophy requires. He was able to cordon off aretē as an area for deep philosophical exploration in a way that the sophists could not, and he was able to use the sophists' own methods of critical questioning to their full philosophical advantage.

This connects naturally to the second likely reason that Plato was interested in the sophists. The sophists' critical insights and methods served as an ideal preparation for philosophical inquiry. I would go so far as to say that they were the necessary precondition for philosophy in the Socratic manner. Plato thus exposes his readers (by having Socrates expose interlocutors) to sophistic arguments of all sorts as a way of awakening their minds. Another way to put this is to say that philosophy begins from and requires wonder; but wonder is not easy to achieve. It is true, as Aristotle would later write, that "all men by nature desire to know." Yet, for the most part, people live not in quest of knowledge but in the belief that they already possess it. When puzzles emerge, we tend to suppress them. Thus the significance of the sophists is that they force intellectual puzzles upon hearers and demand that the world be reengaged in a spirit of wonder. They make weaker arguments seem stronger, overturn traditional claims, and leave their hearers in that most uncomfortable state of confusion and disorientation. And this is precisely what Socratic philosophy requires in order to get off the ground. That is why, when the sophists are not present in Plato's dialogues, we so often find Socrates playing their part, posing uncomfortable questions, refuting traditional beliefs, and generally bewildering his interlocutors until they are willing to admit that they do not really know what is true.[64] For Plato, sophistry was not only a backdrop for philosophy; it was its foundation.

THREE

THE "GREAT SPEECH" IN PLATO'S *PROTAGORAS*

The so-called Great Speech in Plato's *Protagoras* (320c8–328d2) is a lengthy *epideixis*—a "demonstration" (320c)—in which Protagoras reveals to Socrates his understanding of *aretē* and some of the difficulties he faces in teaching it. In this chapter I argue that Plato intended the Great Speech to show Protagoras' extraordinary skills and to suggest some remarkable affinities between Protagoras and Socrates. Through a careful reading of the speech one sees not only why Protagoras would have attracted students of various sorts, but also why Plato would have deemed him a significant interlocutor for Socrates. Socrates is not a sophist, as he himself makes perfectly clear (*Prt.* 314d8); and Protagoras is not Socrates, either. My point is not to assimilate the two or to deny that a fundamental purpose of Plato's *Protagoras* is to lead readers to differentiate Socrates from Protagoras in a critical fashion.[1] But I believe this process of critical differentiation is far more demanding than is often supposed—or, to put it differently: Plato allows Protagoras to be more brilliant and more closely related to Socrates than modern commentators have tended to realize.[2]

But why—one might ask—have commentators failed to recognize the profound tribute Plato pays to Protagoras in this speech? Three reasons come to mind, and these will be useful to consider by way of an introduction to the speech itself. First, the speech arises as a response to a challenge Socrates puts to Protagoras (319a–320c), and the challenge itself is more complex than often realized. Usually, the challenge is treated as a strictly theoretical one—to demonstrate that political virtue can be taught.[3] But, in fact, Socrates calls on Protagoras to demonstrate certain rhetorical skills as well;[4] and the rhetorical side of the challenge is meant deliberately to compete with the theoretical side. That is to say, if Protagoras attends only to the theoretical challenge he will fail the rhetorical one, and *vice versa*. I say more about these complexities later.

Second, commentators have tended more often than not to focus on only one or two famous passages of the Great Speech while neglecting its overarching purposes and structure. This is understandable, because the Great Speech is so long and rich that it is difficult to treat thoroughly in studies whose central purposes lie elsewhere. It has thus been used as a "grab bag" of interesting ideas.[5] But a real danger awaits those who take isolated fragments of this speech out of context. For precisely because the speech is motivated by rhetorical considerations, one cannot safely assume that any given passage simply expresses Protagoras' "doctrine," let alone his complete doctrine. As with Plato's Socrates, so, too, with Plato's Protagoras: he does not always say everything he thinks.

Finally, the speech has been misunderstood because of the demands it places on the modern reader in terms exogenous information. For example, to interpret the grand myth that inaugurates the Great Speech, one must be familiar with Hesiod's two famous poems, *Theogony* and *Works and Days* (see the appendix to this book), for Protagoras' myth is designed to rework and improve on Hesiod's mythopoetic teachings.[6] Plato's educated readers would have recognized this because they would have known the myths being reworked.[7] Moreover, that Protagoras was famous in antiquity for precisely such a critical engagement of early Greek poetry is also helpful to know. I now say a bit more about Protagoras' relation to the poets in order to prepare the way for his speech.

As a teacher of aretē, Protagoras could not have avoided the fact that the subject matter of his instruction was also the subject matter of traditional poetry. The poets were the primary authority in moral matters. Homer in particular, but also Hesiod, Theognis, Pindar, Simonides, and Solon, among others, supplied the core of childhood education in morals. Their poems were committed to memory early on; and one could expect as an adult to be called on to recite these poems at the banquets (*symposia*) that sometimes followed an evening meal. In effect, the world of aretē was a world defined by poets. And thus for Protagoras to put himself forward as a teacher of aretē—as the *best* teacher of it, no less (*Prt.* 328a–b)—would have required him to engage the poets. And so he did.

Echoes of this engagement appear here and there in the sources, though much of the evidence is fragmentary. A passage of Aristotle's *Poetics* (1456^{b}15) refers to Protagoras' semantic critique of the *Iliad*'s opening line. A *Scholium* on Homer by Ammonius (an Alexandrian commentator of the late fourth century AD) mentions Protagoras' literary analysis of a scene from the *Iliad.*[8] And another source tells of a humorous episode in which an angry poet heaped curses on Protagoras for refusing to praise one of his poems—to which Protagoras allegedly responded: "My good sir, I am better off enduring your abuse than enduring your poems!"[9] These passages are merely suggestive, but they indicate that Protagoras engaged the poets and that his engagement was basically critical. This is corroborated by a passage from the middle of the *Protagoras* (well after the Great Speech) in which Plato has Protagoras declare that "the greatest part of a man's education is . . . to be able to understand which of the things said by the poets have been correctly written and which not, and to know how to analyze them and give an account when questioned" (339a).

From these indications it appears that a critical engagement with the poets was a well-known aspect of Protagoras' enterprise as a teacher of aretē.[10] And when one turns to the Great Speech one sees the significance of this. In the myth that inaugurates the speech, Protagoras takes aspects of Hesiodic myth that seem morally and politically harmful and replaces them with newly fashioned material that is more beneficial. It is a masterful rewriting of part of the canon (along the lines of Socrates' critique of Greek myths in book two of the *Republic*). However, Protagoras does not, for various reasons, announce what he is doing. To appreciate what he is doing, one must not only have the details of Hesiod's poems in mind, but also know that Protagoras was an important voice in what Plato elsewhere dubs the "old quarrel between philosophy and poetry."[11] Reading the speech in its proper intellectual-historical context thus proves crucial not only for understanding the speech itself, but also for gauging Protagoras' achievement as a political thinker and rhetorician. I now turn to consider the complexity of Socrates' challenge.

Socrates' Challenge (319a–320c)

A young man, Hippocrates, has knocked on Socrates' door before dawn, abuzz with excitement about the possibility of studying with the sophist Protagoras. Socrates asks Hippocrates what he expects to gain by studying with a sophist, but the young man has not given the matter much thought. Thus does a cluster of questions arise (311b–314b): What is a sophist? What do the sophists teach? Do they *know* whether their intellectual wares are good or bad for the soul? Or do they simply, like wholesalers of exotic foods, praise whatever they happen to have in stock?

To answer these questions, Socrates and Hippocrates decide to interview Protagoras, who is staying with a number of other sophists at the house of Callias, a wealthy Athenian.[12] And after some initial conversation, which I shall return to shortly, Socrates asks Protagoras directly what a student like Hippocrates—a wealthy, young man, eager to make a name for himself in the city—might expect to learn from him. Protagoras' initial responses are vague (he is cautious when it comes to describing what he teaches) but they are nevertheless suggestive. At first he announces simply that Hippocrates will "go home a better man" and "make progress toward a better state" for every day they spend together (318a). "Better" (*beltion*) is a key term in Protagoras' pedagogical vocabulary. In the "Apology of Protagoras" in the *Theaetetus*, Protagoras is said to modify the souls of his listeners so that their opinions and beliefs change for the better (*Theat.* 166a–168c). Here in the *Protagoras*, the sophist does not say in what respect he will make his students "better."

When Socrates presses him on this point, Protagoras explains (318e–319a) that he teaches *euboulia*, "sound judgment," and this in two different spheres: in household affairs, so that one may best manage an estate; and in civic affairs, so that one may best manage a city by becoming most powerful (or capable, *dunatōtatos*) in words and deeds. The statement seems deliberately to conjure up images of Homeric aretē. For, in the *Iliad*, *euboulia* was the intellectual excellence of kings and heroes, the ability to think and speak well in council;[13] and "words and deeds" were the main areas in which the Homeric hero could strive.[14] Protagoras thus presents himself as a traditional educator of political elites—of heroes who wish to save their cities and win glory for themselves.

Socrates asks for still greater clarification. Does Protagoras mean to say that he teaches *politikē technē*, "political skill," and that he makes men into good citizens (*agathous politas*)? To this Protagoras assents. I return in a moment to certain semantic issues that arise from Socrates' questions (e.g., what does it mean to be a "good" citizen?), but for now I stress that Socrates locates Protagoras' instruction squarely in the political domain. Protagoras teaches political skills and abilities. But then comes the challenge. For, Socrates now expresses doubts about whether political ability can be taught. And to support his doubts he offers two arguments before challenging Protagoras explicitly to supply an *epideixis*, a demonstration that political ability can be taught. Consider the grounds for Socrates' doubt.

The Theoretical Challenge: Two Objections

The "Assembly Objection": First of all, the Athenian Assembly does not seem to believe that political ability can be taught. For whenever it meets to deliberate about "political" matters, it welcomes advice from anyone who wishes to speak, regardless of education or credentials. This contrasts sharply with the Assembly's practice when discussing technical matters. If, for example, the question is how to build a bridge or a temple, advice is received only from trained experts. Why should this be? It is—Socrates infers—because the Athenians do not regard political ability as *didakton*, teachable; they distinguish political skill from technical skill (*technē*) in just this respect. And if the Athenians are wise—which Socrates here grants—then their opinion should have some weight.

Second, the "Elite Parent Objection": Nor, Socrates adds, do the "wisest and best" parents of Athens seem to regard political ability as teachable. For the case of Pericles is typical: he educates his children thoroughly in all teachable matters, but when it comes to the very matters in which he himself is held to be "wisest and best"—that is, political matters—he neither educates them himself nor sends them away to others, but lets them wander around in search of wisdom on their own. Humorously, Pericles' two sons, Paralus and Xanthippus, are among the students currently in attendance with Protagoras (315a). Whether they are there on their own accord or at their father's bidding we do not know. And so it is with other leading citizens, too; they themselves are "good" (*agathoi*), but they prove incapable of making anyone—even their own children—"better" (320b2–3).

Such are Socrates' grounds for doubting that political ability is *didakton*. I note that Socrates' own position is not clearly stated. He does not argue that *he* regards political ability as unteachable, only that it seems to be so "in view of" (*eis apoblepōn*) the way the Assembly and the elite parents of Athens behave. Indeed, Socrates confesses that he "wavers" on this issue when he considers Protagoras' own career (320b6). Protagoras' task, therefore, is to remove the ostensible sources of his doubt. However, this is in fact only half the challenge Protagoras faces; for Socrates' objections are deliberately political in nature and designed to solicit a rhetorical, not merely a theoretical, response. How can Protagoras show that political ability can be taught without, at the same time, implying that the Athenian Assembly is unwise and that the elite parents of Athens are pedagogically incompetent?

The Rhetorical Component: Caution toward Masses and Elites

As I interpret Socrates' challenge, then, he is not only asking Protagoras to demonstrate that political ability can be taught, but also asking the sophist to demonstrate his hallmark political "caution" or "discretion" (*eulabeia*). That Protagoras takes great pride in his caution one learns from the gratuitous speech he makes on the subject when he first meets Socrates (316c–317c). There he explains that he faces two basic dangers as a sophist: first, the danger of jealous parents, who do not like to be told that their sons will become "best" by studying with a foreign sophist; and second, the danger of "ill will and hostile plots" forming against him (316d3). About this second danger, Protagoras is vague; he hints only that it is a *political* danger he has in mind (i.e., one arising from those who have power, 317a). And why would the powerful feel hostile toward Protagoras? One is left to draw the inference, but it is not difficult to draw: Protagoras promises to make his students "the *most* powerful in acting and speaking in civic affairs" (319a). If Protagoras can deliver on his promise, his students will be poised to displace, or at least dilute, the current elites in power. The democratic masses are powerful in Athens, too, but they are not such a threat to Protagoras because, as he baldly asserts, they "perceive nothing," but simply "recite whatever the powerful proclaim" (317a4–6).[15]

In the face of such dangers Protagoras announces that he "exercises caution" (or discretion, *eulabeomai*, 316d1) and brags about his techniques to Socrates. What kind of techniques does he employ? His fist move—somewhat counterintuitive, but nevertheless understandable—is to profess *openly* to being a sophist (317b). Better to admit this, Protagoras insists, than to deny it, because one will likely be exposed as a sophist anyway. (Readers are perhaps supposed to think of Socrates here.[16]) Then Protagoras mentions certain "other" cautionary tactics that he has devised (317b6–7), to which he attributes his very survival. He does not say what these are. But then comes a crucial line. He says (317c4–5), "And so it would be much the most pleasing thing for me . . . to fashion a speech before all those who are inside about these things (*peri toutōn*)." The line is wonderfully ambiguous. As I read it, *toutōn* refers at once to the "other cautionary techniques" Protagoras has tantalizingly mentioned but not named, as well as to his more general willingness (see 316c) to show Hippocrates what he teaches. The line is crucial because it signals, well before Socrates even requests a speech from Protagoras, that the sophist wishes to offer a display of (among other things) his cautionary techniques (cf. 317c, where Socrates senses Protagoras' desire to make a display for the other sophists).

This explains why Socrates frames his own two arguments in such pointed political terms. Knowing precisely where the dangers lie for Protagoras (since Protagoras has told him), Socrates challenges the sophist not merely to demonstrate that political ability can be taught, but also to demonstrate how it is possible to speak openly about teaching political excellence without posing a threat to the equality-loving democratic Assembly, on the one hand, or to elite parents, on the other. Moreover, Socrates has reason indeed for wanting to know this, because Socrates *too* speaks about political excellence in public, and faces hostility from these very groups.[17]

Socrates' challenge thus contains a rhetorical component.[18] But to be clearer about its nature, it has sometimes been suggested that Protagoras is somehow facing an *immediate* risk of antagonizing potentially hostile groups and must for this reason conceal his real views.[19] This is to misunderstand the challenge. Protagoras is here safely ensconced in a private home with no one to hear him but fellow sophists and professed admirers. He can thus speak relatively openly if he wishes about his disdain for "the many" (352e, 353a), and the various dangers he faces. The reason Protagoras must exercise cautionary rhetoric is that

Socrates has set him up for the task. Protagoras has bragged about his skills in this; he has announced his desire to deliver a speech about it; and Socrates has (brilliantly) supplied the occasion.

Protagoras has yet another reason to exhibit rhetorical skills in his speech. If one considers his audience (314e–316a, 317d–e), he has a remarkably diverse group of people to impress—other sophists, students of various sorts, and Socrates. But what will impress them? The very diversity of the group poses a challenge. No doubt some of his auditors (Hippocrates included) would be impressed to hear a bit of the "clever speaking" for which Protagoras is renowned (312d). However, there remains the question of genre. Perhaps some would be interested in courtroom oratory, others in public debate; perhaps others still—for example, the sophists in the room, and Antimoerus the Mendaean, who is studying to become a sophist himself (315a)—would be impressed to hear Protagoras' pioneering theories and penetrating insights. Protagoras has to speak in different ways to different members of his audience. And, as I show, this is something he does.[20]

Competing Demands and a Semantic Opening

I close my reflections on Socrates' challenge by noting how impossible it seems to fulfill and by foreshadowing how Protagoras will proceed. The difficulty is that the two components of the challenge, the theoretical and the rhetorical components, tug against each other: if Protagoras speaks openly about his ability to teach political skills to his students, then he is likely to fail at his rhetorical task of exercising caution. On the other hand, if he speaks with caution and discretion vis-à-vis the relevant political factions, he is likely to undercut his ability to respond to Socrates' objections. This opposition or tension within Socrates' challenge constitutes, in my view, a major aspect of the challenge itself. How can Protagoras address both components of the challenge at once?

The key will lie in the dynamic and polyvalent terms Socrates himself employed in the challenge. When Socrates asked whether "political ability" (as I have been rendering it) can be taught, he expressed himself in a number of ways: political ability is aretē (excellence, virtue) and/or *politikē technē* (political skill); and those who possess it are said to be *agathos* (good) and/or *sophos* (wise). But as A.W.H. Adkins has argued in a seminal essay on the Great Speech, commendatory words like aretē and agathos have a wide range of potential meaning in fifth-century discourse. They can refer, on the one hand, to rare and "competitive" excellences such as the elite wisdom of a Pericles; or, on the other hand, to more common, "cooperative" virtues, such as justice and moderation.[21] The fundamental ambiguity of these terms—which corresponds in reality to multiple aspects or types of aretē (virtue, excellence, goodness, skill, wisdom)—supplies Protagoras with a crucial opening. If Protagoras can somehow use these terms in a way that seems unthreatening to the masses and the elite, while at the same time signaling to his immediate audience what he really has in mind, he will be in a position to meet both sides of Socrates' challenge at once.

I now fill out my argument by explaining more concretely what Protagoras' speech accomplishes. The speech is divided into three sections, including (1) a myth, (2) a set of arguments designed to convince the masses that virtue can be taught, and (3) a set of arguments designed to convince elite parents that virtue can be taught. In this way, Protagoras manages to display a range of rhetorical genres—moral fable, forensic rhetoric, and theoretical argument—as well as two additional rhetorical techniques, his art of "making changes" (*metaballōn*) and his art of *antilogikē*, both of which are discussed further in Chapter 7. Second, Protagoras manages (as expected) to reconcile the two competing elements of Socrates' challenge. He does this by artfully manipulating the referents of all the key terms—*aretē, politikē technē, agathos*, and *sophia*—so that their most elite connotations are suppressed and their common or "cooperative" connotations are amplified. This transformation occurs primarily in the elaborate myth with which the speech begins, but semantic manipulations are afoot throughout the speech, and this constitutes one of its most impressive rhetorical features. Finally, Protagoras exhibits in various places his penetrating political-theoretical insight. The major place to see this is likewise in the myth, but other places also contain theories and ideas that prove seminal in the history of political thought. I now turn to the speech.

The Myth (320c8–322d5)

Protagoras' speech begins with an intriguing myth about the divine origins of "technical" and "political" wisdom or skill. As the story goes, the god Prometheus and his brother Epimetheus were in the process of outfitting mortal creatures for life on earth when a mistake occurred: they distributed all the powers at their disposal to lesser animals and forgot to assign powers to man. This was partly Epimetheus' fault: Epimetheus, whose name means "afterthought," attempted to undertake the whole distribution by himself, having prevailed upon his brother for the privilege. But it was Prometheus' fault, too: Prometheus (forethought) did not see what was coming. To remedy their mistake, Prometheus stole technical wisdom (*tēn entechnon sophian*) from Athena and Hephaestus to give (along with fire) to mankind. And thus man began life on earth, equipped with technical wisdom.

But although technical wisdom enabled mankind to do many wonderful things, it did not prove adequate for survival. Men were constantly under attack by wild beasts, and they lacked a crucial power—a power that Prometheus could not steal because it was safely guarded by Zeus: namely, *politikē technē* (also called political *sophia*, cf. 321d4–5, 322b5). Without this, men could not retreat behind city walls, for once there, they would commit injustices against each other and so fall into strife. Nor could they face off collectively against the beasts, since the "art of war" (*polemikē*) was a part of the art of politics. Were it not for a merciful act of Zeus, mankind would certainly have perished. But taking pity on men, Zeus instructed his messenger, Hermes, to deliver two political gifts: *aidōs* (respect for others, shame) and *dikē* (justice) so that there could be "unifying bonds of friendship" and "principles of order" in cities (322c). Moreover, Zeus instructed Hermes carefully about the distribution of these gifts: first, *all* men should receive a share of them; they should not be the preserve of an elite few. And, second, anyone incapable of partaking in them should be killed as a pestilence to the city. Thus did mankind come to possess "political skill."

This is only a bare outline of the myth, but it will suffice to raise the question: What, exactly, does this myth accomplish in terms of Socrates' challenge? Commentators have long thought that it accomplishes relatively little. It does not demonstrate that political virtue can be taught, nor does it respond directly to Socrates' two objections. And if these were indeed Protagoras' only goals, one would have to conclude that the myth misses its mark.[22] However, these are not Protagoras' only goals, and the myth in fact accomplishes a great deal. First, it exhibits a distinct genre of rhetoric (moral fable) for those students interested in the art of public speaking. Second, it is here that certain semantic modulations are performed that enable Protagoras later on to coordinate the theoretical and rhetorical challenges he faces. And third, it demonstrates in a most impressive manner how solid Protagoras' political-theoretical powers are. To appreciate this last point one must (as suggested earlier) read the myth against the background of Hesiod's poems. I take each of these aspects of the myth in turn.

Moral Fable

The genre of moral fable was not unique to Protagoras. One finds it also in Prodicus' "Hercules Speech" and Hippias' "Nestor Speech" (both discussed in subsequent chapters). Sophistic speeches in this genre tended to exhibit certain patterns: they typically drew on well-known mythological material in order to fashion a new scene or vignette, the purpose of which was to exhort large audiences to the life of virtue. The appeal of these speeches was primarily literary and aesthetic rather than logical. Audiences were invited to admire and imitate some heroic individual, himself learning how to be virtuous. That the appeal was to the emotions rather than to reason can be explained by the nature of the audience in question: not all audiences, and particularly not mass audiences, are moved by rational argument.[23] Yet it was precisely mass audiences for whom these speeches were intended. The sophists thus had to consider not only what they wanted to convey, but also how best to convey it. This is clearly the genre Protagoras takes up in delivering his myth. He is, then, in one sense, simply demonstrating his skill in this rhetorical mode.

Yet Protagoras' myth also deviates from this genre in one important way. Where sophistic moral fables typically exhorted audiences to virtue, Protagoras' speech does not. It instead furnishes a new genealogy of virtue. This still allows Protagoras to celebrate certain political virtues by giving them a divine lineage, but it also allows him to influence or reshape his audience's understanding of political virtue itself. Thus does Protagoras show how the beliefs of the many can be manipulated. In other words, and more specifically: prior to the myth Protagoras suggested that he taught certain competitive political skills to elite youths (students were to become "most powerful in words and deeds" so they can "best manage a city," 318e–319); but by the end of the myth political skill looks different: it looks like cooperative virtue (*aidōs* and *dikē*), which can and must be possessed by all men in common. As the competitive side of politics is suppressed and the cooperative side brought out, the fable becomes a tool for manipulating mass perceptions about the kinds of thing Protagoras teaches.

Semantic Modulations: From Competitive to Cooperative Virtue

One can see more closely how Protagoras does this if attention is fixed squarely on the meaning of the word *politikē* (art of politics) as the myth proceeds. When the word is first introduced, it refers to a power, or set of powers, designed to save mankind from wild animals, and it does this in two ways: it enables people to draw together into cities without committing injustices against each other; and it enables people to wage war. This second aspect of *politikē*, the "art of war" (*polemikē*) is every bit as necessary for human survival as the arts of political association. So says the myth, initially. But by the end of the myth the art of war has dropped out. Zeus distributes two and only two political powers to mankind, aidōs and dikē, both of which facilitate "unifying bonds of friendship" and "principles of order" in cities (322c). These are the cooperative virtues that make civic association possible.

But what happens to the art of war? Are listeners to understand that this is somehow included in aidōs and dikē? The hypothesis is tempting but cannot be right. Respect for others and a sense of justice may be necessary for waging war, but they are not sufficient. Military success requires leadership. Indeed, the very notion of an "art of war" (*polemikē technē*) connotes, if anything, the specialized skills of a military leader: foresight, strategy, prudence, courage, physical stature, and, perhaps most importantly, the ability to persuade and to command. Without such skills, war is simply impossible. Nor is the "art of war" something that every man possesses—as we are told is the case with aidōs and dikē.[24] Every man is not a general. The end of the myth, then, seems deliberately to obscure the fact that there is more to war (and to politics in general) than mere "cooperative" political virtue.

I now state more systematically the point that the myth tries to obscure. A significant distinction can be marked between collective living and collective *enterprise* (i.e., collaboration for a common goal or purpose, as in war). With collective enterprise comes the problem of unifying wills, of choosing the best among potential goals and strategies and convincing people to go along. Not only aidōs and dikē are required for collective enterprise, but also leadership. Yet while Protagoras alludes to leadership through his "art of war," (and even through his phrase "art of politics," which naturally evokes the skills of a Pericles), the end of the myth suppresses this aspect of political life. Politics is presented as if it were *nothing but* justice and respect, capacities that almost all humans share.

The myth does this, I believe, for two reasons. One is that Protagoras is here paving the way for the arguments to come. If and only if he can cast the subject matter of his instruction in terms that are agreeable to the masses can he respond to Socrates' first objection, the "Assembly objection," in a suitably cautious way. (We see how this plays out in detail later.) Second, Protagoras is, I believe, demonstrating through his myth *how* public speakers might construe politics for a mass audience. That is to say, they have the power to help audiences see the part they can play in politics while not dwelling on the part that will be played by others. In this vein I argue (below) that the myth supplies an example of Protagorean *metaballōn*, the art of "making changes" that is discussed in the *Theaetetus* (see Chapter 7). But first I turn to the myth's political teaching.

The Political Teaching: Protagoras' Quarrel with Hesiod

The connection between Protagoras' myth of Prometheus and the earlier myth found in Hesiod is established through unmistakable allusions. (Readers unfamiliar with Hesiod's poems may want to consult the appendix to this book.) The fact that Protagoras chooses Prometheus as a main character and includes a virtually identical list of supporting characters: Epimetheus, Zeus, Athena, Hephaestus, and Hermes; the fact that Protagoras focuses thematically on the problem of political disorder and describes aidōs and dikē as gifts from Zeus to man (but not to animals)—these and other striking similarities point us back to Hesiod.[25] But to recognize the allusion is not enough; we must also see what Protagoras is *doing* with it. He is in fact improving on Hesiod's myth, changing it in ways that supply a better foundation for political life.

This becomes clear if one studies the differences between the two myths. The first and most obvious difference is that Protagoras offers a myth of moral-political progress, not a myth of decline. Hesiod's myth begins with gods and men living together in peace and ends with estrangement, disorder, death, and destruction. Hesiod's men start out with *Aidōs, Dikē*, and *Nemesis*,[26] divine bulwarks against evil. But these goddesses eventually depart from the earth and leave mankind to ruin. The Protagorean myth, by contrast, begins with an imperfect creation, one in which human beings are ill-equipped to protect themselves or to live together in cities. But then, eventually, *Aidōs* and *Dikē* are sent to *save* mankind by supplying a foundation for civic order and friendship (322c).[27]

This reversal of trajectory is politically significant: if moral decline is certain and evil is sure to triumph over goodness in the end, then why should individuals be just rather than unjust?[28] Hesiod's answer to this problem was equivocal at best: Zeus *may* reward the just and punish the wicked, at least at present (see *Works and Days* 238–240 and cf. 270–273; I elaborate on this point further in the appendix). Protagoras' answer, by contrast, is unequivocally supportive of justice: aidōs and dikē are gifts from Zeus to man; they are the ground of all social existence and the key to human salvation from violent death; thus "he who is incapable of sharing in *aidōs* and *dikē* must be killed as an illness to the city" (322d). Protagoras bolsters civic justice with a myth that more forcefully supports it.[29]

Another difference, equally significant in terms of lending support to justice, is that in Protagoras' myth, the practice of punishment (so essential to civic order) becomes more coherent, more rational. In Hesiod, Zeus metes out punishments in a state of "thumotic" rage (see e.g., *Theogony* 545–558, 561–589). His retributions take aim at the weak and often impact innocent parties (e.g., the human race and Epimetheus). That the ground of punishment is Zeus' rage means that many unjust deeds go unpunished; and when punishment does occur it is unpredictable and excessive.

Protagoras recasts all this. In Protagoras' myth, Zeus does not punish human beings when they are unjust; he leaves this for humans to do themselves. This removes much of the uncertainty and inconsistency attending a divine system of retribution and yet leaves justice with a divine sanction: the *nomos* comes from Zeus, but punishment is a civic concern. Second, Protagoras surgically removes from the myth all evidence of Zeus' thumotically motivated punishment of Prometheus; for this would supply a bad example of how punishment should be carried out. Instead Protagoras suggests that the very question of Prometheus' guilt or innocence is a complicated matter.[30] On the one hand, Prometheus did, as legend has it, steal fire from the gods. But on the other hand, there were extenuating circumstances (at least on Protagoras' telling). The initial mistake was Epimetheus' not Prometheus' (this is new to Protagoras' story); and Prometheus was motivated by a philanthropic intent: he was aiming at the "salvation" (*sōtērian*) of mankind and was simply "at a loss" (*aporia*) for any other means besides theft (321c7–8). The extent of Prometheus' guilt is thus not easy to determine, and so Protagoras changes the way the punishment is described. There is indeed a rumor of Prometheus' having been "prosecuted on a charge of theft," but this is only "according to what is said" (322a). And nothing is known about how the prosecution went. These subtle adjustments to Hesiod's myth not only shore up the case for justice by making it more rational, less thumotic; they also lay the groundwork for the full-blown theory of punishment articulated later in the Great Speech (323d–324c).

The final and most important difference between Protagoras' myth and Hesiod's concerns the nature of political association as this is portrayed among both gods and men. Here Protagoras' alterations are most elaborate. A major component of politics (human and divine) in Hesiodic myth is what the poet calls "cruel strife,"[31] the conflict that results from the desire to seize the goods of others. At first, Hesiod seems to condemn this force simply as "blameworthy" (*WD* 13, cf. 321ff.); but in fact he does not condemn it simply. He continues throughout his poems to acknowledge the quasi-legitimate role it may play in the affairs of gods and men, especially among men who are wealthy and strong (*WD* 30–32, 202–212). In fact, Hesiod predicts the ultimate triumph of cruel strife over justice (*WD* 192–201) and shows the ways in which the just are perpetually vulnerable. The politics of cruel strife is thus the politics of power; the weak must do the bidding of the strong.

In reworking this material, Protagoras begins at the level of the gods, removing cruel strife altogether as a cosmic principle and inserting in its place a common *telos* or purpose for divine action. That *telos* is philanthropy: the love of, and concern for, man in his state of need. Thus all the divine characters in Protagoras' myth—whatever their differences in ability and whatever mistakes they may make—become joint contributors to a project of offering assistance to mankind. This could not contrast more sharply with the Hesiodic myth, in which the gods cease vying with each other only long enough to contribute to a Zeus-ordained project of *mis*anthropy: the creation of Pandora (*Thg* 570–589, *WD* 60–82). It is, indeed, significant that Pandora is never mentioned in Protagoras' myth. There can be no Pandora, because there is no "cruel strife" and no irrational desire to punish. Thus the Hesiodic tale of Pandora gives way in Protagoras' hands to a truer "*pan-dora*" or "gift from all gods," namely, the benevolent dispensation of the powers (*dunameis*) necessary for human flourishing. The contrast here is especially evident in the character of Hermes: in Hesiod, Hermes delivers life-destroying evils to mankind; in Protagoras, he delivers life-saving goods.

By recasting the way the gods act, Protagoras also creates a better model of political association for men to follow. Here it would be no exaggeration to say that Protagoras invents a divine "politics" (cooperation within a stable community) where in Hesiod there is none. How can we describe this politics? One of its hallmarks is the freedom and autonomy left to each god to exercise unique skills and powers. Thus the gods call on the foresight and hindsight of Prometheus and Epimetheus when it comes to outfitting mortal creatures for life; and Prometheus allows Epimetheus (after some persuading) to undertake the initial distribution. The point here is not that such delegations of authority immediately produce ideal results. (That this is not the case is clear from Epimetheus' colossal blunder and Prometheus' tragic resort to theft.) The point is rather that each god (or person) *does indeed* possess unique and often essential powers, which, when perfected and well exercised, can contribute in substantial ways to the goals of the community. Moreover, there is a point to be made here about aidōs and dikē as well: to deny one the chance of perfecting one's skills and contributing the fruits of one's labor to the community would, it seems, amount to a violation of the justice and respect owed to fellow citizens.

Another hallmark of Protagorean politics (its distributive principle) appears as Zeus and Hermes prepare to distribute aidōs and dikē to man (322c–d): some powers (aidōs and dikē, among them) must be shared by *all* citizens if cities are to exist at all; these are prerequisites for political life. Other powers, however, are not shared by all, but are rather distributed according to the principle that "one suffices for many in the possession of a power."[32] The example Hermes supplies is that of the medical art, where one practitioner suffices for a whole community. Yet this is merely one instance of what must be a very large category of talents and intellectual powers indeed (a category extending even to the political sphere proper where debates over policy occur—though Protagoras deliberately obscures this).[33]

For such a community to flourish, individuals must not only possess discrete talents and cultivate them to the fullest possible extent, they must also *contribute* their talents to the political community as a whole. If there is to be only one skilled doctor for many who lack this skill, the doctor must in fact *serve* others with his talent; he cannot merely serve himself. Stated simply, every citizen possesses powers that render him invaluable to his community. And the corollary of this is also true: no individual possesses powers that enable him to "go it alone." Indeed, the worst thing for a community of this sort is to fail to think and to act together. Protagoras' myth illustrates this forcefully through the utter failure of Epimetheus acting alone to equip man adequately for life. The failure stems precisely from his desire to work by himself, contrary to what the gods as a group had commanded (320d), which was for Prometheus and Epimetheus to work together. This desire to act alone is what sets in motion the string of errors and negative consequences that must, ultimately, be resolved by Zeus.

We find, then, that the myth contains a pair of distributive principles stipulating the two ways in which powers are dispersed in a healthy political community. Some powers (virtues, capacities) will necessarily be possessed by all; others will be possessed by a few. Yet all powers must be carefully developed and used to promote the ends of the community as a whole. Protagoras underscores these principles in two ways. He describes them in connection with the distribution of powers to mankind, and he also depicts them at work among the gods. We thus find Epimetheus who possesses hindsight; Prometheus who possesses foresight; Athena and Hephaestus who possess various technical skills; and Zeus who possesses the "political art." All the gods possess the political art in some minimal sense—they have the power to get along with each other and to work communally for the good of mankind. But Zeus is different: he possesses political powers that are uncommon and guarded.

Now as one considers what Zeus' own powers must entail, one sees, finally, that Protagorean politics also involves a distinct form of political leadership. The Protagorean leader must (like Zeus) allow others the freedom to express their seemingly contradictory views and to contribute their seemingly discrepant gifts. This is the process by which the leader himself acquires pieces of a more complete political wisdom. Patiently and unobtrusively he must wait and observe. Eventually, though, the time will come for him to act. And drawing on all the efforts that have gone before, negotiating a necessary course on the basis of what has been tried and what is needed, and exercising the powers of speech and persuasion at his command, the leader must intervene to set things on a stable and fruitful course. This moment of political possibility, the possibility for leaders to make a positive difference, may be what Protagoras meant by the *kairos* or "right time."[34] It is the time for those capable of leadership to speak and to act.

But even here leadership must be exercised in a delicate and inconspicuous way. For, in the first place, it is built up in part from the powers and insights of others and seems now to surpass those powers. It may thus lead to jealousy. And yet nothing can be more harmful to a community of the sort here described than the spread of political jealously, which leads citizens to neglect their own affairs and to covet the gifts of others. A community of diverse talents that succumbs to jealousy must crumble. Moreover, leadership must be inconspicuous also because the citizens who have contributed to the leader's own, broader view may never be able to see that broad view themselves. Their only hope of seeing it is through some form of persuasion that tries to connect particular viewpoints to some understanding of the whole; but this may not always be possible. And if it is not, then a leader must at least be able to speak in such a way as to acknowledge and to celebrate the various individual perspectives that contribute to the whole.

A rough model for this inconspicuous leadership is supplied by the character of Zeus in Protagoras' myth. Zeus is not exactly a king. He neither assigns powers to man unilaterally (as Hesiod's Zeus attempts to do through the settlement at Mekone), nor does he determine who does undertake the distribution—the community of gods determines that (320d3–6). Zeus simply waits and observes until it is necessary for him to act. But Zeus represents only a rough model because he barely speaks in the myth and thus does not demonstrate deliberative politics at its best. A better model of political leadership is supplied (not surprisingly) by Protagoras himself, the master of persuasion and of a dialectical art that draws diverse views together into a single whole.[35]

Some combination of Zeus and Protagoras, therefore, would seem to be the ideal political leader.

Metaballōn

I have been considering the ways in which Protagoras' myth displays his political-theoretical wisdom. What emerges, in sum, is a full-fledged theory of politics expressed in opposition to the mythopoetic teachings of Hesiod. By replacing politically problematic aspects of Hesiod's myths with healthier ideas, Protagoras takes his place in a line of thinkers running from Xenophanes to Plato himself.[36] I close my consideration of the myth by pointing out that it constitutes a clear demonstration of the art of "making changes" (*metaballōn*) that is attributed to Protagoras in the *Theaetetus* (167c). There, Protagoras is made to say that a rhetor (*rhētoras*) is *sophos* and *agathos* when he effects a change in the belief structure of a city, making sound things instead of pernicious things seem just (*dikaia*). For whatever *seems* just and attractive (*kala*) in any city, *is* so for that city, as long as the city so believes (*nomidzēi*). And a wise man can make sound things instead of pernicious things seem and be just to the city in each case.

Here is exactly what Protagoras does in his paradigmatic myth of Prometheus: he makes sound things instead of pernicious things seem just. The myth is designed for mass consumption, and because the masses are not likely to possess *politikē technē* in the fullest sense of the term, and because they can *and should* possess basic political virtues such as justice and respect, Protagoras celebrates the one and obscures the other. Moreover, I would argue that Plato means for his readers to admire this. One might complain that it is elitist or deceptive in the way it obscures whole sectors of political skill from the masses. But at least from Plato's viewpoint—which is what I am interested in here—I would not count these complaints as strikes against Protagoras' political art. In fact, I would suggest that Protagoras' art of making changes finds a parallel in Socrates' account of civic origins in the *Republic*, beginning with the "city of need" (369b–372d) and culminating in the "myth of the metals" (412b–417b). This is not the place to expand on this parallel in any systematic way, but I do see these Platonic tales as related in essential ways to what Protagoras offers in his own civic genealogical myth.

Democratic Argument that Virtue Can Be Taught (322D–324C)

With his myth complete, Protagoras now turns to Socrates' first objection (the "Assembly objection") and offers three arguments to show that political virtue can be taught. This middle section of the Great Speech has puzzled commentators because of something Protagoras says when it is over, just as the third and final section commences. He says that then and only then does he cease speaking in myth (*mythos*) and start speaking in terms of reason or argument (*logos*). But if the final section alone is to be understood as logos, what are we to make of the three arguments here?[37] Clearly Protagoras' myth has come to an end and yet he regards this section as, in some sense, mythos rather than logos. The key lies in the way Protagoras here combines mythos and logos for rhetorical purposes. We are faced with arguments, to be sure; but they are arguments that depend on the myth for their persuasiveness. The myth is treated, in other words, as a "commonplace"; and Protagoras here demonstrates how it is possible to persuade mass audiences based on beliefs they already possess (or have just been given). If this is correct, then the middle section of the speech does more than merely supply a demonstration that virtue can be taught. It also displays a distinct genre of rhetoric, forensic rhetoric,[38] and reveals how Protagoras (or any speaker) might exercise caution in speaking about politics before a mass audience.

The forensic quality of Protagoras' first argument comes to light most readily if one notices the way Socrates' "objection" exhibited forensic qualities itself: Socrates focused on an observed action and drew an inference about the motivation of the actor. The "action" was the customary practice of the Assembly in distinguishing between political and technical questions—the Assembly allows *anyone* to speak in the political sphere but listens only to trained experts in technical matters. The reason or motive that Socrates imputed to the Assembly was that they do not regard political skill as *didakton*, teachable. In other words, they listen to everyone because they cannot know in advance who will be gifted at politics. Protagoras now responds with a counterargument, and his strategy is to accept the facts of the case as Socrates presents them, but to dispute the alleged motive. The cause (*aition*) of the Assembly's listening to everyone, Protagoras argues, is not that they hold *politikē* to be unteachable, but that they accept—in keeping with the myth—that politikē is possessed by *everyone*. Citing the conclusion of the myth explicitly, Protagoras drives the point home: "it is proper for everyone to have a share in this virtue . . . or else cities will not exist."

Already in this first argument, two defining traits of the middle section of this speech come to light. First, Protagoras here argues like a lawyer or statesman; this will appear even more clearly in a moment. And second, his reasoning (*logos*) truly depends on myth (*mythos*). Protagoras literally points to the myth to explain the cause (*aition*) of the Assembly's practice. Without reference to the myth, the argument would lack persuasive power. Notice also in this connection that Protagoras refers twice to the reasonableness of the Assembly's practice, and both times it is the *myth* that defines what is reasonably done (*eikotōs*, 322e2, 323a2). Later in this section, a similar touchstone is supplied by common opinion and common practices, and not the myth explicitly. But the form of the argument remains the same. Protagoras argues by relating a controversial point to currently held opinions, which (whether true or false) an audience finds attractive. That these opinions are largely unexamined and only conditionally to be regarded as true helps us to understand why Protagoras only later claims to have abandoned myth for unadulterated logos.

A final point to observe about Protagoras' first argument is that it actually outflanks Socrates' attempt to affirm the Assembly in its practice of listening to everyone. On Socrates' argument, the Assembly listens to everyone because political virtue can appear unpredictably in anyone. But Protagoras' argument seems more democratic: the Assembly listens to everyone because everyone indeed possesses political virtue. Moreover, Protagoras goes so far as to suggest a distinct political role to be played by the masses who meet in the Assembly: Just as a basic sense of justice and moderation must be possessed by everyone in order for cities to exist, so too must these virtues supply the foundation for all political decisions. All decisions "must entirely follow the path of" the foundational civic virtues.[39] Thus the role of the people in politics is to ensure that political decisions harmonize with basic, civic moral virtues.

The very idea of a special role for the people in politics suggests that other roles will be played by others—the role of the leader, for example. Protagoras therefore cannot make too much of this point or he will say more than needs to be said and fail to display his much advertised caution vis-à-vis the democratic masses. Perhaps this is why Protagoras now shifts quickly to his second argument, what he calls his "hard proof" that "all human beings really do believe every man shares in justice and the rest of political *aretē*" (323a5–7).[40]

The Hard Proof (Tekmērion)

The word *tekmērion* derives from *tekma*, a "fixed boundary." Protagoras is here attempting to "fix" by other means what he has already argued on the basis of the myth—namely, that Athenians (and indeed all people) believe that political virtue is shared by all. The proof runs as follows.

> If someone claims to be a good flute player but isn't . . . people either ridicule him or treat him harshly, and when his relatives approach him they admonish him as one who is mad (*mainomenon*). But as for justice and the rest of political *aretē*, even if they know someone is unjust, and if he himself tells the truth about himself before many, yet while in the former case they held telling the truth to be knowing one's limits (*sophrosunē*), in this they hold *it* to be madness (*mania*) and assert that all must *say* they are just, whether they are or not, and that anyone who doesn't *pretend* to possess justice is mad. They do so on the grounds that everyone should somehow or other share in it or cease to be among humans. (323a–c, my trans.)

This proof is worth analyzing not only because it is challenging to understand but also because it has been thought (wrongly in my view) to reflect negatively on Protagoras. The argument can be clarified if one notices that it makes observations on three levels. First and most fundamentally, it draws our attention to two types of human failure: failures of technical skill and failures of political skill. Next it draws attention to the way individuals who exhibit these failures might present themselves: they can either admit or deny their failures. And, finally, it points out how people in general receive the various individuals in question. And here is the crucial point: When someone fails to possess some technical skill, people harbor no ill will toward him, unless he presents himself as skillful when he is not; then people censure him for not knowing his limits. The rule here is that one should admit one's limits with respect to those skills that are not universal and thus not expected. But when it comes to *political* skills the situation is reversed: if someone admits frankly to an utter lack of justice, people do not praise this person for knowing his limits, they censure him. This shows that people *expect* everyone to possess basic political skill. (Political skill is presented throughout this proof as though it refers strictly to "cooperative" moral virtues such as justice and respect.)

However, Protagoras goes further; and here is the controversial part: "all must *say* they are just, whether they are or not, and anyone who does not *pretend* to possess justice is mad" (323b). This has been taken, understandably, to indicate that Protagoras is an advocate of lying about one's virtue. However, the text does not permit this interpretation for a number of reasons. First and most fundamentally, Protagoras' argument—however we interpret it—must make sense as a proof of the point Protagoras is making; and he has no reason to encourage his democratic audience to disguise their basic moral virtue—this would not advance his goals in any way. Secondly, Protagoras is not expressing his own view here, but the view of people in general (*pantes anthrōpoi*, 323a5–6); and thus his statement is descriptive: people do, as a matter of fact, regard as insane a person who lacks justice and admits this of himself. The question, then, is *why* they regard it such. And here I believe Protagoras has a point. To admit one's utter lack of justice is madness because justice is indeed normative—it is expected of everyone. And thus when people depart (viciously) from justice, they tend to disguise their departure as virtue. Hypocrisy, as Rochefoucauld has said, is the homage that vice must pay to virtue. In other words, the fact that sane people cover up their vice proves *eo ipso* that virtue is universally expected of all men. Interpreted thus, Protagoras' proof actually demonstrates the point he sets out to make: it demonstrates that all human beings expect people to share in basic political virtue.

The People Believe Virtue Can Be Taught

The final step in this part of Protagoras' speech is to address Socrates' concrete question: Can virtue be *taught*? Nothing in the speech up to this point has actually addressed this. The myth, for its part, merely assigned two political virtues to all human beings; it said nothing about whether these needed to be taught—on the contrary, it seemed to suggest by its silence on this point that virtue simply arises by nature (*phusei*) or automatically (*automatou*). And so Protagoras must now demonstrate that political virtue requires teaching and deliberate care (*epimeleias*).[41] But, again, he must do so in a way that displays his caution toward the masses. For if political virtue is revealed to involve elite skills and to require elite teaching, then the masses who cannot afford such instruction may be shut out of politics, at least at the highest levels. This is the appearance Protagoras needs to avoid, and here is how he does so. First, he continues to modulate the meaning of "political virtue" so that it refers to "cooperative" rather than "competitive" qualities. Second, he proceeds deductively from commonly held views. In this way, Protagoras argues not only that virtue is teachable, but also that the people *themselves* believe it to be so.

The actual argument focuses on the practice of punishment—or, to be precise, on the rationalized practice of punishment as this was developed in the myth. For punishment to be rational, individuals undergoing punishment must have been in control of the deeds for which they are being punished; and the punishment itself must aim at instruction, not vengeance. It is manifestly irrational to punish people for things beyond their control or to punish without the moral improvement of the wrongdoer in mind. Protagoras thus claims that people are not punished for their "natural" defects such as dwarfishness, ugliness, or weakness. And yet people are indeed punished when they fail to practice basic political virtues such as justice and respect.[42] What does this imply? It implies that political virtue (or the lack of it) is not simply natural; it is within our control and a matter of teaching. In other words, if we assume that Athenian practices of punishment are rational, then the very fact that people are punished for acts of injustice proves that political virtue can be taught.

This proof does not demonstrate what Socrates presumably had in mind: it does not demonstrate that political virtue in every sense of the word can be taught. It says nothing about the elite skills of a Pericles. And yet if Protagoras had demonstrated that *these* virtues could be taught, he would have met one challenge at the expense of the other. His challenge in this part of the speech is not simply to demonstrate that political aretē can be taught, but to do so *in a fashion unthreatening to the masses*. And so, what he does is to define "virtue" and "political skill" in the most common and democratic way, and then to argue on the basis of a commonly accepted institution (punishment) that this can be and indeed is taught. In short, he demonstrates that virtue can be taught from the perspective of the masses.[43]

Argument for Elite Parents (324d–328d)

One final aspect of Socrates' challenge remains to be tackled. Socrates had observed (319e–320b) that elite parents like Pericles, the "wisest and best citizens," often fail to impart their own special aretē to their sons. Sometimes they do not even try (Pericles again). This led Socrates to suggest that political virtue is not teachable. What will Protagoras say? Political virtue in this context refers not to cooperative virtues, not primarily at least, but to the competitive virtues of a leader. If Protagoras concedes that this is unteachable, then he calls his own pedagogical enterprise into question. But if he claims that it is teachable, he runs the risk of offending those parents who fail to impart excellence to their sons. Such parents must be either incompetent or neglectful when it comes to education (cf. 316c–d).

Protagoras' strategy is, once again, to exploit the ambiguity of key moral terms. This seems a permanent feature of his cautionary rhetoric. The manipulation is here subtle and ingenious. Socrates had asked about the "wisest and best" citizens of Athens, the *sophōtatoi kai aristoi tōn politōn*—what we might call the *aristocracy*. Protagoras in his response renames these *agathoi*, which is a roughly synonymous term,[44] but carries the secondary meaning of "good men" in the moral sense (just, moderate, pious). By renaming the *aristoi* "*agathoi*," Protagoras can suggest that the virtue which is distinctly theirs is none other than the basic moral virtues he has been considering all along. And the advantage of this comes to light right away. The moral virtues are in fact actively taught by elite parents.

In addition to manipulating terms, Protagoras also demonstrates in this section of his speech how elite audiences can be flattered and thus disarmed. The flattery has two aspects. First, he affirms the elites in their material wealth: not only do elite parents educate their children in virtue, they do so *best of all*, because they have the means to place their children with good teachers at the earliest age and to keep them under tutelage the longest (326c). Second, Protagoras flatters the elites for their intellectual acuity, and he does so by now arguing in a new way. Here is the significance of Protagoras' remark, which opens this section of the speech: "About this, Socrates, I shall no longer tell you a myth, but rather an argument" (324d). The Athenian elites, who in many cases are responsible for crafting laws and policies, do not need to be told myths. They are able to see the truth of things (or so they believe). Protagoras thus argues according to a criterion of truth, which he calls nature (*physis*, 325a, 327b). "Is there or is there not," Protagoras asks, "some one thing that all citizens necessarily share in, if in fact there is to be a city?" There is, Protagoras answers, and it is aretē—"justice, moderation and being pious (325a)." The elite perceive this because it is "such by nature" (325b), and this is why they attend so carefully to the education of their children.

Such is Protagoras' use of flattery and his manipulation of terms. However, a problem arises with the argument in this section of the speech. Unlike his earlier "democratic argument" that virtue could be taught, Protagoras' argument here fails to respond convincingly to Socrates' initial observation. Socrates' observation was that the children of the elite often pale in comparison to their parents, and the example of Pericles' two children, Paralus and Xanthippus, supplied the case in point. But Protagoras' response does not explain this phenomenon. It suggests only that the children of the elite receive the best education of all. If anything, this only deepens the puzzle.

As if sensing the lacuna, Protagoras now addresses the puzzle directly. Building masterfully on the two ideas he has already emphasized—namely that political virtue is *cooperative* virtue and that "nature" is the relevant criterion of truth—his argument runs as follows: in any art that is universally practiced and valued, those who really stand out will be those who have the "best nature" for it (327c), and these are not necessarily those whose parents are exceptionally talented. Nature does not work that way, Protagoras points out. Great talents can be born from untalented parents and *vice versa*. Nevertheless, Paralus and Xanthippus cannot be written off so fast, for they are still young; and the challenge is for all parents to give their children the best education possible, which means looking for teachers, if any exist, who are a little more capable than others of advancing people in virtue. And this is the thought with which Protagoras concludes his great speech: "Indeed, I think I am one of these and that I aid someone's becoming noble and good better than do other human beings and that I am worthy of the fee I charge and still more" (328b).

Conclusion: What the Great Speech Reveals

Protagoras' Great Speech thus accomplishes a number of things. It demonstrates that political virtue (of the cooperative sort, at least) can be taught. It demonstrates Protagoras' way of speaking cautiously to different kinds of audience. It displays several well-known genres of artful speech—moral fable, forensic rhetoric, and arguments from nature. And it presents some of Protagoras' impressive political-theoretical insights. Moreover, the speech goes some way toward demonstrating that competitive political virtue can be taught, too. It does so not in the substance of its arguments as much as in its deeds. The speech itself is an example of competitive political skill. Certainly it demonstrates something of the "good counsel" that Protagoras claims to teach. The ideas and techniques here on display would likely have been discussed more systematically in private sessions. But some degree of teaching has certainly already begun.

Now that this speech has been analyzed with care, it is time to look back at the questions that animate this study. What is the significance of the fact that Plato assigns such a remarkable speech to Protagoras? What does this suggest about Plato's view of this sophist or his purposes in treating him so extensively in the dialogues? Put differently, what does a careful analysis of the Great Speech reveal that would otherwise be obscure? The answer is that the speech reveals something of the depth and complexity of the affinities between Socrates and Protagoras, and, by leading readers to see this, invites them to consider afresh the question of Socrates' singularity. Only on the basis of a correct view of the similarities between Socrates and Protagoras, I would argue, are we prepared to see the meaningful differences.[45]

What then are the similarities? Consider Protagoras' use of myth. Myth supplies a way of speaking persuasively to audiences that might not be moved by bare argument. It appeals to the emotions, aids understanding by presenting ideas in a narrative context, and lends a poetic dignity to the whole. Moreover, by creating a myth Protagoras has an opportunity to subtly rework earlier political-theoretical ideas, rendering them more suitable for civic health. Socrates and Protagoras both create (and re-create) myths in the dialogues, and they appear to do so with similar purposes in mind. They thus appear to have been on the same side in the "ancient quarrel between poetry and philosophy" (*Republic* 607b)—more so, perhaps, than commentators have previously realized. And yet, to say that Protagoras and Socrates both sought to revise myth in accordance with reason is only to begin the comparison. What the comparison makes possible is the question of how Socrates' revisions of myth go beyond those of Protagoras. Here I only suggest that Socrates' myths tend not to focus on the origins of human institutions (something that can be accounted for by reason), but on questions that reason itself cannot determine and that nevertheless impact the health of the city, such as the question of rewards and punishments after death.[46] I am inclined to say, also, that Socrates' gods are not as human (which is to say: flawed) as the gods Protagoras creates.

This leads to another similarity (and difference) between Protagoras and Socrates, namely that they both understand the basic need for *some kind* of account of how and why cities emerge. Protagoras' myth of Prometheus thus finds its counterpart in Socrates' account of civic origins in *Republic* II. These two accounts are not identical, and one of the major differences is that Protagoras begins in the mythic past with a theological explanation of man's basic needs, while Socrates begins with the simple fact of need and moves forward from there. But both accounts entail the recognition that individuals are insufficient on their own, that cities are therefore necessary, that without justice cities cannot exist, and that in a successful city, some skills will be possessed by only one or a few who have the ability to work in the interest of all. In this sense, too, Protagoras and Socrates appear not as antagonists but as allies in the grand and meaningful attempt to describe the foundations of politics in a way that can promote civic health and well-being.[47]

Yet another similarity concerns the practice of artful speech. Protagoras and Socrates both speak in different ways to different audiences, saying less than everything they mean to some, while indicating a more complete meaning to others through subtle hints and suggestions. Moreover, they both appear to have used this technique for pedagogical and prudential reasons. Pedagogically, they sense that some listeners may be harmed or led astray by hearing things ill-suited to their nature or their present needs.[48] With respect to prudence, both perceive the deadly tension that can arise between the city and anyone who inquires too deeply into virtue. Both "take forethought" before they speak,[49] attempting to avoiding direct confrontation whenever possible. But here, too, an important difference emerges. This tension between the philosopher and the city is what leads, ultimately, to Socrates' death; while the Platonic Protagoras is said to have lived to a ripe old age with his reputation intact. Was Protagoras, perhaps, more expert at forethought (prudential calculation) than Socrates?

Merely to pose the question is to expose the most significant difference between Socrates and Protagoras that comes to light in this dialogue. The difference relates to what "forethought" finally means and requires. And this, in turn, depends on what really "saves" a man.[50] For Protagoras, it is necessary to take forethought about matters relating to one's safety and the stability of the city; and forethought equates essentially with strategic calculation and speech. Protagoras anticipates what others will see, what they will believe; and he speaks in ways that foster the ends he deems good. These ends appear to include not only safety and stability, but also the pursuit of personal power and honor. (Protagoras was, ultimately, conventional in his attachment to these familiar goods.)[51] For Socrates, though, forethought does not mean simply the ability to protect his body and his reputation from harm. It means knowing, or, if not knowing, then tirelessly seeking, what *is* good and bad for man. Only on the basis of such an understanding could an individual be said to be truly prudent, or to take forethought in the complete sense. A fundamental difference between Socrates and Protagoras, is, then, that Socrates was engaged in a search for the meaning of aretē that was not limited to or constrained by conventional beliefs; and he was engaged in a search for a "saving knowledge" that did not assume that one's body or one's reputation were the highest goods. As Socrates says elsewhere, for him the good life, not life itself, was most important.

FOUR

PRODICUS

Diplomat, Sophist, and Teacher of Socrates

> Prodicus of Ceos seems to have been the most notable philologist among the major sophists. According to tradition Socrates at some time was his pupil and we still can sense a distinct sympathy for him in the dialogues of Plato. . . . Plato's sympathy for Prodicus may well have been rooted in a craftsman's respect for the valuable work of a predecessor.
>
> —Eric Voegelin, *The World of the Polis*[1]

Prodicus came from the city of Iulis on the island of Ceos in the Cyclades. He served his city as a diplomat and was evidently a good one, for Plato mentions a speech he delivered before the Athenian Council, which won him great respect (*Hipp. Maj.* 282c). While traveling as a diplomat, Prodicus also made money as a sophist, delivering public exhibition speeches (*epideixeis*) and offering private instruction to the young. His public speeches ranged widely in subject matter from lectures on language to elaborate moral fables like his famous "Choice of Hercules." According to tradition, Prodicus once appeared in Boeotia while Xenophon was in prison there, and Xenophon went so far as to post his own bail in order to attend one of Prodicus' lectures. By all accounts his lectures were highly regarded and attended by numerous notable personalities.[2] Regarding his private instruction, little if anything is known, except that his curriculum was probably similar to that of Protagoras. He is mentioned in the same breath as Protagoras in the *Republic* (600c) as someone who taught *aretē* in general and political excellence in particular. In age, he was approximately contemporary with Socrates and a good bit younger than Protagoras.

This much about Prodicus is basic; but what is not basic is the intriguing way in which Plato casts Prodicus' relationship to Socrates in the dialogues. Eric Voegelin was right in the passage quoted earlier to detect a sympathy of spirit. However, the grounds for this sympathy are not easily worked out. There is no dialogue called the *Prodicus*. That in itself is interesting, given Plato's handling of other sophists in distinct works of their own, and it suggests already that Prodicus was somehow different. In order to investigate the status of this great diplomat and sophist in Plato's dialogues, one must consider references to him scattered across the entire corpus. And, in fact, these turn out to be quite remarkable both for their quantity and content. As a quick survey reveals, Prodicus is mentioned in more than a dozen dialogues and actually appears as a character in the *Protagoras* alongside Protagoras and Hippias.[3] As for the significance of all these references, that is the purpose of this chapter to investigate. In what follows, I argue that despite some passages of light and humorous critique, Plato's posture toward Prodicus was actually one of great respect. Plato in fact goes out of his way to record precisely how and why Socrates could learn from this sophist. Though we do not typically think of Socrates as a student of the sophists, his relationship to Prodicus was clearly an exception. Socrates was quite literally his pupil, and the effect of Prodicus' teaching on Socrates' own search for wisdom appears to have been significant.[4]

DEEPENING THE QUESTION: THREE INTRIGUING PASSAGES

It is useful to begin by examining those passages about Prodicus that are at once the most suggestive and the most obscure in meaning. Examination of these prompts certain questions that fuel the remainder of this study.

The first passage (and perhaps the most familiar) is the initial description of Prodicus in the *Protagoras* (315c8–316a2). Socrates has just arrived at the house of Callias, where numerous students and admirers of the sophists are grouped in clusters around Protagoras, Prodicus, and Hippias. Socrates likens the scene in general to the house of Hades, where the wandering Odysseus encountered so many departed souls. When he spots Prodicus, Socrates alludes in particular to the shade of Tantalus ("and I spied Tantalus too," *Prt.* 315c8; cf. *Odyssey* 11.582), and proceeds to describe him in a rather comical way. Prodicus is still in bed, wrapped in "very many bedclothes," in an old storage room that Callias had converted for the occasion. At his side on nearby couches are a number of attractive students—among whom Pausanius and Agathon will be familiar from the *Symposium*. Prodicus is conversing with his admirers about something that Socrates cannot quite make out, the room being too reverberant and Prodicus' voice too deep. However, Socrates (as narrator) professes to be earnestly (*liparōs*) interested in hearing Prodicus, because the Cean seems to him an altogether wise and divine man (*passophos . . . kai theios*).

Like so many passages relating to Prodicus this one will likely strike readers as equivocal in tone. On the one hand, Socrates seems to acknowledge that Prodicus' wisdom is somehow special: "Only in the case of Prodicus," remarks one commentator, "does Socrates make known his (unfulfilled) desire to hear what is being said."[5] On the other hand, Socrates' description of the sophist's posture and his similarity to Tantalus are plainly mocking. And yet, if we ask what these criticisms are meant to convey, the answer is not at all obvious. Tantalus, we know from various legends, was a proverbially wealthy king with a special connection to the gods. Having been admitted to their company, he soon committed the crime of ingesting divine food (thus becoming immortal himself) and delivering this food also to mankind (Pindar, *Olympian* I, 60ff.). For his crime, Tantalus was eternally punished in the manner in which Odysseus observes him in Hades. Standing in water up to his chin, with fruits and luxuriant olives hanging above him, he appears hungry and thirsty, but cannot fulfill his desires; for when he reaches out toward the food it suddenly disperses to the winds, and when he stoops for the water it suddenly recedes into the earth. This much we know about Tantalus, but what any of this has to do with Prodicus, we do not know. Nor do we know what Socrates might mean by describing this sophist as "altogether wise and divine."

Leaving these questions in place, let us turn to another passage—this time from the *Theaetetus*—where Prodicus is mentioned again in fascinating but puzzling terms. The context is Socrates' description of his own art of "midwifery" (149a–151d), by which he delivers pupils of any philosophical ideas they may have while testing to see whether these are in fact sound. This is a service Socrates performs for pupils who seem to him suitably "pregnant" and who suffer the "labor pains" of intellectual perplexity. However, Socrates explains:

> [I]n some cases . . . when [students] do not seem to me to be exactly pregnant, since I see that they have no need of me, I act with perfect goodwill [*panu eumenōs*] as a match-maker and, with god's help, I guess very successfully by whose association they would be benefited, and I have married off many of them to Prodicus, and many others to different wise and divinely-speaking men [*thespesiois andrasi*]. (151b, trans. mine)

Again, the passage is notable for its ambivalence. On the one hand, Prodicus is clearly being put down: to Prodicus go the dullards! But on the other hand, the sophist is, again, singled out for unique attention: to Prodicus *especially* (more than to others) go Socrates' nonpregnant souls. Socrates claims to hand these pupils to Prodicus in good faith, hoping and expecting that they might be benefited by him. And Socrates in fact takes great pride in his "match-making" abilities (*Tht.* 149e–150a). Thus we have the sense, despite the comic put down, that Prodicus is also being commended here as the *best* of the lesser educators. Yet, all this is quite speculative, and what the passage really leaves us with are questions: Why Prodicus? Is there anything about Prodicus' instruction that would make him especially well-suited to teach students who fall short of Socrates' own prerequisites? What is the ground for Socrates' apparent trust in Prodicus?

If the *Protagoras* and *Theaetetus* serve to pique our interest in Prodicus, this is only deepened when we consider another passage—or, actually a cluster of passages—which indicate that Socrates was *himself* a pupil of Prodicus. In the *Cratylus* (384b) Socrates humorously remarks that he cannot answer a question his interlocutors have posed about the correctness of words, because in his poverty he could only afford the one-drachma *epideixis* of Prodicus, not the fifty-drachma course in which the sophist offered a complete education in the matter. Were this the only passage of its kind, one might reasonably dismiss it as mere humor, but there are in my view too many such passages to dismiss. In the *Charmides* (163d), Socrates remarks that he has "heard

Prodicus myriad times making distinctions about words." In the *Protagoras* (341a) he says that he has become well acquainted with Prodicus' art of distinction-making by literally becoming a pupil or disciple (*mathētēs*) of the sophist. In the *Hippias Major* (282c) he refers to Prodicus as his friend or companion (*hetairos*). And near the end of the *Meno* (96d), Socrates again describes Prodicus as his teacher—though now with a tinge of criticism: Prodicus has failed to *educate* Socrates—just as Meno's teacher, Gorgias, has failed to educate Meno—on how exactly men come to acquire aretē and whether being good boils down essentially to knowledge or perhaps to something else.[6]

Such offhand remarks begin to add up, and they render all the more interesting Socrates' remark in the *Theaetetus* that he sends certain students to Prodicus. The connection between Socrates and this sophist was evidently quite real, and Socrates' knowledge of his teaching quite intimate. However, we are still left with a number of questions: What if anything did Socrates learn from Prodicus that was useful or beneficial? What were the sophist's strengths? What, on the other hand, were the weaknesses that would lead Plato to lampoon him (if that is not too strong a word) in the *Protagoras*, to refer to him in such equivocal terms in the *Theaetetus*, and to suggest in the *Meno* that he did not impart enough knowledge about aretē? These are the questions I pursue for the remainder of the chapter. However, I must warn my readers that these are notoriously difficult matters to pin down on the basis of the meager evidence at our disposal and that my reflections (especially in the next two sections) must therefore take the form more of an exploration of certain possibilities than a completely satisfactory account.[7] My decision to press on in spite of the poor state of the evidence is based solely on the fact that the information we do possess turns out to be so fascinating and, to a certain extent, enlightening, even if it does not completely answer the questions I have posed.

Casting a fairly broad net, let us begin by examining what a number of authors other than Plato have said about Prodicus' intellectual characteristics and his achievements. We must not turn away information that comes to us through other channels, and this may indeed help us to understand Prodicus in ways that Socrates and Plato might have understood him. After examining this evidence, I turn to Plato's treatment of Prodicus' art of making distinctions, bcause this facet of his teaching seems, in particular, to account for much of what Plato's Socrates admires and also criticizes in his teacher.

THE CHOICE OF HERCULES

To the ancients, Prodicus was well known for a moral fable he frequently recited before large audiences about the hero Hercules. A version of his fable has come down to us through Xenophon's *Memorabilia* (II.i.21–34), and though it is often taken out of context, the setting in this case proves quite important.[8] In Book II of the *Memorabilia*, Xenophon advances the argument that association with Socrates was morally beneficial, and he adduces as evidence the fact that Socrates could sometimes be found exhorting his companions to practice self-control. Xenophon mentions one pupil in particular—a certain Aristippus,[9] who was especially prone to intemperance—and describes how Socrates tried to assist him through a careful dialectical examination. Unfortunately, Socratic conversation failed in this case to procure the desired result, but Socrates did not give up. Rather he resorted in the last instance simply to reciting (as best he could remember) the speech of the "wise Prodicus" about Hercules. That Socrates was familiar with Prodicus' speech and indeed employed it as a tool for his own pedagogical purposes corroborates (on the basis of non-Platonic evidence) the point we have already been observing—namely, that Socrates and Prodicus were closely connected and that the sophist's teachings contained material that was useful. In fact, the whole episode as Xenophon describes it seems to capture in a metaphorical way the practice of matchmaking described in the *Theaetetus*: when Aristippus fails to respond to the cold logic of Socratic argument, he is turned (metaphorically) over to Prodicus, where, it is hoped, he will find something of benefit.

What did Prodicus' speech entail? According to Xenophon,[10] it depicted Hercules at the verge of manhood, in the throes of a choice between virtue (*aretē*) and vice (*kakia*). In dramatic fashion, Prodicus made the hero's choice stand visually before him as two attractive goddesses, each with her own allurements. Once the setting is established, the first to speak is Vice, who promises a life of comfort, abundant pleasure, and the power to exploit the hard work of others: "you shall . . . never refrain from taking advantage whenever you are able; for to my companions I supply the power to seize benefits from all quarters" (*Mem.* II.i.25).[11] Vice's demeanor is seductive, but her beauty is cheap; and when Hercules inquires of her name, she tells him: "My friends call me Happiness (*Eudaimonia*), but among those who hate me I am called Vice" (Ibid. 26). At this point, Virtue makes the case for her own way of life:

> I shall not deceive you with a pleasant prelude. Rather shall I tell you truly the things that are, as the gods have ordained them: For all things good and fine, the gods give nothing to a man without work and care. If you want the favor of the gods, you must worship the gods; if you desire the love of friends, you must show kindness to your friends; if you desire to be honored by some city, you must aid that city; if you deem it valuable to be admired by all of Greece for *aretē*, you must strive to do good for Greece; . . . if you want to grow great through war and want power to liberate your friends and subdue your enemies, you must learn the arts of war from those who know them and must practice their right use; and if you want your body to be strong, you must accustom it to be the servant of your mind and train it with toil and sweat. (Ibid., 27–28)

Virtue's speech is as frank as her appearance is modest, and it must have appealed to Hercules, for at this point Vice anxiously interjects that the course just described is the long and arduous road to happiness (*euphrosunē*), while her own route and her own happiness (*eudaimonia*) is quick and easy.[12] However, the contest is not over, for Virtue counters at this point with an incisive comparison of the rewards of each life:

> You poor wretch, what good do you really have? And what pleasure do you know, when you are unwilling to do anything for it? You do not even wait for the desire of pleasant things to set in before you fill yourself up with them—finding cooks to give zest to eating, searching out expensive wines. . . . To improve your sleep it is not enough for you to buy soft blankets, but you must have frames for your beds. For not work, but the boredom of having nothing to do makes you desire sleep. You rouse your sexual lusts by means of tricks when there is no need, using men as women. And so you train your friends, debauching them by night and plunging them into sleep for the best hours of the day. Though you are immortal, you are the outcast of the gods and a scourge to good human beings. Moreover, the sweetest of all sounds to hear, self approval, you

> never hear; and the sweetest of all sights, a beautiful deed of your own making, you never see. . . . Who in their right minds would join your throng? While your followers are young, their bodies are weak, when they become old, their souls are without insight. . . . Their past deeds bring them shame, their present deeds distress. . . . But I consort with the gods and with good human beings. No fine deed of god or man comes about without me. . . . To my friends, meat and drink bring sweet and simple pleasure, for they wait until they desire them. And a sweeter sleep falls upon them than upon idlers; they are not angered by waking up, nor for its sake do they neglect the things they ought to be doing. With me, the young delight in the praises of the old; the old are exalted by the respect of the young; all remember with pleasure their own past transactions and take delight in their present well-being. For through me, they are dear to the gods, loved by their friends, and honored by their country. And when their appointed time comes, they lie neither forgotten nor dishonored, but live on, celebrated and remembered for all time. *These things* are for you, Hercules, child of good parents. If you will work in earnest, you shall have the most blessed happiness of all. (Ibid., 30–33)

I quote from this speech at length because it is regrettably not as well known as it once was[13] and because it is relevant to my inquiry in so many ways. In the first place, the moral soundness of Prodicus' fable may well have contributed to Socrates' general admiration for him that we sense in Plato's dialogues.[14] That Hercules went on to choose the path of virtue (rather than vice) can be inferred from Socrates' final description of the fable as "the education of Hercules by Virtue" (Ibid., 34); the same point is made however (independently of Xenophon's account) by a *scholion* on Aristophanes' *Clouds* (DK 84 B1). In fact, its moral outcome is important to emphasize, because already in the fifth century we find Aristophanes offering what appears to be a malevolent spoof of Prodicus' story in his personification of Just and Unjust Speech in the *Clouds* (885–1105). Here it is the unjust speech that wins, and the student (Pheidippides) goes on to commit outrageous acts. Such Aristophanic caricatures are, no doubt, partly responsible for the common opinion, both ancient and modern, that sophistic teaching must be in every case inimical to virtue. But Prodicus' speech was plainly not immoral in nature—quite the reverse. And Xenophon's Socrates is understandably admiring of its pedagogical potential.

However, to recognize that Prodicus' speech was on the side of morality as this was conventionally understood is not yet to give it its full due. One might conjecture also that Socrates would have appreciated the *arguments* that Prodicus offered. Indeed, on the basis of this speech alone Prodicus can be recognized as a key transition figure, reaching back on the one hand to the older moral tradition of Hesiod, and looking forward on the other hand to the Socratic defense of justice in Plato's *Republic*.[15] Like Hesiod (in the *Theogony* and *Works and Days*), Prodicus recommends the life of hard work and honest pursuits. But he improves substantially on the Hesiodic arguments for that life. For like Socrates in the *Republic*, he imagines a concrete and initially tempting case for injustice (vice); he attempts to align the life of virtue with the life of the gods—denying that divine beings are impressed by vice in men *or* gods; and he concludes that justice is ultimately more satisfying, more rewarding, and even more *pleasant* than injustice (thus moving in the direction of the "proofs" of *Republic* IX).[16] In this motion toward Socratic and Platonic arguments for justice, Prodicus clearly improves on the Hesiodic account, but he does not entirely abandon that account. He retains the mythical framework and aspects of its language in order to offer what amounts to a rational as well as an emotional appeal for traditionally educated youths. In the final analysis, even if the "Choice of Hercules" is not yet the philosophical *tour de force* of Plato's "Choice of Glaucon" (that is, the *Republic*), it nevertheless contains arguments that Socrates would understandably admire.

Careful examination of this speech may also help us to understand one of those obscure Platonic passages about Prodicus discussed earlier. I refer to the comic description of Prodicus in bed, where (it now seems) Plato may have intentionally drawn material from Prodicus' own description of the life according to vice. Is it not the way of vice, according to Prodicus himself, to use soft blankets to improve one's sleep, to sleep late into the day, to surround oneself with attractive boys and inflame one's desire for food and drink by consuming these in inappropriate ways and at inappropriate times? The way of virtue, by contrast, entails waiting patiently for food and drink; arising early from bed and getting a head start on the day. Note that in the *Protagoras*, Prodicus arises from bed only when he is enticed to do so by the extremely attractive Alcibiades.[17]

If it is the case that Prodicus' "Choice of Hercules" supplied the material for Plato's colorful portrait of the sophist in the *Protagoras*, then we would still be faced with the difficult question of what to infer from this. Is Plato merely engaging in a little fun at Prodicus' expense? Or is he suggesting, rather more seriously, that Prodicus had difficulties living up to his own moral ideals? Neither option is completely satisfactory. In the first case, one wonders why Plato would want to misrepresent an upstanding moral educator whom Socrates obviously admired.[18] In the latter case, one wonders how Socrates could have sent students to the man. Perhaps the conjecture of Guthrie is correct that Prodicus had difficulties with self-control noticeable enough to warrant the joke, but minor enough to be harmless.[19] The truth is, however, that we simply do not know. What we have here are mere possibilities.

What we do know is that Prodicus' speech itself was intended to bolster the life of virtue over and against the perennial temptations of vice. This is how and why Socrates employs it (without further comment) as a tool in his conversation with Aristippus; and it is on this basis that Xenophon cites the speech as evidence for his claim that association with Socrates was morally beneficial. That Socrates also found other of Prodicus' ideas useful is a point we return to below.

Religious Theory

But before turning completely to Plato, let us take note of another major strand of Prodicus' thought that may lie in the background of Plato's handling of him. According to numerous ancient sources, Prodicus was well known for advancing an innovative theory about the origins of religious worship. Sources for this are neither as ancient nor as complete as one would like. However, to judge from what we do possess, it appears that Prodicus described religious worship as arising initially in two stages. In stage one, certain things that nourished and benefited human life came to be regarded as gods; the list includes the sun, the moon, rivers, springs, and other such basic goods. Then, at a later point (stage two), certain discoverers of food, shelter, and various practical arts came to be worshipped as gods, such as Demeter (for bread) and Dionysius (for wine).[20] This is unfortunately all we know of Prodicus' theory. Modern commentators have likened it, perhaps reasonably, to certain nineteenth-century theories of religion, which, in effect, reduce theology to anthropology by giving religion a human (not a divine) origin. However, we really do not know how, if at all, the theory factored into Prodicus' own teaching or what it was intended to convey about the legitimacy or illegitimacy of specific religious beliefs and practices.

It may be the case that Prodicus was an atheist of some sort. This is certainly how he came to be viewed by later writers. Sextus Empiricus, for example, knows of and accepts a tradition that places Prodicus on a list of fifth-century atheists "who say there is no god" (*Adversus Mathematicos* IX.51). Similarly Philodemus writes: "Prodicus maintains that the gods of popular belief do not exist and that they lack knowledge."[21] And this is evidently how Epicurus also regarded Prodicus, for at an earlier point in Philodemus' work it is said that "Epicurus reproached for their complete madness those who eliminate the divine from existing things, as in Book XII of *On Nature* he reproaches Prodicus, Diagoras and Critias among others, saying that they rave like lunatics, and he likens them to Bacchant revelers, admonishing them not to trouble or disturb us."[22]

But on the other hand, the label of "atheist" may have been attached to Prodicus sloppily and unfairly. Certainly the word *atheos* (literally one who is regarded as "godless," either because the gods seem to have abandoned him, or he the gods, or sometimes both) was a notoriously slippery and indeterminate term, and was often bandied about recklessly by comedians and politicians for reasons having little to do with a thinker's actual beliefs.[23] Was this term attached to Prodicus simply because he advanced a novel theory about the origins of religious belief? It is quite possible: In both Philodemus and Sextus, the allegation that Prodicus denied the gods is followed forthwith by a description of his theory about religious origins, as if this were evidence for his atheism. And yet, if this were the only evidence, one must be careful to recognize that Prodicus' theory, as it has come down to us, does not necessitate an atheistic outlook. Indeed, there are at least four options available him:

1. He could have retained his belief in the gods while trying to show, nevertheless, that human awareness of them emerged from concrete events in the history of our struggle for survival. With respect to the second stage of his theory (man's recognition of gods like Demeter), this would require

Prodicus to believe that human beings somehow became gods after accomplishing significant deeds. This would not be unusual in Greek religion, though it would certainly rewrite the mythology surrounding Dionysus and Demeter in particular.[24]

2. He could have believed that while the gods of *popular* belief (i.e., the gods celebrated by the poets and defended by the city) were illegitimate fictions, nevertheless other gods of some kind were real. Disbelief in the popular gods is actually all that Philodemus ever imputes to Prodicus (see above) and this is the position that Aristophanes also ascribes to Prodicus (see below).
3. He could have disbelieved in all gods as such, but nevertheless supported the worship of them as a valid and important cultural practice (for any number of reasons). This could explain why the "Choice of Hercules" makes constant references to the gods—although option (1) could also explain this.
4. And, Prodicus could have simply been an all-out atheist, who rejected belief in the gods and disdained religious worship of all kinds, as alleged of him by Sextus Empiricus earlier.

Without knowing more about what Prodicus actually argued and *why* he argued it, we cannot rule out any of these options. The doxographical reports of later writers simply do not settle the matter.[25]

When we turn to fifth-century evidence about Prodicus' religious views (scant though it is), we find nothing to corroborate the view that he was an avowed atheist in the full-fledged sense of the term. There is, in the first place, Prodicus' own "Choice of Hercules," which can hardly be classified as an atheistic text—quite the opposite. If Prodicus staked out a position like (3) above, he may well have infused his public speeches with conventional religious images. More suggestive, however, is the fact that in Aristophanes' *Clouds* (357ff.), Prodicus and Socrates are paired together (suggesting once again a connection of some sort between the two) as the sole mortals with whom the Cloud deities will converse. Significantly, Aristophanes does not portray Prodicus (or Socrates) as believing in no gods at all; he portrays them as religious innovators who deny the traditional gods while acknowledging the existence of new and strange deities: Chaos, Clouds, and Tongue. Likewise in Aristophanes' *Birds* (685ff.), the chorus of divine birds mentions Prodicus by name, not as someone who disbelieves in the gods, but only as someone who investigates their nature and origins:

> Weak mortals, chained to the earth, creatures of clay as frail as the foliage of the woods, you unfortunate race, whose life is but darkness, as unreal as a shadow, the illusion of a dream, hearken to us, who are immortal beings, ethereal, ever young and occupied with eternal thoughts, for we shall teach you about all celestial matters; you shall know thoroughly what is the nature of the birds, what the origin of the gods, of the rivers, of Erebus, and Chaos; thanks to us, even Prodicus will envy you your knowledge.[26]

The testimony of Aristophanes cannot be relied on for any detailed information about philosophers' views, but it is at least significant that the comedian nowhere portrays Prodicus as a complete atheist. Rather the evidence leaves ample room for possibility (2) above. Moreover, the pairing of Prodicus and Socrates in the *Clouds* helps us to see in a concrete way how this sophist might have come to be *regarded* as a complete atheist. As Socrates makes clear in the *Apology* (18b–c, 26e), the very same passages of the *Clouds* led in his own case to the popular perception that *he* believed in "no gods at all."

The connection between Prodicus and Socrates in the *Clouds* brings me back now to the issue that interests me most—not the question of Prodicus' religious beliefs per se, but the question of why Plato's Socrates appears to admire and also to criticize this sophist. This question becomes all the more intriguing when we realize that the historical connection between Socrates and Prodicus may have involved conversations relating to divine things. But unfortunately—and perhaps significantly—when we turn to Plato's dialogues we find no explicit mention of Prodicus' theory about the origins of divine cult, much less any direct evidence that this might have been of interest to Socrates. What we do find (and this is as far as I think we can go) is that the language Plato uses to invoke Prodicus and his unique brand of wisdom is often divinely charged. The comparison of Prodicus to Tantalus in the *Protagoras* might be mentioned in this connection: Could Prodicus' theorizing about divine matters, his claiming to know concretely of divine origins, and his delivering of this knowledge to the people in the form of his theory be analogous, perhaps, to Tantalus' ill-fated keeping company with the gods, consuming of divine food, and delivering the same to human beings? I have put the possibility in the interrogative in order to stress the extreme uncertainty of all this. One of the advantages of this interpretation is that it might explain why Socrates goes on to describe Prodicus' knowledge (ironically on this reading) as "altogether wise and divine" (315e7–316a1). Prodicus, in other words, claims for himself a kind of knowledge, which in Socrates' view, only a god could possess. Moreover, a bit later in the dialogue (341a), Socrates describes Prodicus' wisdom as "a certain divine wisdom of long ago, which either began in the time of Simonides or else is even more ancient still." Is this, too, an oblique reference to Prodicus' own view that divine things (his own knowledge included) are discovered (or created) by man at a concrete point in time?

Whether such passages in fact contain faint vestigial echoes of Prodicus' own theorizing about the divine is difficult in the extreme to determine given Plato's delicate style and the incompleteness of the evidence at our disposal. Much less can we tell what these references might imply about Socrates' attitude toward Prodicus. Such is the state of uncertainty we are faced with here. However, as we turn now to other passages in Plato's dialogues where Prodicus' name is invoked, we find much more solid evidence about the way Socrates (and Plato) actually viewed this sophist.

THE ART OF DISTINCTION-MAKING

Aside from those intriguing Platonic passages with which I began this investigation, the bulk of references to Prodicus in Plato's dialogues relate to his art of making distinctions.[27] This in itself is important to note and suggests that here, if anywhere, we shall find (or come closest to finding) answers to the questions posed earlier. In German scholarship, this art is referred to as *synonymik*, because the words whose precise shades of meaning Prodicus distinguishes (e.g., "dread" and "fear") were commonly regarded as synonyms. However, this is a modern coinage, and I prefer to use the Platonic formulations. In Plato, the art is described generically and specifically. Generically, it is an art *peri onomatōn orthotētos* ("concerning the correct use of words," *Crat.* 384b;

Euthyd. 278a), and specifically it is *peri onomatōn diairountos* ("concerning the division or differentiation of words, *Charm.* 163d; *Lach.* 197d; *Prt.* 340b). I thus refer to it as *diairesis* or "distinction-making" for short. That it is not merely a matter of the "correct use of words" is significant. Other sophists—for example, Protagoras—taught the generic art (*Prt.* 339d; *Phdr.* 267c); but only Prodicus took it in the specific direction of diairesis.[28]

For an initial taste of this art we can turn to a short speech Prodicus delivers in the *Protagoras* at the point where the conversation between Protagoras and Socrates breaks down over a disagreement about the proper length of Protagoras' answers. To the interlocutors and the audience alike, Prodicus offers the following sage advice:

> Those present at speeches of this kind ought to listen in common [*koinous*] to both interlocutors, but not equally [*isous*]. That is not the same thing. For they should listen to both in common but not allot equal weight to each; they should instead give more to the wiser, less to the less learned. And I myself, Protagoras and Socrates, I think it right for you to come to an agreement, and to dispute [*amphisbētein*] about the arguments with one another but not to quarrel [*eridzein*]: it is with good will that friends dispute with friends, but those who are at odds and are enemies quarrel with one another. And thus our get-together would come to pass most beautifully. For in this way you the speakers would be especially esteemed [*eudokimoite*] by us the listeners and not praised [*epainoisthe*]—for esteem stems from the souls of the listeners without deception, but praise in argument is often given by those who speak falsely contrary to their opinion. And we the listeners, in turn, would in this way be especially delighted [euphrainoimetha], not pleased [hēdoimestha]—for feeling delight belongs to one who learns something and who shares in prudence by means of the intellect itself, whereas being pleased belongs to one who eats something or who experiences another pleasure by means of the body itself. (*Prt.* 337a–c)[29]

This speech is clearly a parody and intended to be humorous. But it also affords a rich glimpse into Prodicus' art. As for humor, this derives from the fact that Prodicus seems to make more than a few too many distinctions here, as if he were prone to make distinctions merely for the sake of it. This is in fact a running joke in the remainder of the *Protagoras* and elsewhere in Plato (*Prt.* 341d, 358a–b, 358d–e; *Men.* 75e). To put it somewhat crudely, we might call Prodicus a "hairsplitter."[30] But in Plato's hands this point is never made in a mean-spirited way, nor is it meant to be devastating as a philosophical critique. The charge is always lighthearted—so much so, that Prodicus himself can join in the laugh (*Prt.* 358b2: "Prodicus then laughed and agreed").

Setting humor aside, though, we cannot help but notice that all the distinctions Prodicus makes in this little speech are both valid and important. The distinction between listening to various speakers in common (i.e., impartially), on the one hand, and reducing all speakers to intellectual equality, on the other, is fundamental to philosophical discourse. Without listening impartially, one would never be in a position to glean insights from unexpected places. And yet, to treat all speakers as equals in the full sense of that word would be to reduce philosophy to a mere catalog of common opinions. So, too, are Prodicus' other distinctions quite cogent. Indeed, Socrates himself distinguishes sharply in various places between philosophical argument, on the one hand, and quarreling or "eristics," on the other, just as Prodicus does here. And the distinction between intellectual delight and mere hedonistic pleasure is fundamental to many an argument in Platonic and Aristotelian texts. Thus while Plato clearly parodies Prodicus' art, he also allows its potential to shine through.

Now, what I want to argue is that by paying close attention to the various contexts in which Prodicus' art of diairesis appears in Plato's dialogues, one can, first of all, gain a sense of how Prodicus himself may have intended for his art to be used, and, secondly, begin to see why Plato's treatment of this sophist would necessarily be ambivalent. For, on the one hand, Prodicus' art had tremendous power to dissolve all sorts of intellectual confusion and chicanery. But, on the other hand, its potential to advance Socrates' own quest for wisdom must have been severely limited—and this for interesting reasons. All this needs further elaboration, so I begin by considering the contexts in which Prodicean diairesis appears.

These can be divided into three categories, which I label "political," "philosophical," and "anti-eristic." The passage we have just considered from the *Protagoras* is actually a hybrid, hinting at all three contexts. The philosophical and anti-eristic nature of the passage has already been touched on, and we see purer examples of these tendencies later, so I do not dwell on them here. The *political* aspect of the passage, however, is quite important to highlight. This stems from the fact that the speech is really a diplomatic speech. Prodicus enters the scene in order to resolve a conflict that has arisen between two parties (Socrates and Protagoras)—a conflict exacerbated by the fact that the onlookers, too, have taken sides. To resolve the conflict and restore a degree of peace, Prodicus lays down certain clarifying distinctions so that everyone involved can better understand the nature of their joint enterprise.

The assumption behind Prodicus' speech is, interestingly, that the conflict is not real, or not necessary—in other words, that those involved have misunderstood their own situations. And it is worth remarking that this assumption may not always hold true: there are certainly political conflicts that do not reduce finally to a failure to make proper distinctions. However, many conflicts are of a type that could be avoided by careful distinction-making. An example is supplied by an episode in Book I of Thucydides, where a team of diplomats from Corinth attempts (ever so delicately) to censure their Spartan allies for not taking a tougher stand against Athens—to censure, but not to offend. They explain the difference thus: "We hope that none of you [Spartans] will consider these words of *remonstrance* to be rather words of *hostility*; men remonstrate with friends who are in error; accusations they reserve for enemies who have wronged them" (I.69.6). This has long been thought an example of Prodicus' direct influence on Thucydides. On that matter I remain agnostic.[31] But what the passage does supply is a clear example of the potential of Prodicus' art to be used in political (particularly diplomatic) contexts. Although Prodicus' speech in the *Protagoras* is the only Platonic example of this type, we can reasonably suppose that diplomatic rhetoric was one of the major areas in which Prodicus himself would have used diairesis. He was, after all, a diplomat by trade.[32]

That diairesis could be used in philosophical contexts as well as political ones is also plain from Plato's presentation of it. In the *Laches* (197a–c), Nicias uses it to show why, properly speaking, one should not attribute courage to wild animals, no matter how courageous they may appear. Courage (*to andreion*), he argues, should only be attributed to those who have foresight and who know what should and should not be feared. Wild animals, by contrast, exhibit rashness (*to aphobon*), because they fear nothing and lack foresight altogether. The same is true of children, Nicias points out; and many a soldier must be viewed as lacking genuine courage, too, according to this definition. (Compare Aristotle *EN* III.8, 1116a16–1117a28.) That Nicias' method here derives ultimately from Prodicus is made clear by an intellectual genealogy, which Socrates immediately establishes: Nicias "spends most of his time with Damon, and Damon spends most of his time with Prodicus, who has the reputation of being the best of the sophists at distinguishing such words" (*Lach.* 197d).[33] Also traceable back to Prodicus is the use of diairesis that informs the whole of Pausanias' encomium to Love in the *Symposium* (180c–185c). (Pausanias, we recall, appears as one of Prodicus' admirers in the *Protagoras.*) "Our task has been simple," Pausanias begins, "to speak in praise of Love." However, "there are two kinds of Love. . . . There is a Common Love [named *Pandemos*] and a Heavenly Love [named *Urania*]." Pausanias goes on to distinguish between these in such a way as to make clear why performing some actions in the name of love turns out to be vulgar, while, by contrast, submitting oneself to a lover who can make one more virtuous and wise is not only honorable but also valuable to the city as a whole. In both dialogues, diairesis is used to draw out valuable philosophical distinctions and to prevent confusion of a serious sort. Indeed, clear thinking about the difference between courage and rashness, and between healthy and unhealthy love relationships, is no minor philosophical accomplishment.

Finally, diairesis could be used to combat eristic. This is in a sense a philosophical use of the art, too, and thus we might collapse this whole category into the previous one. However, I separate it out for two reasons: (1) because a unique set of circumstances gives rise to the anti-eristic use of diairesis; and (2) because here especially Socrates seems to endorse Prodicus' art. In fact, Socrates himself uses diairesis on two occasions in the dialogues in order to combat eristic, and he consistently acknowledges his debt to Prodicus as he does so. One instance occurs later in the *Protagoras*—at the point where Protagoras tries to analyze a poem by Simonides as a way of demonstrating his own expert knowledge of aretē (339a ff.). Evidently, Protagoras' whole purpose in discussing Simonides is simply to accuse the poet of contradicting himself. Simonides wrote at one point that "it is difficult to become truly a good man," but later in the same poem he criticized the seventh-century sage Pittacus for saying much the same thing—"it is difficult to be noble." Citing these two passages side by side,

Protagoras proudly declares that Simonides was inconsistent in the matter of virtue—that he "does not speak correctly" about it (*ouk orthōs legei*, 339d)—and the implication is that Protagoras himself would be a much more reliable teacher of aretē. However, the question of whether Simonides contradicts himself is not so simple. And to show that it is not, Socrates dramatically invokes Prodicus' "muse-like skill" of diairesis (340a), arguing that "to become" and "to be" are not exactly the same. Thus Socrates reveals that Simonides may well have maintained that it is difficult to *become* good, while yet taking issue with Pittacus' claim that it is difficult to *be* good. In fact, Socrates shows, the same distinction had been made centuries earlier by Hesiod: "Before virtue the gods placed sweat," wrote the great poet; but whenever someone "reaches the apex of it, then it is easy to possess, difficult though it was" (*Prt.* 340d; cf. Hesiod, *WD*, 289–292). Thus, far from contradicting himself, Simonides may have possessed a subtler understanding of virtue than Protagoras; and Socrates goes on to show how, on the basis of the distinction between being and becoming, one might read Simonides' whole poem as a sustained critique of a dangerous error in Pittacus' moral teachings.[34]

Now Socrates' interpretation of Simonides may well be skewed. He certainly twists the poet's words to suit his own purposes.[35] But what interests me here is not the interpretation of the poem as much as the circumstances that give rise to it and that lead Socrates to employ Prodicus' art. Protagoras' gleeful claim that Simonides contradicts himself has more to do with grandstanding than with a genuine interest in thinking about virtue. It is, in fact, a maneuver familiar to anyone who teaches bright undergraduates: there is always one student in the room who, instead of exploring the subtle hints and intimations that all great literature contains, finds more satisfaction in pointing up some apparent contradiction in an author's thought. Whether the contradiction is real or not is neither here nor there when its discovery is motivated by the desire to vault oneself above an author before considering carefully whether his words may in a sense be true. And it is precisely this temperament of contradiction-making, which, in Socrates' judgment, calls for Prodicus' art. In this application, diairesis is an antidote. It slows down the overzealous contradiction-maker by investigating the contradiction itself to see whether some important distinction may have been overlooked, and it invites one even to coin new terms or to use common words in more precise ways in order to reach clarity.[36] The art can be abused and distinctions can be manufactured, which have no basis in fact (see especially *Prt.* 341d); but that is no strike against the art itself.[37] Rather, Socrates' use of diairesis in the *Protagoras* shows at least one way in which it is quite valuable indeed. Those who point out contradictions for the purposes not of seeking truth but of winning victories are not engaged in philosophy. They are engaged in quarreling or "eristic" (as Prodicus calls it in his own speech quoted above). And Prodicus' art supplies a powerful weapon against this tendency.

That Socrates recognized the power of diairesis to combat eristic is confirmed by a passage from the *Euthydemus*. Euthydemus and his brother Dionysodorus were notorious for their eristic assaults on unsuspecting interlocutors, and near the beginning of Plato's dialogue about them they demonstrate their awesome powers on a youth named Clinias. Their initial question to Clinias is whether the best learners are "the wise" or "the ignorant" (275d). When Clinias answers, "the wise," they force him to contradict himself by leading him to see that all learners must necessarily be ignorant of what they learn. However, when Clinias accordingly changes his answer to "the ignorant," they force him to contradict himself again by showing him that ignorant people (now in the sense of dummies, *hoi amatheis*, *Euthyd.* 276c) are never as good at learning as the wise. This goes on and on, until Socrates at last intervenes to save Clinias from utter frustration and confusion. And when he intervenes, it is Prodicus' art of diairesis that he wields, instructing Clinias as follows:

> In the first place, as Prodicus says, you must learn about the correct use of words [*peri onomatōn orthotētos*]. . . . You did not realize that people use the word "learn" [*manthanein*] not only in the situation in which a person who has knowledge of a thing in the beginning acquires it later, but also when he who already has this knowledge uses it to inspect the same thing, whether it is something spoken or something done. As a matter of fact, people call the latter "understand" [*sunienai*] rather than "learn," but they do sometimes call it learn as well. (*Euthyd.* 277e–278a)[38]

That the same word, "learn," is sometimes applied to people in opposite epistemological states accounts for the illusion of self-contradiction. But, as Socrates explains, the word is actually multivalent, and by using

Prodicus' art to separate out its various meanings, all subsequent confusion can be avoided.

The circumstances that lead Socrates to use diairesis in the *Euthydemus* are quite similar to those that govern its use in the *Protagoras*. In both cases we find a sophist (or two) proudly alleging that someone has contradicted himself; in both cases the contradiction is spurious; and in both cases Socrates wants to set the matter straight by introducing a distinction that has been blurred. What do these similarities suggest? They suggest—indeed they demonstrate—that there was at least one context in which Socrates found Prodicus' art valuable, perhaps even indispensable. And because we can assume that Prodicus intended for his art to be used in this way (this is certainly the implication of Socrates' invoking his name in these passages) we can say with some certainty that this was a major point of commonality between the two thinkers. Both Prodicus and Socrates recognized the problem of contradiction-making run amok, and they both saw the need for some method by which to detect and negate merely apparent contradictions. Prodicus' method supplied the perfect tool.

Moreover, Prodicus' method may have had a role to play as a check of sorts within Socratic philosophy itself (leaving aside eristic interlocutors). This is because the avid search for self-contradiction was an integral *part* of Socratic philosophizing, not merely a weapon used by the eristics. What, after all, is Socratic *elenchus* but the exposure of contradictions latent in the thinking of Socrates or one of his interlocutors? Because Socrates' method involves the constant ferreting out of contradictions, there is always the danger that the contradictions he turns up will be merely verbal. Socrates thus needs a method of guarding against this—of distinguishing genuine from spurious contradictions in his *own* thinking. And this is something Prodicus' art could provide. In fact, we see Socrates employ diairesis in just this way in Book V of the *Republic*. After Socrates and Glaucon reach their agreement that women and men should take on the work of the city in common, Socrates suddenly senses a contradiction: he and Glaucon had earlier agreed that each distinct nature must perform its own distinct task; but now they are arguing that two *different* natures should perform the same task. Enter Prodicean diairesis:

> Oh, Glaucon, the power of the contradicting art [*tēs antilogikēs technēs*] is grand. . . . In my opinion many fall into it even

> unwillingly and suppose they are not quarreling but discussing [*ouk eridzein alla dialegesthai*], because they are unable to consider what's said by separating it out [*diairoumenoi*] into its forms. They pursue contradiction in the mere name of what's spoken about, using eristic, not dialectic, with one another. (454a)[39]

In this case the error belongs to Socrates and Glaucon themselves. They have failed to distinguish between the *ways* that female and male natures differ. To say only that they differ is too simple. Because they differ in some ways but not in others, there is really no self-contradiction in their proposal. Although Prodicus is not mentioned by name in this passage, the Prodicean spirit of Socrates' self-correction here is unmistakable, and it indicates that Socrates' appreciation of diairesis was not merely limited to combating eristic tendencies in others.

At the outset of this chapter I asked, "What, if anything, did Socrates learn from Prodicus that was useful or beneficial?" and "What were the sophist's strengths?" In my judgment, Prodicus' art of diairesis supplies the strongest possible answer to both questions. However, this art was not without weaknesses and philosophical limits. Let me briefly consider these before concluding.

Weaknesses of Diairesis

At certain points in Plato's presentation of Prodicus, we perceive hints of criticism. At this juncture I take stock of all these hints in order to evaluate their overall force. Certainly the most humorous and yet least damning of them is the suggestion that Prodicus employed diairesis too often and thus drew distinctions of dubious philosophical worth. We took note of this criticism in passing earlier. A typical instance occurs at *Protagoras* 358d–e, where Socrates asks whether "dread and fear" can be defined as "an expectation of something bad." When Prodicus answers that dread can be defined thus, but not fear, Socrates is moved to voice a frustration that must have occurred to many a listener besides Socrates: "But Prodicus, it *doesn't matter!* What does matter is. . . ." Indeed a similar frustration appears in Aristotle's *Topics*, and is echoed in a later commentary by Alexander of Aphrodisias,[40] who, however, supplies an interesting reason for Prodicus' hyper-scrupulousness about distinctions: "Prodicus," he writes, "attempted to assign to every term its own peculiar significance." This is an interesting piece of information and may explain Prodicus' ultimate goal—in other words, to remove confusion on a mass scale by creating (or perhaps recovering?) a language in which each word signified one and only one thing, a language rich enough to capture all the subtle nuances of human perception and yet precise enough to avoid all ambiguity. If this was Prodicus' hope, it would be easy to imagine that he would make distinctions, which, to the layman, seemed too exact. But, then again, the layman would presumably not have been bothered by intellectual confusion and the appearance of self-contradiction in the way that someone like Prodicus (and Socrates) would. What I suggest is that there was indeed a tendency in Prodicus' use of diairesis that was risible, but that this tendency may have stemmed from a goal that was praiseworthy. We consider the nature of Prodicus' goals vis-à-vis those of Socrates momentarily.

A second criticism is slightly more serious, but only hinted at on one occasion in Plato. I am thus not sure how much to make of it. It is that Prodicus may have employed his art tendentiously in order to undercut certain interlocutors he wished to defeat. This seems to be the upshot of the little episode at *Protagoras* 341c–341e, where Prodicus (at Socrates' prompting) defines the word "difficult" in such a way as to sabotage an argument being made by Protagoras. As Socrates immediately points out, Prodicus' definition is bogus; and it is clear from the context that Prodicus must have known it to be so.[41] This criticism cannot be easily dismissed, but there is also little more that can be said about it. Diairesis was a powerful tool. It could be used in the pursuit of truth or in the pursuit of merely rhetorical victory. In this sense our evaluation of it should perhaps mirror a nuanced evaluation of "scholasticism" as this appeared in the late Middle Ages: scholasticism, too, was an art of distinction-making with tremendous power for good, even though its practitioners could sometimes slip into tendentious quibbling. Was Prodicus himself given over to tendentious quibbling? On the basis of this one passage, tucked away in the middle of the *Protagoras*, we must allow for the possibility. However, every other indication is that this sophist knew well the difference between serious thought and eristic, and was a forceful defender of clarity and truth.

The final and most interesting criticism I consider is one that requires us to contrast Prodicus' art with the ways and means of Socratic philosophizing. We have already noticed that Socrates made use of diairesis. However, his use of it appears to have been largely negative: diairesis supplied a "check" against overzealous contradiction-making. What I stress now is the extent to which Prodicus and Socrates, though motivated by a similar problem, actually moved in different directions in search of solutions. The problem that they both perceived was the sloppiness of common speaking and of common thought. It was this sloppiness that allowed eristic tricksters like Euthydemus to play on various ambiguities and to force interlocutors to contradict themselves. But if the question is how to address this sloppiness, the way one answers will have a great deal to do with one's philosophical outlook, one's perspective on the material world around us. Prodicus' view is, evidently, that this world can be shown to be law-like and consistent if only one uses language in a precise enough way to capture its law-like properties. This, however, is not Socrates' view. By all accounts, the view Socrates holds is rather that the material world is shot through with ambiguity and instability—or at least our perceptions of it are necessarily so. Thus, in order to find law-like consistency, one must ascend above the level of matter and physical perception to the level of "ideas" and "forms." Prodicus and Socrates thus begin from a common problem, but they branch off in radically different directions in their attempt to address it. This can be illustrated most clearly if one simply imagines what the final solution would look like as Prodicus and Socrates each conceives it. In Prodicus' case the challenge is to expand one's vocabulary and one's thought, giving every possible nuance a distinct name, until one attains a vast plurality of terms. The more sophisticated one becomes, the more concepts and names with which one has to grapple. Socrates, by contrast, pushes in the opposite direction, gathering various thoughts and expressions together under fewer and fewer formal categories until eventually he approaches unity in something like the Form of the Good. (I am not interested at this point in whether Socrates himself—or merely Plato—pressed this far; I am only arguing that it is the tendency in Socratic thought to move from plurality to unity.)

The difference between Prodicus and Socrates in this regard could not have been lost on Socrates, and it may well have accounted for his equivocal evaluation of Prodicus in the final analysis. And there is some evidence for this: in the *Euthydemus*, after Socrates makes use of Prodicean diairesis in order to save young Clinias from disaster, Socrates has this to say about the art:

> I call these things "frivolity" because even if a man were to learn many or even all such things, he would be none the wiser as to how matters stand but would only be able to make fun of people, tripping them up and overturning them by means of the distinctions in words, just like the people who pull the chair out from under a man who is going to sit down and then laugh gleefully when they see him sprawling on this back. (278b)[42]

Here Socrates' evaluation of diairesis is bound up with his evaluation of eristic. The most critical part of the passage—the censure against deliberately tripping people up—is reserved for eristic. But Socrates seems to be saying as well that *even if* eristic education were followed immediately by a Prodicean-style explanation of how the tricks are possible, one would still be left knowing nothing more about how matters *really* stand. What does this mean? Well, because one would in fact have learned a good bit about how matters stand regarding the ambiguity of words and the proper distinctions to make, I understand Socrates to be referring to something more serious. What one would still lack is knowledge of things in themselves. In other words, to distinguish between two kinds of learning (as Socrates, following Prodicus, does at this point in the dialogue) is not yet to ask what learning is, or what knowledge is. About these matters, one would remain as ignorant as before. Here I believe we put our finger on the most concrete weakness of Prodicus' method: its inability, despite its many useful applications, to advance Socrates in his search for wisdom about things in themselves.[43]

Conclusion

Prodicus was unique among the sophists for his close connection to Socrates. Plato allows us to see that connection in a number of places; however, without a careful investigation of the matter their relationship seems impossibly obscure. Plato has Socrates describe Prodicus at the beginning of the *Protagoras* in a way that seems at once to signal admiration and criticism. In the *Theaetetus*, Socrates claims to send certain pupils to Prodicus, but only the "non-pregnant" ones. And in the *Meno* Socrates acknowledges his having studied with Prodicus while, at the same time, making clear that the sophist did not teach him the ultimate truths about aretē. My purpose in this chapter has been to shed light on these suggestive passages by investigating any and all aspects of Prodicus' wisdom that might account for Plato's puzzling tone. I began by examining Prodicus' moral teaching in the "Choice of Hercules" and by considering his innovative religious theory, as this has come down to us through non-Platonic sources. Both these areas of his thought proved interesting, but their connection to Plato's presentation of Prodicus could not be established with any certainty. More certain, however, is the importance of Prodicus' art of diairesis. Through a careful examination of this art and especially Socrates' own use of it, one can reach fairly robust answers to the questions posed at the outset. "What did Socrates learn from Prodicus that was useful or beneficial?" As Plato has Socrates say on multiple occasions, he learned Prodicus' art of distinction-making, and its usefulness is well demonstrated by Socrates' incorporation of it into his conversations and into his own philosophical speculation. "What, on the other hand, were the weaknesses that might have led Plato to lampoon Prodicus in various places?" Concerning the portrait of him at the beginning of the *Protagoras* (e.g., his lying in bed and his similarity to Tantalus), it is perhaps impossible to say. I have considered some possibilities. However, one can say with some certainty that Prodicus' art of diairesis had weaknesses that would warrant Socrates' (and Plato's) criticism. Though it was a useful art, it was not a "pregnant" art. That is to say, it was incapable of giving birth to the kind of ideas that Socrates encouraged his pupils to seek. Moreover, unable to pursue such ideas, Prodicus would have failed (as *per* the criticism of him in the *Meno*) to impart to Socrates a satisfactory understanding of aretē.

What Prodicus could do at most (according to Plato) was to teach his pupils the ways of conventional virtue, to bolster the case for this through powerful images and cogent argumentation, and to equip his pupils with an art of distinction-making that might save them from many intellectual errors. This is no small set of accomplishments, and we can easily imagine that Socrates would have been earnest about sending certain students Prodicus' way. It is an incomplete set of accomplishments from the Socratic point of view for the reasons specified earlier. And it would fall to Socrates to attempt to fill in the lacunae left in his teacher's thought and to incorporate his teacher's method into a broader philosophical project. Be that as it may, I think we have seen beyond a doubt that it was not Plato's purpose to present Prodicus in a "very negative" light, as Douglas Stewart has suggested (see n. 4, earlier). Much closer to the truth was the remark of Eric Voegelin with which I began this chapter, that Plato showed a distinct "sympathy" for Prodicus that was "rooted in a craftsman's respect for the valuable work of a predecessor."

FIVE

THE SOPHIST HIPPIAS AND THE PROBLEM OF *POLYTROPIA*

> Also in art a man who makes a mistake voluntarily is preferable to one who makes it involuntarily; but in practical wisdom, as in every virtue or excellence, such a man is less desirable.[1]

Plato treats the sophist Hippias extensively in the dialogues, more so than casual readers may realize. Besides the passing references to him in the *Apology* (19e) and the *Phaedrus* (267b), Plato portrays him in the *Protagoras* (318e, 337c–338b, 347b) emphasizing his pedagogical approach and certain tendencies of his rhetoric. And in two dialogues devoted entirely to Hippias, the *Hippias Major* and the *Hippias Minor*, Socrates engages the sophist on serious philosophical topics. The frequency with which Hippias appears in the dialogues suggests that he was important for Plato. But what was the nature of his importance? Why did Plato want to present this sophist so often?

The present study offers an answer to this question from the vantage point of the *Hippias Minor*, the richest of Plato's portraits of Hippias. I do not offer a separate chapter on the *Hippias Major* here, because its authenticity has been seriously challenged, and I do not want to rest my arguments on a dialogue that can be dismissed as spurious.[2] I do, however, believe that the conclusions I reach in this chapter are compatible with what readers learn of Hippias and Socrates in the *Hippias Major*. And I allude frequently to that dialogue here. My argument is twofold. In part, it is that Hippias, the self-proclaimed polymath, was the perfect embodiment of certain intellectual tendencies that Plato wished to combat.[3] These include (1) the tendency of supposing one is a moral expert when one is merely an expert in some other area of life (cf. *Apology* 21b–2e); and (2) the tendency of allowing mutually exclusive beliefs to reside simultaneously in one's mind on questions of the utmost importance. Neither of these tendencies is unique to Hippias, which is why the dialogue is still so powerful today. But because Hippias represented these tendencies in such an intense, larger-than-life way, he supplied an ideal occasion for Plato to discuss them. However—and this is a second part of my argument—I do not believe that Plato's interest in Hippias was exhausted by the desire to criticize. Rather, as with so many of Plato's interlocutors, Hippias seems most significant in supplying a certain kind of touchstone for readers who want to explore the nature and implications of Socratic philosophy. In other words, the dialogue is not merely about Hippias but also, and more importantly, about the kinds of insights that become available when a character like Hippias is paired with Socrates. Chief among these insights is that Socratic philosophy (as Plato presents it and means for us to understand it) is far closer to sophistry than we might initially suppose. Socrates is shown to employ the techniques of sophistry unapologetically in order to advance his pedagogical and philosophical goals. In fact this dialogue shows that Socrates was more "sophistic" than Hippias, one of the most famous fifth-century sophists. And yet, there is a positive pedagogical and philosophical agenda behind Socrates' use of sophistry, which needs to be investigated and described as well.

Finally, though it is not useful for me to say too much at this point about the literary theme of *polytropia* that courses through this dialogue, I offer this by way of introduction: when Plato explores the relationship between Socrates and Hippias in the *Hippias Minor* he chooses to do so in terms of polytropia. This was a relatively rare term in fifth-century discourse, and it proves challenging to define because of its metaphorical range of meanings. Literally, it means "much-turning." But when applied to a human being it can refer either to physical or to intellectual traits. Odysseus in the first line of the *Odyssey* is described as polytropic. He is "wandering," "turning many ways" in a geographical sense, but also intellectually "changeful," "versatile," "ingenious."[4]

In the *Hippias Minor*, the sophist Hippias regards Odysseus' polytropia as a villainous trait. Yet as the dialogue unfolds it becomes clear that polytropia admits of many forms and that Hippias and Socrates each in different ways possess polytropic tendencies. The dialogue, then, explores Hippias and Socrates in terms of their polytropia and raises important questions about how to compare their various embodiments of this trait.[5]

Hippias Minor: Setting

The *Hippias Minor* is set chronologically two days after the *Hippias Major* and immediately after Hippias' grand exhibition speech about Homeric moral customs.[6] In the earlier dialogue Socrates questioned Hippias about the nature of "*to kalon*," the noble or fair. The outcome was aporetic and more than a little unfriendly. Hippias attacked Socrates' method (mere "scrapings and clippings of speeches divided up into bits") and exalted his own method of addressing "the whole of things" (301b, 304a–b). At the beginning of the *Hippias Minor*, it is not clear that Socrates will question Hippias again. We may assume that Hippias' speech was quite successful for what it was. Eudicus (Hippias' host in Athens) praises it enthusiastically, as do other members of the audience. But Socrates does not praise the speech and in fact sits silently until most of the audience has dispersed. Then it is Eudicus who draws Socrates into a renewed conversation with Hippias by demanding that Socrates either praise the speech or refute something in it.

With Eudicus' encouragement, Socrates poses the question that drives the entire dialogue, a question designed at once to remind Hippias of their prior exchange and to raise the stakes for the present one.

> Indeed, Eudicus, . . . I used to hear from your father, Apemantus, that the *Iliad* of Homer is a more noble [*kallion*] poem than the *Odyssey*, and more noble in the measure that Achilles is a better man than Odysseus. . . . I would with pleasure inquire about that, then, if Hippias is willing—what his opinion is of these two men and which he asserts to have been better.[7]

To ask whether Achilles or Odysseus is nobler is to beg the very question Hippias failed to answer two days earlier: What is the noble? But

Socrates now raises the stakes by invoking the name of Apemantus (Eudicus' father), requesting that Hippias relate his own understanding of nobility to that of Apemantus. The challenge is not difficult in one sense, for Hippias in fact endorses Apemantus' understanding.[8] But it does raise the question of what Hippias will add in order to demonstrate his superior wisdom and skill.

What Hippias adds is his confident knowledge of Homeric formulations. "Homer," he proclaims, "represented Achilles as the best man [*ariston andra*] of those who came to Troy, Nestor as the wisest [*sophōtaton*] and Odysseus as the most polytropic [*polytropōtaton*]" (364c). Here is the first mention of polytropia. It is worth noting that Hippias is not here making an unusual claim, but merely recalling the *Odyssey*'s first line and comparing Odysseus' epithet to those of other heroes. But there is a moral assessment here, too. Hippias interprets polytropia as an opprobrious term, or at least one that seems markedly less noble than the traits associated with Achilles and Nestor, their manliness and wisdom.

It is useful at this point to summarize the course of the dialogue and to consider its meaning at the most general level. The dialogue unfolds in six steps.

1. Socrates leads Hippias to affirm his negative view of polytropia—that it is essentially the same as lying, that it is villainous, and that it is the opposite of the truthfulness and simplicity he associates with Achilles.
2. In response, Socrates crafts an argument that concludes that liars and truth tellers are not different but the same and that, therefore, neither is better or worse than the other.
3. Hippias disagrees with this conclusion but cannot fault the argument. He admonishes Socrates to abandon such arguments altogether and to listen to him demonstrate "in an ample speech with many proofs" that Homer represented Achilles as better than Odysseus and not a liar while he represented Odysseus as a treacherous liar.
4. Though Socrates does not allow Hippias to make a speech, he does turn to a brief consideration of the Homeric texts and advances an esoteric interpretation according to which Achilles, not Odysseus, is the most polytropic and the most expert at lying.

5. Hippias concedes that Achilles makes contradictory statements but insists that he does so unintentionally. He still maintains that Odysseus lies on purpose.
6. Socrates argues that if Hippias is right, then Achilles should be less esteemed than Odysseus. He supports this with an argument that concludes that voluntary wrongdoing is always better than involuntary wrongdoing.

Viewed at this level of abstraction the dialogue appears to be, first and foremost, a comic debunking of Hippias' major claims of expertise and wisdom. Hippias claims (*a*) to be an expert interpreter of Homer, but he in fact proves less expert than Socrates. Socrates exhibits the greater facility with the text and the more sophisticated hermeneutic approach. Hippias claims (*b*) that lying is villainous and that truth telling is good, but under the pressure of Socratic questioning he agrees that liars and the truth tellers are the same and thus no different from a moral point of view. Hippias claims (*c*) that involuntary wrongdoing is better than voluntary wrongdoing, but he cannot resist Socrates' argument that voluntary wrongdoing is better. Hippias comes into the conversation claiming (*d*) that he is undefeatable in argument and has nothing to fear from Socrates, while, in fact, he proves quite incapable of handling Socrates' questions. Socrates refutes his every claim—or, worse, he makes Hippias refute *himself* by leading him to state opposite positions again and again. Finally, Hippias claims (*e*) that Achilles is a morally better man than Odysseus. In so doing he professes moral knowledge. However, by the end of the dialogue, everything seems unclear. Odysseus appears to be the better man in a certain sense, and because Hippias cannot explain this, his claim to moral knowledge seems bogus.[9]

Again, at this level of abstraction, the dialogue seems primarily comic.[10] But it is not possible for serious readers to remain at this level for long. Certain aspects of the dialogue simply cry out for further consideration. One is the fact that Socrates' arguments against Hippias seem to involve fallacies, and we wonder what the significance of this might be.[11] We also wonder about the shockingly immoral flavor of Socrates' conclusions—that truth tellers are no better or worse than liars and that voluntary wrongdoing is better than involuntarily wrongdoing. Why would Socrates steer the conversation to such morally dubious ends? Until we can account for these aspects of the dialogue, we have not fully understood its purpose.[12] There appears to be a dialogue beneath this dialogue, some meaning or purpose that cannot be explained by merely recounting the plot. As I argue here, the key to understanding this subplot is the significance of polytropia. We must begin by realizing the ways in which the term can be applied not only to Odysseus, but also to Socrates and even to Hippias.

FORMS OF *POLYTROPIA* IN SOCRATES AND HIPPIAS

When Hippias impugns the character of Odysseus for being polytropic, he touches a nerve in Socrates, who immediately questions him about his use of the term: Does Homer not represent Achilles too as polytropic? No, answers Hippias, for Achilles is truthful (*alēthēs*) and simple (*haplous*)—just the opposite of polytropic. To demonstrate this he quotes from a central scene of the *Iliad* (IX 308–314), where Achilles tells Odysseus:

> Son of Laertes, sprung from Zeus, much-devising Odysseus,
> One surely must speak out without regard to consequences,
> Just as I am going to do and as I think it will be fulfilled;
> For that one is hateful to me as the gates of Hades
> Who hides one thing in his mind but says something else.
> But I will speak, as it is also going to be fulfilled.

To hide something in one's mind while saying something else is the essence of polytropia, as far as Hippias is concerned. And it is indistinguishable from lying, so that, for Hippias, Odysseus becomes *polutropos te kai pseudēs*, polytropic and lying (365b). In fact Hippias goes even further in vilifying this trait: polytropic people are *panourgoi*, "willing to do anything, unscrupulous, treacherous," and also *kakourgoi*, "evil doers" (365e).

One might at this point observe that Hippias' view of Odysseus reflects a fairly poor understanding of the Homeric texts. Odysseus is more complicated than Hippias presently allows; and in fact Hippias mutates the Homeric texts (probably unconsciously) in a way that renders the contrast between Odysseus and Achilles sharper than it really is.[13] Such problems are typical of Hippias' own polytropia, to which we shall return in a moment. But first, why should Socrates care as much as he evidently does about Hippias' misrepresentation of Odysseus? Why bother taking this up? The answer seems to be that Hippias' attack on Odysseus' polytropia cuts dangerously close to Socrates' own character. Socrates is in fact polytropic himself insofar as he routinely and expertly engages in irony. Like Odysseus, Socrates "hides one thing in his mind but says something else." Thus in Book 1 of the *Republic* (336e–337a), for example, Socrates praises Thrasymachus for his superior wisdom and cleverness while deprecating his own intellectual abilities—this before he roundly defeats Thrasymachus in argument; and in the *Theaetetus* (150b–151b), Socrates describes himself as a mere midwife, bereft of ideas, when in fact he deposits ideas into Theaetetus' mind throughout the dialogue.[14] Irony is polytropic. But if irony is a form of polytropia, is it also a form of lying? Hippias' treatment of Odysseus certainly suggests so. Hippias leaves no room for a form of polytropia that might be different from lying. Thus he would condemn Socrates along with Odysseus if he knew how polytropic Socrates really was. Moreover, Hippias is not alone in this. One of the problems Socrates faces not only in his conversations with "wise men" but also at his trial is that his interlocutors often know he practices irony and view this as deceitful, perhaps even wicked.[15]

Moreover, Socrates is polytropic in other ways as well—for example, in the distinctive way in which he turns questions around in his mind, shifting from one possibility to another, and also in the way he compels other minds to do this. Thus, with Cephalus in Book 1 of the *Republic*, who views justice as telling the truth and giving back what one owes, Socrates demonstrates that justice is also (on some occasions) *not* telling the truth and *not* giving back what one owes (*Rep.* 331c). In other words, Socrates is able to move himself and others into intellectual positions that seem untenable at first. He makes weaker arguments appear stronger and is in this sense wily, versatile, twisty, or in a word, polytropic. But, again, this raises the question: What is the moral status of Socratic polytropia? Is it deceitful and wicked? Or, if not, how is it to be distinguished?

The *Hippias Minor* explores such questions just below the surface. At the same time, it explores questions relating to Hippias' polytropia. Hippias is polytropic in the way that most human beings are so: he holds manifold opinions in his mind on particular questions and "wanders" back and forth between and among these without noticing (a) that he holds manifold opinions and (b) that these conflict with each other either directly or in various implications they entail. He, too, then, hides something in his mind and says something else. An example of Hippias' polytropia can be found in the *Hippias Major*—in fact that whole dialogue is a prolonged demonstration it. When Socrates asks Hippias to define "*to kalon*," (the beautiful or noble or fine), he does so in seven different ways![16] As it turns out, none of these proves adequate; and that is one message of the dialogue. But just as important is the bare fact that Hippias possesses *seven* different accounts of the same thing, accounts that do not agree with each other in crucial yet undetected ways. Hippias is polytropic because he wanders blindly from opinion to opinion like a sailor lost at sea, never knowing exactly what land he will alight upon or what troubles may await him there.

Now, the question of the *Hippias Minor* concerns the moral status of polytropia—so much we can see from the surface. But this question arises not merely explicitly (and rather trivially) with respect to Odysseus, but also implicitly (and more profoundly) with respect to both interlocutors who exhibit their polytropia throughout. Moreover, the question is complicated because the forms of polytropia one observes in Hippias and Socrates differ so fundamentally. Socrates' polytropia is voluntary and skillful. Hippias' is involuntary, unconscious, and unskillful. In the final analysis, then, we are led to pursue two questions: first, whether polytropia as such is morally censurable, as Hippias' remarks about Odysseus suggest, or whether some distinctions might be made concerning types of polytropia. And, second, whether the involuntary form that Hippias exhibits is better or worse than the voluntary form exhibited by Socrates. In order to answer these questions, we need to observe each form in action.

SOCRATIC *POLYTROPIA* IN ACTION

In his role as an expert polytropist, Socrates crafts three arguments, all of them counterintuitive and designed, at least in part, to move Hippias from positions he currently holds to positions he thinks he rejects. The arguments are brilliant and delightful to consider.

1. Liars and Truth Tellers Are the Same

Hippias maintains that polytropic people are liars, that liars and truth tellers are opposites, and that truth tellers are better than liars (365a–c,

366a). Against this view, Socrates argues that liars and truth tellers are the same, not opposite and not distinguishable from a moral point of view. How does he do this? Largely by considering the epistemological requirements of lying. Lying is actually demanding, because one must first of all say what is false and not what is true, which requires a degree of knowledge. And then one must *maintain* one's lie in the face of exogenous facts and implications that could potentially reveal its falsity. The more complex the subject in which one hopes to lie, the more intellectual connections one must master and the more intelligent one must be. Lying thus requires not only a degree of knowledge but also something approximating wisdom, the ability to see how one idea connects to others in the vast matrix of intellectual experience. From this vantage point, it is possible to distinguish expert liars from those who merely approach or approximate the expert. Sometimes people speak falsely because they lack knowledge—they accidentally say what is untrue. But these are not liars. To lie, one must *know* one is speaking falsely. Similarly, people sometimes speak falsely in the hope of lying, but end up revealing their lie. They accidentally say something that either directly or indirectly contradicts the position maintained in their lie. These are indeed liars, but not good ones. What then is a good liar? The best liars are those who are most capable in the subjects in which they lie and, just as importantly, whose knowledge extends to many subjects so that their lies can be maintained in all possible connections. Such a person would be a wise man.

Presented in bare form, Socrates' argument thus runs,

1. Liars need to be capable, prudent, knowing and wise (366a).
2. Whoever is most capable of speaking the truth on a topic is also most capable of lying on that topic (366e).
3. The same man is a liar and truth teller (367c).
4. Therefore, the truth teller is no better than the liar (367c–d).
5. If Odysseus were a liar, he becomes also truthful, and if Achilles were truthful, he becomes also a liar (369b).

This is a clever argument, but it is intentionally false. In other words, it is a lie of sorts. Where is the fallacy? There appear to be several.[17] One involves the shift from potentiality to actuality, from the fact that wise men are potentially good liars to the suggestion that they *are* good liars.[18] They may be, or they may not be. Indeed, they may not *be* liars at all. In addition, Socrates commits the classic sophistic fallacy of *secundum quid*: "for he is the *same man* and does not possess characteristics that are most opposite" (367d). It is plain that the truth teller and the liar are the same with respect to certain characteristics. But it does not follow that they are the same *simpliciter*. This is obscured in step (3), which runs roughshod over a moral consideration: truth tellers and liars may differ decisively in their moral acceptance of lying. And thus in addition to qualifying step (3), we must also qualify step (4): Truth tellers may be no better than liars in their knowledge of the facts about which they lie, and yet be "better" in the moral sense: better for refusing to lie.

Socrates reveals much about his polytropia here. He reveals that he is capable of leading himself and others to conclusions at odds with initial impressions. Indeed, he succeeds in forcing Hippias to admit an appearance that stands flatly at odds with the sophist's initial claim. The liar appeared at first opposite to the truth teller, but now, Hippias admits, "he does not appear to [be opposite], at least not here" (367d). Let me now give a name to the technique Socrates employs. It is unmistakably the Protagorean art of *antilogikē*, of leading overly confident interlocutors into admitting opposite appearances. More specifically, and insofar as it employs fallacies, it is also that subset of *antilogikē* called eristic. Socrates, in other words, is a master of sophistic argumentation.[19]

In the first argument as I have considered it so far, Socrates makes opposite appearances emerge. But this is not all he does. He also places Hippias in the spotlight in an interesting way. By showing that expert liars are capable, prudent, knowing, and wise, and especially by showing that they must possess a vast knowledge of many subjects, Socrates suggests (quite intentionally, as we shall see) that the best liar of all would be Hippias himself, at least as this sophist presents himself. Now we need to be careful how to interpret this. The point is not, evidently, that Hippias is *in fact* a liar. Hippias must know of himself that he is not. And we should know it, too, not only because Hippias has expressed extreme contempt for liars, but also because (as we are no doubt supposed to understand) Hippias is not quite as clever as he thinks; he does not really meet the criteria. The point is rather to make Hippias feel the force of the argument. Hippias now finds himself inextricably bound up with this matter. If he cannot find an argument to oppose the identification (liars = knowers = truth tellers = Hippias), then he stands to lose something important, his reputation for being a morally upstanding sophist and a speaker of truth.[20]

By conceding that the liar "does not appear" opposed to the truth teller, "at least not here" (367d), Hippias admits he is in trouble but tries, at the same time, to contain the trouble to one counter appearance. The case they had been considering was the case of mathematics (one of Hippias' areas of expertise) and what they discovered was that the expert mathematician would be most capable of lying about numbers and would be able to do so most consistently. In the remaining space devoted to the first argument (368d–369b), Socrates does something quite humorous and thoroughly polytropic. He moves methodically through Hippias' entire list of specialties, demonstrating that in every case the same argument obtains. In geometry and astronomy, as well as in all Hippias' other arts (handicrafts, poetry, prose composition, rhythms, harmony, correctness of letters, and even in the art of memory), the *same man* appears most capable of telling truths, and lies. Nor can Hippias deny this when Socrates asks for a single case in which the argument does not apply. Hippias will never find such a case, according to Socrates, if the argument Socrates is making is "true" (369a). However, Socrates' argument is not true, not at least in the implications Socrates draws from it. Socrates thus shows not only that he can lie, but also that he can maintain his lie across several different areas of intellectual experience. Socrates is an expert polytropist. And Hippias, for his part, seems helpless.

2. Achilles, Not Odysseus, Is Most Polytropic

Hippias' only recourse is to flee from the types of questions Socrates is asking. He thus berates Socrates for perpetually weaving arguments that fasten onto small details and fail to contend with the "whole matter" (369b–c). Hippias' counterstrategy is to drag Socrates into a grand rhetorical bout, "to display [to Socrates] in an ample speech with many proofs that Homer represented Achilles as better than Odysseus and not a liar, while he represented the latter as treacherous, frequently lying, and worse than Achilles" (ibid.). However, Socrates will not allow this. Or rather, he will not allow the big speech, but he does allow the conversation to turn briefly to an exegesis of Homer. That Socrates and Hippias here argue over exegetical issues marks the present section of the dialogue as an interlude of sorts. It is an interlude because, as Socrates makes clear, he regards textual exegesis as basically a waste of time.[21] However, the interlude in this dialogue is not strictly playful (*ludus*). For, in fact, the seeds for the dialogue's final phase are planted here, too.

Ironically and thus polytropically, Socrates announces that the whole reason he has been conversing with Hippias is that he regards this sophist as wiser than he. (Socrates' silence at the beginning of the dialogue suggests otherwise.) Socrates wishes to be benefited by Hippias' superior wisdom. And yet Socrates cannot be benefited, at least not readily, because what appears true to Hippias (namely, that Odysseus is most polytropic and lying) does not appear true to Socrates. Or so he says. Rather, it appears that Achilles, who is never explicitly labeled polytropic actually is so, or at least he lies (370a). In order to demonstrate this, Socrates reminds Hippias that Achilles twice proclaimed he would be sailing home for his native Phthia and yet never did sail home, nor did he even prepare to do so. Achilles, it appears, had a "quite a well-born contempt for speaking the truth" (370b–d, cf. *Iliad* I 169–171 and IX 357–363). Thus it is not clear which hero was more excellent. Indeed, both seem excellent "with respect to lying and truth and the rest of virtue" (370e).

Socrates' argument is brilliant in three respects. First, it proceeds in classic Protagorean fashion to exploit Hippias' confidence in an initial appearance. Hippias believes that polytropia is identical to lying. But if this is true, then Hippias has to allow that Achilles is polytropic, too (because he lies). Yet this is the opposite of Hippias' initial claim that Achilles is simple and truthful. Hippias must therefore either contradict himself or give up the equation of polytropia and lying. Second, Socrates here shows that, for his own part, he can maintain a lie quite far afield from the context in which he initially introduced it. Socrates' initial lie was that liars and truth tellers are the same and that neither is better than the other. Here he "demonstrates" this concretely by showing that Odysseus and Achilles are roughly the same with respect to lying and that "it is hard to distinguish which one might be better" (370c). Socrates thus demonstrates his own expert polytropia by maintaining his lie. Finally, Socrates demonstrates that he is more skilled than Hippias at Homeric interpretation. Or he has begun to demonstrate this. Consider how the argument proceeds after Hippias has a chance to reply.

Hippias does reply, and his position is quite sound. He suggests, first of all, that Socrates' interpretation of Homer is forced—another instance of Socrates' failure to "examine in a noble manner" (370e). Secondly, and more importantly, Socrates has failed to notice a crucial distinction. There is a difference between voluntary and involuntary lying, and the difference is relevant to the present case. For Achilles' lies are, it seems to Hippias, entirely unintentional. They arise from this hero's inability to foresee that the misfortune of the army will compel him to stay and help. Odysseus' lies are, contrariwise, always "voluntary and from design" (370e). Odysseus, therefore, is the only liar in the technical sense of the term, and he cannot be forgiven or excused in the way that Achilles can.

But here comes Socrates' superior exegetical skill. Though Hippias' defense of Achilles seems sound, Socrates doubts (or so he says) that it can be true. Moreover, he doubts (the height of irony now) that Hippias is earnest in offering it: "You are deceiving me, Hippias! And you are yourself imitating Odysseus!" (370e). Socrates supports these counter appearances by pointing out that Achilles' lies are simply too glaring to be unintentional. It is not merely that Achilles says one thing and does another. He actually says opposite things to different people. Thus immediately after he tells Odysseus that he will sail away from Troy at dawn (*Iliad* IX 537–563) he tells Ajax that he will remain at Troy to fight Hector (*Iliad* IX 650–655). How can such a blatant contradiction be interpreted as anything but intentional? Certainly the option of assuming that "the son of Thetis, who was educated by the most wise Chiron" was a dolt and someone so utterly forgetful as to say opposite things without noticing it would be an unacceptable interpretive posture. Thus it must follow that Achilles' lies are intentional and that his reputation for honesty is a ruse. In fact, Achilles must have been such a "cheat and designing plotter" that he even outfoxed Odysseus (371a). And Hippias, too, must know this, because Hippias is wise. Hippias is thus trying to pull the wool over Socrates' eyes by advancing a commonly held but untenable interpretation of Achilles.

Both in his irony and in his ability to move from one appearance to another, he reveals his similarity to Odysseus. Indeed, now we might add that he also resembles Achilles, or rather that esoteric Achilles who can lie without being detected by someone who ought to know how to detect a lie (Odysseus, Hippias). More important at this point is to reintroduce the question concerning the moral status of Socrates' lies. Through the twists and turns of the interlude, this question has become slightly more involved. There is, on the one hand, the question of lying as such. But there is now also the question of whether voluntary lying is better or worse than involuntary lying. Hippias' opinion (conventional wisdom) was that if Achilles' lies are involuntary, they are blameless; whereas to lie voluntarily is wicked.[22] Socrates, however, challenges that assumption as the interlude draws to a close: If Achilles' lies are mere accidents, then Odysseus must indeed be better than Achilles. For it was agreed in the earlier discussion on the difficulties of lying (see esp. 366b–367c) that those who lie voluntarily are "better" not only at lying but also at *knowing* than those who lie involuntarily. If Hippias accepted those claims, which he did, then he must also admit that Odysseus is better than Achilles, not the other way around, as he initially claimed.

Socrates, for his part, remains agnostic as to whether Achilles or Odysseus is meant to appear better at lying. Who can be sure what Homer was trying to say? But the philosophical issue whether voluntary or involuntary lying is "better," becomes the focus of Socrates' final argument.

3. Voluntary Wrongdoing Is Better than Involuntary Wrongdoing

"To me it appears, Hippias, that all is the opposite of what you say it is. It appears that those who harm human beings, who do injustice, lie, deceive, and go wrong voluntarily . . . are better than those who do so involuntarily" (372d). How can this be so? It is an inference Socrates draws from a number of examples, the first of which concerns a footrace. Watching runners in a race, we are accustomed to distinguish between good runners and bad. Good runners are those who can run swiftly, bad ones those who cannot. But what if a good runner *decides* to run slowly for some reason? Does he not remain a good runner? We are inclined to say, "Yes." But even if we hesitate on that point, we must at least agree that he remains a "better" runner than one who runs slowly, who cannot run fast. In a footrace, then, where running slowly is bad, it seems that he who does the bad thing voluntarily is better than he who does it involuntarily. Moreover, the same argument can be made for a host of other activities. In singing, he who sings out of tune voluntarily is better (i.e., a better singer) than he who does so involuntarily (374c).

As Socrates methodically applies this argument to ever more elevated matters, the same conclusion seems to hold. Indeed, we become more and more committed to the claim that to do wrong voluntarily is better than to do so involuntarily. But then comes the example of the human soul in its moral capacity, and things seem suddenly unacceptable: "What of this?" Socrates asks Hippias, "would we wish to possess our own [soul] in as good a condition as possible . . . and will our soul be better if it effects badness voluntarily and goes wrong, or if it does so involuntarily?" The answer implied by the previous examples is unambiguous: we should hope for souls that go wrong voluntarily. But this cannot be right, and Hippias indeed vociferously protests: "It would, however, be a terrible thing, Socrates, if those doing injustice voluntarily are to be better than those doing so involuntarily" (375d).

What exactly has gone wrong in Socrates' argument?[23] Like the first argument Socrates made about the identity of liars and truth tellers, this one is not necessarily fallacious on its face, but it is fallacious in what it is meant to imply. In other words it contains an ambiguity of some kind. In this case, the word "better," which in the present context can only mean "more capable," is being stretched to include "morally better," which would seem to involve something completely different. Thus, although it may be true that a runner who voluntarily runs slowly is more capable (better) than one who involuntarily does so, it does not follow that he is morally better. Nor in the moral realm are we comfortable with the claim that to do wrong voluntarily is better. To do wrong voluntarily may demonstrate one's abilities, but it will also demonstrate one's baseness. Before this chapter is done, I return to this argument and consider it more carefully. For I believe that although it is fallacious, one can only declare it so if one asserts something that in fact needs to be questioned: the disjunction between one kind of human excellence relating to capability (and ultimately to power) and another kind relating to moral goodness. I return to this later.

For now, consider the upshot of Socrates' argument in connection with the problem raised earlier of evaluating Socratic polytropia. What are we to make of this? On the one hand we have an argument suggesting that intentional lying is morally better than unintentional lying, which would exculpate Socrates for his own polytropia, if it were true. On the other hand, the argument is not evidently true, and in fact it seems morally repugnant. Thus, polytropic Socrates seems to lack a defense. Worse, he seems by this very argument to have proven that he is base, or at least that he speaks in ways that lend support to a life of vice. We might at this point pause to recall that prejudice that attached to Socrates and plagued him at his trial: that Socrates does injustice by making the weaker speech stronger and by teaching others to do the same (*Ap.* 19b–c). It would take a strong moral constitution indeed to listen to Socrates' arguments here and not be affected—either moved to moral outrage or, for a less-grounded soul, subtly corrupted in one's attachment to conventional morality.

Hippias' *Polytropia* in Action

Hippias, for his part, possesses just such a moral constitution. At no point in the dialogue does he accept the morally dubious conclusions reached by Socrates. In fact he consistently repudiates them. And yet, Hippias seems surprisingly unable to detect where Socrates' arguments go wrong. He is forced to "wander" from views he initially holds to views he does not hold, or does not want to hold but cannot resist. This is what we described earlier as Hippias' own polytropic tendency. It is different from Socratic polytropia in being unintentional and unwelcome. Like the Achilles whom Hippias admires, Hippias desires to be straightforward and truthful, but cannot be so, because circumstances force him to contradict himself. What is the significance of this? I think there are several points to observe.

First, there is something fundamentally inconsistent in Hippias' character. On the one hand, he is a sophist who prizes expertise, knowledge, and omnicompetence. On the other hand, he finds Achilles the most admirable hero, even though Achilles is less expert, less knowledgeable, and less competent than Odysseus. This inconsistency can be explained, I would suggest, by reference to a well-known incongruity in the Greek moral outlook. On the one hand, human excellence (*aretē*) is understood as the attainment of certain powers (whether in the form of technical skills or knowledge or speech), powers that are supposed to secure oneself and one's associates from harm. On the other hand, aretē is understood to involve certain moral qualities such as justice, truthfulness, fairness, and reverence, which are not identical to the "powers" in question and are, at least potentially, in tension with them. This latent tension in the Greek conception of human excellence occasionally boils to surface,[24] but it usually remains submerged, undetected by individuals seeking to do well and live right. And yet, individuals unavoidably place an emphasis on one or the other conception in choosing to pursue particular goals or to act in particular ways. Thus Hippias, for his part, is fully committed in his professional life to the view of aretē that emphasizes competence and power. To be a good man, Hippias' teaching suggests, is to be capable.[25] And yet Hippias is not unaware of the moral dimension of human excellence. Indeed, it is precisely this that leads him to rank Achilles above Odysseus, even though both men possess a high degree of competence.

Hippias, then, emphasizes aretē-as-power in his teaching while acknowledging aretē-as-moral goodness, too.[26] But this leads to a second observation. Hippias turns out to be shockingly power*less* against Socrates. And yet this is the opposite of what we would expect. Socrates is supposed to be the exemplar of the moral conception of aretē. He spends his life asking such questions as, What is justice? What is virtue? What is piety? Socrates is not supposed to be a sophist. And yet here we find him using powerful, fallacious arguments to force his interlocutor into morally dubious positions. Socrates is not only sophistic; he is more sophistic than one of the greatest fifth-century sophists.

Now we come to the question: Why is Hippias unable to detect, and why does Socrates insist on performing, logical maneuvers of such a manifestly sophistic sort? This is a question which, I believe, can be answered. I answer it in three stages, focusing first on Hippias' unique form of sophistry, next on Socrates' pedagogical strategy with Hippias, and finally on Socrates' practice of philosophy, which, I argue, often begins with and builds on his own expert sophistry.

Regarding Hippias' unique form of sophistry, we must appreciate that his commitment to aretē-as-power is not a commitment to power of all kinds. It is a commitment to those forms of intellectual power that might plausibly be put to use in saving a man or a city from ruin. And when Hippias thinks of "ruin," he has specific things in mind—primarily personal defeat in a courtroom or civic defeat in a diplomatic exchange, but also the sort of ruin that might come from failing to understand nature and its properties. (This accounts for Hippias' intense interest in the natural arts and sciences.) What Hippias is *not* interested in is "logic chopping." Why not? To a certain extent he seems to find this simply undignified and aesthetically repellent. But more importantly, he finds it useless for his primary goal of ensuring personal and public security. Here, again, is Hippias admonishing Socrates at the end of the *Hippias Major* (304a–b):

> But Socrates, what do you suppose all these things together are? They are scrapings and clippings of speeches . . . divided up into bits. But the alternative is both beautiful and worth much—to be able to compose a speech well and beautifully in a law court or council chamber or in any other ruling group to which the speech is addressed and to go away having persuaded them and taking off not the littlest but the largest of prizes, the salvation of oneself and one's money and friends. So one ought to cling to these things, bidding good-bye to those little speeches, in order that one not seem exceedingly unintelligent by engaging in babblings and drivel.

As we can see from this passage, Hippias is unprepared to defend himself against Socratic or sophistic *antilogikē*, because unlike other sophists (Protagoras, Euthydemus, and Dionysodorus), Hippias does not think this technique is valuable. In fact, he thinks it is useless. And he is right, but only insofar as his own goals are concerned, the goals of marking clear moral boundaries and using rhetoric to persuade people of what is clearly right and wrong. It does not follow, though, that Socrates' polytropic techniques are useless in every connection. Now we see how they work pedagogically and philosophically toward goals that are valuable from a Socratic point of view.

Pedagogical Significance of Socratic *Polytropia*

It is when readers reflect back on the *Apology* and what Socrates says there about his interviews with wise men that we gain the most insight into the pedagogical significance of Socrates' fallacies.[27] Socrates notices that the purportedly wise men he interviews make the categorical mistake of thinking that their wisdom in certain technical subjects is equivalent to moral wisdom. They think their expertise in various crafts or in poetry or politics entitles them to hold forth on what people *ought* to do. But it does not. Nor is this problem unique to intellectuals of the fifth-century BC. Part of the reason why Socrates' encounters with the "experts" are so instructive even today is that we, too, have our experts—scientists, doctors, policy wonks, and economists—who feel entitled to offer gratuitous moral advice on the basis of research that does not begin to explore the moral terrain. This is what Max Weber complained of when he upbraided the social scientists of his day for their tendency to preach, as if their empirical studies could tell a man how he ought, finally, to live his life.[28] And it is what Hannah Arendt complained of, too, as she reflected on the dangers of twentieth-century science to human values and ideals.[29]

Socrates' fallacious arguments in the *Hippias Minor* are fallacies with a strategy: they are designed to highlight the point of disjunction between two kinds of knowing or, more fundamentally, two kinds of search: the search, on the one hand, for all kinds of facts and capabilities; and the search, on the other hand, for knowledge of right and wrong, knowledge of what a human being ought to do in order to be good. For his part, Hippias has engaged in the first kind of search at the expense of the other, with the result that he stands utterly unprepared to offer anything like genuine moral wisdom. Worse, he presents the results of his quite impressive search for knowledge and capability as if it were moral wisdom, a kind of aretē all its own.

To reveal this problem, Plato's Socrates does something ingenious.[30] He designs arguments that assume the kind of aretē advanced by Hippias but which lead to a morally repugnant conclusion. The arguments are fallacious insofar as they reduce all aretē to mere knowledge and skill. And in order to diagnose the fallacies, the interlocutor must see the distinctly moral dimension of aretē. Only when we see the moral side of aretē can the fallacies be resolved and the repugnant conclusions be avoided. More concretely, Socrates argues (1) that the liar and the truth teller are the same man and thus morally equivalent. Indeed they *are* in terms of their factual knowledge and capability, but not in terms of moral orientation. Again, Socrates argues (2) that voluntary wrongdoers are "better than" involuntary wrongdoers. And this is indeed true, but only if the word "better" is limited to the wrongdoer's factual knowledge and capability. As soon as the word is given its full moral connotation, the fallacy is exposed and the whole problem of moral action is suddenly illuminated.

With respect to Socrates' argument about Homer—namely, that Achilles is more polytropic than Odysseus—I take this to be pedagogically significant in trying to break Hippias from the belief that one can find moral wisdom by simply consulting the "great books" in a factual manner. Homer's text admits of multiple interpretations. We cannot know once and for all what Homer understood human excellence to entail; and even if we could, it would not follow that he was right. Thus Socrates teases out of Homer a moral teaching that will strike Hippias as repellent: Odysseus and Achilles were more or less equals with respect to lying and the rest of virtue (370e).[31]

But what are we to make of the fact that Hippias fails to diagnose these fallacies that Socrates has so brilliantly and polytropically presented? This can be interpreted in a number of ways. Hippias may be so professionally invested in his own brand of aretē that he cannot recognize or will not *say* he recognizes the problem Socrates exposes. Alternatively, Hippias may be so inexperienced in logical analysis and so repelled by Socratic questioning that he prefers simply to let the matter drop. Either way, Socrates' pedagogical strategy appears to have failed. And yet even in failing there is something to be said for it. Hippias has been shown that his own approach to aretē leads to problems he cannot explain. He is thus placed in a position to learn, whether he does so immediately or not.[32] Second, the auditors of this exchange—the immediate audience as well as the readers of the dialogue—are placed in this position, too. The natural response to Socrates' strange (sophistic) arguments is to wonder at them, and the more this wonder becomes active, the more it must follow a course that leads to the insight that what Hippias (and others like him) teach does not constitute moral wisdom, though it often masquerades as such. Finally, then, Socrates' polytropic practices in this dialogue seem justifiable from a moral-pedagogical point of view, even if they remain dangerously prone to be misunderstood.

Philosophic Significance of Socrates' Fallacies

Moreover, there is a straightforwardly philosophical defense to be made of Socrates' polytropic arguments. This can be brought into view if we focus again on that quality of wonder. Socratic philosophy (and perhaps philosophy in general) *begins* with wonder. One must wonder before one can explore. And yet wonder is not always easy to engender. By far the more common epistemological posture is one of trust, simple acceptance of the world as it comes. We take almost everything for granted and only rarely bring questions or curiosities into clear focus in our minds. This is perhaps especially so in the matter of aretē, where we encounter so many well-entrenched opinions along with strong structural incentives to accept them (and disincentives to question them). Here, as the philosopher George Santayana once remarked, "if you refuse to move in the prescribed direction, you are not simply different, you are arrested and perverse."[33] Thus, wonder in matters relating to human excellence is less common than we might initially suppose. We perhaps puzzle over small things—"Was I right to do this?" "Should I have done otherwise?"—but we tend to leave the larger questions of human excellence largely unexplored.[34]

Socrates' polytropic arguments are significant because they generate wonder not only for the interlocutor but more importantly for Socrates himself. Moreover, the specific topics of wonder engendered in this dialogue are of fundamental philosophical importance. I now try to defend that claim. When Socrates reveals that there is a disjunction between two conceptions of aretē, one favored by Hippias that emphasizes factual knowledge and technical capabilities, another that emphasizes notions of moral goodness, he emphatically does *not* claim that only one side of that disjunction should count as genuine aretē. He rather shows, merely, that by emphasizing one side at the expense of the other, Hippias has exposed himself to criticisms from that other (moral) side. But this only raises the question—it does not resolve it—of whether and to what extent human excellence might consist of *both* sides of this disjunction.

There is indeed something to be said for "knowledge and capability" as an answer to the question of human excellence. In this sense, Hippias appears to be on to something. This point is more concrete with an example from contemporary culture. When we watch a film like *Ocean's Eleven*, we find ourselves attracted to characters engaged in crime. Why? It is not, I argue, because they are criminals, but rather because they are such talented criminals. We are attracted to their excellence, not their crime. This is why we are not at all attracted, for example, to the average bank robber who, high on drugs and fumbling in his pocket for a handgun he has forgotten to pack, is arrested as he communicates his demands to the teller. The average bank robber lacks the excellence we admire in the protagonists of *Ocean's Eleven*. But what does "excellence" mean in this context? It must refer, as in the *Hippias Minor*, to the possession of extreme knowledge and skill. Thus there is something we admire and deem excellent quite separate from the matter of moral goodness. In other words, both sides of the disjunction referred to earlier seem to capture a genuine aspect of aretē, something valuable per se.

The question, then, that is raised by the *Hippias Minor* is not (or not merely), "what has Hippias failed to see?" It is also, "what has Hippias succeeded in seeing that is, at least in part, true?" And this leads to the fundamental question of how to balance the two competing visions of aretē, which surface in the dialogue.

Now, we might suppose that this question of balance is irrelevant to the Socratic life, because Socrates is one who so manifestly cares for justice (moral goodness) above all else. "My whole care," he says in the *Apology*, "is to commit no unjust or impious deed" (32d). But the fact that Socrates takes moral matters so seriously does not mean he neglects the other kind of aretē altogether. And in fact, I think he is far more invested in it than we might suppose. Here are two reasons to think this. (1) Socrates shows throughout the *Hippias Minor* that he is exceedingly capable. He is never forced to concede a single point to Hippias, but rather wields relentless power over him and over the conditions of the conversation. Socrates has the better memory, the better logical faculty, the better facility with sophistic arguments. Such capability does not come accidentally. It reflects Socrates' careful mastery of certain processes of thinking and speaking. (2) Besides this, we see that Socrates possesses a great deal of factual knowledge as the dialogue proceeds. He appears to know his Homeric texts better than Hippias, a self-professed Homerist. And he knows at least enough about Hippias' many areas of expertise to use these as fodder for eristic manipulations. All this makes Socrates look quite excellent and admirable, and it suggests that he attends well to that side of aretē that is usually thought to be characteristic of Hippias. Indeed, Socrates appears to be more invested in this than Hippias himself.[35]

By bringing these two types of aretē into view and revealing that Socrates is attracted to them both, the *Hippias Minor* brings us to the brink of a philosophical question. It invites us to ask how these types of aretē should be blended with and modulated by each other. That the dialogue does not go on to answer this question for us means that it is primarily propaedeutic. But we should not discount the achievement of a work that brings us to a state of genuine wonder. The force of the dialogue consists in its revelation that we have two ideas in our heads about aretē that do not always harmonize. According to one conception, it is better to do wrong involuntarily, if one must do it at all; for involuntary wrongdoing is blameless. According to the other, it is better to do wrong *voluntarily*, if one must do it at all; for voluntary action (which necessarily implies knowledge and capability) is praiseworthy as such. There is nothing remotely fallacious about this contradiction that Socrates brings to our mind, and he thus forces us to wonder about it and invites us to explore it further.

Finally, once we see this philosophical quality of Socrates' polytropic arguments, I think we are in a good position to appreciate Socrates' description of himself (372d–e, 376c, cf. *Hippias Major* 304c) as someone who "vacillates" (*planōmai*). According to Socrates, a certain "seizure" befalls him while he is talking to Hippias. He is suddenly struck by the notion that "those who voluntarily go wrong . . . seem better than those who do so involuntarily." However, Socrates says, the opposite view seems to strike him at others times. Thus he is forced to vacillate or wander back and forth.

This is one of those instances where Socratic irony blends so seamlessly into nonirony that it is virtually impossible to separate them out. Socrates makes it sound as if he is the special victim of some epistemic seizure he cannot control. Is he? The answer is yes and no. He is indeed the victim of a kind of intellectual seizure, but this he has in common with all of mankind (376c). We *all* have opposing ideas in our minds, which shift uncontrollably back and forth as we move from context to context. We are all polytropic in this (Hippian) sense. But is Socrates really the victim of this seizure in the same way that we are? Not at all. For one thing, we do not tend to notice the contradictory ideas floating around in our heads. Socrates is unique in noticing them. Second, Socrates is able to *induce* the seizure in a way that few others can. In other words, he uses his polytropic skills as a philosophical tool to invoke puzzles and thus wonder. This also is something rare that Socrates possesses, although he did not develop it alone. As I have shown here and elsewhere, he adopted this technique from certain sophists like Protagoras and turned it to his own pedagogical and philosophical purposes.

Conclusion

At the beginning of this chapter I asked: Why did Plato find Hippias so significant? What might have been his purpose in casting this sophist as an interlocutor for Socrates? These questions have now been answered in several ways. Because Hippias exemplified that general intellectual tendency of supposing he knew more than he really did, Plato's dialogue has a prominent comic aspect: Socrates reveals (as the *Apology* would lead us to expect) that Hippias is not as wise as he thinks. Further, because Hippias so vividly exemplified that categorical mistake of treating technical expertise as moral knowledge, the dialogue has a more serious, critical aspect: it exposes the disjunction between these two kinds of knowledge, and thus speaks to us even today. However, Plato's purpose in the *Hippias Minor* is not exhausted by critique, or so I have argued. There is also a positive side to the dialogue, and we were able to subdivide this into pedagogical and philosophical potentialities. Here, Hippias' status as a sophist is set against Socrates' apparently superior sophistic skills, and we are led to ask why someone like Socrates would have argued so spuriously. Or to put this in the language of the dialogue itself, we are led to inquire into the value of polytropia in its various forms. What we find is that despite Hippias' initial contempt for polytropia, this turns out to be an unavoidable human trait. Whether by accident or by design, we are creatures who hide one thing in our mind while saying another. In other words we experience conflicting impulses and ideas. And yet, by making our polytropia active and intentional, as Socrates does, there seems to be some hope of remedying our confusion. Active polytropia (sophistry) seems to have pedagogical and philosophic power.

Such is the potential of polytropia, but this is not the end of the matter. Finally, the dialogue calls us to make some judgment about the moral status of this activated power, and this proves no easy task. In fact, the dialogue shows us that this question must be subsumed under the broader question of the relationship between two competing conceptions of human excellence, one that emphasizes competence and power in general, the other moral goodness. The two conceptions are not perfectly compatible, and yet they are both compelling and, to varying degrees, assumed by us all. In this context, Socrates' practice of polytropia becomes doubly significant. It is polytropia that enables him to bring this conflict to the forefront of his mind and to reveal it as a puzzle. At the same time, his very use of this power implicates Socrates in one of the two conceptions; it reveals him to be strongly committed to excellence as power, a commitment we initially (but wrongly) limited to Hippias. As a result, we the readers are moved to wonder about the final form that human excellence should take—how to balance or otherwise reconcile the tension between these two competing forms.

SIX

BROTHER SOPHISTS

Euthydemus and Dionysodorus

> Virtue, Socrates, is what [we teach], and we think we can impart it better than anyone else and more quickly.
>
> —Plato, *Euthydemus* 273d

Euthydemus and Dionysodorus have been oddly neglected by scholars of the Greek sophists. They were erroneously omitted from Hermann Diels and Walther Kranz's *Die Fragmente Der Vorsokratiker*. There is no mention of them in Mario Untersteiner's work on the sophists.[1] They are almost completely ignored by Guthrie.[2] And although they are at least recognized as sophists by Jacqueline de Romilly, they are yet deemed so obscure and unimportant that she proceeds simply to set them aside.[3] However, there can be no doubt that Euthydemus and Dionysodorus were important (if also notorious) fifth-century sophists.[4] Plato devotes an entire dialogue to them, the *Euthydemus*, in which they are not only labeled sophists (271c1), but also portrayed as paid teachers of *aretē* (273d). (They thus meet even the strictest definitional criteria.) Their historical existence, moreover, is confirmed by a number of references outside of Plato.[5] And Aristotle goes so far as to devote an entire treatise (the *Sophistical Refutations*) to the task of discrediting the type of fallacious argumentation for which they were well known.

A good reason to consider Euthydemus and Dionysodorus in some detail is, then, that they represent precisely the type of intellectual chicanery to which negative words like *sophistry* and *sophism* apply. These were arrogant, disputatious hair-splitters who would seize on any word and, by means of utterly spurious arguments, proceed to contradict whatever anyone might say, whether true or false. Without studying these sophists, then, we would have no basis for appreciating what, for example, Aristotle means when he refers to "sophistry" as the semblance of wisdom without the reality, aiming at mere contentiousness and apparent victory (*Soph. Ref.*, 165a20–25, 171b30–35). Nor could we make sense of the Eleatic Stranger's conclusion in the *Sophist* that sophistry is in essence "the art of contradiction making, descended from an insincere kind of conceited mimicry of the semblance-making breed, derived from image-making, distinguished as a portion not divine but human, of production, that presents a shadow play of words."[6] Both Plato and Aristotle here equate "sophistry" with a particular breed of sophist, and if we fail to take notice of the breed, we shall be ill-equipped indeed to understand the criticisms.

Yet, the status of Euthydemus and Dionysodorus as the worst breed of sophist presents a challenge, it would appear, for the thesis of this book. If, as I have been arguing, Plato treats the sophists more seriously than modern interpreters tend to recognize and uses them in ways that are essentially propaedeutic and protreptic, then what about Euthydemus and Dionysodorus? What could possibly be gained by taking *these* sophists more seriously? And is there any reason to suppose that Plato does so? If we look at traditional interpretations of Plato's *Euthydemus*, we discover that the dialogue is chiefly remarkable for its comic qualities.[7] And yet more recent interpreters have come to see that beneath its comic veneer the *Euthydemus* contains a sustained treatment of some serious philosophical issues—the question of what philosophy *is*, on the one hand, and its relationship to other human goods and activities, on the other.[8] In the pages that follow, I advance this line of interpretation by showing not only how the *Euthydemus* engages serious philosophical issues, but also (in keeping with the thesis of this book) why the inclusion of the sophists in the dialogue is essential for doing so.

The Frame: Crito as "Lover of Hearing"

The argument that we should—and perhaps must—engage the sophists in order to better understand certain features of Socratic philosophy is emphasized in the dialogue's fascinating frame.[9] As the dialogue opens, Crito is found plying Socrates for information about his conversation partners of the day before. One might expect Socrates to say something critical or cautionary at this point about his sophistic interlocutors, Euthydemus and Dionysodorus.[10] But in fact just the opposite occurs. Socrates praises the sophists' wisdom to the skies, calling it marvelous or wonderous (*thaumasia*, 271c). He extols their omniscience and their argumentative skill. And he urges Crito to join him forthwith in becoming their pupils. In fact, Socrates goes further still, suggesting that they enlist Crito's own children as bait—in case the sophists find Socrates and Crito too old: "I feel sure," Socrates says, "that their desire to get the boys will make them give us lessons too" (272d).[11]

Such praise and enthusiasm for the sophists is, of course, ironic coming from Socrates. And yet this aspect of the dialogue has understandably vexed interpreters, who see the irony as a bit cruel in light of Crito's rather desperate situation.[12] In the closing frame of the *Euthydemus*, we learn that Crito's questions at the beginning are motivated by a deep anxiety about the education of his oldest son, Critobulus. And we learn, too, that Crito has discussed this matter with Socrates before. Crito explains:

> As I am *always* saying to you. . . . Critobulus is at an age when he needs someone who will do him good. Now whenever I am in your company your presence has the effect of leading me to think it madness to have taken such pains about my children in various other ways, such as marrying to make sure that they would be of noble birth on the mother's side, and making money so that they would be as well off as possible, and then to give no thought to their education. But on the other hand, whenever I take a look at any of those persons who set up to educate men, I am amazed; and every last one of them strikes me as utterly grotesque, to speak frankly between ourselves. So the result is that I cannot see how I am to urge [*protrepō*] the boy towards philosophy. (306d–307a, with slight alterations to Sprague)

As Socrates already knows from past conversations, Crito has arrived at an impasse (*aporia* 306d3). Torn between a desire to have his son educated in philosophy and a basic disgust for the "practitioners of philosophy," he cannot see how to proceed. The problem, though, stems from

Crito's own ignorance about the true nature of philosophy. He cannot distinguish philosophy from sophistry. And Socrates must know this. And yet, if this is the case, why does Socrates not set Crito straight immediately by explaining in no uncertain terms that his conversation partners of the day before were sham philosophers who would likely corrupt Critobulus? Why does Socrates encourage Crito to take them so seriously? This is the puzzle of Socrates' irony in the *Euthydemus*.[13]

The key to solving this puzzle lies, to my mind, in a remark Crito makes at the very beginning of the dialogue's closing frame. The remark is strongly emphasized by its structural position. Socrates has just finished narrating his account of the sophists' wisdom and reiterating his desire for Crito to join him in studying with them, when Crito formulates his initial reaction thus: "Well, Socrates, I am indeed a lover of hearing [*philēkoos*], and I gladly *would* learn something [*manthanoimi*], but I am afraid I am not one of Euthydemus' sort" (304c6–8). The significance of the potential optative, *manthanoimi*, will become clear momentarily. It relates to the epithet that Plato here assigns to Crito and that scholars have not, to my knowledge, adequately explored. *Philēkoos* is a rare word in Plato's dialogues.[14] It makes its most significant appearance in *Republic* V, where it is a technical term symbolizing a certain type of nonphilosopher—or someone who experiences a certain obstacle to philosophy. A brief consideration of this term in *Republic* V will shed light at once on Crito's character, his philosophical needs, and Socrates' ironic tone.

At the point in the *Republic* where the "lover of hearing" appears (475d–480a), we find Socrates engaged in the so-called third wave—trying to defend his argument that philosophy and kingship must coincide if there is to be happiness in the city.[15] In an effort to indicate what philosophers might be like, Socrates suggests that they will have an insatiable desire for wisdom, not just some wisdom, but all of it. And this leads Glaucon to object that the "lovers of hearing" as well as the "lovers of sights" (*philotheamonas*) would then have to be classified as philosophers.[16] Not so, Socrates responds, as he makes the distinction clear. While philosophers are willing to taste every kind of learning with gusto, the lovers of hearing and sights manifest a peculiar limitation (hence the potential optative above; Crito cannot see what Socrates can see in these brother sophists). What is the nature of that limitation? In effect, they wish to delight only in what appears to them beautiful and good, while eschewing what seems ugly and base (see *Rep.* 475e–476b, 479a–b). And yet in this they commit a fatal philosophical error, as Socrates promptly shows. For not only is it simply impossible to embrace good and beautiful appearances in human experience while avoiding their opposites entirely (what is good may turn out to be bad; what is beautiful may also appear ugly), but doing so actually breaks off the philosophical ascent to the forms before it can even begin. It is precisely the *problem* of opposite appearances that motivates the Socratic search for a higher, purer form of knowledge. Thus, by turning a blind eye (or a deaf ear, as it were) to the inescapable contrariety of things—the lovers of hearing and sights see no need for the ascent to forms. In Socrates' words, "their thought is unable to see and delight in the nature of the fair *itself*" (476b).

The *Republic* goes on from here to propose a course of instruction for the stubborn *philēkoos* (476d–480a). The first step is, simply, to attempt an ascent with him toward recognition of the forms (476c). But in the event that this fails, a different approach is required. He must be shown the "doubleness" of worldly things—that the fair and the just can also appear ugly and unjust, that pious things can appear impious, and so on. In general he must be shown that all worldly perceptions admit of opposite appearances, that everything is so ambiguous (*epamphoteridzein*, literally, admitting of doubles, 479c3) that it is not possible to think of things fixedly. Even doubles (*diplasia*, 479b3), Socrates points out, may strike us as halves.

All this is directly relevant to the *Euthydemus*. As a lover of hearing, Crito is preoccupied with material goods and conventional notions of value.[17] Anxious about his children's welfare, he has gone to great lengths to furnish them with nobility on their mother's side and plenty of wealth. But what about education? It seems to Crito—especially when he is around Socrates—that "philosophy" is another good he should attempt to provide for his son. But the truth is that Crito does not know what philosophy is or why it should count as a good.[18] It is with these questions in mind that he queries Socrates at the beginning of the dialogue about the conversation Socrates had the day before with Euthydemus and Dionysodorus.

> Who was it, Socrates, you were talking to in the Lyceum yesterday? There was such a crowd standing around you that when I came up and wanted to hear [*akouein*], I couldn't hear anything distinctly. But by craning my neck I did get a look, and

> I thought it was some stranger you were talking to. Who was it? (271a)

Scholars have noticed that Crito's desire to hear combined with his inability to hear distinctly is symbolic of his posture toward philosophy.[19] This insight is strongly reinforced by our understanding of the lover of hearing in general. The opening lines also foreshadow the essential lesson that the lover of hearing must learn. Crito notices only *one* interlocutor; he cannot see that they are, in fact, "doubles." And so Socrates must show him (271a6–7, 271b8) that there were indeed two interlocutors and that they both participate in (*metechei*) the arguments. Just as the lover of hearing must come to see the opposing sides of the things he observes, so, too, must Crito see both sides of this sophistic duo and listen to their dueling claims before he can make sense of the Socratic enterprise, which attempts to transcend them. Moreover, not *until* Crito comes to terms with all this can he possibly see the value in—much less actually succeed at—turning his own son toward philosophy.

On my reading, then, Crito's encounter with the sophists via Socrates' carefully narrated account promises to be the perfect antidote for his sickness as a lover of hearing.[20] The potential lessons from the encounter would seem to be twofold. First, the sophistic paradoxes and refutations might just shock Crito into seeing the doubleness of things—how easily something can appear now one way, now another. We recall that the sophist Protagoras employed *antilogikē* for just this purpose—as an antidote for dogmatic one-sidedness and a preparation for more serious instruction.[21] Yet Euthydemus and Dionysodorus seem much less thoughtful than Protagoras; they seem to possess no *serious* instruction at all—which leads to a second potential lesson for Crito: not only do all good things admit of doubles, but philosophers, too, admit of a double. To understand philosophy, then, one must ascend somehow above the level on which philosophy and its double oscillate back and forth. By exposing Crito to the eristics, Socrates is thus preparing him at once to take part in the philosophical ascent while, at the same time, forcing him to notice and distinguish between the mere appearances of philosophy, on the one hand, and its essential nature, on the other.

Since this can be done fruitfully (if not exclusively) through a careful examination of the double-sophists themselves, Socrates must get

Crito to hear their lessons. It is precisely in order to pull this off that Socrates assumes his well-known ironic stance. He exaggerates the sophists' wisdom, endorses their curriculum, and even involves Crito's own children in the appeal. Moreover, by the end of the opening frame we see that Socrates' appeals have actually worked. Although Crito remains skeptical about the proposed endeavor of studying with these sophists, he now requests considerably more information about their wisdom: "Describe to me in full," he asks, "what the wisdom of the two men is, to give me some idea of *what* we are going to learn" (272d). Crito, the finicky lover of hearing, is now committed to hearing these sophists out—at least through a *narrative* account. And the opening frame draws to a close with Socrates promising Crito that he will presently be hearing (*akouōn,* 272d5).[22]

Socrates' Introduction to the Encounter

I emphasize the narrative aspect of Crito's encounter with the sophists because it reveals an important qualification to my central thesis—that Socrates wishes for Crito (just as Plato wishes for us) to take the sophists more seriously. The qualification is that one's encounter with the sophists might ideally be mediated by a philosophical guide. In the *Euthydemus*, Socrates mediates the sophists' impact in a number of important ways and for three different characters: Crito, Clinias, and Ctesippus. Socrates' concrete maneuvers as mediator are best discussed *en passant*, but the groundwork for his mediation is laid in the short introduction that precedes his account. Here we are also given the basic premise of the story.

Socrates was preparing to leave the Lyceum when his mysterious divine sign suddenly signaled him to wait. Soon afterward two sophists arrived, Euthydemus and Dionysodorus, with a large group of disciples. Not long after that, the beautiful young Clinias arrived, followed by a group of admirers (*erastai*). Clinias, who sat down immediately next to Socrates, attracted the attention of the sophists. And they were soon on him, advertising their wares. What did they offer? Not instruction in generalship, or martial arts, or in legal speechwriting—their previous courses of instruction. They now claimed to offer something much greater, namely, instruction in aretē, which they promised to impart better and more quickly than anyone else.

Just as the sophists prepared to demonstrate their skill, however, Socrates intervened to modify the focus of their demonstration in a crucial way. As he says:

> To give a complete demonstration would obviously be a lengthy business; but tell me just this: are you able to make only that man good who is already persuaded that he ought to learn from you, or also he who is not yet persuaded on this point—either because he believes that this thing, virtue, is not teachable, or because he thinks you two are not teachers? Tell me, does the task of persuading a man in this frame of mind both that virtue is teachable and that you are the ones from whom he could learn it best, belong to this same art or to some other one? (274d–e with alterations to Sprague)

The sophists replied that it all belongs to the very same art. And Socrates responded: Then you are the people "best able to urge [*protrepsaite*] a man to philosophy and the practice of virtue?" (275a1–2). And in this way the topic of the dialogue is established. The sophists are not asked to demonstrate their own course in virtue. They are asked for a demonstration—using Clinias as an example—of protreptic, that is, how to persuade a person that it is necessary to love wisdom (*philosophein*) and attend to virtue (*aretēs epmeleisthai*).

Commentators often see a shift at this point in the dialogue toward Socrates' own philosophical interests and concerns.[23] There is, to be sure, something to be said for this. But there is also, significantly, a shift towards Crito's concerns. It is Crito, more than Socrates, who has been preoccupied with the question of "protreptic." This is not a word that Plato's Socrates often uses.[24] And if Crito is not behind the doubts whether virtue can be taught,[25] he is certainly someone who doubts whether the sophists, in particular, are its teachers: "every last one of them strikes me as utterly grotesque," he tells Socrates in the closing frame (306e). Socrates, for his part, knows of Crito's doubts and concerns. He knows that Crito wonders whether and how to submit his son to protreptic. And he knows, too, that the young Clinias who took part in the conversations the day before reminds Crito of his own Critobulus. Socrates thus capitalizes on these basic facts to tell a story about protreptic that is very much *for* Crito. The story is designed to expose Crito to the sophists' lessons, making certain positive and negative insights possible, while, at the same time, guarding against the dangers that can arise from sophistic encounters.

These dangers, and Socrates' ways of mediating them, are all brought to our attention in Socrates' introduction. We can distinguish between the danger of becoming corrupted by the sophists, on the one hand, and the danger of a too hasty and contemptuous rejection of them, on the other. One danger is typical of the young, the other of the old.[26] And within Socrates' general guise as mediator, one can distinguish between what, for convenience's sake, might be called his role as "protector of youth," his role as "narrator," and his role as story "maker."

Socrates the protector of youth appears in the introduction when his divine sign signals him to stay seated; he is thus poised to prevent Clinias and his followers from falling prey to the sophists. Socrates is worried that someone might corrupt Clinias (275b). Thus, seated on Clinias' left, he literally blocks Euthydemus and Dionysodorus from surrounding him (273b), just as he will later prevent their arguments from surrounding him (277d).[27] What would have happened had Socrates not been there? Clinias, a somewhat timid youth, would likely have become permanently disgusted with arguments. It is a well-known danger, and precisely what Socrates intervenes to prevent later in the dialogue.[28] And although Clinias' principal lover, Ctesippus, would have surely stepped up to defend him, Ctesippus himself would have been harmed in the attempt. Ctesippus, like Crito, is a "lover of hearing" (274c3), not a philosophical guide or protector. He is youthful and somewhat too filled with passionate love to make sound decisions in battle. Thus, Socrates intervenes repeatedly in the dialogue to save Ctesippus, too, from a somewhat different kind of corruption, as we shall see.

Socrates the narrator is also at work in the introduction. This is the voice that, in describing past action, also colors it with interpretive judgments and suggestive images—as, for instance, when Socrates describes Ctesippus as "well-bred except for a certain youthful hubris" (273a8). Of all Socrates' roles, his role as narrator is at once the least conspicuous and the most powerful in terms of shaping interlocutors' perception of events. And it will be used not only to affect Crito's perceptions of the entire sophistic encounter, but also to shape Clinias' and Ctesippus' perceptions of events as they unfold. In describing *what* has just transpired, and coloring this with his own perspective, Socrates can profoundly mediate the effect of the sophists' teachings.[29]

And, lastly, Socrates the story *maker* is at work in the introduction. Just before Socrates turns to his account of the brothers' demonstration, he pauses to invoke *Memory and the Muses*, just as the poets do (275d). This is our first indication that Socrates will not merely be recalling events, but also reshaping them. We see small instances of this reshaping later in the dialogue when Socrates chooses to abbreviate arguments or omit them entirely (e.g., 280b1, 291b). But there are more conspicuous instances that profoundly shape the overall account. Right at the beginning of his introduction, Socrates tells Crito (272d7–9): "I cannot pretend I paid no attention to the pair; rather I paid careful attention and I remember (*memnēmai*)." And yet at the dialogue's highest point, when Socrates has at last led Clinias to shine with intelligence, Crito bursts into the dialogue to protest (290e1–2): "What do you mean, Socrates? Did that boy utter all this?" And Socrates, who earlier said he could not pretend he paid no attention, now does just that: "You're not convinced of it Crito?. . . . Dear me, then perhaps after all it was Ctesippus who said this, and I have not remembered (*ou memnēmai*). . . . Do you suppose, my good Crito, that some superior being was there and uttered these things?—because I am positive I heard them" (290e–291a). The superior being must be Socrates himself (at least in some sense), as Crito suspects.[30] Socrates the story maker has refashioned the encounter in fundamental ways so that Crito can see the potential of protreptic and also be drawn into the process himself. Certainly, Socrates is not simply "remembering" when, just after this, he drops Clinias from his account altogether and allows Crito to take over the role of respondent. Rather, we find here the work of Socrates the story maker, mediating Crito's experience by literally shaping the story to suit his needs. One even suspects that Socrates' initial and decisive shifting of the conversation to the topic of protreptic may, itself, be an artifact of Socrates' making. That an actual conversation took place involving eristic sophists, we can be sure.[31] But was it really about protreptic?

The importance of Socrates' role as a mediating force cannot be overstated. Athenian youths were often attracted to the sophists for dubious reasons, and the danger of corruption was quite real. A youth might grow too fond of arguments, or too frustrated with them—in either case harming his potential for sound judgment.[32] And older Athenians were in danger, too—not of corruption, but of rejecting the sophists too roundly. Why should this be viewed as a danger? Well, at the very least it might shut these Athenians off to any positive lessons the sophists might offer. It might also render them ineffective parents of their intellectually ambitious children. (In this sense, Socrates is perhaps the most responsible "parent" of bright Athenian youths, because in understanding the sophists, he can serve as their guide.) But there is another, more disastrous, consequence to note. In rejecting everything to do with the sophists, older Athenians might well reject Socrates, too. For how can one distinguish Socrates from the sophists if one is not willing to know who the sophists are?[33] Socrates thus encourages experience of the sophists.

As we proceed now to the dialogue's inner rings, we have a number of things to watch out for. There is the issue of Crito's educational needs as well as the question of what differentiates Socrates from the sophists. These issues seem diverse at first, but they merge together in fascinating ways. If Crito is going to learn how properly to educate (*protrepein*) his son, he is going to have to learn what philosophy is and is not, and this will entail distinguishing Socrates from the sophists. Yet, as we see, the problem of making such distinctions, in fact, runs significantly deeper than Crito can go. On one level, certain obvious and almost comical differences come to light (and it is not clear that Crito fully appreciates even these); while, on a deeper level, a number of surprising and even vexing similarities emerge. Because these similarities well elude Crito's grasp, their inclusion in the dialogue cannot be part of Socrates' project to educate him. Yet, as we see, they are crucial for the dialogue's meaning in other ways and must, therefore, be carefully considered.

Eristic Scene I

The sophists begin their demonstration by confronting Clinias with the following question (275d): "Which are the men who learn—the wise or the ignorant?" Like so many of the brothers' questions, this addresses a serious topic.[34] Socrates has asked for a demonstration of protreptic, and the brothers would seem to be suggesting that before one can discuss the *how* of protreptic, one must first consider the condition of the learner. We are indeed put in mind here of that all-important lesson from Plato's *Meno* that it is necessary to recognize one's ignorance before one is suitably positioned to learn. But, as we soon find out, the brothers' questions are not meant to be taken seriously at all. Rather, as Dionysodorus divulges to Socrates, they are but a carefully orchestrated trap: "whichever way the boy answers, he will be refuted," and "*all* our questions are of this same inescapable sort" (275e5–6, 276e5).

When Clinias cautiously responds that it is "the wise" who learn, not the ignorant, he is forced to run the gauntlet of sophistic double arguments (276a–c): When you were learning, asks Euthydemus, did you already know the things you learned? No, replies Clinias. Then in the process of learning things you didn't know, you learned while you were ignorant? asks Euthydemus. Yes, replies Clinias. Then it is the *ignorant* who learn, not the wise, Euthydemus asserts to the applause and laughter of his followers. At this point Dionysodorus jumps in: But when the writing master would give you a dictation, which of the boys learned the piece—the wise or the ignorant? The wise, replies Clinias. Then it is the *wise* who learn, not the ignorant, asserts Dionysodorus, as the followers laugh again.

Just as Dionysodorus had said, there is no answer to their question that cannot be refuted. But they have not yet exhausted their tricks, for they now add a confounding "double twist" to their display.[35] Do those who learn learn things they know or things they don't know? asks Euthydemus. What they do not know, replies Clinias. (It was Euthydemus who had earlier shown him that the learners are the ignorant, not the wise.) Yet, Euthydemus asks, when someone gives you a dictation, doesn't he dictate letters? Yes, replies Clinias. And don't you know your letters? Yes, replies Clinias. And don't you learn what is dictated to you? Yes again, replies Clinias. Then you learn what you *know*, asserts Euthydemus, and your answer was wrong. Then, once again, comes Dionysodorus to show that this answer was not wrong, or that it has just been made wrong again, since (as he shows) "it is those who do *not* know who learn, and not those who know" (277c).

It is not clear when, or how, the sophists might have stopped their display. But at this point Socrates intervenes to prevent Clinias from losing heart. And this affords us a good opportunity to consider how this scene relates to the issue of Crito's educational needs. In one sense, we can say that Crito is here offered precisely what the *Republic* prescribes for the lover of hearing: a shocking demonstration of the "doubleness" of things. These double sophists possess the power to make people's statements seem both true and false. Reality itself seems to bend this way and that in their hands. Not only can they maintain opposite answers to the questions they pose, they can also switch sides halfway through, lest we ascribe some stability even to their own positions. What is true—this display suggests—can be made to seem different not only for different people, but also for the *same* person at different times. This is indeed something like the problem of instability which Socrates wants Crito to face. But is Crito really witnessing something sound?

Here is where Socrates' role as mediator becomes so important. For as he narrates the story to Crito, he supplies ample indications that things are not right. We note, first, Socrates' use of game-like metaphors to describe the events that unfold. Socrates likens the brothers' adoring fans to "a chorus" on a stage; he compares Euthydemus to a "skillful dancer," and describes the way Dionysodorus picks up an argument "as though it were a ball" (276b6, 276d6, 277b4). Even the metaphor Socrates offers at the point of his intervention—Clinias is about to be "thrown down for a third fall" (277d1)—suggests something of a wrestling match in which the sophists have the upper hand. These metaphors pile up to indicate that the sophists' technique is somehow less than serious—that it is better understood as a game than as a serious pursuit.

And yet Socrates' imagery also makes clear that there is something deadly serious about the effect these sophists are having on young Clinias. In the early stages of the encounter, he is described as blushing and in doubt (275d6). Then Clinias is turned this way and that. He is denied a chance to catch his breath (276c2–3). And by the end of the sequence, he is described as drowning—literally dipping below the surface (*baptidzomenon*) and in danger of turning coward (277d2–4). The metaphors of downward motion and sinking are quite significant. Protreptic is supposed to lift a student up, encouraging him to ascend toward wisdom. But the brothers are throwing their pupil downward, twisting and turning him away from wisdom.[36]

Then comes Socrates' analysis of what the sophists are doing. Interrupting their display and protecting Clinias from harm, Socrates puts his own narrative spin on the events that have transpired (277d–278c): "Don't be surprised, Clinias, if these arguments seem strange to you, since perhaps you don't take in what the visitors are doing." In a lengthy speech, Socrates recasts the brothers' actions as a friendly but trivial initiation rite in which the sophists are merely showing Clinias something preliminary. They are showing him that certain words like "learner" can be applied somewhat carelessly to opposite sorts of men—those who have no knowledge of a thing and attempt to acquire it, and those who possess some knowledge that they put to use in acquiring more. This can admittedly lead to confusion. But it is a problem that can also be adequately addressed by simply attending to what Prodicus calls the correct use of words (*onomatōn orthotētos*). One must distinguish precisely between the senses of words, and perhaps choose different words to denote different ideas. We might distinguish, for example, between "learning" and "understanding."[37]

More fundamentally (from Crito's perspective), Socrates goes on to explain why the paradoxes these sophists propound are not, in fact, genuine paradoxes at all. Because the ambiguities they capture are merely verbal, they reveal nothing of interest about *being*.

> If a man were to learn many or even *all* such things, he would be none the wiser as to how matters stand but would only be able to make fun of people, tripping them up and overturning them by means of the distinctions in words, just like people who pull a chair out from under someone who is about to sit down and then laugh gleefully when they see him sprawling on his back. (278b–c)

The eristic brothers are mere verbal pranksters. They have not presented Crito with the genuine problem of doubleness or ambiguity in being. They offer only a semblance of this problem at best. And far from seeming awe-inspiring or threatening, they in fact appear frivolous. They are engaged in neither philosophy nor protreptic, but simply in "play."

The effect of Socrates' intervention here is to supply aid to Clinias and helpful interpretive clues to Crito. Socrates goes on at this point to insist that the brothers deliver what they initially promised: a demonstration of their protreptic wisdom (*tēn protreptikēn sophian*). And to encourage them in this direction, Socrates now announces that he will offer a rough demonstration of his own. It is (as he significantly describes it) the sort of thing he *himself* "would desire to hear" (*epithumō akousai*, 278d4–5). And it will in essence enable Crito (and us) to compare Socrates and the brothers.

Protreptic Scene I

The first point of comparison comes with the caveat Socrates issues at the very beginning of his demonstration. He warns the brothers that his technique may seem unprofessional and extemporaneous compared to theirs (278d–e). This is ironic because Socrates adroitly leads Clinias to new heights. But it is also, in a sense, quite accurate: for Socrates, every protreptic *must* be an improvisation since every pupil is different. Some students will be overly dogmatic and require aggressive refutation; others like Clinias may need their spirits built up before they can proceed.[38] It is significant in these terms that when Socrates had earlier attempted to introduce Clinias to the sophists, offering crucial information about the boy's situation (275b), they dismissed this with contempt: "It makes no difference to us, Socrates, so long as the young man is willing to answer" (275c). Because these sophists have (ostensibly) turned teaching into a *technē* —a "one-size-fits-all" affair with standard rules and procedures, they need not concern themselves with the particularities of individual patients. Socrates, by contrast, does concern himself with particularities. Because he intends to lead his pupils from one place to another (not just around in circles) he must necessarily take stock of their condition. He slows down when they are confused, speeds up when they feel confident, and generally addresses his questions to their individual needs and concerns.[39] All this is symbolized beautifully in Socrates' first words to Clinias as his demonstration begins. Unlike the sophists, whose first question could have been asked of anyone ("who is it who learns, the wise or the ignorant?"), Socrates begins with a particular soul in mind: "*you*, son of Axiochus, answer me" (278e).

That Socrates also has Crito in mind as he narrates the story of his model protreptic will become evident as we proceed. Socrates begins by asking Clinias whether all men wish to do well.[40] Securing his assent to this foundational fact, Socrates next asks about the many good things (*polla k'agatha*) that might make a man do well and collaborates with Clinias to form a list. The list includes wealth, health, beauty, and the things the body needs, followed by certain political goods such as noble birth, power, and honor, as well as moral virtues such as self-control, justice, and courage. At last, the list is topped off by wisdom, which Clinias readily acknowledges to be a good, and Socrates now leads him to agree that the list is complete. But at this point something strange occurs (279c–d): Socrates dramatically "remembers" a good they have failed to consider—namely, good fortune—and gets Clinias to acknowledge its place on the list (thus refuting Clinias' earlier assent to the list's completion). Then Socrates suddenly "reconsiders a second time" and rejects good fortune as abruptly as he introduced it, on the grounds that "wisdom surely *is* good fortune" and that, in placing it on the list, they have essentially said "the same things twice" and made themselves look ridiculous (279d). What is the meaning of this strange boomerang-like consideration of fortune?[41]

For starters, there is humor in the passage, to be sure. It was the sophists who, in offering their "double twist" on the theme of learners, essentially said the same things twice. But there is more going on here than just humor. By controverting agreements that Socrates and Clinias have reached, Socrates appears to be slowly nudging his pupil toward greater involvement with argument. Clinias cannot simply agree with everything Socrates says and expect thereby to avoid the rough and tumble world of refutation. He must be willing to consider and reconsider how things seem, and possibly even see his own views refuted. It is significant that Socrates here subjects Clinias to a *double* refutation, just as the sophists had done. Clinias first vouches for the completeness of their list, only to be forced to retract that statement when Socrates introduces fortune. Yet after coming to accept the place of fortune on the list, Clinias is forced to retract *this*, *too*. Like the sophists, Socrates tugs him this way and that, and leaves him in the end right where they began. But is there a difference between Socrates' and the sophists' approach? To be sure, one difference is that when Clinias appears stunned and amazed by Socrates' turns (279d7), Socrates slows down significantly to explain the entire argument at a pace Clinias can handle. The sudden consideration and reconsideration of fortune thus gives way to a lengthy digression on why, exactly, fortune should not count as an independent good.[42]

One purpose, then, for the strange turns in Socrates' protreptic may be to reengage Clinias in the to-and-fro of argument, introducing him to refutation in a way that is more gentle and constructive. And yet there may be still more to Socrates' design. Why a digression on *fortune* in particular? This was not, after all, something *Clinias* was tempted to regard as a good before Socrates introduced it; and the whole episode could easily be omitted (or replaced with some other controversial good) without changing the essential course of the protreptic. So why does Socrates go out of his way to discuss fortune? It is certainly noteworthy that in Plato's *Crito* the question of the relationship between fortune and wisdom proves a major point of contention between Crito and Socrates. In that dialogue Socrates tries to convince Crito that one's fortune (whether good or bad) should not lead to the modification of one's philosophical positions (46b–c). If one's positions result from sound argument and stand unrefuted, then one must hold on to them come what may. Crito, for his part, attempts to convince Socrates that the incredible bad fortune of being sentenced to death should lead him to abandon certain positions he holds (chief among them his political obedience). Crito, in other words, places fortune ahead of wisdom in considering what Socrates should do (43b–c, 44b, 44d). Could this be Crito's usual position? I will not stake anything on it, but it may well be that the digression on fortune in the *Euthydemus* is Socrates' attempt to dislodge Crito's belief that fortune, more than wisdom, is a key to human happiness.

In any event, fortune is decisively rejected in Socrates' protreptic as he and Clinias proceed to consider whether their list of goods is adequate for human happiness. But is it adequate? they now wonder. Wouldn't these goods need to be *used*, not just possessed, in order to be of advantage? And wouldn't they, moreover, need to be used rightly? It appears that some sort of "knowledge of right use" would be necessary to ensure that everything "good" has its desired effects.[43] But, then, this seems to challenge the very status of goods *qua* goods: For wouldn't a man do more harm using a thing wrongly, Socrates now asks, than if he simply let it alone? "In the first case there is evil, but in the second case neither good nor evil" (280e–81a). And again, without knowledge of right use—or some kind of prudence and wisdom—wouldn't a man do better who does *less*? For if he does less, he makes fewer mistakes; and if he makes fewer mistakes, he does less badly; and if he does less badly then he would be less miserable. (281b–c). And so, as Socrates now shows Clinias, "all the things we called good in the beginning" are not good in themselves by nature, but rather as follows: "if ignorance controls them they are greater evils than their opposites, . . . but if prudence and wisdom control them, they are greater goods. In themselves, neither sort is of any value" (281d–82e1).[44] The conclusion, which Socrates gets Clinias to embrace wholeheartedly, is that "every man should prepare himself by every means to become as wise as possible," and that it is necessary, therefore, to "philosophize," or love wisdom (282a, 282d).

Socrates' protreptic thus moves Clinias to embrace wisdom, but consider now how it also addresses Crito's needs as a lover of hearing. One way it does so is by demonstrating for Crito precisely what the *Republic* suggests a lover of hearing should hear: that the conventional "goods" he desires for himself and his children come necessarily with opposite "bads," which cannot be simply avoided and must, therefore, become the springboard for some higher understanding.[45] Constructing a list of conventional goods with significant parallels to Crito's own list (cf. 306d–e), Socrates slowly but surely rejects the idea that these goods are pure or that the pursuit of them alone can secure happiness. Like the sophists, Socrates reveals the instability and ambiguity of things, but unlike the sophists, his lesson is real: it is no mere artifact of language that goods like wealth can become potentially harmful to their possessor if used without wisdom.[46]

Second, Socrates pauses at the end of the protreptic to draw out a conclusion that can only be intended for Crito (and Athenians like him). Having secured Clinias' assent to the thought that "every man should prepare himself by every means to become as wise as possible" (282a), Socrates hastens to add that,

> For a man who thinks he ought to get this from his father much more than money . . . there is nothing shameful (*ouden aischron*), Clinias—nor disgraceful if, for the sake of this, he should become the servant . . . of *any* man willing to perform any honorable service in his desire to become wise. (282a–b)

Crito, who has taken such pains to secure his son's well-being, is doubly implicated by Socrates' remark. He is implicated for his failure to impart wisdom (or even *guidance* in wisdom) to his son. And he is implicated, too, for his misplaced sense of shame in this regard. As we learn from the frame of the dialogue, Crito is ashamed to mingle too closely or indiscriminately with "philosophers." He has difficulties distinguishing good ones from bad, and he worries that engaging in philosophy might tarnish his reputation.[47] We have seen, too, that this resistance to philosophy is typical of the lover of hearing. And so, here, Socrates presses the point for Crito in an indirect but powerful way. Allowing Crito to "listen in," as it were, on the protreptic with Clinias, Socrates leads Crito to hear that one should pursue wisdom wholeheartedly, that parents should do this with their children, and that there is no shame in the effort.[48]

Thirdly and finally, Socrates' protreptic seems designed to *help* Crito with his difficulty of distinguishing between good and bad philosophical education. The task requires that Crito be willing to examine both forms closely, side-by-side; and this is precisely what the structure of Socrates' narrative allows him to do. What are the differences that emerge? Certain obvious differences strike us first: Socrates tailors his protreptic to the needs of his pupil, whereas the eristics treat every pupil alike; Socrates converses with his pupil in a cooperative way, whereas the eristics approach conversation competitively; Socrates leads his pupil toward the pursuit of philosophy, whereas the eristics seem to lead him away from it. These are by far the easiest distinctions to see. They are, indeed, exaggerated almost to the point of comedy in Socrates' account. The fact that Crito does not adequately grasp them in the end will have to be factored into my interpretation (in due course). But what is certain at this point is that conspicuous differences between Socrates and the eristics are on display.

However, the matter of separating Socrates from these sophists does not rest with such simple distinctions. This is one of the most interesting aspects of the *Euthydemus* and, in my judgment, an essential element of its meaning. To a surprising degree, what at first appear to be clear differences between Socrates and the sophists give way on closer inspection to deeper similarities. And this from both sides of the equation—that is, the *sophists* appear more like Socrates than we might initially suppose; and, in different ways, Socrates appears more like the sophists. And what might be the purpose of all this? This is an interpretive question. But it is my view that Plato has woven these similarities into the dialogue for two reasons: on the one hand to help readers appreciate how Socrates' jurors could have plausibly mistaken him for a sophist (more on this in the final section of this chapter); and, on the other hand, to invite readers themselves to seek a deeper understanding of Socratic philosophy. On this second point, it is my view that the similarities between Socrates and the sophists do point ultimately to deep insights into Socratic philosophy itself. But this can only happen if we take those similarities seriously. This seems to me to have two important implications: (1) most Athenians—even if they could grasp certain surface differences between Socrates and the eristics—might still have a hard time separating Socrates out. And (2) the exercise of taking the sophists seriously—of experiencing their teachings and comparing them to Socrates—proves, in the end, to be a most effective protreptic for Plato's readers.

I expand on these interpretive suggestions as I move forward, but, for now, we briefly examine a sample of the "deeper similarities" that emerge. A good example of the way the sophists appear uncannily like Socrates relates to the hierarchical character of their career. Socrates, as we noted, takes his pupils *from* somewhere *to* somewhere. He moves them from certain low-level pursuits such as that of wealth and honor, to certain higher pursuits such as that of virtue and wisdom. The sophists, by contrast, seem to take the opposite approach, moving their pupils downward and away from virtue and wisdom. Yet, if we look more closely at the way the brothers present themselves early in the dialogue (see 273c–d), we find a simulacrum of the vertical pattern of Socratic inquiry. Not only do the brothers boast a new and improved occupation—instruction in aretē—they now take the view that their earlier pursuits were all subordinate (*parergoi*) to this one. They thus seem to mimic the Socratic ascent toward aretē. In fact, when Socrates mistakenly introduces the brothers as mere teachers of martial and forensic arts, they respond by literally "thinking down" on him (*katephronēthēn hup' autoin*) from their new heights. Here, then, is a similarity. But it also points to a crucial difference with profound implications for philosophy properly understood: where the sophists claim to *possess* knowledge of aretē and to be able to teach it, Socrates does not. And this is no mere accident. Socratic philosophy does not issue in confident knowledge about aretē because it reveals, rather, that the ground of aretē rests in a wisdom that exceeds (at least to some degree) human grasp. The evidence for this is yet to come in the second protreptic. But suffice it here to say that from the vantage point of genuine Socratic philosophy, the sophists' boast about aretē can only mean one of two things: they are either liars or gods.[49]

The question of aretē leads to another surprising similarity between Socrates and the brothers—this one from Socrates' side of the equation. We might initially be inclined to differentiate Socrates from the eristics on the basis of successful and failed protreptic: although these sophists claim to be able to lead a pupil toward aretē, they in fact teach only their eristic wisdom; Socrates, on the other hand, engages in genuine protreptic. But does this distinction hold up? Does Socrates actually lead Clinias to devote himself to aretē, or is it rather that case that, like the sophists, he allows the issue of aretē to drop silently away? In fact, neither Socrates nor the sophists actually address the question of aretē. Why not? Once again, the similarity leads to an important insight about Socratic philosophy. If by aretē we mean conventional notions of virtue, Socrates cannot persuade his pupils to devote themselves to this because, in fact, its value is shown to be conditional. Moral virtues such as courage, justice, and self-control are among the very "goods" on Socrates' list, which turn out to be neither good nor bad by nature (281d), but depend for their goodness on knowledge of right use.[50] Socratic philosophy, then, does not increase one's devotion to aretē in any conventional sense of that word; it could, perforce, weaken it by directing one' energies elsewhere. And yet philosophy does increase one's devotion to aretē understood as the pursuit of wisdom itself. What Socrates initially describes, then, as a two-pronged protreptic—"persuading a man that he ought to devote himself to wisdom *and virtue*" (278d)—resolves necessarily into one thing: the quest for wisdom.

A final similarity between Socrates and the eristics that proves somewhat shocking is that they both make use of spurious arguments in their efforts to nudge Clinias into positions they desire. In fact, Socrates employs some of the *very fallacies* the eristics employ. This similarity has been noted by multiple commentators, but it has not to my knowledge been adequately situated within the complex web of strange semblances that is here taking shape.[51] Socrates' diversion on the subject of fortune supplies a case in point. By the conclusion of this argument, Socrates has convinced Clinias that good fortune and wisdom need not be counted separately as goods, because wisdom simply *is* good fortune. To illustrate this he shows Clinias (279e–280b) that in multiple cases were individuals possess knowledge, they also do well: a knowledgeable flute player plays better; a knowledgeable pilot more ably pilots his ship. And so they conclude on the basis of these cases that "wisdom makes men fortunate in every case," and that "if one has wisdom, one has no need of any good fortune besides" (280a6, 280b1–3). But, as Francisco Gonzalez has ably shown, Socrates' logic here is riddled with fallacies. Chief among them is a shifting of terms and meanings: "His argument begins with the claim that wisdom is good fortune (*eutuchia*)," but his examples "only show a close connection between wisdom and 'acting well' (*eupragia*) in the sense of succeeding (*eutuchēs einai*) at that particular endeavor of which one has knowledge."[52] But this leaves the whole question of genuine *fortune* aside. What about the skillful flute player who, unfortunately, suffers from arthritis? Or the unskilled pilot who happens to catch a good wind? Moreover, Socrates' argument maintains that if knowledge leads to good fortune or success in some art, then it must also lead to good fortune and success *simpliciter*. It is the fallacy of *secundum quid*, which the sophists will make great use of in their upcoming arguments.[53]

What are we to make of this? Socrates' fallacies are not likely to be inadvertent;[54] thus he appears to be knowingly subjecting Clinias to bad arguments. But here again comes an essential insight into Socratic philosophical education. As Gonzalez sees: "the charge of fallacy is a devastating one only when the sole intent of an argument is to *prove* something, that is, to *force the universal acceptance of a conclusion which otherwise need not be accepted*."[55] But neither Socrates nor the sophists are engaged in such an enterprise. The sophists, for their part, want simply to lure their respondents into contradicting themselves—or, at least, into appearing to contradict themselves. The uses for such a technique may be political, legal, or merely comical, but it does not stand or fall by good logic. Socrates in turn has ulterior purposes, too. He wants to persuade Clinias to embrace a certain way of life—the pursuit of wisdom—and he appears to be willing to use good and bad arguments alike in the attempt. The point to take from this is that while the means that Socrates employs may resemble the sophists' means even to the point of employing the same fallacies, those means are not in fact the same, because they are contributing to radically different ends.[56] Thus, if we want to understand Socratic philosophy we cannot only examine its means (the arguments); we must also examine its ends (the turning of the soul).

Thus the *Euthydemus* invites readers to engage the question of Socrates' resemblance to the eristics on multiple levels. There are, on the one hand, relatively obvious similarities and differences to note. On the other hand, there are more subtle ones, which can be explored at great length and which yield essential insights. It is not likely that the deeper levels of the dialogue are intended for Crito's benefit. (We know that Crito was not a subtle thinker.) They are most likely intended for us, Plato's readers, so that our *own* encounter with the eristics *via* Plato's text becomes a kind of protreptic itself, nudging us toward a better understanding of Socratic philosophy.

And yet the issue of Crito's education does not fade away as the dialogue operates on these multiple levels. Rather, we are continually reminded that Crito is the principal target of Socrates' narrative account. Indeed, in the transition between Socrates' first protreptic and the sophists' second eristic display, the theme of what a person should want "to hear" becomes dominant once again. Socrates tells Crito how delighted he was to hear (*akousas*, 282d4) Clinias' strong affirmation of the search for wisdom. And as Socrates now prepares to explain what the sophists did next, he recalls that "everyone expected to hear some wonderful words [*akousomenoi thaumasious tinas logous*]" (283a7). Finally resuming his ironic stance, he tells Crito that "it *was* certainly wonderful, in a way, and *worthy* to hear [*axion akousai*], since it was an incitement to virtue" (283b2). Thus Socrates leads Crito to pay close attention to the eristics' second display.

Eristic Scene II

The first thing to notice about the next eristic display is the conspicuous absence of Clinias as an interlocutor. So far from leading Clinias to love wisdom and virtue, the sophists now fail to address him entirely. The scene consists of six eristic arguments addressed to Socrates and Ctesippus. Ctesippus is drawn into the verbal melee only because the sophists say something that so offends him, he cannot let it stand. The offending argument is their lead one with Socrates, which maintains that if Clinias' friends really wish for Clinias to become wise, they must also wish to utterly destroy him, since becoming wise would entail his becoming something he is not. The thought of wishing to kill Clinias so angers Ctesippus that he explodes onto the scene to contradict it: you have spoken a lie, he tells Dionysodorus, and "were it not a rather rude remark, I would say the same of you" (283e).

Having thus placed himself in the center of the ring with these champion warriors of words, Ctesippus must now be prepared to bear the brunt of their blows. Euthydemus is the first to attack, asking him whether it is even possible to tell a lie. Of course it is, replies Ctesippus. But then comes the inevitable refutation: speaking always entails saying something, it must be agreed; and that something is itself something that *is*; yet speaking falsely proves impossible because it entails speaking what *is not*, and what is not cannot be spoken. It is therefore impossible to tell a lie, and it follows that Dionysodorus was speaking the truth. Ctesippus' anger now leads him to abandon whatever scruples he earlier had. As Dionysodorus takes over and attempts to position him for another round of preprogrammed questions, Ctesippus meets his every line with a jarring insult. Dionysodorus is surprisingly brought to a halt, and Ctesippus appears to be coming into his own. And yet, the tone of the conversation has so deteriorated that Socrates now takes it upon himself to intervene.

Looking back at Ctesippus' initial foray into the discussion, Socrates recalls the word "to utterly destroy" (*exollunai*), which understandably set Ctesippus off, and asks him why they should quibble with the sophists over a mere word? Rather,

> if they really know how to destroy men so as to make good and sensible people out of bad and stupid ones, and the two of them have either found out for themselves or learned from someone else a kind of ruin or destruction by which they do away with a bad man and render him good, if, as I say, they know how to do this—well, they clearly do, since they specifically claimed that the art they had recently discovered was that of making good men out of bad ones—then let us concede them the point and permit them to destroy the boy for us and make him wise—and do the same for the rest of us as well. (285a–b)

Ctesippus readily agrees to go along in this manner and even to offer himself along with Socrates for the slaughter, if the younger boys prove too afraid. But even so, he does not exactly accept that his tone with Dionysodorus had gotten out of control. His aim was not to abuse Dionysodorus, he insists, but merely to contradict (*antilegein*) those comments that were objectionable.

With the intervention complete Socrates and Ctesippus now await a demonstration of that art that causes pupils to die to their former selves so that new, better selves can be born. But no such demonstration emerges. Instead, Dionysodorus fastens on one of Ctesippus' final words, "contradiction," and slides into a well-prepared trope to show that contradiction is impossible (285e–286b): if it is true that no one can speak things that are not, then what is really occurring when two people appear to contradict each other? Either they are both describing the things they are describing and saying the same things; or they are neither of them describing that thing, in which case they cannot be contradicting each other; or one is describing the thing and the other not, in which case one is speaking, the other not, and contradiction is, again, impossible.[57] It is a perplexing argument, to be sure, and Ctesippus is left (humorously, given the terms of the argument itself) speechless by it.

But what are the implications of this bizarre anti-argument, which, as Socrates points out (286c), seems to undercut itself along with everything else? An argument that denies all possibility of argument? A refutation that proceeds by denying all refutation? What can be left standing once this doomsday device is unfurled? Socrates now plays his most active role cross-examining the sophists in order to tease out the implications of this argument. Must a person speak the truth or not speak at all? Can he *think* what is false? Is there such a thing as false *opinion*? Is there no ignorance at all? Can a person at least err in his *actions*? To all these questions, the sophists respond in the negative as they challenge Socrates to refute their doctrine. But if refutation is impossible, how can Socrates refute them? They are asking the impossible. But if false speaking is not possible either, how can they even request this impossible refutation? The claim that refutation is impossible seems to undercut not only itself, but the entire enterprise of eristic refutation as well. And, what is more, it undercuts one of the sophists' earliest and most fundamental claims: their boast to be teachers of aretē. For, as Socrates now shows them (278a–b): "If no one of us makes mistakes either in action or in speech or in thought—if this really *is* the case—what in heaven's name do you two come here to teach? Or didn't you say just now that if anyone wanted to learn virtue, you would impart it best?"[58]

Socrates has skillfully ensnared these deniers of contradiction in a deadly contradiction of their own. Their whole livelihood is now on the line. What reply is left open to them? They cannot *contradict* Socrates' suggestion that they have contradicted themselves; yet if they do not contradict it, then Socrates has shown contradiction to be possible. Either way their doctrine must fall. There is but one option open to them: subterfuge. Calling Socrates an old Cronus for dragging past parts of the conversation up into the present,[59] the sophists now attempt to question their way stealthily into a new eristic trope. Socrates detects the maneuver and attempts to drag the sophists back for an explanation of their doctrine, but there will be no looking back for these sophists. Socrates is accused of refusing to answer questions until, eventually, he must give in to the new trope. And yet where can these sophists now hide? If all their tropes are at root refutations (attempts to impute error to their respondents) then how can they find any trope that Socrates cannot turn back to the point? How can there be error and contradiction if these are not possible? This is precisely the question that Socrates does in fact bring back to the sophists once their final trope runs its course (288a). Their efforts have gotten them nowhere.

Now what are we to make of this second eristic scene from the perspective of Crito's educational needs, or in terms of our question about Socrates' relationship to the eristics? The sophists do not address Clinias at all; they do not unveil their long-promised art of turning bad men into good; and they manage, on the contrary, to have a severely negative effect on Ctesippus. Angry at first, but somewhat hesitant to part with polite modes of discourse, Ctesippus slowly gives way to outright belligerence, even as he begins to find his own use for some of the sophists' techniques. If Crito is supposed to see that all things—even teachers—come in positive and negative guises, he should certainly be able to discern the negative aspects of this set of teachers. Besides the problems just mentioned, we notice, too, that the *topics* that the sophists here take up have begun to slip into morally dubious terrain. The first eristic display had focused on issues of pedagogy such as the relationship of learning to wisdom and ignorance; but now the conversation has changed. Participants are suddenly speaking of killing and lying in a way that blurs lines and invites confusion. If, as Dionysodorus suggests in his first trope, to teach is also to kill, then perhaps to kill is but to teach. And if everything everyone speaks is necessarily true, then why not speak whatever one desires? As a parent, a citizen, and a respectable man, Crito has ample grounds for concern.

In the meantime, Socrates himself appears as saint and savior through all this. He intervenes once to save Ctesippus from losing his composure or, worse, from adopting the very warlike outlook the sophists try to promote. He then *shows* Ctesippus by example how to cross examine these sophists in a more serious way. And after this he intervenes again to put the sophists' failure in proper perspective for Ctesippus and Crito alike:

> Let me say to you [Ctesippus] the same things I was just saying to Clinias, that you fail to recognize how remarkable the strangers' wisdom is. It's just that the two of them are unwilling to give us a serious demonstration, but are putting on conjuring tricks in imitation of that Egyptian sophist, Proteus. So let us imitate Menelaus and refuse to release the pair until they have shown us their serious side. I really think some splendid thing in them will appear whenever they begin to be in earnest, so let us beg and exhort and pray them to make it known. (288b–c)

Irony, it seems, is the proper device for dealing with pretenders to knowledge. But there is something else in this as well, something especially relevant to Crito. One must be willing to engage pedagogical pretenders and ask them—again and again, if necessary—to share their most serious wisdom. Only in this way can either their ignorance come to light, or else some "splendid" thing emerge, which might aid in the search for wisdom. There is nothing to fear (or to be ashamed of) and everything to gain from such persistent questioning, especially of those who claim to possess the art of teaching aretē.

The lesson for Crito, then, seems altogether negative and stark. These are not good teachers; Socrates is. And yet in the midst of such a stark contrast this scene throws another strange similarity our way. The sophists' argument about killing the unwise self in order to give birth to a wise self parallels a well-known Socratic theme of dying. The theme is in fact one of those several areas in which Socrates and the great sophist, Protagoras, come very near to agreement. Protagoras (whose ghost seems to hover over this section of the dialogue), is portrayed in the *Theaetetus* (168a) as one who can change his pupils so profoundly for the better that they essentially "become different people, rid forever of the men they once were." Socrates would make no such claim of his own ability to teach, and yet he does regard philosophical education and growth as akin to a kind of death of the former self (see, e.g., *Phd.* 64a, 68a). Moreover, he has already begun such a transformation with young Clinias, leading him to question goods he formerly desired and to commit his whole life to a way of seeking wisdom he had never before known.[60] Our eristic sophists have thus given voice to a most serious pedagogical doctrine, though for purposes entirely other than those for which it was created.

The significance of this semblance seems to lie, once again, in the grounds on which one must seek the difference between Socrates and the brothers. *Materially* they now appear more similar than ever. Not only do they share a similar approach to argument involving question-and-answer, refutation, and the use of fallacy, they also (we now see) give voice to similar doctrines. And yet they are obviously radically different. (Socrates and the sophists themselves thus appear like those "goods" such as wealth and strength, which Socrates described earlier: their ethical characters swing to opposite extremes even while their material nature remains essentially unchanged.) How, then, are we to account for the difference between them if not in terms of what they say and how they say it? What else is there to explain what intuition tells us is a monumental divide? Perhaps we must do what Socrates instructs Clinias to do in the first protreptic speech, which is to look somehow beyond the material aspect of goods and practices in search of a higher, controlling knowledge or wisdom that determines their ethical value. In practical terms this means looking for that final or ultimate knowledge from which Socratic education on the one hand, and eristic education on the other, springs. But this final knowledge has not yet been revealed. This remains the task of the final two displays.

PROTREPTIC SCENE II

Under the pretense of showing the sophists once more the sort of protreptic he has in mind, Socrates now offers a second demonstration beginning where the first left off. What is the knowledge (*epistēmē*) we seek? He and Clinias agree that it cannot be any knowledge that does not know "how to use." For then it would suffer the same fate as other conditional goods—it would depend for its goodness on something else. And even if someone could discover, for example, a way of producing unlimited wealth or of making oneself immortal, such knowledge would not help. For without knowledge of how to *use* unlimited wealth or unlimited life these assets would seem to carry no advantage (289b2). What is needed, they agree, is a kind of knowledge that *combines* the discovering or making aspect of ordinary arts with a "knowing how to use" what it finds and makes.[61] This in effect rules out all arts like lyre making and flute making in which the manufacturing skill is distinct from use (flute making is an altogether different art from flute playing).

And, by the same token, this knocks the art of speechwriting out of the race, even though, as Socrates humorously suggests, one would not gather this from the image of speechwriters themselves, who appear surpassingly wise, marvelous and lofty (289e). Could it then be the art of generalship they seek? No, indeed, replies Clinias as he hastens (with surprising acuity) to explain. For generalship is a species of manhunting and thus a subspecies of hunting broadly conceived, and no hunting art ever extends beyond pursuing and capturing to the knowledge of use. So, for example, with geometry and astronomy, which are hunting arts in a sense: their job is strictly to find out certain angles or to discover certain stars, but not to use these angles and stars; that is the job of the dialectician (*dialektikos*). And so, too, with generalship: its job is to capture cities, not to use them, which is the job of the statesman (*politikos*). It follows that if what is needed is an art that combines using with finding or making, then generalship cannot be that art and we must look elsewhere for the knowledge that will make us happy. It is quite a remarkable little speech, not least for its amazing awareness of the role that dialectic might play in using the products of subordinate intellectual arts.[62] Crito, for his part, doubts that Clinias could be its author, and halts Socrates' narrative at this point to say so (290e).

It is now clear that Crito has been paying close attention. His reason for intervening at this point in particular is susceptible of multiple interpretations. He may doubt that Clinias could have made such rapid intellectual progress or he may doubt that Socrates has done anything to bring it about.[63] In any event Crito is fully engaged and, what is more, one can tell from his next question to Socrates that this engagement extends beyond a mere interest in Clinias' (and, by extension, Critobulus') potential education: "And after this did you still go on looking for the art? And did you find the one you were looking for or not?" (291a) Crito exhibits an independent interest in the fate of the argument. *He* is now engaged in the search for the knowledge in question and desires to hear of its outcome.[64] At this point, Socrates hardly needs to maintain the device (not to say the pretense) of his narrative account with Clinias. That Socrates does in fact gradually replace Clinias with Crito himself as his interlocutor (see 291e) reveals something fundamental about Socrates' purpose all along.

We are at the high point of the dialogue. And yet, just at this point of Crito's deepest involvement comes what can only be described as a reversal. Socrates informs Crito that they did *not* in fact find the knowledge they sought, but rather, appeared utterly ridiculous, "like children chasing after crested larks": every time they attempted to grasp the knowledge, it would somehow slip away.[65] The biggest letdown, Socrates explains, came when they turned to consider the kingly art (*hē basilikē*), which they equated simply with statesmanship (*politikē*).[66] As they were examining this to see whether it was indeed the knowledge they were seeking, they found themselves suddenly "trapped in a labyrinth" (291b7). At first the kingly art seemed promising, because it hovered above the art of generalship and governed its products. But what is the product or result of the kingly art itself? This proved hard to determine. As Crito now takes over Clinias' role, he and Socrates agree that it must be some form of *knowledge*, and this in turn leads them to a significant insight, namely that all the conventional "goods" people usually attribute to statesmanship—making citizens rich, free and undisturbed by faction—are not really goods at all (292b). They are rather like those conditional goods on Socrates' earlier list, which turned out to be "neither good nor evil" unless wisdom makes them so. But does the kingly art actually produce any wisdom or knowledge? Crito is willing to grant it, but then Socrates presses the point. What is this knowledge? It cannot be anything neutral, like the other goods, so it must be nothing other than itself (292d3–4). It *itself* must be the knowledge by which statesmen make others good. But good in what respect? Socrates and Crito cannot say, except to say, "Good in making others good," which begins an infinite regress without shedding any light on *what* this knowledge is. They have reached, as Crito now concludes, a mighty impasse (*pollēn ge aporian*).

Socrates' search for "knowledge of how to use" thus founders on the question of the highest art, and the significance of this cannot be underestimated.[67] At the end of the last eristic scene we determined that the best hope of distinguishing Socrates from these sophistic brothers lay in examining the end or result of each of their methods. But now the end of Socratic wisdom has turned out to be no end at all. "When we thought we had come to an end," Socrates tells Crito, "we turned around again and reappeared practically at the beginning of our search in just as much trouble as when we started out" (291c). If this is the case, then what distinguishes the Socratic enterprise from the eristic one, which also appeared to twist and turn without ever coming to an end? Or, to put the question more forcefully, what is the *justification* for protreptic and even philosophy itself if it cannot articulate its final goal? As we recall, Socrates' criticism of the sophists after their first demonstration was that "if a man were to learn many or all such things, he would be none the wiser as to how matters really stand" (278b). The same thing, it now appears, can be said of Socratic protreptic. Moreover, does not Socrates' method produce the same disheartening effects we attributed to eristic? At the end of the sophists' first display, Socrates intervened to prevent Clinias from sinking and drowning in argument. Now, at the end of Socrates' protreptic, we hear:

> As far as I was concerned, Crito, when I had fallen into this difficulty, I began to exclaim at the top of my lungs and to call upon the two strangers as though they were the Heavenly Twins to rescue both myself and the boy from the third wave of the argument. (293a)

The heavenly twins (*Dioscuri*) are the proverbial protectors of seamen.[68] Socrates and Clinias are drowning, and *Socrates* now looks to *the sophists* for help! It is a reversal indeed, as Socrates appears suddenly no better at protreptic than the sophists themselves.

And yet, once again, this striking similarity points in the direction of essential insights about Socratic philosophy and protreptic. The full force of these insights can only be formulated once we see how the sophists end their last display. But at this point I can at least insist that while the Socratic search for a ground of ethical knowledge may end in aporia, it is far from utterly vacuous or unsuccessful. Crito has been shown in no uncertain terms the doubleness of everyday goods. And this lesson has now been transposed for him into the register of politics: civic goods, too, admit of doubles and wisdom alone can determine whether they are in fact good or evil. Moreover, the most prestigious careers that parents may wish for their children to take up—those of orator, general, and statesman—are now revealed to be deeply problematic. Like Socrates himself, the occupants of these offices prove unable to account for the knowledge that certifies their very worth. But, unlike Socrates, they proceed anyway as if they possess that knowledge after all. They are in this sense, posers and pretenders all; and this insight is in no way lessened by Socrates' own failure in his search. Finally, it is not at all clear that the effect of Socrates' failure should be one of dismay. We are not told how Clinias reacted in the end, and we shall learn that Crito's reaction is equivocal at best. But for some at least, the failure of the search to acquire the knowledge in question might constitute a profound insight all its own into the limits of human knowledge and the conditions of human life. We *do not possess* the divine knowledge that illuminates all activity with ethical light, desire it as we may. And yet in desiring it and seeking it (like children chasing crested larks) we are at once engaged in an intrinsically (perhaps *the* intrinsically) pleasing human activity and, at the same time, made soberly aware of that which we do not have. The danger in political life is not that citizens will be depressed about the knowledge they lack, but rather that they will delude themselves into believing they possess it and thus engage in activities of a potentially evil nature.

There is, then, much wisdom to be found in what would appear a failed search for wisdom. The dialogue could almost end at this point, but there is one more sophistic display to come, and, with it, a further insight into the matter of "ends."

ERISTIC SCENE III

The third eristic scene begins with an argument that helps clarify a fundamental difference between Socrates and the brothers. Taking up the matter of Socrates' confessed ignorance about the highest things, Euthydemus commences to argue that Socrates has actually possessed the knowledge in question all along. "Do you know *something*," he asks (293b). Yes, replies Socrates. "Then you are knowing (*epistēmōn*), if you really know." And, as the argument runs, if Socrates *is* knowing, then he must know everything, including whatever knowledge he has been seeking. It is the fallacy of *secundum quid*: from the premise that one is knowing in some respect, it is concluded that one is knowing *simpliciter*. Socrates, for his part, attempts to counter that he knows only some things and not others, but this gets him nowhere with Euthydemus. For if he really knows some things and not others, then he is in danger of being knowing and not-knowing at the same time, which is a contradiction in terms. This is all very comical, but it also epitomizes the difference between Socrates and the brothers with respect to their posture toward knowledge. For the brothers, there is neither a philosophical aporia nor a shipwrecked protreptic to worry about, because the supposedly missing knowledge has been with us all along.[69]

Socrates' incredulity over the suggestion that he, and everybody else, already knows everything leads Euthydemus and Dionysodorus to insist on this all the more. And as Socrates' protestations become more pronounced, Euthydemus offers to "prove" to Socrates that he does indeed know, and has *always* known, all things. Socrates' response reminds readers of what is at issue:

> But . . . there is nothing I would like better than to be refuted on these points. Because if I am unaware of my own wisdom, but you are going to demonstrate that I know everything and know it forever, what greater godsend than this would I be likely to come across my whole life long? (295a)[70]

The sophists promise to solve Socrates' aporia once and for all and, in effect, to rewrite the script for the human condition itself. Unfortunately, Euthydemus' "proof" at this point amounts to little more than another *secundum quid*: if one knows everything by means of the soul, then one knows everything *simpliciter*, or, in other words, if one always knows by means of the soul, then one always knows. Socrates attempts to run this fallacy aground by insisting on appropriate qualifications: "Always, *whenever I know*, I know by means of the soul" (296a), he says. But such qualifications get him nowhere. They lead only to the charge that he is a recalcitrant and shameful student. Like Strepsiades in the *Clouds*, Socrates is in danger of being deemed too old and uncouth (*skaios*, cf. *Clouds* 790) to undergo the course of sophistic instruction. And so, in order to avert this outcome, Socrates does his best from here on to comply with the sophists' method.

By complying, however, Socrates also manages to expose certain deeply disturbing aspects of the eristic procedure. One is its unsurprising but nevertheless troubling relationship to the love of power. As Euthydemus concludes his argument, he exclaims to Socrates, "You *will* always know, and know everything, by heaven, *if I want it that way*!" (295d). Such arrogance bordering on outright blasphemy is—readers should understand—a likely effect of the teaching that man is omniscient. It may also, in a deeper sense, be the *underlying cause* of this teaching. The desire to escape, by hook or by crook, the human condition of partial knowledge and partial ignorance leads to repeated attempts to pretend one somehow possesses the knowledge one does not have. The eristic arguments for omniscience are just one such attempt, appealing to the natural desire for more knowledge and more power, which characterizes humans as such.

Another disturbing aspect of eristic that Socrates exposes is its potential to obliterate moral distinctions. If I know everything, Socrates inquires, "how shall I say I know that good men are unjust?" (296e). This at first catches the sophists by surprise. Dionysodorus mistakenly assumes Socrates to be asking for confirmation that good men are *not* unjust. But Euthydemus sees what is really at stake. If the sophists deny that "good men are unjust," Socrates will turn out to be knowing and not knowing at the same time (not to mention speaking something that is not), and thus their whole argument for omniscience will crumble. Their argument requires that Socrates be simply knowing. And yet, if they affirm Socrates' proposition, they commit themselves explicitly to a radical transvaluation of values, which they would, no doubt, prefer to leave implicit.[71] There appears to be no way out except, as before, through subterfuge. Dionysodorus simply switches to another eristic topic.

However, before I let this topic go completely, I point out that Socrates in fact can and *has* argued, in effect, that "good men are unjust." If we take good men to mean the conventionally good men of Athens (the *agathoi*), then Socrates' entire protreptic has shown precisely that their goodness might just as well be wickedness, their justice injustice, because they lack the knowledge that determines ethical value itself. When Socrates thus asks the brothers, "how shall I say I know that good men are unjust?" he asks a question to which a potentially serious answer can be given. The serious answer involves the rudimentary philosophical awareness of the doubleness of things, the awareness that gives rise to the search for wisdom. That the sophists blush and equivocate in the face of this decisive question therefore reveals a great deal: not only that they might be willing to consider injustice as a possible extension of their teaching, but also that they are utter pretenders when it comes to the genuine philosophical problem of doubles in everyday experience.

Now in the midst of this prolonged exchange between Socrates and the brothers, Ctesippus' character begins to develop in significant ways. When Dionysodorus proudly proclaims his own knowledge of everything, Ctesippus intervenes to run the sophist through a battery of specific questions—questions that Socrates the narrator describes as shameless and disgraceful (294d). We can only imagine what the questions were that follow and thus deteriorate from the question whether Dionysodorus knows how many teeth are in Euthydemus' mouth. That Ctesippus is falling into considerable psychological danger is further indicated by a clever allusion Socrates makes to the fabled battle between Hercules and the Hydra. Euthydemus is like the Hydra whose many-headed arguments grow back as fast as Socrates can chop them off. Socrates cannot defeat the Hydra on his own because, like Hercules, he is distracted by a crab (Dionysodorus) that has appeared from the sea to nip at his ankles. As the fable goes, Hercules was forced in his distress to call on his nephew, Iolaus, for help, which the nephew successfully provided. But here in the *Euthydemus*, Socrates worries: "If my Iolaus should come, he would do more harm than good" (297d).[72] We are expected, no doubt, to remember the argument of Socrates' first protreptic, which maintained that "there is more harm done if someone uses a thing wrongly than if he lets it alone" (280e). Were Ctesippus to attempt (in his youthful hubris) to engage in a battle of refutations with this chronically contentious duo, the effects on his own and others' souls could be disastrous.[73]

As it turns out, Ctesippus *is* drawn into the battle (298b) and his performance is in some ways quite remarkable. He reduces Euthydemus to complete silence at one point (299d) by running one of his fallacies in reverse.[74] And after an intense back and forth through at least two more sophistic topics, Ctesippus manages to trap Euthydemus in such an inescapable snare that Dionysodorus must rescue him with the ultimate copout response: "It is neither and it is both! And I am sure you will be helpless in dealing with *that* answer" (300d). Ctesippus has so masterfully acquired the sophists' tricks, and in such short order,[75] that he is able to hoist Euthydemus on his own petard. Ctesippus finishes out his performance with a loud and (as I imagine it) almost diabolical laugh, which emboldens young Clinias to laugh loudly as well. Socrates, however, is not amused. That all this refuting has not been good for Ctesippus is made plain by Socrates the narrator who suggests that Ctesippus has gotten himself too "worked up" (*hyperagōnian*, literally hypercontentious) and calls him a truly awful name (*panourgos*).[76] Ctesippus has defeated Euthydemus, but at what cost? He has become a master wrangler himself.[77]

And how does this grand exchange between Socrates and the brothers draw to a close? It concludes with the apparent victory of

Dionysodorus over Socrates, and thus of eristic over philosophy. In a few decisive maneuvers, Dionysodorus manages (or appears) to topple the command center of Socratic philosophy, the idea of forms (300e–301c), and to replace this with two ultimate doctrines of his own. What are the final goals of wisdom for Dionysodorus? The exercise of power over other men (301c–e), and the exercise of power over the gods (301e–303a).[78] We have reached the end, as it were, of eristic. Socrates now falls silent and the contest is quickly brought to a close.

But what is the significance of Socrates' apparent discomfiture? We must remember at this point that Socrates is telling a story, one over which he has complete control. Here the dramatic indications help to keep things in perspective. Socrates has deliberately drawn the sophists out in order to observe the ultimate goals and implications of their craft. He began by calling on them for help in his distress as though they were the Heavenly Twins. He next made a point of bending over backward to comply with their eristic procedures. He then allowed Ctesippus to reengage the sophists, even though he could have predicted the outcome. And, at last, as the argument against him builds steam he issues nothing but words of encouragement: the brothers are "bringing the art of argument to a fine pitch of excellence, like craftsmen who bring to completion whatever work constitutes their proper business," and they are really "putting the finishing touches" on their wisdom (301c, 301e). Meanwhile, Socrates the narrator indicates that he is going along with the arguments only to hear as quickly as possible the knowledge in which they culminate (301b, 302a).

In other words, Socrates has artfully facilitated Crito's (and our) comparison of the ends of Socratic and eristic pedagogy. And what does the comparison reveal? Although Socratic protreptic ends in aporia, there is nothing remotely aporetic about the end of eristic. In practical terms it ends in decisive verbal victory of one party over another—it is a fight to the death where death means snuffing out or silencing one's adversary. In theoretical terms, it ends in arguments that justify this competitive worldview and that fan the flames of individuals' lust for power. To wit:

> Then it is clear that if someone kills the cook and cuts him up, and then boils him and roasts him, he will be doing the proper business; and if someone hammers the blacksmith himself, and

> puts the potter on the wheel, he will also be doing the proper business. (301d–e)

> And [if] you consider those things to be yours over which you have control and which you are allowed to treat as you please. . . . [and] you admit that Zeus and the other gods are yours, then, do you have the right to sell them or give them away or treat them in any way you like, as you do with the other living creatures? (301e–302a, 303a)

Meanwhile we are able to judge the psychopathological dangers of eristic pedagogy in the glee that Ctesippus experiences after winning a few rounds and in Clinias' surprising pleasure in seeing the sophists receive their comeuppance. Clinias' pleasure is surprising because the verbal death-blow that makes him laugh is not unlike the blows that nearly undid him earlier in the dialogue. And his laughter is indistinguishable from the earlier laughter of Euthydemus' admirers. Clinias' laughter thus betokens a contradiction in his own soul. Clinias enjoys seeing Ctesippus stick it to the sophists, but this is not a world in which a Clinias would fare well.

To see all this is perhaps the best endorsement possible of Socrates' own protreptic approach. If it is a choice between Socrates' aporia in which the structure of reality places constraints on what can be known, and the brothers' eristic method, which repeatedly contradicts itself as it tries to submit the world and everything in it to the sophists' will, who would not opt for aporia? Crito and Athenians like him may choose neither, especially if they do not take the necessary steps or possess the necessary acumen to distinguish them. But the choice for eristic would seem perverse in the extreme after the demonstration Socrates has just supplied. What will Crito make of Socrates' elaborate and helpful narrative?

Socrates' Conclusion and the Closing Frame

I begin by quickly reviewing the issues. Crito is a lover of hearing who is anxious about his son. Blocked from understanding philosophy by his complacent commitment to everyday goods, he cannot distinguish Socratic from sophistic *paideia*. To educate him (along the lines of the course set out for lovers of hearing in the *Republic*), Socrates exposes him to the eristic brothers Euthydemus and Dionysodorus and enables him (at least potentially) to see not only that all things admit of doubles, but also that philosophy and protreptic, too, have doubles. The sustained contrast between the Socratic and eristic methods where so many obvious differences appear along with such vexing similarities should show Crito that while materially these methods are much the same, they can be distinguished ultimately by their ends, even if the end of the Socratic method is, in an important sense, incomplete. Once the methods are thus distinguished, they must also be properly evaluated or ranked. In one sense this seems simple: the Socratic method is good and the sophistic method is bad, both in terms of their grasp of reality and in terms of their pedagogical effects. Yet we have seen that the distinction is not so simple. In fact, the decisive and final evaluation of these two methods would require possession of that very knowledge of "right use," which it is the business of the Socratic method to seek. This is a de facto endorsement of the Socratic method, but it is not a decisive and final answer to the problem of evaluation.

So do matters stand, on my interpretation, as we enter the conclusion of Socrates' narrative and the closing frame of the dialogue. There, however, we are confronted with another reversal, this time on a higher interpretive level of the dialogue.[79]

As Socrates wraps up his narrative, he maintains his ironic posture to the very end. In a concluding gesture, he tells Crito how he heaped praises on the sophists for their miraculous and magnificent abilities. On the one hand, he did acknowledge that very few people would have the stomach for the brothers' arguments—most would be "more ashamed to refute others with arguments like these than to be refuted by them" (303d).[80] But, on the other hand, Socrates himself beseeched the brothers to enroll him along with Clinias as their pupils. If one listens carefully to Socrates' praises in this section one can sense that they are in fact a series of gibes, not full-fledged praise. This does not mean that Socrates would *not* try to learn something further from these sophists. (One of the recurring themes of the dialogue is that one must seek wisdom wherever there is a chance of finding it.) But it does mean that the lessons Socrates would draw would likely differ substantially from those the sophists intend to teach. In any event, Socrates praises the sophists and reiterates his desire to study with them, and it is now time for Crito to sort out an appropriate response.

And so Socrates confronts Crito again with the invitation that began this dialogue, the invitation to study with Euthydemus and Dionysodorus. How does he respond? His initial response includes a line I took note of early on:

> Well Socrates, I am indeed a lover of hearing and *would* be glad to learn something;[81] but all the same I am afraid I also am not one of Euthydemus' sort. Instead I am one of those you mentioned who would rather be refuted by arguments of this kind than use them to refute. (304c–d)

The response identifies Crito as a *philēkoos* and registers his distaste for Euthydemus' arguments.[82] Crito has now *heard* the sophists' lessons through Socrates' narrative account; and because Socrates has stressed that, when it comes to eristic, one lesson may do the trick, Crito may legitimately be done with Euthydemus and Dionysodorus.[83] But the question remaining concerns the *grounds* on which Crito would distinguish himself (and Socrates) from these sophists. In other words, what has Crito learned?

The answer is, disappointingly little. Crito now divulges that he has, in fact, already heard (*ēkouon* again, 304d3) a report about Socrates' encounter of the day before from a speechwriter who was present. Crito does not name him,[84] but he does give Socrates a taste of what was said and indicates that he gives this report some credence.

> Crito, aren't you a disciple of these wise men? Heavens no, I said—there was such a crowd that I was unable to hear, even though I stood quite close. And yet, he said, it was worth hearing. What was it? I asked. You would have heard men conversing who are the wisest of the present day in this kind of argument. And I said, what did they show you? Nothing else, said he, than the sort of thing one can hear from such people at any time—chattering and making a worthless fuss about matters of no consequence. (These are his approximate words.) But surely, I said, philosophy is a charming thing. Charming, my innocent friend? he said—why it is of no value whatsoever! And if you had been present, I think, you would have been

> embarrassed on your friend's account, he acted so strangely in his willingness to put himself at the disposal of men who care nothing about what they say, but just snatch at every word. . . . But the fact is, Crito, he said, that both the activity itself and the men who engage in it are worthless and ridiculous. (304d–305b)

Crito, the lover of hearing, whose weakness it is to give too much credence to conventional moral evaluations has heard a conventional moral evaluation of the discussion that took place. The critic is right that the eristics snatch at every word,[85] and it is true that in the brothers' hands eristic refutation seems worthless and ridiculous. But what is significant is that the critic extends this criticism to *philosophy*, and Crito is unable, despite an intuition to the contrary, to correct him. Now this is all prior to Crito's hearing of Socrates' narration, so hope remains that he might now perceive what he could not perceive before. But does he?

Not exactly. Accepting the critic's perspective he now reproaches Socrates for participating in the discussion (305b). That Socrates' participation was a help to Clinias and a potential boon to Crito has not registered. He then attempts to shield Socrates and his beloved "philosophy" from the full force of the speechwriter's criticism by saying that there is nothing wrong with the activity so long as one does not engage in it in front of a large crowd. Crito is echoing a piece of ironic advice Socrates had offered the sophists (304a), but his meaning is quite different. There is something to be ashamed of in philosophy, and Crito still has not recognized that the "activity" comes in different varieties. Socrates would do well, he suggests, to indulge such habits in private.

What can Socrates do? As he often does when his pupils need help making elementary distinctions—and as he earlier did with Clinias—he invokes the name of Prodicus.[86] In an attempt to knock the speechwriter down to size, and taking full stock of Crito's obsession with reputation,[87] Socrates describes speechwriters (*ad hominem*) as desperately insecure middlemen between statesmen and philosophers. Since philosophers in particular can expose their middling ways, speechwriters like nothing more than to take pot shots at them while deluding themselves into believing that some halfway house between politics and philosophy is the best place to reside. Crito is tempted by this view as well (305e), but Socrates hastens to discredit it: "the fact of the matter is that, while partaking in both, they are inferior to both with respect to the object for which either philosophy or politics is of value" (306c).[88] Crito cannot take refuge in the speechwriter's perspective and hope thereby to dodge the question of philosophy. And he knows better than to repair to the statesman's art, because this was the source of the vexing aporia, which derailed Socrates' second protreptic. There is no choice then, but to face the possibility of philosophy as a worthwhile enterprise. Can Crito do it? It is possible, but unlikely. As the dialogue draws to a close, Crito is found complaining to Socrates that the teachers of philosophy are all grotesque. He has still not seen that the teachers come in doubles. He has still not distinguished Socrates from the sophists on the matter of teaching. And so the dialogue closes with Socrates offering Crito the following sage advice: "Do not do what you ought not to, Crito, but pay no attention to the practitioners of philosophy, whether good or bad. Rather give serious consideration to the thing itself: if it seems to you negligible, then turn everyone from it, not just your sons. But if it seems to you to be what I think it is, then take heart, pursue it, practice it, both you and yours, as the proverb says" (307b–c).

Clouds, *Apology*, and Conclusion

That Crito fails to distinguish philosophy from eristic despite his affection for Socrates and his prolonged exposure to the sophists through Socrates' narrative account is troubling in the extreme. What does this mean for the dialogue's interpretation? The proper handling of this question requires that we pay some attention to the ways the *Euthydemus* speaks to issues central to Socrates' trial. That trial, as we recall, involved two different sets of charges. There were the official charges brought by the likes of Meletus and Anytus—that Socrates was guilty of corrupting the young and of not believing in the gods of the city but in other, novel *daimonia* (*Ap.* 24b). And then there were unofficial charges, prejudices Athenians had formed from the way Socrates was lampooned in Aristophanes' *Clouds*. Among these charges was the claim that Socrates could make weaker arguments stronger and teach others to do the same (*Ap.* 19b–c). Now these charges amount in a nutshell to the suggestion that Socrates was a dangerous sophist not unlike the sort we encounter in the *Euthydemus*, and Socrates' defense, therefore, would require him to distinguish himself from such sophists. And yet, if we learn one thing from the *Euthydemus* it is that such distinctions are a matter of some delicacy and no small intellectual task.[89] There were, obviously, limits to what could be accomplished in the format of a trial. Were Socrates really to educate his jurors, he would need to present his philosophical conversations side-by-side with their sophistic counterparts so that the similarities and differences could be observed.

In this way it is possible to read the *Euthydemus* as a longer, more nuanced "apology" of Socrates, which not only addresses the charges against him, but also (brilliantly) takes the form of a parody of Aristophanes' *Clouds*. To pursue this line of interpretation in detail would require a separate study,[90] but let me here mention only two pieces of evidence to support it. First of all, from beginning to end, allusions to the *Clouds* run through the *Euthydemus*. Some of these are verbal allusions to rare Aristophanic words and phrases;[91] others are more thematic: a father considers whether to send his son to be educated by the sophists; he is shown a sham education in which weaker arguments are made stronger; an elderly pupil proves somewhat intractable while a younger one learns quickly and uses his new skills to attack his teachers.[92] Second, all three elements of the official charges against Socrates are treated in the *Euthydemus*. Socrates' *daimonion* makes a rare appearance in which we see its beneficent effects. There is a discussion of Socrates' (qualified) belief in the gods of the city. And Socrates' role as defender, not corrupter, of youth is emphasized. Let us assume, then, that the *Euthydemus* can be read as Plato's quasi-comic response to Aristophanes' comic portrait of Socrates,[93] and that the role Socrates plays in educating Crito and mediating the sophists' effects on the young—a role facilitated by Socrates' *daimonion*—is Plato's answer to the charges against him.

Now, in this context, what does it mean that Crito fails to learn the lessons Socrates makes available? There is, in my view, a darker and lighter interpretation of this, and they are not mutually exclusive. On the darker side, Crito's failure seems to signal a deep pessimism about the outcome of Socrates' trial. Whatever the numerical difference between the votes for death and those to acquit,[94] the *Euthydemus* suggests that the outcome was not *intellectually* close. That is to say, if Crito—one of Socrates' closest companions—could not be moved to distinguish sufficiently between Socrates and the basest of sophistic pretenders, even after a prolonged narrative designed precisely to help him do so, then what would it have taken for those jurors who voted to convict Socrates to change their minds? Crito would not have voted to convict. He was enamored of Socrates. But this affection must, to some extent, be merely accidental, because it is not based on reason. Were Crito another man, less connected to Socrates than he happened to be by chance,[95] then he might well have been among those who voted to convict. Crito's failure in the *Euthydemus* thus seems to indicate something of the extreme barrier separating certain types of Athenians from an adequate understanding of Socrates' philosophic and pedagogic enterprise.

On the other hand—and this is the more optimistic side of the dialogue—we as readers are invited to observe Crito's failure in the *Euthydemus* and to understand it. But what does this imply? It implies that we can grasp at least some of the insights that Crito (and Socrates' jurors) cannot. And this means that the *Euthydemus* is protreptic on yet another level. It is not only protreptic for Clinias, and on a higher level for Crito, it is also, on its highest level, protreptic for the reader. Like Clinias and Crito, we, too, are taken through a guided tour of the eristic and Socratic enterprises. But we are given more to consider than either of these characters. We are given the story of Crito's failure. Crito, then, becomes the negative side of a pair of potential doubles, which we are invited to complete. The *Euthydemus* invites *us* to engage our minds in the protreptic that is offered and to improve on Crito's response by appreciating the Socratic enterprise with all its subtle difficulties and to engage in that enterprise ourselves.

SEVEN

PROTAGOREAN SOPHISTRY IN PLATO'S *THEAETETUS*

That the figure of Protagoras features prominently in Plato's *Theaetetus* is widely known. In an effort to answer Socrates' question, "What is knowledge?" a young student of geometry proposes that knowledge is "nothing but perception," which prompts Socrates to discuss Protagoras' ideas at some length. Occupying more than half the dialogue, the discussion leads ultimately to Protagoras' apparent refutation; and the interlocutors move on to discuss other things. However, the true extent of Protagoras' role in the *Theaetetus* has not always been appreciated. Socrates does not simply refute Protagoras' ideas, but also endorses them to a certain extent.[1] Moreover, he uses Protagorean insights and techniques as he attempts to reorient his interlocutors properly for the practice of philosophy, the "love of wisdom."

Wisdom, as Socrates conceives it, is not knowledge of this or that aspect of Being, much less this or that department of science. It is knowledge of the whole—all the parts of Being as well as their interrelations. Protagoras is important in this connection because he was expert at exposing a quality of Being that is all too often neglected or even denied, namely, the vexing instability and relativity of things we experience. However, Protagoras was also prone to hyperbole and claimed that relativity characterized "all things" in a way that was demonstrably false. Protagoras' mistake was classic. He mistook a part of Being for the whole. In particular, he failed to attend to the intimations of permanence in human experience, intimations that Socrates articulates in the language of "forms." Moreover (and necessarily) he did not pursue the challenge of understanding the *relationship* among the various aspects of Being—material and formal, changing and permanent, evanescent and eternal.[2] And because he did not investigate this, he could not have really possessed the expertise in human *aretē* that he claimed to possess. For humans live precisely at the intersection of the changing and the fixed, and it is here, too, that ethics and politics come to life. Wisdom in the full-blown Socratic sense described here is impossible of human achievement, but it is not impossible of pursuit. And the recognition that one does not already possess it stands as a kind of wisdom all its own—what Socrates calls "human wisdom" in the *Apology*.

Socrates' two interlocutors in the *Theaetetus* are fascinating to consider in this light. As geometers (or, "number people," in general), they are experts in one of the purest, most certain branches of knowledge. They specialize in formal entities and relations, and they suppose this makes them wise. At the same time, though, they are admirers of Protagoras and particularly of what Protagorean relativism suggests about ethics and politics. (Like many empiricists today, these geometers do not regard "value judgments" as susceptible of knowledge.) Perhaps initially this combination of traits—scientific precision on one level mixed with relativism on another—may seem promising to a certain cast of mind as an approach to wisdom: Formal and material Being are both given a place, and their relationship is accounted for in terms of degrees of certainty. On the other hand, though, there is something fundamentally wrong in this view of things insofar as it does not explain the way humans—Theodorus and Theaetetus included—actually live (more on this later). The formal and the material world are not quite as disjointed as these geometers suppose.

My argument in this chapter is that Socrates' relationship to Protagoras in the *Theaetetus* is more nuanced than it first appears. After Socrates familiarizes himself with Theodorus' and Theaetetus' outlook, he attempts to reorient them slightly, breaking their inordinate attachment to Protagoras while trying at the same time to help them retain what is valuable in this sophist's teaching. It is an extremely difficult task because of the interlocutors' different dispositions. Theaetetus (the younger of the two) is prone to reject Protagoras completely the moment Socrates begins to criticize the sophist. Socrates must therefore work hard to keep the true aspects of Protagorean relativity before Theaetetus' eyes. Theodorus, by contrast, is more willing to let go of some aspects of Protagoras while retaining others; yet what he wants to retain is deeply problematic (and dangerous): a moral relativism that fails to account fully for his own or his students' conduct. Socrates thus attempts to steer Theodorus permanently away from relativism.

In the end, neither Theodorus nor Theaetetus find themselves properly positioned for a life of philosophy. Though Theaetetus seems to hold out more promise than Theodorus, he is nevertheless deemed "no longer pregnant" after Socrates finishes examining him. This suggests that he must either abandon philosophy or find some way of becoming "pregnant" again. (The meaning and significance of this metaphor becomes clear below.) However, readers of the dialogue are in a potentially better position, for we are able to learn from the ways in which Theodorus and Theaetetus fail. Moreover, we learn concrete things from the dialogue as a work of Platonic art. In other words, we are not limited to Socrates' arguments but also have the interplay of structure and content to consider. In this respect, the most important part of the dialogue may be the section where Socrates likens the examination of Protagoras to a battle in which Heraclitians stand at one extreme and Parmenideans stand at the other. Read in light of the dialogue's opening frame (which I analyze at the end of the chapter), this image helps readers understand how and why Socratic philosophy must stake out its claim in the middle of these two extremes. Readers also come to see why Protagoras, who leans hard to the Heraclitean side, is pedagogically useful but also dangerous.

Socrates Meets Theodorus and Theaetetus

On his way to receive his indictment for impiety and corrupting the young, Socrates crosses paths with an old acquaintance, a foreign teacher of geometry, astronomy, arithmetic, music, and "everything else connected with education" (145a). His name is Theodorus (literally, "gift of god"), a former student and friend of Protagoras (since deceased) who makes his living by maintaining a sizable school of associates. Socrates asks him about his most promising Athenian students: he inquires if any of those who make "geometry or something else of philosophy their concern" are expected to become capable (*epieikeis*). Theodorus' willingness to answer the question formulated in this way suggests that he understands himself to be engaged in philosophy.

Theodorus' background and current status are interesting. He was educated by Protagoras but broke rather early from his teacher because he preferred the methods associated with geometry to the "bare speeches" used by Protagoras (165a). Now a teacher himself, Theodorus specializes in all subjects involving numbers, measurement, and calculation. In this sense he may be thought of as a valuable teacher for future students of philosophy because he works in "forms" and teaches students to think in terms of forms (see *Republic* 521d–531d). But it is clear that Theodorus does not see his role as merely propaedeutic, for when Socrates describes him as an expert not only in numbers, but also in virtue and wisdom (*aretē te kai sophia*, 145b), he does not protest. For Theodorus, the pursuit of knowledge through numbers can be simply equated with philosophy and human excellence.

Theaetetus, whose name means "something asked of the gods; a godsend," is Theodorus' prize Athenian student. Theodorus describes him as interestingly ugly in just the way Socrates is ugly—bulging eyes and snub nose—only less so. Yet despite his ugliness, Theaetetus possesses the rarest combination of intellectual gifts. He is a good learner, an exceptionally gentle soul and yet manly (*andreios*) beyond compare; he is good at remembering things and takes effortlessly to his studies. Moreover, he is not especially attached to money but is rather amazing liberal; and (as readers can piece together) he is neither a boaster nor a coward nor unjust.[3] Theaetetus is, then, as commentators have pointed out, a nearly perfect example of the ideal guardians and potential philosophers described in Plato's *Republic*.[4] No wonder he is a godsend! However, this is not the language Theodorus uses to describe him. To Theodorus, he is rather the best student ever "perceived by the senses" (*aisthanomai*, 144a).

It is significant that Theodorus describes Theaetetus in terms of sense perception, as this foreshadows the definition of knowledge as perception (*aisthesis*) that occupies the bulk of the dialogue and hints at Theodorus' abiding attachment to Protagorean ideas. At the same time, Socrates foreshadows the refutation that he and Theodorus will level against the definition of knowledge as perception: If to know is simply to perceive, then everyone must have immense and inscrutable knowledge, and there is no place for experts—people who know more, or better, than others. Yet Theodorus and Theaetetus are indeed experts (e.g., in math).[5] Therefore knowledge cannot be reduced to perception. Socrates foreshadows this refutation now in his opening questions to Theaetetus (144e–145b): Shouldn't we simply ignore Theodorus' claim that we are alike in our ugliness, because he is no expert in faces? Yet mustn't we take him seriously when he claims you are good and wise, because he indeed has knowledge of this? Contrasting, already, the material and intelligible planes on which the search for knowledge in this dialogue unfolds, Socrates' question leads Theaetetus to admit (rather reluctantly, for he is not a boaster) that he is in fact an exceptional student. Socrates thus gets him to agree to a conversation.

The series of questions that follows and which leads to the main question (what is knowledge?) are crucial for understanding what is really at stake in this dialogue. Socrates gets Theaetetus to affirm the following propositions. (1) When Theaetetus studies various subjects such as geometry and astronomy with Theodorus, he plainly learns something; (2) to learn (*manthanein*) is to become wiser (*sophōteron*) about the thing one is learning; (3) what people are wise about are the things they know; and therefore (4) knowledge (*epistēmē*) and wisdom (*sophia*) are the same. Socrates at this point asks for a definition of knowledge, and Theaetetus' attempt to articulate one fills the dialogue. However, Socrates' question about knowledge emerges from the assumption that knowledge and wisdom are the same. And this I take to be the real issue of the dialogue. If knowledge and wisdom are the same (as Theodorus obviously believes and encourages his students to believe) then the path to wisdom would entail the acquisition of more and more facts. Further, the more certain the facts (think here of math as well the application of math to the phenomenal world, i.e., "empiricism") the more certain one's wisdom. On the other hand, if wisdom is not merely knowledge of numerical facts, but something more—knowledge of the whole of Being including, crucially, of oneself and one's relation to the rest of Being (material and formal)—then Theodorus and Theaetetus have no special claim to wisdom at all. In fact, they would seem particularly unwise insofar as they mistake a sliver of what can be known (albeit a sliver that permits of considerable certainty) for the whole. At its core, then, the *Theaetetus* is about the problem of wisdom. And the drama of the dialogue consists in the humorous fact that the geometers, for all their rigor and love of knowledge, cannot say what knowledge is, for this is not a geometrical question; nor can they say what knowers are: They are unknown to themselves, these men of wisdom.

First Definition: Enumeration of Sciences and Arts

In his first attempt to answer the question "what is knowledge?" Theaetetus proposes that knowledge is precisely what he has been learning from Theodorus—the various sciences (*epistēmai*, literally "knowledges") such as geometry and astronomy. To this he adds a handful of arts (*technai*) such as shoemaking, perhaps recognizing that Socrates often refers to such arts in his conversations.[6] Knowledge, then, is everything a person acquires by studying the arts and sciences. This answer is not a surprise because Socrates has just suggested rhetorically to Theaetetus that what he learns from Theodorus is knowledge (and that knowledge is wisdom). However, it will not do. Theaetetus has failed to abridge the instances of knowledge into a single formula; and even if he tried at this point to do so, his formula would be flawed insofar as his list of "knowledges" is too partial. It is partial both in the sense of failing to capture the whole and also in the sense of being biased. He has considered only his favorite, and what he takes to be Socrates' favorite, topics.

The Midwife Analogy

In response to this initial failure, Socrates counsels Theaetetus not to feel frustrated and attempts to embolden him by means of a pedagogical analogy. He likens himself famously to a midwife, an intellectual version of his mother, who was a midwife in the normal sense. The comparison is complex.[7] Like a midwife, Socrates possesses a special ability to determine who is "pregnant" or not. Moreover, he is able to amplify or diminish the labor pains of his patient through certain techniques resembling the drugs and incantations used by classical midwives; he knows when and how to deliver the offspring, but also when and how to abort if the health of the "mother" is at stake; and he is, moreover, an expert when it comes to pairing people up with one another so that the best possible offspring are produced. However, Socrates differs from ordinary midwives in four important ways. He uses his art only on men. He examines only their souls not their bodies. He scrutinizes the offspring not in physical but in intellectual terms (true versus false, real versus image). And he is himself completely barren, having never been pregnant with wisdom (150c).

This last point is especially important to Socrates, and his amplification of it takes on a suddenly religious character. Ordinary midwives must always be women who have given birth before, though they must also be beyond childbearing age. The reason is that (as convention holds) Artemis, who is the goddess of midwifery, is herself barren; and she therefore wants midwives to be similar. Yet human midwives (as opposed to divine) cannot work without experience: "human nature is too weak to grasp an art of which it is inexperienced" (149c). Therefore, Artemis allows that midwives experience birth but insists they not be currently fertile. This is the case for all ordinary midwives. However, Socrates is different insofar as he (like Artemis) can perform his midwifery having had no personal experience of birth. He describes his situation to Theaetetus as follows.

> The god compels me to midwife and prevented me from generating. Now I myself therefore am obviously hardly wise at all, and I have not had a discovery of this sort as an offspring of my soul. But whoever associate with me (some even appear very foolish at first), all, whomever the god allows, as the association advances, make an amazing lot of progress. It's their own opinion and everyone else's too. And this too is plain as day, that they never learned anything from me, but they on their own from themselves found and gave birth to many beautiful things. (150c–d)[8]

The god compels him. Socrates even goes so far as to weave his unique *daimonion* (divine voice) into the account, claiming that students who leave his care too soon and want to come back later, sometimes discover that the diamonion will not let them. From Artemis to "the god compels me" to the admonitions of Socrates' daimonion, the whole analogy is religiously charged.

But why does Socrates present himself here as a midwife, and why does he employ such divinely charged language? The midwife analogy is unique to the *Theaetetus*. Nowhere else does midwifery come up in Plato's dialogues or in any other account of Socrates. Nor does it appear to be a perfect representation of Socrates' pedagogical activity. For one thing, he manifestly does deposit ideas in his students' heads—as he will do momentarily to Theaetetus. He thus teaches more than the analogy suggests. At the same time, he is not known ever to have led a student to full-blown wisdom as he suggests he has done here. Thus he teaches somewhat less than the analogy suggests.

Perhaps one way to account for Socrates' use of this analogy is to appreciate how artfully it places Theaetetus in an ideal position to learn. Theaetetus is flattered by being told he is pregnant, and yet he is not led to believe that every attempt at birth will succeed or that every issue will be tenable. Moreover, it creates space for a teacher who, like Socrates, is less interested in depositing information than in leading pupils to look critically at their own ideas and, if necessary, to abort a cherished belief. Perhaps another way to account for the analogy is to remember that Socrates is on his way to court where he will receive an indictment for corrupting the young and not believing in the civic gods. Both charges are to an extent addressed by the midwife analogy. Someone who does not teach cannot corrupt. Someone who views himself as rigorously obedient to a god analogous to Artemis is not in this respect impious.

But there is another way, not incompatible with these considerations, of understanding why the midwife analogy appears in the *Theaetetus*. It is because the Protagorean outlook under consideration for the bulk of the dialogue views everything in the world, including ideas, as "offspring" (*ekgonos*) generated by the mating of things in motion (cf. the eye and the visible object at 156a–b).[9] This is what Socrates refers to later in the dialogue as Protagoras' "hidden away truth" (155e). By casting his own engagement with Theaetetus in terms of Protagoras' philosophical outlook, Socrates is able partly to endorse the sophist's view while at the same time exposing its limits. The partial endorsement involves Socrates' implicit acknowledgment that things, including people and their thoughts, are sometimes best understood as offspring. Individuals may indeed become pregnant (physically or intellectually) through their encounters with others. Socrates thus describes Theaetetus' second definition (knowledge is perception) not as a mere utterance, but as a newborn child (*to neogenes paidion*, 160e). Socrates' job is to deliver and examine it to see if it is sound.

That the midwife analogy also exposes the limits of the Protagorean view can be seen by considering the oddity of Socrates himself.

Socrates qua midwife is a glitch in the Protagorean system not only because he is incapable of begetting (*agonos*, 157c–d), which the system does not offer as a possibility, but also because he is able to control the birth process of others, slowing it down and speeding it up as suits his will. Moreover, he stands as judge over the intellectual offspring of his patients, determining whether the newborns are true or false, good or bad, beautiful or ugly—none of which can be explained in terms of the theory itself. Evaluative judgments such as these are not the same as the things they judge; they stand apart as a kind of meta-thought and thus must hail from somewhere other than from the bare mechanics of begetting. If the Protagorean outlook is accurate and exhaustive, then Socrates must somehow be a god or be empowered by a god. For unlike everyone else whose thoughts are mechanistically determined by whatever influences happen to produce them, Socrates stands outside the system as a free and powerful will. Socrates is not a god. And although he may or may not have regarded himself as acting in the service of some concrete god, he nevertheless recognized a divine element in human nature that could not be accounted for by Protagoras' teaching. That divine element is the freedom of our mind and will, and the midwife analogy exposes it.

Second Definition: Knowledge Is Perception

Encouraged by Socrates' midwife analogy, Theaetetus tries again to define knowledge by asserting now that it is "nothing but perception" (151e). When Socrates criticized Theaetetus' first proposal, he stressed that good definitions should be simple and unaffected (*haploos, phaulon*). Now he praises Theaetetus for his forthrightness but not for his answer. So far from being unaffected, this definition seems rather to have been directly influenced by the great sophist Protagoras. Someone has been doing some reading.[10]

Socrates' treatment of this definition divides into two parts, one in which the idea is "born" and one in which it is "tested." The birth, which I treat presently, involves relating it genealogically to kindred ideas—especially those of Protagoras—and runs through 161a, where Theodorus is made to reenter the dialogue for structural emphasis. Apparently the midwife analogy serves, among other things, as an excuse for Socrates to teach Theaetetus how to think like Protagoras—and "teach" here is the operative word, because Theaetetus learns far more about Protagoras from Socrates than he could ever have discovered from reading the sophist's books. That this is the true purpose of the section running through 161a is evident, moreover, from the fact that the refutation of Theaetetus' second definition can be (and eventually is) executed in very few steps. But Socrates does not take those steps until after he has exposed a whole Protagorean worldview including its fascinating underlying assumptions. Why, then, does Socrates deepen Theaetetus' understanding of Protagoras if this is not essential to the topic? He does so, I suggest, for two reasons—because exposure to Protagoras moves interlocutors to a state of wonder, which is a pre-condition for philosophy, and also because Protagoras' ideas are partly true. Let me now consider the "birth."

The initial relationship between "knowledge is perception" and the ideas of Protagoras may not be obvious at first, but Socrates quickly connects the dots. Protagoras began his book *On Truth* with the line: "Of all things, man is the measure: of those that are, that (and how) they are; of those that are not, that they are not" (152a).[11] What does this mean? Socrates and Theaetetus agree: it meant, according to Protagoras, that things often appear (*phainetai*) differently to different people, that there is no criterion of truth beyond the individual perceiver, and that, therefore, truth is relative.[12] Socrates then helpfully offers the example of the wind: Sometimes when the wind is blowing, one person is cold, another is not. But how can one and the same wind be both cold and not cold at the same time? The answer as Protagoras taught is that "the wind itself in itself" is neither cold nor hot but rather "cold for whoever is cold and not for whoever is not," which is to say that its coldness is relative to the person (152b).[13] This amounts to saying that perception is knowledge, because whatever a person perceives or feels at any moment is something for which he and only he is "the measure."[14] Thus everyone's perceptions are certain and inscrutable. Who can tell a person that he does not perceive what he manifestly perceives?

So much is familiar to Theaetetus, but now Socrates introduces a complication. Protagorean relativism rests on certain unspoken assumptions that on investigation turn out to be, surprisingly, incompatible with the very terms of the man-measure doctrine itself. By this Socrates does not mean to suggest that Protagoras was confused; he means rather to suggest that the man-measure doctrine was an exoteric teaching with a deeper, esoteric teaching beneath it. Socrates' case turns on the fact that the man-measure doctrine refers to a single human being (a "man") perceiving a stable object (a "thing"), which, ontologically speaking, "is." However, the ontology required to support Protagoras' relativism ultimately rules out such stable language. Neither the perceiver nor the object can simply "be," but must rather be bound up in a process of becoming (*gignesthai*). Why else would the wind or any other "thing" seem different on different days? Both the wind and the person who perceives it are constantly changing. Such a view was, according to Socrates, endorsed by thinkers from Homer to Heraclitus, even though they tended to communicate it secretly. As for Protagoras, he seems to Socrates to have offered the man-measure doctrine as a tantalizing morsel for the common herd while transmitting the more complicated doctrine to his pupils as an unspeakable secret (*aporrētos*) or a concealed truth (*tēn alētheian apokekrummenēn*).[15]

For our purposes the more complicated doctrine can be boiled down to a number of essential claims, which Socrates dubs the the Protagorean "myth," perhaps because it outstrips what can be known by unassisted reason. (1) From the beginning everything is motion and there is nothing beyond this. (2) There are different kinds of motion: locomotion, alteration, and mixing. (3) Nothing ever *is*, everything always becomes. (4) Perception, both physical and intellectual, occurs (or is born) when something with the power to affect comes into contact with (or mates with) something with the power to be affected by that sort of thing. For example, when something with the power to affect the ears or eyes comes into contact with those organs, a sound or a sight is born just at the same moment that a hearing or sighting is born. Most importantly, (5) when either of these two things changes (the person or the thing coming into contact with it) the perception is not the same. Consequently, (6) nothing is one "itself by itself," but everything comes to be *for* (or in relation to) something. And lastly, (7) though people habitually use words like "be" and "is," these are actually inaccurate. Strictly speaking, nothing can be described statically.[16]

What is the purpose of all this? Again, Socrates imputes this hidden truth to Protagoras as a way of undergirding the sophist's relativism. It helps illuminate why perceptions differ not only from person to person but also for the same person at different times. The same wind seems cold and not cold because it relates differently to different people in different states. Moreover, this "hidden truth" helps explain the puzzle of the dice that Socrates introduces. Imagine, says Socrates, that a group of six dice is set next to a group of four. The group of six appears to be "more." But when the same group is placed next to a group of twelve, it appears "less." How can the same group of six become less and more without altering in any way—without increasing or decreasing? The answer is easy once relativity is understood: things are what they are in relation to their surroundings.[17]

Puzzles such as those of the wind and the dice—and there are many others humorously embedded in the dialogue[18]—are familiar to Theaetetus, but he says he was never able to explain them—not, at least, until Socrates introduced the esoteric doctrine. In fact, he says such puzzles make him dizzy. The question is why Socrates introduces them in the first place and why he then clears them up by introducing Protagoras' "hidden truth." If we read forward to the two grounds on which Theaetetus' definition of knowledge as perception is overturned, we noticed that neither refutation depends on familiarity with Protagoras' man-measure doctrine, much less on the expert understanding of it conveyed by the "hidden truth." The whole tour of Protagorean ideas appears, then, as unnecessary. Or, to reframe the issue, we might ask: for what purpose *is* the tour of Protagorean ideas necessary (since we may assume that it is in the dialogue for a reason)?

Some insight can be gained from what Socrates' tells Theaetetus after his confession of dizziness. Socrates says (155d):

> The reason, my dear, is that Theodorus appears not to have guessed badly about your nature, for this experience is very much a philosopher's: to wonder (*to thaumadzein*). For nothing else is the beginning of philosophy than this and, it seems likely that whoever said Iris was the offspring of Wonder (*Thaumas*) didn't trace the genealogy badly (*ou kakōs genealogein*).

Wonder is "the beginning of philosophy." In other words, one cannot move toward a better understanding of something unless one first appreciates its puzzling qualities. But the difficulty is that wonder is so hard to engender and so easy to suppress. As I have remarked before, the natural tendency is to accept conventional accounts of things unquestioningly, for example, that what is true, good, and beautiful is as unproblematic as math. But the puzzles introduced by Protagoras reveal how complex such matters really are. The virtue of exploring

Protagorean ideas, then, is that they awaken students from their conventional slumber and kindle the wonder that ignites philosophy. And Philosophy, construed in this light, can be understood as the wonder-driven attempt to free oneself from the world of partial beliefs (cf. the cave analogy in *Republic* VII).[19] Philosophy resembles Iris (whose name contains the double meaning of rainbow and messenger) insofar as it is open to, or receptive to, the "message" of the wonderful qualities of being that stretch all the way from earth to heaven and from heaven back down to earth.[20]

Is it not a problem, though, that Protagoras' man-measure doctrine and the relativity it exposes are exaggerated? After all, it is one thing to recognize that some claims are relative; something else entirely to extend relativity to "all things." Does this not taint whatever good Protagoras might have to offer? This is an understandable worry, but I think it can be set aside. Such hyperbolic tendencies might indeed taint Protagoras' benefit if philosophy required its practitioners to accept dogmatically whatever was presented as truth. But philosophy entails no such thing. It demands, rather, that its followers question relentlessly the accounts they receive until an account is reached that stands free from contradiction as much as humanly possible.[21] The sophists are useful in this sense not so much because their teachings are *true* as because they are wonder producing. At the very least, listeners may wonder just enough to desire to explain their tricks.[22] But more importantly, listeners may become habituated to wonder in general. Indeed, we may say (as Socrates suggests in the *Euthydemus*) that a would-be philosopher who does not have sufficient wonder to take sophistic puzzles seriously is simply not ready for philosophy.

At the same time, though, it must be stressed that not everything the sophists teach is untrue. I have noted this many times in the preceding chapters, but here I want to stress that the relativity that Protagoras exposes is quite accurate as a description of a certain class of phenomena. The puzzles of the wind and the dice really are explained by realizing that cold and warm, less and more, are relative terms. The question is how far the class of relative phenomena extends. Does it, for example, extend into questions of ethics and politics? This question is not explored in the process of "birthing" Theaetetus' definition, but it is explored in the section in which Socrates tests it. That test runs through 186e and includes four different refutations before the definition is finally pronounced fruitless, a "wind egg."

Pig Is the Measure

Reminding Theodorus, who now reenters the dialogue, that he (Socrates) merely takes speeches from others and has nothing to offer of his own, Socrates immediately offers something of his own. He "wonders" (*thaumadzō*) why Protagoras didn't say "Pig is the measure of all things," or any other animal with perception, because, according to Protagoras, everyone is equal with respect to the veracity of perceptions. Humans, beasts, and gods must all be reduced to the same level if every perception is true; so the question is, why privilege human beings? Moreover, if all perceptions are true, then what is the basis for anyone calling himself a teacher as Protagoras does, or for bothering to examine the opinions of others for their truth as Socrates does? Teaching and learning become nonsense if everything anyone perceives is true (161e–162a).

This line of refutation seems to hold out great potential to expose the limits of Protagoras' relativism, for we suddenly see the extent to which the whole theory flattens out commonsense distinctions among types of being: animals, humans, and gods. This is something that Socrates might explore further. However, Socrates' purpose here is not only to test Protagoras' theory, but also to test Theaetetus' posture with respect to philosophy—can Theaetetus place himself in a state of wonder about Protagoras and use his wonder to propel philosophical investigation further? Socrates' experience of wonder is mentioned twice at the outset of this initial test (161b, 161c4). Socrates is thus showing the way. But Theaetetus' reaction is crucial to observe. By the end of the test, what for Socrates began as a "wonder" strikes Theaetetus as such a complete wonder (*panu thaumadzō*) that he is ready to abandon the Protagorean orientation entirely—knowledge must not be perception (162d). But this is not how wonder should function. It should initiate inquiry, not end it. Thus Socrates must do something to turn Theaetetus back. What he does is to criticize (in the imagined voice of Protagoras) his own refutation as mere rhetoric (*dēmēgoreō*). To say that humans are no better than beasts or that they are as knowing as gods may serve to frighten or flatter people, but it is something else entirely to determine whether the theory in question is true (162d–e).[23] Theaetetus (comically) agrees wholeheartedly.

We learn something important about Theaetetus from this exchange. He is impressionable. In fact, he is so impressionable that he seems to personify the very notion that all thoughts are derivative. Like a ball of putty, he takes the form of whatever is pressed on him. (He is thus like the wax block mentioned later in the dialogue.) This helps to explain why Socrates plays the sophist with him in a new way in this part of the dialogue. He now uses sophistic maneuvers both to generate wonder and also to address Theaetetus' impressionableness. By rapidly luring Theaetetus in contradictory directions, one after another, he tries to get the lad to appreciate—from fatigue if from nothing else—the value of examining things more carefully before changing one's view. The outcome of this eristic strategy is not a "given" and the stakes are high: If Theaetetus cannot learn to reflect on what he hears before he accepts it as true, he has no hope of becoming philosophical.

Knowing While Not Knowing

That this is indeed Socrates' pedagogic strategy is confirmed by the unmistakably eristic flavor of his second round of tests. If perception is knowledge, then what happens when someone perceives something in one way while not perceiving it in another? Knowing and not knowing would occur at the same time, which is impossible. Therefore, knowledge cannot be perception. To his credit, Theaetetus initially rejects this line of argument, the examples of which are quite humorous: if one hears a foreign language, but has never learned the language, then he must know and not know the language at the same time. Or if he sees some letters, but has never learned to read, he must know and not know his letters. Theaetetus sees that this does not refute the theory that knowledge is perception. To know and perceive what letters look like is different from knowing and perceiving what they signify.

But then Theaetetus immediately falls victim to the same trick played in another register: If someone sees something and then shuts his eyes and recalls what he saw; does he know the thing in his memory, or not? The problem here is that memory is not obviously perception; and yet common sense tells us we *know* what we remember. Thus again we seem to be knowing and not knowing at the same time. Or, put differently, if seeing is knowing, then not seeing is not knowing; and therefore something we recall with our eyes closed is not known; and yet we know it. Moved by this argument, the implications of which he calls "a monster" (163d), Theaetetus again swings hard toward rejecting the definition of knowledge as perception.

But Socrates now pulls the rug out from under Theaetetus again by claiming that they have been arguing in an "antilogical" manner as if they were competitors (*agonistai*) rather than philosophers. Theaetetus has again been too easily impressed, "crowing like an ignoble cock," before anything has really been settled (164c). Socrates thus again characterizes his own test as sophistic and flawed.

In order to restore Theaetetus' confidence in the definition of knowledge as perception, Socrates now volunteers to offer a full-blown defense of Protagoras. The defense has two parts, an illuminating lesson in sophistic refutation followed by a prolonged speech. The lesson in refutation purports to explain why Socrates' second test was sophistic through and through. Socrates (Protagoras would say) merely took advantage of ambiguities in the verb "to know," which may sometimes mean "perceive," "understand" or "recall."[24] Socrates could also have taken advantage of the multiple channels of perception, as he now shows, by asking Theaetetus to hold a hand over one of his eyes while viewing an object with the other. If knowledge is perception, then Theaetetus would have to know and not know the same object at the same time. Such tricks are legion, Socrates says, but they do not actually disprove the theory that knowledge is perception; they merely raise questions that would have to be addressed if one were to pursue the theory further. In other words, one does not disprove something by showing that it leads to apparently absurd implications; one merely casts doubt, since absurd implications can often be removed by introducing a distinction (166b–d).[25]

The second part of Socrates' defense of Protagoras is a sustained speech in the sophist's name—a speech to show how the man-measure doctrine might yet overcome Socrates' charge (in the first test) that it obliterates wisdom and teaching by making everyone equal with respect to truth. Often referred to as the "Apology of Protagoras" (166a–168c), the speech likens education and politics to caring for plants and other physical bodies. Such engagements have nothing to do with truth, says the defense, but rather with changing (*metaballōn*) the condition of patients so that what appears to them is healthy rather than harmful. For example, in medicine, when a physician encounters someone who thinks all food tastes bitter, he does not deem the patient foolish or pronounce his perceptions false; he rather attempts to bring about a change toward "a better condition" (*ameinōn hexis*).[26] So, too, in education, when a sophist finds a pupil full of harmful and disadvantageous opinions, he does not (despite how it seems) transform false opinions into true ones—"for it's impossible to opine . . . things beyond whatever one experiences, and these are always true" (167a–b). But he rather uses speeches like a doctor uses medicine, so that what is "better" appears to the pupil in place of what is worse. Finally, the same thing occurs in politics: "the wise and good public speakers are those who make cities be of the opinion that useful things [*ta chrēsta*] are just [*dikaia*] instead of useless things" (167c).

Socrates thus defends the possibility of wisdom in a world in which all perceptions are true at the moment of their occurrence for the individual or group that experiences them. And it must be said that the defense is fairly compelling, as far as it goes.[27] Individuals and cities really do have opinions that guide them, and these are indeed true for them as long as they are held. The American understanding of criminal justice, for instance—whatever it happens to be at any point in time—*is* what Americans find true about criminal justice as long as they hold it to be so. And wise public speakers really might, as Socrates' speech suggests, help cities to embrace politically healthy rather than harmful opinions about things such as justice. Rhetoricians and sophists are thus like doctors for the city and the soul. In other dialogues Plato has Socrates doubt whether rhetoricians and sophists possess valid criteria of health for the city and the soul;[28] but this is a separate question from whether they see their role as attempting to change people for the better. This is a fundamental commonality between Socrates and Protagoras.

Socrates concludes his defense of Protagoras with a powerful exhortation to philosophical rather than competitive conversation (167d–168c)—an exhortation baffling to many commentators for its surprisingly Socratic tone. Recall that Socrates is speaking in the name of Protagoras here. "In conversation," Socrates imagines Protagoras urging, "be in earnest." Do not try to trick your opponents, but rather assist them to see precisely where they have been led astray by themselves and their associates. In this way interlocutors will grow to "hate themselves and flee from themselves into philosophy so that, once they've become different, they may be rid of who they were before" (167e–168a). Is this not Socratic rather than Protagorean?[29] If so, how are we to make sense of Socrates' ascribing the thought to Protagoras?

Perhaps one way to understand this is in terms of Protagorean theory itself, which Socrates partly endorses. If, as Protagoras maintains, all things are the product of motion and of mating, then nothing (including Protagoras himself) can remain itself or himself for long. What Socrates thus does is to demonstrate *ad oculos* the effect of Protagorean flux theory on Protagoras himself. If all things are the product of mating, then nothing prevents Socrates from mating Protagorean and Socratic ideas so that a hybrid of sorts, a "Soctagoras," is produced.[30] Commentators have often surmised or complained that the sophist in the *Theaetetus* is not pure Protagoras, but they have failed to consider why this may be the case, in terms of the dialogue itself.[31] The point is made explicit later on (182c–183c): if *everything* is by definition flowing and changing, then even Protagoras and his ideas must give way to flux; Protagoras cannot resist being changed any more than anyone else can. That this is indeed a change from Protagoras' original position is made perfectly clear (169d–e, 171e). Socrates has thus morphed the sophist into something closer to Socrates himself. A condition of Socrates' ability to do this is that he and Protagoras be closely related enough to enable breeding—for example, like an eye and a visible object. This is another way of stating my argument about the basic kinship that serves as the backdrop for the fascinating differences between Socrates and the Protagoras.

Expertise

Halfway through Socrates' elaborate testing of the brainchild, "knowledge is perception," he shifts from sophistic-style refutations to a sounder examination and, at the same time, switches interlocutors, taking the older Theodorus as his partner. Why? He does so because he imagines Protagoras objecting to the employment of a youth to test his theories. The shift from Theaetetus to Theodorus thus foreshadows what becomes the heart of the third test: the question of expertise. To complain that what appears to a youth (Theaetetus) is not the best measure of the truth of Protagoras' doctrine is to admit that not everyone is equal with respect to discerning the truth. Thus Protagoras (at least as Socrates reconstructs him) does not act as if he believes his own theory. Experts know more than mere novices. And this is precisely what Socrates now wants Theodorus to consider: "whether you, after all, must be the measure of geometrical theorems or whether all are as competent for themselves as you are in astronomy and everything else in which you are charged with excelling" (169a). If Theodorus is an expert, then he cannot be equal to others as a measurer of truth, and Protagoras' theory seems to fail.[32]

But does it? Protagoras did not exactly say that all men are equal judges of all things. He said (according to Socrates' example of the wind) that each man is the judge of what is true *for him* at the moment of perception. And this is a hard theory to refute if it is possible to refute it at all.[33] What Socrates does, then, in pointing to expertise as a problem is not to refute Protagoras' theory but rather to circumscribe the domain in which it has anything interesting to say. It is both interesting and indeed true to say that the wind is hot or cold depending on the perceiver, or that beauty is in the eye of the beholder; but Protagoras' theory ceases to be interesting precisely when and where one begins to discuss something other than present perceptions. So, for instance, it may be true that what tastes sour for a person is sour for him, as long as it tastes so. But something different is going on when one speaks of what will cure an illness. Here people can be simply wrong. One might insist that what appears medicinal to a person is so for him, as long as it appears so. But this is certainly a trivial claim compared to the fact that some things really are curative of certain diseases, whether the patient knows it or not. What then is the line of demarcation between the areas where Protagoras' teaching is enlightening and those where it is trivial? And what, in particular, about things like justice and holiness, which now come to the surface of the conversation (172a–b)? Are these merely relative to the person and the city? Or can one speak of expertise in these areas as well as in geometry?

This question is never explicitly answered in the *Theaetetus* though various options are made available. Let me itemize them. The rhetorical thrust of Protagoras' man-measure dictum seems to suggest that no truths beyond subjective experience exist. This is one option. But it is rendered questionable by the problem of expertise, which does not seem merely subjective. A second option is to allow that most things are relative to time, person and place (including justice and holiness) but not questions such as what is healthy or advantageous. This option may resemble some varieties of modern pragmatism;[34] and Socrates attributes it to certain half-hearted followers of Protagoras (172b). They can't go with Protagoras all the way, but they can do so until questions of advantage arise. A final option, however, is delicately suggested by the concern for justice exhibited throughout the dialogue by all the conversationalists including Theodorus and Theaetetus. For example, Socrates suggests and Theaetetus agrees that sophistic refutations are not just (163a). Similarly Socrates worries about treating Protagoras unjustly (164e) and even has Protagoras himself complain that he is being treated unjustly by Socrates (167d). Moreover, Theodorus seems especially concerned that he may, in criticizing Protagoras' views, seem like an unjust friend to the now deceased sophist (162a, 171c). What this suggests is that the first and second options (as tempting as they may be for someone like Theodorus) are simply not a robust explanation of the way people act. None of these characters acts as if justice is merely subjective.

Digression: Philosophy and the Courts

At this point, Theodorus and Socrates embark on what appears to be a digression. However, appearances can be deceptive (as this dialogue itself teaches). And in fact all the principal themes and questions that have animated the discussion up to this point remain poignantly in play as the "digression" unfolds. The purpose of the digression, as I understand it, is for Socrates to test whether Theodorus subscribes to the first, second or third ways of understanding justice and—upon learning that he fits in the second category—to drive a wedge between him and Protagoras once and for all.[35] What appears as a digression from one perspective, then, turns out to be essential from another. (This instability of impressions remains, at least for the dialogue's readers, a residual truth that Protagoras helps to illuminate—so that even while Socrates and Theodorus move away from relativity, readers are encouraged not to move away too far.)

The digression begins after Socrates realizes that the problem of expertise he has been exploring fits into a broader problem with Protagoras' doctrine (the problem of learning over time, 178a). Thus he says that a "bigger argument from a lesser one is overtaking us" (172c). The question is whether they have sufficient leisure to pursue this bigger argument, and while Theodorus seems confident that they do, he is unaware—as readers are, too, at this point—that Socrates "must go to the porch of the king to meet the indictment of Meletus" (210d). Socrates is thus not completely free. He only "appears" to be (172c). And yet in another sense (qua philosopher) Socrates is more free even than those who compel him to appear in court. This, or something like it, has to be the unspoken train of thought that leads Socrates to digress into an extended comparison of philosophers and those who spend their time in the courts.[36]

Philosophers appear laughable in court, Socrates claims, because of their unfamiliarity with public speaking. They appear to be foolish and slavish. However, the truth is quite the reverse. Those who spend their time in the courts lack freedom to such a degree that they forgo even the possibility of loving wisdom. Always in the press of business, they must tailor their speeches and even their thoughts to the immediate issue at hand. Moreover, they necessarily become corrupt from their preoccupations due to the impossibility of supporting every cause with true words and just deeds, whereas philosophers avoid corruption by avoiding the courts and politics altogether. In fact, philosophers regard such affairs with a degree of contempt, which is why they lack knowledge of some of the most basic political things. They do not know how to find the marketplace or the court; they never attend banquets where citizens gather; they know nothing of family status (whether a person comes from noble or base parents). Instead, they calculate that everyone has thousands of ancestors both noble and base, and they turn their minds to matters below and above the earth. They "geometrize the planes," gaze at stars, and explore the nature of each whole of the things that are (173e). Moreover, they ask questions such as "what is 'human' being?" "How does 'human' being relate to the rest of being?" "What is justice?" "What is kingship?" and "What is human happiness?" When those who spend their time in the courts try to engage such questions, they find out that it is they rather than philosophers who are stupid and inept.

Theodorus really likes this comparison, and that is no accident. Socrates has designed it with him in mind. This is why the description of the philosophical type includes so many references to calculation, geometry, and astronomy.[37] The classic Socratic questions are mentioned, too ("What is justice?" etc.). However, Socrates is not as exclusively oriented toward the abstract as the philosopher he describes here. Socrates *does* know his way to the marketplace and to the court; he does attend banquets (such as the one in the *Symposium*), and he does know the names and social status of the people he meets. It is Theodorus who does not. Thus at the beginning of the dialogue, when Socrates asked Theodorus who Theaetetus' father was, Theodorus did not remember, though he had heard the name many times (144b). Socrates, by contrast, takes one look at Theaetetus and knows he is the "son of Euphronius from Sunium," a noble and good man with considerable wealth (144c). The description of the philosopher, then, which Socrates contrasts with the political type of man is not a portrait of Socrates as much as an image that incorporates traits from both Theodorus and Socrates alike; it is a mating of the two, designed for a purpose.

The question is why Socrates does this, and the answer is not far to seek. By showing Theodorus the contrast between the philosophical and political ways of life, Socrates in effect drives a wedge between Theodorus and Protagoras. Theodorus fancies himself a philosopher. This has been clear from the beginning and it is clear from his love of this comparison. But he is not the same kind of philosopher as Socrates, and he will in fact never come close to loving wisdom in the fullest sense until he expands his interests to include the concrete as well as the abstract, as Socrates does. But Socrates suppresses all that for now. The purpose here is to show Theodorus that if he loves philosophy as now defined, Theodorus should not have much affection for Protagoras. Why? Because if a line were drawn between men who spend their life in philosophy and those who spend their life in the courts, Protagoras would fall unmistakably on the side of the courts. And Theodorus knows this to be true (178e). Theodorus, then, should forget about Protagoras.

But the way in which Theodorus praises Socrates' comparison reveals that he is not ready to abandon Protagoras completely. He praises the speech in consequentialist terms (or in terms of "advantage") as follows: "If you should persuade everyone, Socrates, of what you're saying as you did me, peace would be more widespread and evils less among human beings" (176a). Theodorus thus speaks as if he has Socrates' "defense of Protagoras" still in mind. No person's view is more or less true than another's, but some beliefs are more advantageous, and these should be the focus of persuasion. Given this response, we can now speculate that what Theodorus finds attractive about Protagoras, despite the fact that the sophist is tainted by involvement in quotidian affairs, is his teaching that moral values are relative (to put it in modern terms). In other words, like many geometers, mathematicians, and astronomers even today, Theodorus views questions of justice and holiness as matters of mere opinion, which, like people's taste in wine or music, vary from individual to individual or from culture to culture. *De gustibus non est disputandum*. Theodorus thus clearly embraces the second of the three options concerning justice sketched out above. He is a half-hearted Protagorean—or he thinks he is.

But if this is the case, then there is an easy way to get Theodorus to abandon Protagoras' teaching altogether. He need only be shown that the relativist outlook is not advantageous, or not as advantageous as some other set of beliefs. Because Theodorus accepts persuasion of this sort as legitimate, Socrates has the opportunity to offer an alternative to the Protagorean myth. And this is precisely what he does (176a–177c). Borrowing the title from Protagoras' book, *Truth*, Socrates' alternative "truth" (176c) would maintain that god is in no way unjust but is rather as just as is possible to be. Nothing is more similar to him than a person who becomes as just as possible. The recognition of this is wisdom and true aretē; ignorance of it is folly and vice. And the true penalty for injustice is not what people suppose—beatings and executions, which, after all sometimes happen to the just as well—but rather something unavoidable. The penalty is a life lived in the paradigm of the godless and miserable instead of the paradigm of the divine and happy (176c–177a).

We now analyze this alternative myth. The basic problem of political order is that while things work best when everyone practices justice, individuals stand a good chance of faring even better by practicing injustice, as long as they can get away with it. To be unjust while appearing or seeming just is thus a tempting policy. In this light, Protagoras' doctrine that nothing exists *except* appearances, that the good has no being of its own beyond how it appears to me at any given moment is politically dangerous in the extreme. It encourages the very conduct that undermines political life. What is needed, then, is a ground for just conduct that does not rest on appearances. People need to prize justice not because they want to "seem to be good and not bad" (176b)—for seeming can be managed easily enough—but because of something more serious. They need to believe that justice is personally advantageous and injustice disadvantageous, whether one seems to possess these or not. And this is what Socrates' "truth" accomplishes by referring to paradigms of divine happiness and godless misery. God, not man, is the measure of all things.

But there is more. Protagoras' teaching is also flawed in the unbounded hope it places in political persuasion—the ability of "wise public speakers" to change the condition of whole communities for the better. For even if people were told about a most extreme kind of punishment—that the unjust will not be received by the region free of the bad after they die—they would still not change. Of this Socrates is certain (177b). So, the power of persuasion is markedly limited.[38] And yet Theodorus has imbibed this unhealthy optimism about persuasion, as is clear from his remark to Socrates that "peace would be more widespread and evils less among human beings," if Socrates would simply speak to everyone (176a). Socrates' truth, therefore, must replace this dangerous belief with something better. Socrates thus maintains that "It is not possible for the evils to perish, for there must always be something contrary to the good," and that the goal of life is not to transform the world but *oneself* by assimilating oneself to god as far as possible (176a–b). As for what assimilation entails, Socrates says only that it involves striving to become just and holy through prudence (*phronēsis*, 176b). This should be enough. If Theodorus believes these things instead of his hodgepodge of numerical certainty, moral relativism and political optimism, he will believe something that is not harmful to himself, his students or his community—and which may even be true.

The digression ends when Socrates protests that they will "choke off" their former discussion if they persist in this digression for too long. The question that the digression raises is why Socrates steers Theodorus so hard away from Protagorean relativism while he attempts to keep Theaetetus in mind of it. The answer, I suspect, has everything to do with the different dispositions of the two. Theaetetus has some potential for a life of philosophy. Not only does he love the domain of "forms" as these factor into geometry and other kindred sciences, but he also has a capacity to wonder about puzzles of all sorts and a willingness to venture into uncharted territory even when his reputation is at stake. Theodorus shares the first of these traits, but not, evidently, the second or the third. His *modus operandi* throughout the dialogue is to avoid getting pulled into the conversation. He finds the topic unfamiliar and difficult, and he fears cutting a bad figure. Socrates thus leaves him with the next best thing to philosophy itself, a set of opinions that are unlikely to do any harm and may even do some good.

In the remainder of Socrates' examination of "knowledge is perception," three things occur. (1) Socrates resumes his critique of Protagoras on the basis of expertise and thereby gets Theodorus to repudiate, once and for all, the Protagorean teaching, "man is the measure of all things." (2) Socrates shows Theaetetus quite easily that knowledge cannot be perception by considering the need for a common sensorium of some kind in order to make sense of various perceptions. And in between these two accomplishments, Socrates (3) describes their effort to wrestle with Protagoras in a vivid and memorable way—as participation in an epic battle between Heracliteans and Parmenidians over the nature of being. This middle scene in between Theodorus and Theaetetus affords a glimpse of the dialogue's most profound teaching, an account of what wisdom requires and therefore what philosophy must do.

After these three steps are complete, Theaetetus and Socrates go on to consider two other possible definitions of knowledge: "knowledge is true opinion," and "knowledge is true opinion with an account." Theodorus never reenters the conversation. And Theaetetus, for his part, fails to reach a satisfactory definition of knowledge before Socrates deems him "no longer pregnant." Much could be said about the wonderful images and arguments that occupy the second half of the dialogue. However, because my overarching purpose here is to understand Plato's use of the sophists, I want to focus now rather structurally on how this dialogue's beginning, middle and end bring the challenge of philosophy into clear focus and how Protagoras fares when this challenge is properly understood.

Heraclitians and Parmenideans

The digression, which constitutes the center of the dialogue (172c–177c), contrasts philosophers with denizens of the court. Shortly after this (179c–184b), Socrates' battle imagery contrasts the philosophical outlook of Heracliteans and Parmenidians. Though the two contrasts do not serve the same function in terms of the dialogue's argument on the surface, they do, interestingly, illuminate each other. Or, more precisely, the latter contrast supplies a broader perspective according to which the initial contrast can be reinterpreted. Moreover, the whole dialogue takes on new meaning in this light, as I show shortly by considering the dialogue's beginning and end.

Socrates introduces the battle image just as he and Theodorus move to consider Protagorean relativism (in other words, each individual is the measure of what is true for him) on its strongest ground, namely as a description of *present* experience. They have already concluded that as soon as one takes the future into consideration (e.g., will it rain tomorrow?) it becomes possible to speak of genuine expertise, and the theory must give way. But the question is whether everything a person experiences in the present is, qua experience, "knowledge" and "true" (179c). In order to test this, Socrates proposes to examine more closely the Heraclitean theory of "sweeping Being" that undergirds Protagorean relativism and to contrast it with the "immovable" or "resting" Being of the Parmenideans. These are the two sides of the battle; and Socrates sums up the predicament he and Theodorus face in the following way.

> How shall we handle all these, Theodorus? For in advancing little by little, we have, without being aware of it, fallen into the middle of both, and unless we somehow manage to defend ourselves and escape, we'll pay the penalty. . . . [by being] seized by both sides and dragged in contrary directions. Now I'm of the opinion that we must examine first . . . the flowing ones (*tous rheontas*).[39] And if they appear to be reasonable, we'll drag ourselves off with them and try to avoid the others. But if the arresters (*stasiōtai*) of the Whole seem to be saying truer things, we'll flee over to them and away from those who set the immoveable things in motion (*tōn ta akinēta kinountōn*). And if it's evident that there's no measure of sense in what both are saying, we'll be laughable, convinced that we're making sense though we're nobodies, and having rejected upon scrutiny (*apodedokimakotes*) very ancient and all-wise men. (180e–181b)

The terms Socrates uses to describe the contenders in this battle suggest that more is at stake than just theories of Being. The "flowing ones" are described as "those who set the immoveable things in motion," which is a proverbial expression for a violation of the sacred. The "arrestors" are *stasiōtai*, which is a pun—literally people who make things stand still (*stasis*), but also and more commonly "members of a political faction or party." Finally, Socrates imagines rejecting both sides "upon scrutiny," which alludes to the *dokimasia*, the process of examining elected officials to determine whether they meet the qualifications for office.[40] The upshot of these verbal associations seems to be that the way one views Being has important religious, political, and philosophical implications.

The appearance of similar terminology in the digression on philosophy and the courts confirms that the battle between Flowing ones and Arrestors does indeed have wide implications. Philosophers are described there as people who are always trying to hit on that which *is*. The denizens of the court are described, by contrast, as "always speaking under the pressure of water in flow (*rheon*)" such that they lack the freedom to discuss whatever they want (172e). This is on the surface a simple reference to the water clock that measured the time allotted to each speaker in court, but it also serves to connect the courtroom speaker's lack of freedom to the theory of the "flowing ones" who comprise one side of the battle. The implication: Just as the courtroom orator is constrained in his freedom by the pressure of the clock, so, too, are human beings constrained on the theory that everything is flux. If human beings and their ideas are constantly being changed by the impact of other things on them, then our thoughts, speech, and indeed our *selves* are not really within our control. There is no room for a "self" that stands outside or endures through the process of change. Moreover, because everyone's process of change is idiosyncratic, there can be no stable community—no association based on shared understandings.

Certainly there are further political implications of the theory that everything is constantly changing due to internal and external forces: push this too far and political life becomes impossible for numerous reasons. But there are also philosophical implications, and Socrates hints at these when he ends the digression on philosophy and the courts in the following way: "Now let us stand apart and withdraw from these things—they were in fact said as bi-products—for if we don't, always more will keep on flowing in [*epirrheonta*] and bury the argument with which we began" (177b). Philosophy becomes impossible, too, if everything, including the inquirer and his search, is constantly succumbing to change. Philosophy requires a relatively stable investigation into a relatively stable subject, and it presupposes inquirers who are stable enough to concentrate attention even while numerous interesting digressions might carry them away. By ending the digression, then, Socrates tacitly rejects the theory that all is flux. The theory cannot account for—indeed would obliterate—a sustained philosophical search.

Socrates' rejection of flux theory in the digression thus anticipates and, in retrospect, deepens his rejection of it as a contender in the battle over Being.

But what about the other side of that battle? Does the Parmenidean camp make a more reasonable case? Interestingly, Socrates is not willing to consider the question. Why not? He says (183e–184b) he feels shame before the deceased Parmenides who seems to Socrates to have had profound depth. They met once when Socrates was young, so Socrates has firsthand knowledge of his stature. But Socrates says they will never succeed in understanding what the man was thinking when he spoke. Second, they lack time to consider adequately Parmenides' thought if they hope, at the same time, to continue their investigation of Theaetetus' thesis that knowledge is perception. So they abandon the plan to investigate both sides of the battle.

This means that for the participants of the dialogue, the outcome of the battle strategy is inconclusive. Socrates and Theodorus know not to side with the Heracliteans, but they do not know whether to flee toward the Parmenidians or to reject them, too, remaining somehow in the middle. However, careful readers are not left in doubt about the necessary course, because we are not left in doubt about the inadequacy of the Parmenidian option. It is decisively criticized by the events of the dialogue's opening frame (as I show). Moreover, readers are evidently supposed to ponder the dialogue in this way. After all, why does Socrates bring up the battle between Heraclitians and Parmenidians, and why does he propose to examine both sides? A simple examination of Heraclitian flux theory alone is all that was required to undermine Protagorean relativism. Parmenides need not have been mentioned. That he was mentioned in such a vivid way as to suggest that he must either be sided with or else, somehow, rejected for a middle position of some sort, suggests that the issue cannot simply be set aside. Happily the beginning of the dialogue is there to point the way.

The Dialogue's Opening Frame

The *Theaetetus* is one of Plato's dialogues in which an important prologue or opening scene precedes the dialogue itself.[41] In this case, the scene is set in Megara sometime after Socrates' death. A character named Euclides (the founder of the Megarian school of philosophy) has just been to the harbor where he happened upon Theaetetus. Theaetetus was en route from Corinth—where had been participating in a military campaign—to his home in Athens.[42] He was, tragically, on the brink of death from war wounds and dysentery. Having said his farewells to Theaetetus, Euclides now remarks to a friend named Terpsion "how prophetically" Socrates had spoken about Theaetetus (142c) when he "expressed great admiration for his nature" and predicted that Theaetetus would necessarily "come into account [*ellogimos*] if he reached maturity."

Socrates' impressions of Theaetetus are known to Euclides, because Socrates—just before his execution—chose to narrate to him the conversation that forms the body of our dialogue. Euclides took notes ("reminders," cf. *Phaedrus* 278a) and later attempted to expand these into a full account. Though Euclides could not remember everything Socrates had said, he did have the opportunity on several occasions to return to Athens to question Socrates about various details before the end of Socrates' life.[43] The result was a nearly perfect written version of Socrates' account—but with one important exception: Whereas Socrates had told the story in such a way as to offer narrative reflection on the conversation, Euclides intentionally omitted these remarks, perhaps deeming them too cumbersome or unimportant.[44] The dialogue proper now begins when Euclides proposes to read his written version to Terpsion or, rather, since they are both fatigued and in need of rest (*anapausasthai*), to have a servant read the text.

There are many fascinating things to observe about this opening scene, but I wish to stress only three related points. First, for readers willing to consider it in retrospect, it seems designed to suggest that Theaetetus never grew out of his two chief character traits—his attraction to Protagorean/Heraclitean flux and his (related) tendency to be overly impressionable. This is subtly revealed in the few things we are told about him. He is first described as being "carried along" (*pheromenō*) by others from Corinth to Athens (142a). This is, significantly, the term Socrates and Theodorus later use to describe the Heraclitians, who propose a theory of "sweeping being" (*pheromenēn ousian*) and are themselves perpetually sweeping (*pherontai*) along (179d, 179e). Next, we learn that Theaetetus is dying not so much from his war wounds as from dysentery (142b). He is dying, in other words, from diarrhea or, quite literally, "the flow."[45] Finally we learn that when Euclides begged Theaetetus to remain in Megara for his own good, Theaetetus refused. This is a person who is not willing to lodge himself somewhere or come to rest (*kataluō*).

The second thing to observe about the opening frame is the extent to which it prompts readers to take a critical view of Parmenidianism by mocking how Euclides—who was himself a follower of Parmenides—behaves. That he was a Parmenidean would have been known to Plato's readers, but modern readers can acquire the relevant facts from Diogenes Laertius.[46] In the opening frame, Euclides and Terpsion opt to have the *Theaetetus* read to them while they are resting (*anapauomenois*, 143b). The word "rest" is stressed both through repetition and placement in the opening frame. We may take this, then, as an allusion to the Parmenidean philosophy of rest. And in this connection it seems significant that the *Theaetetus*, unlike the *Euthydemus*, has an opening but not a closing frame. In other words, where readers would expect to hear Euclides' and Terpsion's closing *reflections* on the dialogue that was read to them, we in fact hear nothing. They appear to have fallen asleep. Motionlessness, as Socrates aptly remarks in the *Theaetetus* (153b–c) and elsewhere is inimical to learning.[47]

By associating Euclides with Parmenides and then calling his ability to learn into question, the opening frame in effect prompts readers to take a critical stance toward the Parmenidean side of the "war" described later in the dialogue. And the weakness of Euclides' Parmenidean outlook is not limited to his desire to rest. Why *does* Euclides decide to delete Socrates' narrative remarks from his account of the conversation between Socrates and Theaetetus? He must deem the narrative perspective inessential. But is it? Socrates' narrative remarks certainly contained invaluable information not only about what he intended in conversing with Theaetetus, but also what, in retrospect, he thought of the conversation.[48] In other words, human intentionality as well as the human ability to reflect are something beyond (and not captured by) the raw experience of an event. By deleting the narrative remarks, then, Euclides reveals his assumption that all one needs to know about a thing (a conversation, for instance) is contained in the thing itself. Perspective is neither required nor possible. This fits nicely with the Parmenidian theory that "all is one," but does it not render philosophy as futile as it was revealed to be at the opposite Heraclitean extreme, which reduced everything to a matter of perspective? If we cannot get *some* perspective on the things, events, and selves we encounter in human life—because everything is one—then philosophy, which is the attempt to put things in their proper perspective, is simply impossible.

Tying together now these two observations about the opening frame—namely, that Theaetetus is overly prone to flux and Euclides overly prone to rest, such that neither maintains a workable posture for the practice of philosophy, which is defined by its motion (love) toward stability (the source of Being)—I think it is reasonable to propose that Euclides would not be capable of properly interpreting the prophecy which Socrates issued concerning Theaetetus. Socrates' prophecy was that "there was every necessity that he [Theaetetus] would become held in account [*ellogimos*] if he reached maturity." What this means to Euclides is that Theaetetus would become an object of praise. And Euclides finds confirmation of this when, as he remarks, "I was listening even now to some people highly praising his conduct in the battle" (142b). But is Socrates likely to have cared about, much less predicted, Theaetetus' fame—Theaetetus whom he deems no longer pregnant, dangerously impressionable, and radically unprepared to grasp the problem of wisdom? This seems unlikely. But then again, Socrates' prophecy does make sense when read in light of the dialogue's ultimate use of terms. To be "held in account," is to be contained or captured by a single *logos*—which is impossible as long as Theaetetus shifts from perspective to perspective without adequate reflection. Theaetetus cannot reach an account of knowledge, much less of himself. Socrates' prophecy, then, seems to mean that if Theaetetus can somehow survive to manhood without being killed as a result of his impressionableness (e.g., by overdoing it in battle, as he apparently did), then it will be *because* he has begun to hold himself to a more fixed and stable account—it will be because he has sought and begun to find self knowledge.

The Role of Protagoras in the Search for Wisdom

Once the problems with the Heraclitean and Parmenidean options are exposed, we are prepared to move gradually back to the question of Protagoras: What role does this sophist play in Socratic philosophy and pedagogy? Recall that when Socrates described the predicament of existence in between Heraclitean and Parmendidean extremes, he spelled out four possible courses of action: (1) side with the Heracliteans; (2) side with the Parmenideans; (3) suffer the fate of being pulled apart by both; or (4) somehow defend the middle ground. He and

Theodorus then rejected the Heracliteans, but they could not consider the Parmenidians without abandoning and thus sacrificing the question, "what is knowledge?" They had therefore to set aside a profound philosophical problem, in order to remain true to another, antecedent problem. Such is the condition of philosophy in the middle ground between Parmenides and Heraclitus. By allowing a degree of digression, but not an all-out change of subject, Socrates shows that he is living in this middle ground and that he indeed feels the pressure, the "pull" from both sides.

Such is Socrates' partial response to the predicament. But readers are afforded a tremendous opportunity that Socrates himself, in the press of events, did not have. This opportunity is presented to us intentionally by Plato, who himself stands outside the pressure of the moment. We are encouraged through the opening frame to consider and reject the Parmenidean side and thus to turn to the fourth option as the only attractive alternative. We are encouraged, in other words, to "somehow defend the middle ground."

As I understand it, then, a defense of the middle ground might entail understanding the human condition not as "torn" between permanence and change but rather as "contained" within a tension between these two poles while yet enabling a degree of movement toward permanence through human reason and reflection. However the effort to live in this way is open to several dangers worth identifying:

First and foremost is the danger of not perceiving the tension at all, of allowing convention and complacency to occlude the problematic nature of being strung between the relative and the absolute. I list this danger first because it seems to threaten the greatest number of people.[49]

Second is the danger of giving oneself over to relativism upon discovering that human experience indeed admits of considerable relativity. Plato's Socrates cautions against this danger in the Republic (539b–c), and it can be thought of as especially threatening to bright young men.

Third is the danger of reeling so hard away from the initial experience of relativity that a false security is sought in a dogmatized absolute. This is as much a falsification of the human condition as the belief that everything is relative. However, it has, perhaps, two things to be said for it: it is at least a movement in the proper direction, and it may be—depending on how it is approached—basically harmless to politics.[50] As I interpret Socrates' interaction with Theodorus, his goal is to nudge the old Geometer into a position of this sort, which involves in his case a healthy eschewal of political life.

Fourth and finally is the danger of living in the tension but experiencing it as a torture of sorts, because the loving motion within it proves too difficult or is thought to be either impossible or unsatisfying. Certainly, Theaetetus shows signs of being tortured in this way (155c), and a fine line separates such anxiety from the genuine agitation or wonder that propels philosophical investigation. Socrates, on my interpretation, does not give up on Theaetetus in the way he gives up on Theodorus. Rather, he attempts to moderate the lad's amazement at relativity while emboldening him (and testing his fitness) to explore the hints of permanence. The results are inconclusive. When Theaetetus leaves Socrates' care he has shown himself to be a good pupil but rather too impressionable and not yet ready for the climb. Tragically, his death comes before his improvement, perhaps because Socrates himself did not live to help him.[51]

Now, against this backdrop I consider the likely significance of Protagoras for Socrates and Plato. As I see it, he is important for pedagogical and for philosophical reasons. Pedagogically, Protagoras' teaching masterfully exposes students to the relativity of human perception on the physical and intellectual plane. Not only the coolness or hotness of the wind, but also the justice or injustice of particular policies may indeed appear different to different people depending on their condition, and this is not simply because some people see "the truth" more clearly than others.[52] Relativity is a fact of human experience. The virtue of Protagoras' teaching, then, is to expose relativity to the minds of the overly complacent (thus steering listeners away from the first danger listed above); and I think he does this not only through his written teaching, which takes its departure from the (no doubt exaggerated) claim that man is the measure of (*all*) things, but also through his private teaching, which emphasizes making weaker arguments stronger and contradicting anything and everything an adversary may say.[53] Notice that in both these ways, Socrates appears intimately bound up with Protagoras. He imparts Protagorean teachings to his pupils (or deepens their knowledge of this sophist's teachings) and, at the same time, uses Protagoras' technique of refutation and of making weaker arguments seem stronger. Socrates, in a word, "incorporates" Protagoras into his own pedagogy so as to awaken students to the phenomenon of relativity. (Notice that Socrates' practice of "relativizing" Theaetetus' answers to the question of knowledge, continues to the end of the dialogue even after the sophist is supposedly dismissed.)

While Socrates enlists Protagoras to help students avoid the first danger described above, he runs the risk, at the same time, of plunging students headlong into the second or third dangers. This is because Protagoras makes such a compelling case while also exaggerating the sphere of instability. Students who absorb Protagoras thus become less attuned to the call of permanence and do not therefore see the problem of relating the various levels of being, one with another. This is, I believe, why Socrates consistently attempts to mediate the impact of Protagoras on people for whom he cares. We have seen this occur in the *Protagoras* with Hippocrates, in the *Euthydemus* with Clinias, Ctesippus, and Crito, as well as here in the *Theaetetus*. Socrates thus depends on, but carefully mediates, the insights and techniques of the sophist Protagoras.

This much is strictly pedagogical. But what about Socrates' own philosophical enterprise and its relationship to Protagoras? Here, too, I see a strong connection. The challenge of philosophy is to gain insight into the nature and structure of Being. Such insight is not possible without noticing and accounting for the instability of phenomena in everyday experience. The kinds of puzzles, therefore, which Protagoras exposes are—whether spurious or not—extremely useful for philosophical investigation. If the puzzles are genuine, they need to be incorporated into our understanding of Being. If they are spurious, they need nevertheless to be explained; and someone in possession of wisdom should be *able* to explain them. They therefore serve as an invaluable test. On this reading, Socrates is genuinely interested in everything Protagoras has to say about the nature of Being, and he (Socrates) paves the way for texts such as Aristotle's *On Sophistical Refutations*, which likewise takes up the challenge of articulating precisely how sophistic arguments go wrong.

But this is not all. A final way in which Protagoras proves useful to the Socratic search for wisdom concerns the challenge of the moral life in the absence of an absolute conception of the good. Socrates and Protagoras are both, fascinatingly, moralists without a moral ground. They both regard man and the matter of human virtue as a central intellectual concern. And both see that the moral life must go on, and does go on, in the absence of a fixed "knowledge" of the good. But they do not respond identically to this challenge. Protagoras seems content to live life in the rough-and-tumble world of flux and relativity. He teaches students how to manipulate appearances in the service of things they presently desire. He teaches cities how to arrange themselves such that what appears "just" is advantageous rather than disadvantageous.[54] But he does not, as Socrates does, yearn ardently for something more. The Socratic response, which stands in sharp contrast to the Protagorean one, is to find the meaning of life in the search for clarity about the good. And it may well be that Socrates conceived this approach in dialectical reaction to the Protagorean approach, having been aware of its inadequacy.

That inadequacy in a nutshell reduces to the problem of human reason. Protagoras, for all his stunning intellectualism, is consigned to a life of irrationality inasmuch as his understanding of Being necessitates endless contradiction at the individual and social level. If individuals are indeed the measure of all things and if all things are constantly changing, then individuals (to the extent they can be said to "exist" at all) will inevitably exist as now this, now not-this. People and their communities will be characterized by contradictory impulses, desires, speeches, and actions. Protagoras' response to this problem was likely simple: he maintained that no real contradiction exists, because contradiction requires opposition in the same being at the same moment in the same way. But if all is flux, then *apparent* contradictions are in fact nothing but changes of condition.[55] But this response, for all its cleverness, does not really satisfy. It does not, most importantly, do justice to the feeling of embarrassment people have when they notice the contradictory ideas they possess. In other words, feeling embarrassed about self-contradiction is itself an intimation of permanence in the world of flux, and it is one of many such intimations that Socrates recognizes in himself and exploits in others as he engages his search for wisdom.[56]

Compared to Protagoras' response to the problem of the moral life in a world without absolute knowledge of the good, Socrates' response seems more rational not only because Socrates strives to avoid self-contradiction, but also because he never forsakes the architectonic role of the good in the structure of human thought and action. Human deliberations and action reveal themselves to be teleological in nature, in relation to various goods. And we proceed as if a final good animates our attachment to various particular goods. The problem is that we cannot say what that final good is, which means that all our deliberations and actions turn out to be at best conditionally good—conditional on their attunement with the true good we cannot describe. In such a condition as this, it is rational indeed to search as ardently as possible for that architectonic good on which all our actions depend for their goodness. And this is exactly what Socrates does. This entails bracketing off much of the activity that ordinarily comprises man's attempts to satisfy himself. But in the absence of knowledge concerning the ultimate value of such actions and satisfactions the thought of bracketing seems rational. It does not necessitate the negation or eschewal of the ordinary acts of human life, but it does entail a suspension of judgment about their ultimate worth.

This is not the place to go into any greater detail about the Socratic way of life. My point is a general one about the role of Protagoras, not a particular one about Socratic philosophy. The point is simply this: because Protagoras was, like Socrates, so keenly aware of the problem of relativity in human experience, including moral experience, he likely served a special role in helping Socrates to think through the options of how to live under such conditions. Their outlook was similar enough for some dialectical interchange to be worthwhile. There is no way to prove that Protagoras served as an important philosophical aid to Socrates' own thinking, but it is indeed possible to show that Plato incorporates Protagoras into the dialogues in such a way that he (Protagoras) can serve as such an aid for interlocutors and readers. Readers of the *Theaetetus* especially are invited to consider the problem of relativity as Socrates presents this through Protagoras' work. We are then invited to consider how Protagoras and Socrates respond differently to this problem in their own pedagogical and philosophical enterprises. And in making such comparisons, we are not only led to see the rationality of the Socratic response; we are, perhaps led to engage in philosophy itself. In fact, the act of differentiating Socrates from Protagoras comes so close to the search for wisdom itself that it blends into that search and, just possibly, becomes identical with it.

EIGHT

PLATO'S CRITIQUE OF THE SOPHISTS?

> The study of great philosophers is an education in concrete consciousness, but it can easily degenerate into a support for abstractions. . . . This is why Plato and many others wrote in a form resembling poetry in which all explicit generalizations are false and the real generalizations are left to the reader to make for himself on the basis of the experience provided by the book. Thus the books are not only educations in concreteness but provide powerful lessons in the deceptiveness of easy generalizations and, properly studied, liberate us from them.
>
> —Allan Bloom[1]

The previous chapters have examined Plato's concrete treatments of particular sophists. These have proven more complex and philosophically significant than commentators usually recognize, and the details of these accounts have consistently frustrated such easy generalizations as, for example, that Plato was "profoundly hostile" to the sophists or that he was "a declared foe" of all they stood for.[2] Plato appears, rather, to have gone to great lengths to show readers the deep affinities between sophistic and Socratic thought and to suggest that a thorough and serious engagement with the sophists is an excellent propaedeutic to philosophy. Plato does expose the defects of particular sophists. Yet such defects seem frequently idiosyncratic. They do not extend in a general way to every sophist. Indeed, Plato's portraits of the sophists vary so widely that it seems scarcely possible to speak of a Platonic critique of the sophists as a class.

However, Plato does not merely treat particular sophists, each with his own distinct strengths and weakness; he does also treat "the sophists" as a class in various dialogues. And these more generic accounts present something of a puzzle. For although the particular treatments seem by-and-large amicable in tone, the general treatments seems markedly more critical, disapproving, even dismissive. In fact, the general treatments appear so consistently negative that one may be tempted to conclude—as G.B. Kerferd did—that whatever positive indications one may find in particular dialogues about particular sophists, these are nothing compared to Plato's "outright condemnation" of the sophists in general.[3]

But is this the right conclusion to draw—the right way of understanding the disjunction between the rich particulars and the easy generalizations one finds in Plato? My argument here is that it is not. If we examine more closely the passages that purportedly represent "Plato's condemnation of the sophists," what we find are not Platonic criticisms per se, but rather the partial (that is to say, imperfect) assessments of various Platonic characters in diverse contexts, assessments that seem to be articulated for radically different purposes. That the generalizations about the sophists do not harmonize with the concrete particulars as Plato himself presents them is in keeping with the methodological insight expressed earlier by Bloom that Plato does not give his readers easy doctrines or generalizations. He offers, on the one hand, bountiful particulars with which one must labor in order to reap the harvest of insights these make possible, and, on the other hand, provocative but ultimately inadequate generalizations that beg questions and prompt deeper reflection. Plato thus constantly orients his readers first toward particulars and, from there, to the formulation of one's *own* generalizations. He does not direct readers to accept at face value such flawed accounts as he puts in the mouths of his own characters.[4]

In this chapter, I consider four such accounts of the sophists: those of Anytus speaking to Socrates in the *Meno*, Socrates speaking to Adeimantus in the *Republic*, Socrates speaking to Polus in the *Gorgias*, and the Eleatic Stranger speaking to Theaetetus in the *Sophist*. Although all these appear to stand as general critiques of the sophists, none is successful as such, nor, I argue, does Plato mean for us to accept them as such. These accounts are obviously defective both in their own terms and in light of what we know of the sophists from other dialogues. At the same time, however, I want to argue that these passages of general criticism have a broader scope than merely attempting to criticize the sophists. They also call into question the very lines of demarcation between such categories as "sophistry," "philosophy," and "good citizenship," thus leading inevitably to the possibility of self-reflection, whether one understands oneself to be a philosopher or merely a citizen. In other words, what is usually taken rather facilely to be "Plato's critique of the sophists" in fact cuts more deeply into common thinking and doing than readers may like to admit. Widely accepted and even cherished political, philosophical, and pedagogical practices are implicated in these accounts.

Before I begin, let me emphasize what I am not attempting in this chapter. It is not my intention to offer an exhaustive catalog of the various criticisms that Plato's Socrates levels against particular sophists. I am here interested only in those accounts that address the sophistic movement as a whole. Thus, many of the best known charges are not discussed here—for example, that the sophists were hairsplitters, or makers of big speeches, or practitioners of sham logic. The previous chapters have treated these charges well enough and demonstrated that while they do apply to particular sophists, they do not apply to sophistry as such. Nor do I address here a criticism, which does apply to the sophists as class, though it does not appear to be consistently made—that the practice of taking fees is somehow vicious or aberrant. I have written on this at length elsewhere and am convinced that despite the presence of this theme in several passages of Plato (and Xenophon) it does not constitute a severe criticism of the sophists.[5] Like other criticisms, though, it does tend to implicate more people than the sophists—including us moderns who accept a paycheck to teach young people and believe we can impart virtue. With this caveat in mind, I turn to the relevant passages.

Anytus

In Plato's *Meno*, the democratic politician Anytus makes a brief cameo appearance, just long enough for Socrates to question him about teachers of civic virtue: Does Anytus consider the sophists to be good teachers, able to impart to youths the wisdom and virtue by which households and cities are well managed? The very question sparks a furious reply: By Hercules, Socrates, watch what you are saying! The sophists are nothing but the ruin and corruption (*lōbē te kai diaphthora*) of all who associate with them, and they should be expelled from every city they enter (91c–92b). Anytus' view that the sophists are "corruptors of youth" was widely held among Athenians. Socrates refers to it at one point in the *Republic* as the view of "the many" (492a), and we recall that Aristophanes advanced this position to great comic effect in the *Clouds*. But does Plato also mean to endorse it, and does he intend for his readers to do so?[6]

This question can, I believe, be answered, but the answer is not simple. On the one hand, Plato gives readers ample reason to doubt, if not to reject outright, the testimony of Anytus concerning the sophists. Not only is Anytus one of the accusers who would eventually bring Socrates to trial on charges relating to sophistry, he is also someone who (as he concedes to Socrates) has never experienced the sophists in person; *nor needs to* in order to know who they are (92c). Socrates thus exposes Anytus' view for what it is, a mere prejudice. Moreover, in the *Republic* (492a–e), in a passage considered more closely below, Socrates explicitly counters the claim that the sophists are corruptors of youth, laying the blame for this instead on the Athenian people. Such indications as these support the conclusion that Plato (or at least Plato's Socrates) does not regard the sophists as corruptors, whatever else he might hold against them.[7]

But on the other hand, we know from the preceding chapters that the question cannot be so easily dismissed; for Plato shows in no uncertain terms that the danger of corruption by sophists is quite real. In the *Protagoras*, for example, Socrates rebukes the young man, Hippocrates, for his willingness to entrust his soul to a sophist without consulting with his family or friends. The sophists are like retailers of food for the soul, Socrates cautions: they may not know whether the wares they sell are genuinely good or bad, but they sell them nevertheless; and once one ingests them, as it were, there is no going back—the effect on the soul is immediate (313a–314b). Similarly in the *Euthydemus*, Plato indicates the danger of corruption by showing the effects that Euthydemus and Dionysodorus have on the young man Ctesippus, fanning the flames of his most violent passions and furnishing him with the tools to refute every claim one makes, whether true or false. Finally, in Book VII of the *Republic*, in the discussion of the curriculum for philosopher-kings, Socrates remarks on the severe harm that comes to students who are exposed to the art of sophistic-style refutation at too early an age (537e–539d): when they witness the refutation of conventional beliefs about what is just and fair, the beliefs instilled in them by parents and enshrined in the laws, they fall quickly into a profound nihilism (literally, believing *nothing* of what they formerly believed, *to mēden hēgeisthai hōnper proteron*). They arrive, then, at the view that what the law says is no more fair than foul. And eventually they are filled with lawlessness (*paranomias*) and are ruined. Such is the danger stemming from sophistic education.[8] In light of passages such as these, the view expressed by Anytus in the *Meno* seems suddenly more plausible. On the Platonic evidence itself, the sophists appear as corruptors of youth.

And yet it is a position between these two extremes, which, I believe, Plato's dialogues prompt readers ultimately to take—that the sophists were and were not corruptors of youth, depending on the context. Such a position is required for two reasons. First, the heterogeneity among the sophists themselves: figures like Hippias and Prodicus stand at a distant remove from figures like Euthydemus and Dionysodorus on the point of corruption; they were neither experts at contradiction nor prone to challenge conventional moral views, at least not as Plato portrays them. Thus to characterize all sophists equally or essentially as corruptors of youth would be to paint with too broad a brush. Second, the vantage point from which one defines corruption matters as well, for what looks like corruption from a popular or civic point of view may not be corruption at all from a philosophical point of view, and vice versa. Thus, it becomes necessary to ask whether sophistry corrupts *philosophy*, not merely whether it corrupts popular morality. And the answer is, again, yes and no. Socratic philosophy, as we have seen, tends to incorporate sophistic techniques into its own processes. The techniques of *antilogikē*, *diairesis*, revisionist myth-making, and eristic, for example, play essential roles in what Socrates does in his own conversations with interlocutors. In this sense, the sophists appear not as corruptors but as potential resources for philosophy itself. On the other hand, the sophists may yet be corruptors from Socrates' point of view insofar as their pedagogical practices are not tempered by the humility that comes from awareness of one's ignorance or by the virtues of love and friendship that animate Socrates' own conversations. The sophists appear consistently motivated by the desire to compete, or to "protect friends and harm enemies," or to win honor, and so on. These are indeed corrupting influences from the Socratic point of view, but they are, significantly, perfectly in step with Greek popular morality.

All in all, then, some sophists may have had a corrupting influence, whether viewed from the perspective of civic life or from that of philosophy, but others did not, or not in every respect. In other words, Plato does not offer a uniform view. One thing that is uniform, however, is Plato's attitude toward the mentality of characters like Anytus, who would expel the sophists from every city and have nothing more to do with them. Theirs is the opposite of a philosophical attitude, which requires engaging the sophists vigorously but cautiously as a way of both advancing and critically clarifying the pursuit of wisdom.

Socrates and Adeimantus

Another passage in which the sophists come in for general criticism occurs in Book VI of the *Republic* (492a ff.). There Socrates asks Adeimantus whether he, too, believes, as do the many, "that certain young men are corrupted by sophists . . . to any extent worth mentioning?"[9] Socrates, for his part, does not believe so, or suggests he does not. And he urges Adeimantus to adopt another opinion (*doxatō* in the imperative), namely, that each sophist teaches nothing but the convictions of the many (*ta tōn pollōn dogmata*), which arise when citizens gather together in assemblies or courts or any other public forum (492b–493a). The so-called wisdom of the sophists is thus merely conventional morality. As Socrates explains:

> It is just like the case of a man who learns by heart the angers and desires of a great, strong beast he is rearing, how it should be approached and how . . . it becomes most gentle and, particularly, under what conditions it is accustomed to utter its several sounds, and, in turn, what sort of sounds uttered by another make it tame or angry. When he has learned all this from associating and spending time with the beast, he calls it wisdom [*sophian*] and, organizing it into an art [*technēn*], turns to teaching. Knowing nothing in truth about which of these convictions and desires is noble or base, or good, or evil, or just, or unjust, he applies all the names following the great animal's

> opinions—calling what delights it good and what vexes it bad. He has no other account [*logon*] about them. . . . (493a–c)

This is one of the best known descriptions of the sophists in Plato. However, it is in Socrates' own words only an opinion or supposition he urges upon Adeimantus, not a set of facts to be accepted without question.[10] As such, it involves three rather exaggerated claims: (1) that the sophists' power to corrupt is insignificant; (2) that their "wisdom" entails nothing more than the convictions of the many; and (3) that they can offer no truthful *logos* about the just, beautiful, and good. That these claims are all, to a certain extent, false, can be easily shown. But they also, I argue, contain a degree of truth, which, when considered carefully, has the effect of exposing the "sophistry" in everyday moral and political life. The account is thus exaggerated, but enlightening.

The falseness of the claims is revealed, again, by Plato's own presentations of the particular sophists. We have just seen, for instance, how the *Protagoras*, the *Euthydemus* and even the *Republic* itself (Book VII) reveal a Socrates who is much concerned about the potential corruption stemming from sophistic teachings. Socrates does not regard their corruptive powers as insignificant. Nor can we accede to the second claim that the sum and substance of sophistic education involves nothing beyond the "convictions of the many," when we have observed at numerous points in the preceding chapters the degree to which the sophists challenged and even undermined traditional views through their methods and doctrines. Ought we, then, to accept the third claim, that the sophists could adduce no true logos about the just, the beautiful, and the good beyond what the average Athenian might supply? This is perhaps the most plausible of the criticisms, if by logos we are to understand a Socratic-style account that admits no exception. On this plane, the sophists were likely no better equipped than anyone else to meet Socrates' demands. However, this still seems to sell the sophists short. For was it not Prodicus who argued so cogently in his "Choice of Hercules" that the good life, the life of virtue, is ultimately more pleasant than the life of vice, thus anticipating one of the arguments in Book IX of the *Republic*? And was it not Protagoras who, in the dialogue bearing his name, made the very Socratic observation that many things commonly thought to be "good" can be shown to be bad as soon as they are viewed in a different connection or in relation to different people (333e–334c, cf. *Euthyd.* 281d–282e)? If the sophists were unable to adduce a Socratic definition of the noble or the good, they certainly deepened the way people understood these concepts.

That Socrates here downplays the importance of the sophists is thus a given. But there is also something behind this distortion—an insight or set of insights it facilitates. This comes to light if one notices that the consistent effect of the distortion is to blur or even collapse the line of demarcation between sophistic and *civic* education. The citizens, Socrates argues, are the biggest sophists of all (*megistous sophistas*, 492a8–b1); while the individual, professional sophists are at root nothing but civic educators. This is, to be sure, a shocking equation to make. For it flies directly in the face of the view articulated by Anytus and embraced by "the many," the Athenian citizens themselves. But by deliberately questioning the line between sophistic and civic education, Plato in effect compels readers to consider the mutual entailment of these forces—their similarity to and dependence on each other.

The relationship of dependence is perhaps best revealed in the laws of supply and demand, which animate the sophists' transactions. The sophists come to the city in order to make money; and students seek the sophists out in order to acquire a certain set of skills. If the sophists did not supply these skills, they would not make money (consider *Soph.* 232d and *Prt.* 312d in this light). Nor need anyone wonder what these students sought. They sought the powers of speaking persuasively and thinking strategically, of influencing people's judgments and effecting political outcomes—powers that were key to success in every aspect of democratic and commercial life. Yet in order to teach these skills the sophists needed to know thoroughly the sentiments of the people. They needed to become psychologists and sociologists in a sense, directing their attention to popular sensibilities and reactions at the empirical level. Indeed, if their teachings appeared to stray too far from this all-important touchstone, the sophists might find themselves without customers or, worse, expelled from the city.[11] Thus, Socrates' account in the *Republic* suggests that the sophists are not at bottom *free* in the sense that Socrates is free. They are repeatedly compelled as if by necessity (*anangkē*, *Rep.* 492d1, 493c5), to return to the views of the many for the raw material of their art.

This is one insight that Socrates' blurring of the line between sophistry and the city makes possible: readers see something of the constraints on sophistry. But we also learn something about the "sophistry" of the city. The people and their leaders are described as the "biggest sophists" not only because they dictate the terms of the sophists' art, but also because they are themselves the most powerful and effective educators. Their collective outlook, their loves and hates, the cadences of their praise and blame become the air that young people breathe. Youths are thus, in effect, indoctrinated into popular culture and cannot escape its grip. Indeed, for those who by some miraculous occurrence manage to see beyond popular sentiment (the nonconformists, dissidents, criminals, and the like), there is punishment in the form of dishonor, fines, and even death (*Rep.* 492d). The city, then, plays the role of sophist *par excellence* in relation to its own youth; it educates in "virtue," as it conceives this, but it does so with a degree of hegemony and ferocity unparalleled by any professional sophist.

Finally, there is an epistemological connection to observe between sophistic and civic education. That the passage presently under consideration occurs in Book VI of the *Republic*, one of the more epistemological books, facilitates this insight. From the point of view of Socratic philosophizing—which is to say, from the point of view of inquiring into the form or being of things—the moral teachings of the sophists and the city seem equally dogmatic. For sophists and citizens alike are content to accept mere opinions (*dogmata*, 493a8) about the most serious questions of human life. Although it is true that the sophists frequently raised doubts and attempted to dislodge dogmas, their powers of dissolvent criticism could not, it seems, extend to the very roots of ethical and political action. There is no evidence in Plato (or elsewhere, as far as I am aware) that the sophists ever posed the sorts of questions Socrates posed about fundamental moral concepts—what *is* the just, the good, and the noble?—thus calling into question the conventional attachment to such goods as wealth, honor, and power. Rather, they appear to have operated entirely within these conventional parameters and expected their students to do the same. In this sense, the sophists and the city are as one compared to philosophy, which stands radically apart, questioning and doubting the most fundamental starting points of human action.

What readers may conclude, then, is that Socrates' critique of sophistry in Book VI, while exaggerated in serious ways, is yet penetrating in others. And it reveals connections between sophistry and the city that might otherwise remain obscure. And yet to see this is also, perhaps, to get more than one bargains for. It is not possible, I would argue, to appreciate the broader implications of the passage just examined without realizing that we modern citizens, too, as participants in civic life and civic education, are very much implicated in the sophistic endeavor. Socrates' critique of the sophists becomes, in other words, an invitation to self-reflection.

Socrates and Polus

Having examined Plato's handling of the sophists in the *Meno* and *Republic*, I turn now to another well-known account. In Plato's *Gorgias* (463a–466a), Socrates gives voice to an appraisal of the sophists similar to that found in the *Republic*, but more developed and more critical. The context is an investigation of the nature of rhetoric. Socrates' interlocutor Polus suffers from a lust for rhetoric; he wants only to praise it for all its supposed powers. Socrates attempts to raise the philosophically prior question of *what* rhetoric is, but this fails to diminish Polus' lust. Thus, Socrates tries a bolder approach: he denounces the art of rhetoric by claiming that it is not art at all, just a pseudo-art or knack, and also by grouping it with sophistry (see Figure 8.1).[12]

Figure 8.1. Rhetoric and Sophistry in the *Gorgias*

		ART	NONART
SOUL	*Politics*	Legislative	Sophistry
		Justice	Rhetoric
BODY	*Care of Body*	Gymnastic	Cosmetic
		Medicine	Cookery
		Good Condition	**Seemingly Good Condition**

Just as there is a division between the body and the soul, Socrates explains, so there is a division among arts, such that one art cares for the body and another, politics (*politikē*), cares for the soul.[13] Moreover, each of these arts can be divided in two: the art of gymnastic keeps the body healthy, while the art of medicine attends to any physical problems that may arise. Analogously for the soul: the art of legislation (*nomothetikē*) keeps the soul well maintained, while the art of justice (*dikaiosunē, dikastikē,* cf. 520b) addresses any problems that arise. Thus, there are four genuine arts that "take care" of a person, always in accordance with what is best.

However, right alongside these arts appear four phantoms or pseudo-arts, which pretend to know what is best, but in fact aim only at pleasure. Next to gymnastic stands the practice of cosmetic, which makes the body appear healthier than it really is. Next to medicine (which for the Greeks often involved dietary remedies) is the practice of cookery, which makes foods taste better than they really are. And so, too, in the soul: next to the legislative art appears sophistry, and next to justice appears rhetoric. Socrates does not gloss the specific work that sophistry and rhetoric perform, but he does underscore the similarity between these two pseudo-arts and those of cosmetic and cookery, for they all guess at the pleasant without knowing what is best. They are thus "evildoing, deceitful, ignoble and unfree" (465b).[14] More generally, they are all forms of flattery (*hē kolakeutikē*, 464c), which is to say, they belong to a soul terribly clever by nature at associating with human beings, but not in possession of an art (463a–b).

This well-known passage from the *Gorgias* offers an apparently devastating appraisal of sophistry, ancillary though it is to Socrates' primary purpose of ridiculing rhetoric. As in the *Republic*, sophistry is here designated as lacking knowledge of the specific goods it extols. However, the criticism now runs deeper. Because it lacks knowledge, it is not really an art at all, and because it deliberately misleads people into accepting pleasure in place of what is genuinely good, it is wicked and shameful.

Yet, once again, readers might ask whether this account should be taken at face value as "Plato's critique of the sophists."[15] That it should not is revealed by the same kinds of obstacles encountered in connection with the passage from the *Republic*. In the first place, Plato's own portraits of the individual sophists in other dialogues do not generally support the claim that they were deliberate deceivers or evildoers. We may want to make an exception here for Euthydemus and Dionysodorus. But on the whole, Plato presents the sophists as more or less earnest educators, committed to the value of, indeed the *good* of, the education they had to offer, even if some irony and even esotericism were required when speaking of their education in public, as with the case of Protagoras. No matter how philosophically naive the sophists may have appeared from the Socratic point of view, no matter how inadequate their conceptions of the good may have been, they were not, on Plato's account, deliberately duping people into accepting false goods as true ones.

The second reason not to accept this account without question relates to the porousness and ultimate instability of its own lines of demarcation. That the line between sophistry and rhetoric is not as stable as Socrates here suggests has been frequently discussed.[16] Socrates himself acknowledges this when he says near the end of his account that although sophists and rhetoricians are distinct by nature, they seem in practice to be "mixed together in the same place and about the same things" (465c, cf. 520a–b). In other words, the sophists are as likely to teach the art of forensic rhetoric as the rhetoricians are apt to make speeches about policy and law. Socrates does not seem to have captured the genuine point of difference between them. But this is not the only problematic division. Even more doubtful is the fundamental structural divide between art and nonart as this pertains to the soul. With respect to the body there are, to be sure, genuine arts of medicine and gymnastic. And one can perhaps allow that by comparison to these, the practices of cookery and cosmetic appear somehow less noble, perhaps even deceitful. But when we turn to the soul, we are struck by the problem of identifying the practitioners of the purportedly genuine arts. Who are the real experts in "legislation" and "justice," who meet Socrates' strict criteria of art and supply the comparison by which the sophists and rhetoricians appear less noble?

The answer would seem to be, simply, statesmen and judges. (The idea that the sophists were nothing but pseudo-statesmen would certainly have resonated with Plato's contemporaries.[17]) But as the conversation in the *Gorgias* unfolds, it becomes clear that this is not what Socrates has in mind. Rather, Socrates asserts, *no statesman* either in Athens' past or in her present has ever practiced the genuine art of statecraft, thereby improving the condition of the Athenian people. To a man, statesmen have consistently rendered the Athenian people worse off than they were before (503c–d, 515c–517c). The passages in which Socrates makes this claim are well known, but their implications have not always been appreciated. Socrates' critique of Athenian statesmen effectively obliterates the distinction between statesmanship and sophistry established earlier in the dialogue. Once again, Socrates' supposed criticism of the sophists turns out to be less restricted than it initially appears. As far as art (*technē*) is concerned, there is no difference whatever, Socrates suggests, between the most widely celebrated statesmen of Athens and the sophists. This conclusion is shocking, but it is also inescapable as the conversation in the *Gorgias* proceeds past the initial charting out of categories.

Is there, then, no distinction at all to be drawn between genuine politikē (care of the soul) and sham politikē in the *Gorgias*? Perhaps Socrates' distinction is meant finally to capture the difference not between the sophists and Athenian statesmen, but between the sophists and Socrates himself. This possibility is lent some support by Socrates' arresting statement near the end of the dialogue that he alone (or virtually alone, "so as not to say myself alone") puts his hand to the true political art, practicing politics with a view not to pleasure, but to what is best (521d). Socrates, in other words, is the only true statesman. Does this not rescue something of the division that Socrates draws for Polus? It seems to. However, it does so at the cost either of relaxing the criteria for genuine *technai*, which Socrates earlier established, or else exaggerating what we usually assume to be the limits of Socratic knowledge. If an art is to be genuine, according to Socrates, it must have fixed rules; it must be able to give an account of itself; and it must, above all, be grounded in a knowledge or science of the subject at hand; but that Socrates himself possesses no such science of the good for the soul or the city is a constant refrain in the dialogues.[18] At best, we might say, Socrates *aims* at the good and never knowingly trades what is right for mere pleasure. But this is a far cry from an "art of politics," as this phrase is used in the *Gorgias*.

Socrates' distinction between legislation and sophistry—between genuine and sham arts of the soul—thus boils down in the end to a distinction between all ethics and politics as it is conventionally practiced, on the one hand, and the Socratic *ideal* of ethical knowledge, on the other; or if we prefer, between the presumed knowledge of all human action, on the one hand, and the awareness of ignorance characteristic of Socrates, on the other. In any event, the supposedly devastating critique of sophistry in the *Gorgias* is neither as devastating nor as restricted to sophistry as it initially seems. My point here is not to deny the fecundity of Plato's distinction between the pursuit of pleasure and that of truth as this appears in the *Gorgias*. This distinction is certainly crucial. My point is rather to question whether it serves as an adequate vehicle for condemning sophistry. I would argue that it does not; and Plato shows this by showing that it does not isolate the sophists. And yet this leads now to the questions: What is it, then, that makes sophistry distinct? And is there anywhere that Plato criticizes sophistry as such—sophistry *and only sophistry*? So far, we have seen nothing that stands as a straightforward "Platonic critique of sophistry."[19]

The Eleatic Stranger and Theaetetus

If there is one place more than any other where Plato is thought to present his own fully developed view of sophistry, it is in the dialogue entitled (appropriately enough) the *Sophist*. Here one is supposed to find Plato's "outright condemnation" of sophistry as an enterprise which, *inter alia*, concerns itself with "semblances" rather than truth.[20] In the remainder of this chapter, however, I argue that nothing as simple as outright condemnation can be the purpose behind Plato's *Sophist*. As with the texts discussed earlier, this dialogue generates more questions than it answers through the disjunction between the generalizations it offers and the particulars it portrays. Only this time the questions center not on the relationship of sophistry to the city, or to statesmanship, but on its relationship to *philosophy*.

The complications commence immediately with the dialogue's opening lines, where Socrates (who plays only a minor role in the dialogue) is introduced to the chief speaker, a Stranger from the city of Elea. This mysterious figure is described by the mathematician, Theodorus, as "very much a philosopher" and an associate of the schools of Parmenides and Zeno.[21] Yet his status qua philosopher (and thus as a possible mouthpiece for Plato's views) is shown to be far less than certain.[22] We know from the *Theaetetus*, a dialogue set one day prior to the present conversation, that Theodorus is no qualified judge of what philosophy is or is not. Moreover, Socrates' response to Theodorus here in the *Sophist* also raises doubts:

> This genus [i.e., that of philosophers] is scarcely much easier to discern than that of a god. For on account of the ignorance of everyone else, these men—those who not in a fabricated way but in their *being* are philosophers—certainly show up in all sorts of apparitions and haunt cities, looking down from on high on thc lifc of those below. And in the opinion of some they are worth nothing and of some everything, and at times they take on the apparitions of statesmen, and at times of sophists, and there are times when they might give some the impression that they are altogether crazy. (216c–d)

Thus Socrates implicitly calls into question the status of the Stranger whose understanding of sophistry this dialogue presents. Who is this Stranger? And if he is not a philosopher, what is he?

If the Stranger's very status as a philosopher is problematic for the attempt to identify his views with those of Plato, so, too, is the question he attempts to answer and the way he goes about answering it. The question is not "what is a sophist?" or even "what, to the Stranger, is a sophist?" but rather whether, and how, those in the Stranger's own *region* (*hoi peri ton ekei topon*) distinguish among sophists, statesmen, and philosophers.[23] According to the Stranger, those in his region do regard these as three separate things; and yet "it is no small or easy task," he continues, "to distinguish with clarity whatever they severally are" (217b). At this point Theodorus informs Socrates that the Stranger "has heard" and "has not forgotten" a full account of this matter from someone else, but has been reticent to disclose it—at least to Theodorus. When Socrates, in turn, presses for the account, the Stranger agrees to supply it, but not as a simple speech; he feels a certain unease or shame (*aidōs tis*), he says, about lecturing *ex cathedra* to such new acquaintances. The Stranger thus proceeds by a method of question-and-answer, and takes as his interlocutor the precocious Theaetetus, who is supposed to be tractable, but nevertheless affects the course of the conversation through the answers he gives.[24] All of this, then, complicates the question of *whose* view of the sophists Plato presents in this dialogue. Is it Plato's view, or that of the Stranger, or that of some unknown teacher whose account the Stranger recalls? Or is it, rather, an impromptu account, conditioned in part by what the Stranger "has heard" and in part by the present audience and interlocutor? We do not know, and indeed Plato seems deliberately to place obstacles in the way of speculation.

Finally, as far as preliminary matters go, the Stranger's unique method of division or diairesis also frustrates the attempt to attribute his views simply to Plato. This method, which differs sharply from the procedure Socrates employed only a day earlier with Theaetetus, is illustrated in the Stranger's sample-definition of an angler (219a–221c). He begins by asking Theaetetus whether an angler is in possession of a technē. On the assumption that he is, the two proceed in the manner of biologists or genealogists, treating technē as a sort of genus in which the angler (and later the sophist) must appear.[25] Accordingly, they subdivide the arts into smaller and smaller branches until they finally pinpoint the angler's specific qualities (see Figure 8.2). All technai are first divided into a productive (*poiētikē*) and acquisitive (*ktētikē*) branch, the anger belonging clearly to the latter. The acquisitive technai are then divided into those of exchange and of conquest; conquest is divided into open fighting and stealthy fighting (hunting); hunting into its focus on lifeless and living prey; and so on, until at last the anger (and only the angler) can be defined by his unique way of pulling fish up out of the water with a barbed hook.

Although the Stranger's elaborate method is not entirely without precedent in Plato's dialogues,[26] it differs from the usual Socratic procedure in at least three crucial respects. (1) Its general motion is from genus to differentia rather than vice versa. That is to say, it reasons downward in the direction of multiplicity, not upward to unity. (2) It does not examine or refute the answers the interlocutor gives. It is thus static or dogmatic with respect to its own unfolding.[27] Or if this is too strong, one might say it involves an extremely gentle form of refutation, which, unlike Socratic refutation, operates always implicitly, never explicitly.[28] And (3) the Stranger's method strives to be "value free" in a way not unlike contemporary social science. Its business is to separate "like from like" *without considering the good or bad* in the objects it examines (227a–c).

Because the Stranger's method ultimately fails (as I demonstrate) to offer a successful account of sophistry—one that stays true to its value-free ideals and captures *all* the sophists while, at the same time, exempting Socrates and the Stranger himself from the charge of sophistry—it is doubtful whether Plato intends for us simply to admire it. And if this is doubtful, doubtful, too, is whether we should interpret this dialogue as offering anything like "Plato's critique of the sophists." It turns out to be as much a critique (or a throwing into question) of philosophy in its various appearances as it is a critique of the sophists. We now examine the basic contours of the Stranger's account.

The Stranger and Theaetetus initially consider six (or at least six[29]) different appearances of the sophist by considering a number of genetic descents. As he first comes to light, he appears as a distant cousin of the angler, practicing an acquisitive art that hunts living animals. Where the angler sought his prey in water, however, the sophist seeks his prey on land. More precisely, he seeks young men of wealth and rank, and by persuasion undertakes to educate them privately in opinions about aretē for a fee (221c–223b). This seems a plausible (though not exhaustive) account of the sophists as we actually encounter them in Plato's dialogues.[30] But it leads to interpretive difficulties. First, it is noteworthy how significantly this account diverges from the description of sophistry in the *Gorgias*. Now the sophists are credited explicitly with a technē; moreover, their audience is always private, never public (the *Gorgias* was ambiguous on this point); and their art is now, in a final dramatic move, distinguished sharply from flattery (223a). That this does not harmonize in any respect with the account in the *Gorgias* alerts us to the hazards of attributing views too hastily to Plato. Another problem concerns Socrates, who is evidently barely distinguishable from the sophists according to this account. This is suggested by the reference at 222e to a form of "erotic art" (*erōtikēs technēs*, see Figure 8.2), which differs from sophistry only in operating without pay. In other words, Socrates, too, turns out to be a member of the sophists' family, a "private hunter" employing persuasion in pursuit of youths.[31] This issue of Socrates' proximity to (and even his possible identity with) the sophists becomes from here forward a major theme of the *Sophist*.

The Stranger now informs Theaetetus that the art they are seeking is quite motley and that it appears also in another genus (*genos*, 223c). Sophist II—as we might call him for exposition's sake—thus comes to light as a practitioner not of conquest (the generic art under which Sophist I appeared), but of "exchange," its neighboring art. Sophist II sells a kind of "food for the soul" (223e–224a, cf. *Prt.* 313c–314b) in the form of teachings (*mathēmata*) about aretē, and as the Stranger initially describes him, his teachings are not his own but are acquired from others, as he travels from city to city. Sophist II is a kind of "merchant" of knowledge of virtue. But no sooner is he defined than

Figure 8.2. First Five Sophistic Appearances in the *Sophist*

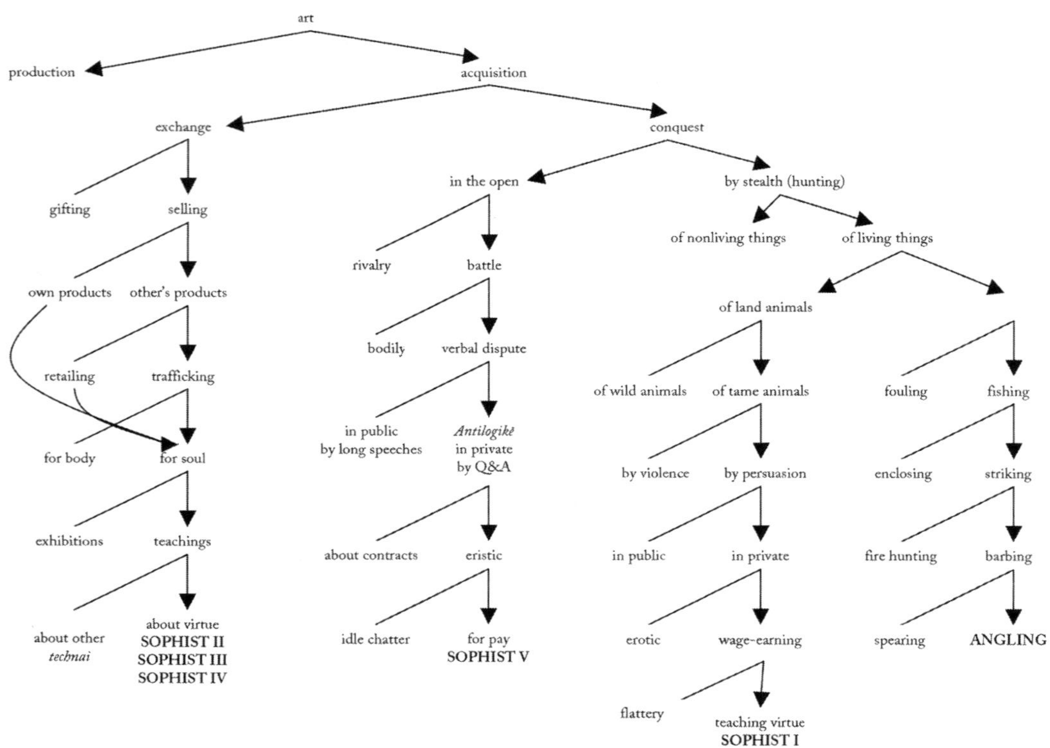

a number of other closely related sophistic types also appear: Sophist III is like Sophist II, except that he settles down in only one city to sell his wares; and Sophist IV sells wares of his own design as well as those he acquires from others (224d–e). At this point the complexity of the sophists' art seems to overwhelm the Stranger's own art of division. There are evidently more sophistic types lurking in the present genus than the Stranger and Theaetetus can count.[32] Nor is it clear that all the Stranger's divisions are sound. For example, the sharp division between sophistry and the art of display (*epideiktikē*, 224b5) seems dubious in the extreme given the sophists' common practice of delivering *epideixeis*. And a final division between (a) the sophist, who sells knowledge of aretē, and (b) the technē-seller who sells knowledge of all remaining arts, certainly fails to address the claim made by some sophists that their art entails expertise in all other arts.[33] This is a problem which the Stranger must recognize, since he cites the difficulty later in the dialogue (232d–e) and attempts to remedy it through his discussion of "semblances" in his final determination of the sophist. Yet it essentially discredits the present cluster of accounts.

As if to compound these difficulties, the Stranger next leads Theaetetus to another account of the sophist within the art of conquest, the original genus under which both the angler and Sophist I were found. The distinctive feature of this new appearance, Sophist V, is his "agonistic" quality of open (as opposed to stealth) fighting.[34] He employs an art called *contradiction* (*antilogikon*), which proceeds by question-and-answer in private conversation More specifically, he uses the technique of "eristic" in disputes about justice itself, injustice, and *everything else*," and makes money from this enterprise (225a–226a). What emerges at this point in the discussion is, no doubt, the Euthydemus-type of sophist with his roots in Protagorean *antilogikē* . But, once again, aspects of the account lead to difficulties. One of the crucial distinctions along the way to Sophist V involves rending the art of controversy in two, producing one art that practices a clash of long speeches against long speeches on matters of justice and injustice in public; and another that practices private contradiction by question-and-answer. It is only the latter that leads eventually to Sophist V, while the former is treated not as sophistry but as something else: "forensic." Yet we know from the case of Hippias, for example, that not all sophists were skilled at eristic; Hippias in fact despised eristic and commended long forensic speeches.[35] Nor is Prodicus well-captured by this fifth determination, since he was not known for refutation. We know too that all sophists, including Euthydemus and Dionysodorus (the eristics par excellence), taught the art of crafting long, forensic speeches in addition to their other teachings.[36] The division between forensic and sophistry thus seems forced. Indeed, it collapses in light of the particulars presented in this and other dialogues. In any event, by excluding sophists like Hippias and Prodicus from its domain, "Sophist V" does not capture "sophistry" as such, but only one of its aspects. This, again, is a problem which the Stranger must recognize (see 332a), but whether his final account can effectively remove it remains to be seen.

Another problem with the Stranger's path to Sophist V is that it once again nearly—indeed too nearly—identifies Socrates with the sophists. Only in the very last division does the Stranger distinguish between two types of eristic art—one that makes money (this is the sophist), and another that does not and, in fact, "neglects its own affairs" for the sheer enjoyment of argument, even when many who hear it find no pleasure in it at all (225d). This is redolent of the Socrates of Plato's *Apology* (23b–d, 30b–c). And, in fact, the Stranger seems to be homing in precisely on Socrates as the dialogue proceeds. For, although in the first determination, an image of Socrates appeared only two steps away from the sophist, here in the fifth determination the image appears only one step away. If the dialogue proceeds any further, we might suppose, Socrates will become one with the sophist.

In fact, the sixth and penultimate attempt at definition brings the problem of Socrates to a head. Reiterating his claim that the sophist is a motley and elusive kind of beast, the Stranger now proposes to pursue him by another route (226a–b). He begins by drawing Theaetetus' attention to a general category of arts called "discrimination" (*diakritikē*), which divide or separate things (see Figure 8.3). The Stranger does not make clear how, if at all, this new beginning relates to the five preceding accounts, but readers are aware that the Stranger himself practices some art of division; so this promises to be a telling account. Their next step is to divide the art in two, revealing one form that "separates like from like" and another that "separates better from worse." The first, evidently the Stranger's own art, does not receive a name; but the second is called *purification* (*katharmos*) and begins already to remind one of Socrates (cf. *Phaedo*, 67c–d). But before the Stranger proceeds any further, he offers a brief comment on his own method (which, again, can only be the unnamed art), so as to distinguish it more sharply from "purification." It is here (227a–c) that he emphasizes the value-neutrality of his logos, which attempts to discern what is and is not kindred in all arts. It is necessary, he explains, to treat the art of generalship and that of lice-killing as "equivalent" (*ex isou*) in value, as one maps out their relationship to one another. No art should be viewed as "better" or "worse" than another.

Here, it would seem, is a crucial weakness in the Stranger's method. Indeed, if there is one reason why he and Theaetetus have been so far unable to isolate the sophist without, at the same time, capturing Socrates, it must relate to this refusal to view beings through the lens of value. Plato shows us, in other words, not only *that* the Stranger has failed so far to isolate the sophist, but also (at least in part) why he has failed.

This much on the method of separating like from like. Now the Stranger and Theaetetus close in on Sophist VI, racing down the path of purification until at last they reveal an art that endeavors to purify the soul (as opposed to the body) by removing vice and leaving virtue. This it does by addressing people's conceit, that is, by showing interlocutors that they do not know what they suppose they know. The famous passage on the practitioners of *elenchus*, which follows has been

Figure 8.3. Sixth Sophistic Appearance in the *Sophist*

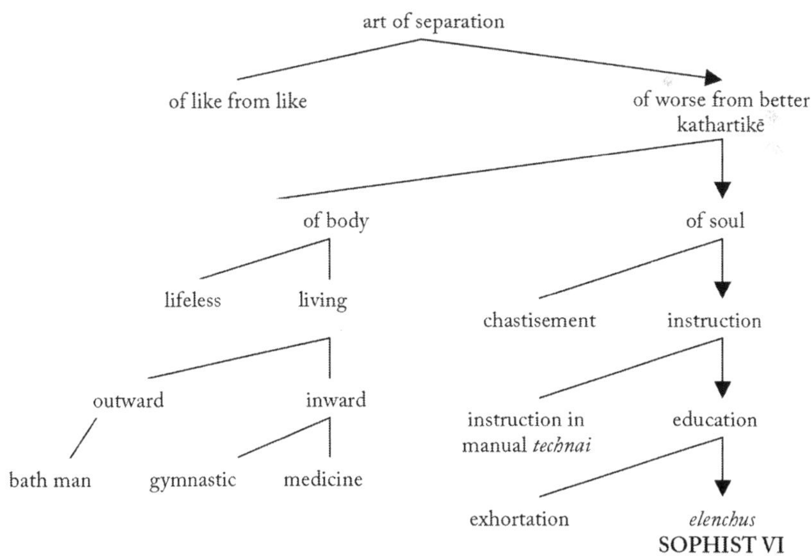

almost universally taken to be a description of Socrates, or at least to include him in its scope.[37]

> They question a man's words, when he thinks he is saying something and is really saying nothing. And because those questioned wander, they examine their opinions with ease, and once they bring the opinions together into the same place by their speeches, they put them side by side, and in so doing, show that the opinions are simultaneously contrary to themselves about the same things in regard to the same things in the same respects. . . . The reason, my dear boy, is that those who purify them hold the view—just as physicians of bodies have held the view that a body would be incapable of deriving any advantage from the sustenance to be applied before one casts out the internal impediments to it—so with the soul, it will not have the benefit of the teachings to be applied before one puts, by way of refutation [*elenchōn*], the one being refuted into a state of shame, takes out the opinions that are impediments to the teachings, and shows him forth purified [*katharon*] and believing he knows just the things he does know and no more. (230b–d)[38]

If commentators are right to see in this passage a reference to Socratic elenchus, then the Stranger has now perfectly identified Socrates with the sophists. For this is Sophist VI, who uses elenchus, that is, refutation, to purify interlocutors of their inconsistent beliefs. Thus, it emerges that despite the Stranger's awesome powers of discrimination, he either does not or cannot distinguish between Socrates and the sophists.[39]

And yet, it is precisely at this point that the Stranger is compelled to acknowledge the violence caused by his methodological imperative of value-neutrality. For he clearly perceives value in the practice of elenctic catharsis practiced by Socrates. It is the "greatest of all purifications," he tells Theaetetus, and whoever has not undergone it is, *a fortiori*, impure, uneducated, and ugly, 230e). These are not value-free terms. Moreover, the Stranger balks at referring to the practitioners of this art as "sophists," for fear of ascribing to sophists "too great an honor" (231a; compare the Stranger's earlier remark at 227b about the "equal honor" accorded to all arts). Readers can feel the strain on the Stranger's method, too, when he suggests to Theaetetus that the elenctic types perhaps relate to the other sophists as "a wolf to a dog" or "the most savage to the most tame" (231a). He cannot bring himself to put Socrates and the sophists on the same plane. And, although he does in the end arrive at a compromise of sorts by designating the present class as "sophistics of *noble* descent" (*hē genei gennaia sophistikē*), we observe that the use of the word "noble" itself violates the Stranger's principle of neutrality. Plato, thus, allows readers to see that a system of classification barred from referring to values is not only inadequate but finally impossible. The Stranger offers no reasonable way (and certainly not a Platonic way) of accounting for his own recognition of the uniqueness of Socrates.

Nor do the problems with the method stop there. The Stranger and Theaetetus have still failed—at least thus far—to offer an adequate account of the sophists. They have now considered six different accounts. The problem is thus not a lack of definitions, but an overabundance of them. Too many arts and activities have been described under one indeterminate name, "sophist," thus rendering the term equivocal and uncertain. Recognizing this difficulty, the Stranger and Theaetetus now attempt one final account of the sophist, hoping, as they set out, to discover some single, unifying trait that might be definitive (see Figure 8.4).

At the Stranger's urging, the trait they home in on is the practice of contradiction-making: "we surely said that he was a contradictor (*antilogikon*)," recalls the Stranger, "and that he proved also to be a teacher of this to others" (232b). "Yes," says Theaetetus. But on what subject, asks the Stranger, does the sophist promise to turn out contradictors? Do they not address *every* subject from invisible divine things, to all that is visible in the sky and on earth, to laws, to policies, and to all of the technai? How can this be possible, the Stranger wonders; for surely a man cannot know everything; and yet how can a man who does not *know* a subject successfully controvert one who does? Somehow the sophists must merely "appear to be knowledgeable on those very things about which they contradict others" (233c).[40] This insight leads in turn to a lengthy and dense digression on the problem of being and not-being, or, more precisely, on how a person can possibly speak what *is not*. As many have pointed out, this problem had a history. The Stranger in effect wrestles here with a defect in Parmenidean thought (cf. 216a).[41] Parmenides had argued that thinking and being are one, and that therefore what is not cannot be spoken. But if this is true, there can be no way of distinguishing between sophists and philosophers by considering the truth of their speech. Everything that is spoken becomes, in some sense, true. Yet this conclusion is repugnant to the Stranger. Thus, he and Theaetetus must find some way of accounting for the possibility of false speech. One is tempted to linger over this fascinating and rich section of the dialogue. It is indeed the part that has received the most attention from commentators. But for present purposes, it is more important to see how the account of Sophist VI unfolds and to return to the basic question of whether the Stranger offers an adequate account of sophistry—one that might count as "Platonic."

After establishing that the subject-matter of the sophist's contradictions is some kind of image or appearance, and that appearances are indeed possible, the Stranger and Theaetetus resume their attempt to hunt down the sophist once and for all (264c ff.). Because he has turned out to be some kind of "image-maker," they must now assign him to a different branch of art than that in which the other sophists appeared (see Figure 8.4); his general enterprise is one of production (*poiētikē*) not acquisition (*ktētikē*).

The next step is to divide image-making in two, revealing an art of making of likenesses (*eikastikē*) and another of making semblances (*phantastikē*). This is a crucial distinction. A likeness is a nearly exact copy of an original, while a semblance involves some degree of distortion, often intentional, as, for instance, when an artist creates a colossal statue and enlarges the uppermost parts so that the statue will appear well-proportioned to the human observer. The sophist is just such a maker of semblances, the Stranger suggests; but, at the same time, he occupies a very large class (cf. 236c, 268a). (The significance of this aside will become clear as the Stranger gradually reveals that Socrates and the Stranger himself are both included in the class.) The art of semblance making is now divided into one art, which makes use of tools, as sculptors do, and another, which uses only the person, as actors (and sophists) do. This is referred to as *mimēsis*, imitation, and divided again into two types—one based on knowledge of the thing copied and another based on ignorance or mere opinion. The sophist belongs in the latter group, because it was already established that his claim to know all arts cannot possibly be true. He is thus an opinion-based imitator (*doxomimētikē*), as opposed to an imitator who operates from knowledge or science (*epistēmēs*).

Figure 8.4. Seventh Sophistic Appearance in the *Sophist*

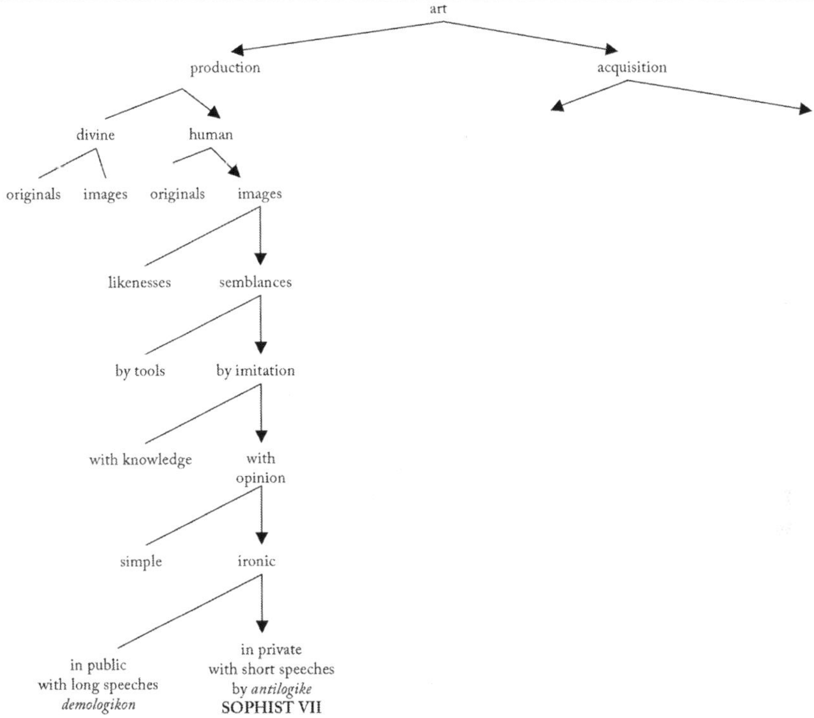

But just as the Stranger and Theaetetus close in on the sophist, readers are treated to a final surprise. The Stranger's penultimate step is to sever opinion-based imitators in two. One of its forms, he says, can be defined by the practitioner's *belief* (a false one, as it turns out) that he knows the things that he imitates; this is referred to as "simple" or "naive" imitation. The other is, strikingly, defined by his "suspicion and fear that he is ignorant of those things which he has embodied in a figure before everyone else as if he knew" (268a). This is labeled "ironic imitation" (*ton eirōnikon mimētēn*), and its affinity to Socrates is unmistakable (compare, e.g., *Rep.* 506a–d). But this is also *the* sophist (Sophist VII), for the Stranger's final move is simply to divide "ironic imitation" in two, removing one type that speaks before multitudes with long speeches—the "public speaker" (*dēmologikon*)—and leaving another type, Sophist VII, whose enterprise is private. The unique enterprise of the sophist thus finally comes to light in the famous closing lines of this dialogue as "the ironic part of the opinion-based mimetics of making contradictory *logoi*, stemming from the semblance class of the image-making art that conjures in speeches and is distinctly set apart as the human not divine part of production."[42]

Is this, at last, *Plato's* definition (and critique) of the sophists? As I have tried to show, the obstacles to this view are simply insurmountable. First, this final determination captures not only the sophists, but also Socrates. Could Plato have decided that his teacher was a sophist after all? The extreme improbability that this is the purpose behind Plato's *Sophist* is revealed by the almost cartoonish quality of the Stranger's method and the superficiality of his view of Socrates. That Plato would have moved from a more to a less nuanced understanding of Socrates and his relationship to the sophists is virtually unthinkable. Second, the Stranger's account of the sophists is fatally flawed. The seventh and final definition purports to capture the unifying element that all sophists have in common and which all the earlier accounts contained. But by homing in on the art of contradiction making (*antilogikos*), the Stranger incorporates only *two* of the previous six definitions. Sophists II–IV involved no reference to contradiction making at all. They were described merely as sellers of teachings about aretē. By thus forcing the peculiar quality of contradiction making onto all sophistic activity as such, the Stranger produces a classically flawed definition of the sort Socrates' interlocutors often produce when pressed for a generic account. The Stranger, in other words, mistakes an accident for an essence, a particular for a universal.[43]

Last, one must observe that the Stranger himself is caught in the net of his final definition—and Plato must intend for readers to see this. I have already remarked that the Stranger's art of diairesis falls within the general class of distinction-making that also houses the sophist. But how far down its branches does the Stranger's art go? Certainly, he produces "images" of the sophist by means of speech for Theaetetus. Are his images to be understood as "likenesses" or "semblances"? Their multiplicity and imperfection prevent us from classing them as likenesses. The stranger is, then, a maker of semblences, like the sophist. Is he a "knowing imitator" or an "opinion-based imitator"? It is not easy to say. This is to ask whether the Stranger distorts his subject with the intent of making the sophists seem more realistic from the vantage point of the interlocutor, in the way an artist distorts a colossal statue, or whether he distorts out of ignorance. In either case, the bulk of (and perhaps all of) the final determination of the sophist proves true of the Stranger as well.[44] And because Socrates and the Stranger are both bound up in this account, it can hardly be Plato's final and damning critique to suggest that the sophist is a mimicking semblance maker, aware of his ignorance and ironic in his private conversations as he refutes interlocutors' dogmatic beliefs. That *this* is Plato's deathblow to all sophistic pedagogy simply strains credulity. The *Sophist* rather ends in something like *aporia*. The failure is implicit rather than explicit, but the dialogue offers nothing like a successful final account.

As for Plato's actual purpose in the *Sophist*, a number of interpreters have taken stock of the kinds of complexities highlighted in this chapter. Catherine Zuckert's study of the dialogue suggests that the Stranger is as much a sophist as Socrates if philosophy is defined as *knowledge* of the whole or even of the self.[45] If, on the other hand, philosophy is only the *pursuit* of knowledge, then the Stranger and Socrates represent different routes to wisdom, each incomplete, but capable of throwing critical light on each other. The Stranger's account of sophistry turns out to be flawed in Zuckert's view because of the particular weaknesses of his philosophical method, and the dialogue turns out to be more about the nature of philosophy than about the nature of sophistry as such.

A somewhat more elaborate interpretation is offered by Jacob Howland,[46] who argues that the Stranger's effort to reveal the nature of sophistry operates on two levels, that of words and deeds. On the level of words, the Stranger's account is obviously flawed, but by deliberately making it so, the Stranger effectively exhibits through his deeds what sophistry is. The Stranger is not a sophist, but he dons the appearance of one in order to educate Theaetetus; and the reason the sophist must be imitated thus, rather than verbally defined, is that sophistry resides finally in the soul, and speech cannot adequately reflect the human soul. Both Zuckert and Howland recognize that the Stranger is no spokesman for Plato and that his presentation of sophistry breaks down in crucial ways.[47] These are the fundamental points that I, too, have been trying to make. My purpose in turning to the *Sophist* in this chapter has not been to add to the interpretations already in print, but to show that the traditional approach that reads the dialogue as Plato's final condemnation of sophistry simply cannot be sustained.

CONCLUSION

I have now considered four different treatments of the sophists in four different dialogues and found these to be in every case defective as general critiques. In the first place, the criticisms diverge radically from dialogue to dialogue so that the sophists are said to be (1) subversive corruptors of youth, (2) slaves to conventional civic values, without the power to corrupt, (3) flatterers devoted to pleasure rather than truth, and (4) antilogical semblance makers. To a certain extent these accounts overlap, but in other ways they are quite incompatible. Anytus' diatribe in the *Meno*, for example, stands virtually opposed to Socrates' remarks to Adeimantus in the *Republic*. And although the sophists are said in the *Gorgias* to be flatterers with no genuine technē of their own, they are described in the *Sophist* as distinct from flatterers and given an art—even if this turns out in the end to be one of semblance making.

Not only do the four accounts differ from each other, they also stand at odds with the more detailed portraits of the sophists in such dialogues as the *Protagoras*, *Hippias Major*, *Hippias Minor*, and *Euthydemus*, nor do they prove stable on their own terms. Thus we have seen how the lines of demarcation between sophistry and statesmanship slowly collapse in the *Gorgias* and how the final determination of the *Sophist* fails at once to capture the empirical variety of the previous six determinations and to separate sophistry from philosophy. In none of these dialogues does Plato seem to offer a general criticism of the sophists that holds up.

But this is puzzling indeed. Why would Plato offer four explicit and at times quite elaborate appraisals of the sophists if these were not meant to be taken seriously? Why would he do so, especially, given what I have been arguing throughout this book, that Plato means for his readers to take the sophists very seriously indeed? Wouldn't such conspicuous and apparently damning criticisms turn readers away from the sophists rather than toward them? If my argument about the speciousness of these criticisms is correct, then I must try to account for why Plato would offer them at all.

There are a number of possibilities. Certainly the least acceptable in my view is that Plato was not in control of his own text and thus unwittingly contradicted himself across and within the dialogues. This view not only violates the standards of hermeneutical charity, which should constitute the starting point of any interpretation, it also flies in the face of the mastery that is evident at every turn in the dialogues. From the macro to the micro level, Plato seems to know exactly what he is saying and how he is saying it, so that it becomes fruitful to interrogate his texts as closely as we can. At another extreme is the view that Plato meant to communicate his true meaning only to a small segment of his readers, the philosophical elite, while throwing the average reader off the scent by offering false or misleading doctrines. I do not deny that many, indeed most, readers of Plato have tended to fasten on exoteric doctrines without adequately appreciating the extent to which Plato himself complicates and subverts these doctrines in the very dialogues in which they are expressed. And there is no doubt, besides, that Plato is deliberately obscure. But I do not think that the problems we have been examining with "Plato's critiques of the sophists" are of the sort that can be perceived only by elite readers. That the problems are rarely noticed has more to do with modern habits of reading than with deceptiveness on Plato's part. Anyone who reflects on these accounts can perceive their inadequacy.

We do better in my judgment to look for an explanation in the pedagogical aspect of the dialogues. In each of the general accounts assayed above, what begins as a critical view of the sophists turns ineluctably to questions and criticisms at once more far reaching and consequential. Socrates' questioning of Anytus, for example, exposes the seriousness of the issue (central to the *Meno* as a whole) of "epistemological dogmatism": one cannot learn what one assumes he already knows. The issue is abstract, thusly stated, and yet it affects Anytus himself, just as it affects other characters in the *Meno*. Indeed it is a ubiquitous problem of human life, one so consequential that it led to Socrates' trial and death. The critical view of the sophists expressed by Anytus in the *Meno* thus opens up (when interrogated) the whole problem of dogmatism and truth.

So, too, in the *Republic* and *Gorgias*, the negative view of the sophists is one Socrates advances more for pedagogical reasons than for its own merits. In both cases, the view turns ineluctably to questions about the grounds of civic action and civic knowledge, as Socrates exposes the degree of "sophistry" inherent in mass politics and statesmanship alike. Finally, in *The Sophist*, the explicit accounts of sophistry turn slowly but surely toward a self-questioning of philosophy in its various forms from Parmenideanism to Socratism to the Stranger's own value-free sorting of beings into kinds.

The sophists thus represent something of a springboard when they are critically discussed in the dialogues. Because the negative view of them was so widely held, Plato could assume his interlocutors (and his readers) would initially accept the critical perspective; but because the sophists were multifaceted (motley), and essentially bound up with civic and philosophical enterprises, Plato could also delicately turn the criticisms toward his interlocutors themselves. This, it seems, is the ultimate purpose behind Plato's generalized critiques of the sophists. Again, it has not been my argument that Plato offered no valid criticisms of the individual sophists. But it seems that the *general* criticisms he offered are not, in the final analysis, his own "teachings" on the sophists, as much as views that emerge in the midst of particular movements of thought among particular interlocutors. Plato's own views on the sophists' significance are better found in those dialogues that treat them individually rather than collectively; and these dialogues suggest that most of the sophists contributed important insights and techniques to the development of Socratic philosophy, even if they stood apart from Socrates in other important ways.

And what did the sophists contribute to Socratic philosophy, or what did they have in common with it? As the previous chapters have shown, various individual sophists related to Socrates in markedly different ways. In the chapter on Protagoras' "Great Speech" I noted that Protagoras and Socrates had a common awareness of the dangers attending the pursuit of excellence in democratic Athens. And I showed that they negotiated those dangers through similar rhetorical strategies including myth-making, esotericism, and irony. Moreover, Protagoras' brilliant reworking of mythical material from Hesiod resembled Socrates' reworking of myth at various points in Plato's dialogues, especially in the early books of the *Republic*. In both cases, mythical content that was deemed socially destabilizing was reworked into something more beneficial. In the chapter on Plato's *Theaetetus*, Protagoras' art of making changes for the better in civic belief structures was given a name—*metaballōn*. And I argued that Socrates engaged in a similar art, even if he had no reason to join Protagoras in eschewing the category of "truth" while doing so.

In the section on Prodicus, I shed light on those passages scattered throughout Plato's dialogues suggesting that Socrates studied with Prodicus. I demonstrated that Socrates sometimes employed Prodicus' art of *diaresis* for pedagogical and philosophical purposes. Even though

Prodicus' art could not take Socrates where he ultimately wanted to go—to a unified view of the Whole—it served nevertheless as a useful tool for combating confusion in himself and others by ensuring that important distinctions were not overlooked. Moreover, Prodicus seems to have anticipated the problem that Socrates in Plato's *Republic* set out to solve in his own distinctive way: the problem of defending the life of justice against those who claim that injustice is ultimately more profitable. Prodicus' "Choice of Hercules" thus relates closely to what I called the "Choice of Glaucon," which is Plato's Republic—and we should not be surprised that Socrates, according to Xenophon, used Prodicus' speech as a pedagogical tool on at least one occasion.

With Hippias the commonalities are not so obvious because of the thick comic veneer Plato places over his handling of this overly confident polymath. But by focusing on the central theme of *polytropia* in the *Hippias Minor*, I was able to show the ways in which Socrates and Hippias were both polytropic in different ways, and to show how Hippias represented one (permanently attractive) way of pursuing human excellence, a way that Socrates did not so much reject as try to balance with his deep concern for truth and justice.

Finally, with Euthydemus and Dionysodorus, as well as with the Protagoras of the *Theaetetus*, I was able to demonstrate what may be the most fundamental reason why the sophists were so important to Plato's Socrates, namely that they could engender wonder, which is the starting point of philosophy. Many commentators have noted in the past the extent to which Plato's Socrates argues fallaciously or sophistically at various points in the dialogues. But by examining the *Euthydemus* and the first part of the *Theaetetus*, I was able to show why he does so. It is because the quest for wisdom is impossible for interlocutors who suppose they already possess it. And thus Socrates recommends exposure to the sophists as a way of awakening interlocutors from their dogmatic slumber. So important is the wonder engendered by the sophists, that when they are not present in a dialogue, Socrates plays the sophist himself, either by crafting arguments like the ones they make or by alluding to specific sophists and their teachings for consideration. Pedagogically and philosophically the practice can be justified. Pedagogically, a spurious argument may work as well as a valid one to show an interlocutor he is confused. Philosophically, spurious arguments stand as an invitation to analyze their error. Thus, Socrates had no fear of the sophists and rather saw engagement with them as useful.

Such are some of the ways the sophists and Socrates relate in Plato's dialogues. I said from the start that my goal is not to collapse Socrates and the sophists into one another. They were distinct in the most monumental of ways—in the loves that animated them, in what they valued and devalued in human experience, and in how they lived. No one from the ranks of the sophists seems to have lived the life of intellectual honesty and integrity that Socrates did. And there is no indication that any of the sophists would have died for such a life. But the differences notwithstanding, I believe readers of Plato suffer a great loss if they (like Anytus in the *Meno*) dismiss the sophists out of hand. In fact, the process of attempting to differentiate Socrates and the sophists is such a rich and enlightening enterprise, as Plato constructs it, that progress can only be made by those who are willing to look at the problem from a Socratic point of view—that is, to become a Socratic philosopher. I am reminded of something the late professor Eric Voegelin once wrote about people who try to reject ancient metaphysics. The attempt would be "self-defeating," he thought. For "by the time the would-be critic has penetrated the meaning of metaphysics with sufficient thoroughness to make his criticism weighty, he will have become a metaphysician himself."[48] Something similar seems to be the case with Socrates and the sophists. By the time the student can differentiate them successfully, he will be engaged in Socratic philosophy: he will, for instance, have to begin by admitting that the problem is more difficult than it first appears; he will then inevitably take up and reject various theories and methods of differentiation (much as the Stranger does in the *Sophist*); and he will then at last come to see that the difference lies in an understanding of what ultimately counts in human life, an understanding that, however, cannot leave a person unaffected by its pursuit.

APPENDIX

A Primer on Hesiod's Myth of Prometheus

For readers unfamiliar with Hesiod's poems, I offer here an analysis of his myth of Prometheus with special attention to the moral and political problems to which the account gives rise. The myth of Prometheus appears twice in Hesiod: once in the *Theogony* (510–616) and once the *Works and Days* (42–105). The two accounts are complimentary even though their functions are different within each poem. In the *Theogony*, the myth is part of Hesiod's elaborate account of the relationships and power struggles among the gods. Man factors into the account only incidentally. In the *Works and Days*, by contrast, Hesiod's purpose is primarily anthropological and pedagogical. Here the myth serves (along with the myth of Five Races) as support for a moral message directed at Perses, Hesiod's ne'er-do-well brother who has conspired with local judges to rob the poet of his inheritance. Thus, although each poem contains a version of the Prometheus myth, neither is complete without the other. In what follows I piece together the fullest version of the myth by combining material from the two sources.[1]

In the *Theogony*, the myth begins at a place called Mekone, with Prometheus dividing up portions of a sacrificial ox on the occasion of some sort of settlement between gods and men (*T* 535ff.).[2] In an effort to corrupt the settlement and to match wits with Zeus, Prometheus devises a "crafty trick": he wraps the edible parts of the ox (the parts that should go to Zeus) in the unattractive skin of the ox's stomach; he then wraps the bones and other inedible parts (the parts that should go to man) in the choicest fat. The portions are thus set out to fool Zeus into taking the human share. Seeing through the trick, Zeus anticipates evils to befall mankind; but he plays along. Seizing the portion assigned to man, he discovers the bones and becomes deeply enraged. He responds by punishing mankind, depriving them of fire. Thus far the myth centers on the theme seizing, taking more than one's share. Prometheus attempts through trickery to seize more for man than man's allotted share. Zeus responds by seizing what he believes to be the better share, though it turns out to be worse. Thus the conflict begins.

In the *Works and Days*, the debacle with the ox is alluded to but not developed. Its place at the front of the myth is occupied instead by a "real-life" story about portions and seizing, the story of Perses (Hesiod's brother). Reenacting, in a sense, the event at Mekone, Perses corrupts a settlement reached with Hesiod over their mutual inheritance: "For we had already divided our inheritance, but you seized the greater share and carried it off" (37–39). Hesiod then uses the myth of Prometheus as a way of warning Perses about the likely consequences of such conduct.

The two poems dovetail at the point of Zeus's first punishment, where Zeus hides fire from men. This is followed by a second Promethean crime: Prometheus conceals fire in a hollow fennel and steals it back again for man. At this point, Zeus seems to be completely outwitted (*T* 565; *WD* 47–55), but not for long. Upon discovering the far-seen light of fire among men, Zeus, enraged in his heart, devises a new punishment—this time for Prometheus as well as for mankind. Prometheus he chains to a column and sets an eagle to gnaw on his liver by day. (The liver heals itself by night, thus creating a cycle of daily pain.) The punishment for men—the creation of the first woman, Pandora—is similar in effect. Zeus orders Hephaestus to mix earth and water into the maiden-like form of the goddesses. Athena then bestows certain charms on her, outfitting her with robes and jewels (in the *Theogony*) or with skill in needlework and weaving (in the *Works and Days*). In the latter poem, Aphrodite and other gods and goddesses have a hand in the work as well, particularly Hermes, who gives her a "shameless mind," "crafty words," and a "deceitful nature" (68). When she is all finished, she is named "Pandora" (gifts from all), because all the immortals contributed to her making.

Next Zeus instructs Hermes to deliver Pandora to Epimetheus as a gift.[3] Epimetheus had been counseled by Prometheus never to take a gift from Zeus lest some harm should come to men, but he has forgotten. Receiving Pandora as his wife, he only afterward understands that she, like the fennel stalk in which Prometheus concealed fire, is but a deceptive container. Inside are the ills that men must suffer for their theft of fire. Pandora is irresistible. She is perceived as good (*T.* 585), and yet like a drone in a hive, she reaps the work of others (*T* 595–600). Or, as the *Works and Days* puts it: she opens the lid of her jar and scatters ills, hard toil, and heavy sickness among men where before, there was comfort.

What are the moral and political implications of Hesiod's myth? Hesiod uses the tale of Prometheus (particularly in the *Works and Days*) as a vehicle for explaining the human condition and for considering appropriate responses to it. The human condition is a fallen one, consisting of toil and suffering, dishonesty, sickness and death. It is not purely evil, but goodness and badness are mixed together. However, things are getting worse.

This condition is amplified by the account of the Five Races that are described in *Works and Days*. Beginning with a golden race of men who live like gods, beyond the reach of evils, Hesiod describes a decline that culminates in an iron race of men (Hesiod's own race) who never rest from labor and sorrow. Eventually, Zeus will destroy the human race entirely, but not until it becomes more corrupt than it presently is. Men will know that fateful hour, for:

> There will be no favor for the man who keeps his oath or for the just or for the good; but rather men will praise the evildoer and his violent dealing. Strength will be right (*dikē*), and respect (*aidōs*) will cease to be; and the wicked will hurt the worthy man, speaking false words against him, and will swear an oath upon them. And then *Aidōs* and *Nemesis*, with their sweet forms Au wrapped in white robes will go from wide-pathed earth and forsake mankind. . . . and bitter sorrows will be left for mortal men, and there will be no help against evil. (*WD* 190–201)

Speaking in terms of *aidōs* and *dikē*, Hesiod presents the human condition as one of continual decline. Man once lived happily, beloved by the gods, enjoying many good things with ease in peace. Man now suffers a life of hardship, commits evils, and forsakes the gods. There are still good people and good things, but evil ways are prevailing, and the current trajectory (one that Hesiod's brother, Perses, has furthered along through his unjust seizing) is the path toward destruction.

What would be an appropriate response to this grim condition? As far as his advice to Perses goes, Hesiod is unambiguous. Perses should listen to right (*dikē*) and cease thinking of violence. In particular, he should earn his own sustenance by *working*, not by seizing. For Zeus has ordained a "*nomos*" for men—that "fishes and beasts and winged fowls should destroy one another, for dikē is not in them, but to mankind he gave dikē, which is much more noble" (*WD* 275–278). The person who knows justice and defends it will prosper, and he will bring prosperity on his family, city, and progeny. The person who violates justice, however, will be punished (238–240) by far-seeing Zeus. Sometimes, indeed, a whole city may suffer for one presumptuous man, as when Zeus sends famine and plague to destroy a people.

This is Hesiod's message to Perses, counseling him to work and to be just. However, two striking problems confront the poet in offering this moral—and these I take to be problems that Protagoras intends to address through his reworking of the myth. The first is that Hesiod's myths (the myth of Prometheus and of the Five Races) seem susceptible of an opposite moral conclusion. That is, if Zeus has ordained evil and hardship for men, and both are to increase until the race is utterly destroyed, then why should men be just? Why not join in the violence and cheating, which seem so much more profitable?[4] Hesiod clearly recognizes the problem but he does not adequately resolve it: there will indeed come a time, Hesiod admits, when might will make right, and when that time arrives, "may neither I myself be righteous among men, nor my son—for then it is a bad thing to be righteous. . . . . But I think that all-wise Zeus will not yet bring that to pass." This is less than a ringing endorsement of justice.

The second problem pertains to princes and other powerful men in the city. For they seem—Hesiod admits—to be governed by an altogether different nomos, a different moral code, than that which governs poor men like Hesiod and Perses. The first indication of this problem appears in Hesiod's description of "two kinds of strife" at the beginning of the *Works and Days*, one that is cruel and warlike, the other that is more wholesome and kind. Perses should keep company with wholesome strife (striving jealously to work harder than one's neighbors) and steer clear of cruel strife (striving to seize another's goods)—at least, that is, until he has produced enough stock of his own to keep him strong; *then* he can "raise disputes and strive to get another's goods" (11–34). It gradually becomes clear that Hesiod's advice to Perses is not necessarily advice for man qua man, but for man qua poor man or weak man (214).

This complication is then forcefully illustrated in the fable of the hawk and the nightingale, which , Hesiod says, is for "rulers themselves to understand":

> Thus said the hawk to the nightingale with speckled neck, while he carried her high up among the clouds, gripped fast in his talons, and she, pierced by his crooked talons, cried pitifully. To her he spake disdainfully: "Miserable little thing, why do you cry out? One far stronger than you now holds you fast, and you must go wherever I take you, songstress as you are. And if I please, I will make my meal of you, or let you go. He is a fool who tries to withstand the stronger, for he does not get the mastery and suffers pain besides his shame." So said the swiftly flying hawk, the long-winged bird. (*WD* 201–212)

The fable indicates again that power places its possessor above the moral constraints of the weak and the poor. Princes may do as they like, and the weak would do well not to resist or to challenge them. Hesiod is quick to remind princes that there is always someone more powerful than they—namely, Zeus, who sees crooked judgments and unjust minds (248–266); moreover, Hesiod insists that Zeus may punish princes for their folly (1–10, 248), or punish a prince's people (261), which amounts ultimately to the same thing. But this is, again, hardly a ringing endorsement of justice.

The problem with the moral universe as Hesiod portrays it is traceable ultimately back to the nature of the gods themselves. Zeus's rule is the rule of power. It was seized by power and is maintained by power. He uses his power—it is true—to propound something called *justice* (*dikē*), but this may be interpreted as nothing other than that which preserves Zeus's rule by keeping those who oppose him in check.

"Justice" for mankind is *work* and *toil.* This is so because Zeus has punished his challenger, Prometheus, by punishing his people. If there is a foundation or ground for justice besides Zeus's power, it is not clear what it might be; and the gods (who themselves engage in violent strife and never work) seem rather to undercut than to support the idea of a well-grounded justice. Thus, the violent power that tempts kings and tempts Hesiod's brother, Perses, is something real; it has its origin in the gods.

NOTES

Chapter 1. Introduction

1. *Apology, Cratylus, Theaetetus, Sophist, Statesman, Symposium, Phaedrus, Theages* [Sp.], *Charmides, Laches, Lysis, Euthydemus, Protagoras, Gorgias, Meno, Hippias Major, Hippias Minor, Republic, Timaeus, Minos* [Sp.], and *Laws*.
2. See, for example, Joseph Moreau, *Platon devant les sophists* (Paris: J. Vrin, 1987); Edward Schiappa, *Protagoras and Logos: A Study in Greek Philosophy and Rhetoric* (Columbia: University of South Carolina Press, 1991), esp. 5–7; Barbara Cassin, "Qui a peur de la sophistique? Contre l'ethical correctness," *Le Débat* 72 (1991): 52–64, translated into English by Charles Wolfe as, "Who's Afraid of the Sophists? Against Ethical Correctness," *Hypatia* 15 (2000): 102–120; John Poulakos, *Sophistical Rhetoric in Classical Greece* (Columbia: University of South Carolina Press, 1995); Cassin, *L'effet sophistique* (Paris: Gallimard, NRF Essais, 1995); Robert W. Wallace, "Plato's Sophists, Intellectual History after 450, and Socrates," in L.J. Samons II, ed., *Cambridge Companion to the Age of Pericles* (Cambridge: Cambridge University Press, 2009), 215–237; and Håken Tell, *Plato's Counterfeit Sophists* (Cambridge, MA: Center for Hellenic Studies, 2010).
3. "The art of contradiction making, descended from an insincere kind of mimicry of the semblance-making breed, derived from image making, distinguished as a portion, not divine but human, of production, that presents a shadow play of words—such are the

blood and lineage which can, with perfect truth, be assigned to the authentic Sophist." *Sophist* (268c–d), F.M. Cornford, trans., in Edith Hamilton and Huntington Cairns, eds., *The Collected Dialogues of Plato* (Princeton: Princeton University Press, 1961).

4. *Meno* 91c, Robert Bartlett, trans., in Bartlett, *Plato: Protagoras and Meno* (Ithaca, NY: Cornell University Press, 2004).
5. Ibid., 92b.
6. *Protagoras* 315c–316a, 337a–c, 339e–342a, 357e, 358a–e; see also *Apology* 19e; *Charmides* 163d; *Cratylus* 384b; *Laches* 197d; *Meno* 75e, 96d; *Euthydemus* 277e, 305c; *Hippias Major* 282c; *Phaedrus* 256b; *Symposium* 177b; *Republic* 600c; and *Theaetetus* 151b. He is also discussed in the pseudo-Platonic *Axiochus*; *Eryxias*, and *Theages*.
7. Terrence Irwin, "Plato's Objections to the Sophists," in C.A. Powell, ed., *The Greek World* (London: Routledge, 1995), 568–587, also casts doubt on these familiar claims about Plato's purposes. For one example among many of such claims, see Hans-Georg Gadamer, *Dialogue and Dialectic: Eight Hermeneutical Studies on Plato* (New Haven, CT: Yale University Press, 1980), ch. 5.
8. Here my argument dovetails with observations made by George Grote, *Plato and the Other Companions of Sokrates* (London: J. Murray, 1868–1870), 521; Hans Raeder, "Platon und die Sophisten," *Proceedings of the Royal Danish Academy* (1938), 11; E.R. Dodds, *Plato: Gorgias* (Oxford: Clarendon Press, 1959), 6–10; A.W.H. Adkins in *Merit and Responsibility* (Oxford: Clarendon Press, 1960); Terrence Irwin, *Plato's Moral Theory* (Oxford: Oxford University Press, 1979), 35; C.J. Rowe, *Plato: Poets, Orators, Sophists* (Brighton: Harvester, 1984), 145 and 147; and Irwin, "Plato's Objection to the Sophists," 588, n. 2.
9. Terms such as sophist, rhetorician, and philosopher were in flux in fifth-century discourse. Thus Plato's use of these terms may or may not correspond with their use by others. Alcidamas and Isocrates are especially interesting to compare in this connection. See Marina McCoy, "Alcidamas, Isocrates, and Plato on Speech, Writing and Philosophical Rhetoric," *Ancient Philosophy* 29 (2009): 45–66.
10. Aristotle *Part. An.* 642a28; Cicero *Tusc.* V.4.10.
11. Some of the best studies include W.K.C. Guthrie, *The Sophists* (Cambridge: Cambridge University Press, 1971), first published

as part 1 of *History of Greek Philosophy*, vol. III (Cambridge: Cambridge University Press, 1969); G.B. Kerferd, *The Sophistic Movement* (Cambridge: Cambridge University Press, 1981); Jacqueline de Romilly, *The Great Sophists in Periclean Athens*, trans. Janet Lloyd (Oxford: Clarendon Press, 1992); John M. Dillon and Tania Gergel, *The Greek Sophists* (New York: Penguin, 2003); and Mauro Bonazzi, *I Sofisti* (Roma: Carocci Editore, 2010).

12. One result of this enterprise has been the production of various collections of sophistic fragments, the first of which was H. Diels and W. Kranz, *Die Fragmente der Vorsokratiker*, 2nd ed., 3 vols. (Berlin: Weidmann Verlag, 1906–1910). English language collections include Rosamond Kent Sprague, ed., *The Older Sophists* (Columbia: University of South Carolina Press, 1972); Robin Waterfield, *The First Philosophers: The Presocratics and Sophists* (Oxford: Oxford University Press, 2000); and Dillon and Gergel, *The Greek Sophists.*
13. Eric Havelock, *The Liberal Temper in Greek Politics* (New Haven, CT: Yale University Press, 1957), 161, my italics.
14. Kerferd, *Sophistic Movement*, 1.
15. Dillon and Gergel, *Greek Sophists*, xix.
16. Especially Catherine Zuckert, *Plato's Philosophers: The Coherence of the Dialogues* (Chicago: University of Chicago Press, 2009); Marina McCoy, *Plato on the Rhetoric of Philosophers and Sophists* (Cambridge: Cambridge University Press, 2008); Ruby Blondell, *Play of Character in Plato's Dialogues* (Cambridge: Cambridge University Press, 2002); Zuckert, "Who's a Philosopher? Who's a Sophist? The Stranger vs. Socrates," *Review of Metaphysics* 54 (2000): 65–97; Francisco Gonzalez, *Dialectic and Dialogue: Plato's Practice of Philosophical Inquiry* (Evanston, IL: Northwestern University Press, 1998); Roslyn Weiss, *The Socratic Paradox and Its Enemies* (Chicago: University of Chicago Press, 1998); Charles H. Kahn, *Plato and the Socratic Dialogue: The Philosophical Use of a Literary Form* (Cambridge: Cambridge University Press, 1996); Thomas Chance, *Plato's Euthydemus: Analysis of What Is and Is Not Philosophy* (Berkeley: University of California Press, 1992); David Roochnik, "The Serious Play of Plato's *Euthydemus*," *Interpretation* 18, no. 2, (Winter 1990): 211–232 ; C.J. Rowe, *Plato: Poets, Orators, Sophists* (Brighton: Harvester, 1984); and Hans Raeder, "Platon und die Sophisten," *Proceedings of the Royal Danish Academy* (1938): 1–36.
17. For useful accounts of this change, see Gerald A. Press, "The State

of the Question in the Study of Plato," *Southern Journal of Philosophy* 34 (1996): 507–522; and Miriam Byrd, "The Summoner Approach: A New Method of Plato Interpretation," *Journal of the History of Philosophy* 45 (2007): 365–381. For a fuller discussion of what is meant by "literary" and "dramatic," see Ruby Blondell, *The Play of Character in Plato's Dialogues* (Cambridge: Cambridge University Press, 2002), 14–66.

18. Malcolm Schofield, "Socrates versus Protagoras," in Barry S. Gower and Michael C. Stokes, eds., *Socratic Questions: New Essays on the Philosophy of Socrates and its Significance* (London and New York: Routledge, 1992), 122.
19. On the problem of the shifting mouthpiece in Plato, see Mary Whitlock Blundell, "Self-Censorship in Plato's *Republic*," in *Virtue, Love and Form: Essays in Memory of Gregory Vlastos*, eds. Terrence Irwin and Martha Nussbaum (Edmonton: Academic Publishing, 1994), 35–36. On the fallacy of attributing characters' views to their author, see the classic study by J.J. Mulhern, "Two Interpretive Fallacies," *Systematics* 9 (1971): 168–172. See more recently Gerald A. Press, ed., *Who Speaks for Plato? Studies in Platonic Anonymity* (Lanham, MD: Rowman & Littlefield, 2000), especially the essays by Debra Nails and Gerald Press (Chapters 1 and 2) against the backdrop of Lloyd P. Gerson, "Plato *absconditus*" in the same volume (Chapter 13). The comparison between Shakespeare and Plato interpretation was famously made by Leo Strauss, *The City and Man* (Chicago: University of Chicago Press, 1964), 59.
20. For an historical account of the rise of the "developmental" approach, see E.N. Tigerstedt, *Interpreting Plato* (Stockholm: Almqvist and Wiksell, 1977), 25–51. Pioneered by Karl Friedrich Hermann, *Geschichte und System der platonischen Philosophie* (Heidelberg: Winter, 1839), the approach soon became so dominant that even to question it seemed perverse. Prominent twentieth-century examples include J.E. Raven, *Plato's Thought in the Making: A Study of the Development of his Metaphysics* (Cambridge: Cambridge University Press, 1965); J. Gould, *The Development of Plato's Ethics* (New York: Russell & Russell, 1972); Richard Robinson, *Plato's Earlier Dialectic*, 2nd ed. (Oxford: Clarendon Press, 1984); W.J. Prior, *Unity and Development in Plato's Metaphysics* (LaSalle, IL: Open Court, 1985); and George Klosko, *The Development of Plato's Political Theory* (New York: Metheun, 1986).
21. Chronological studies up to 1981 are usefully reviewed by Holger

Thesleff, *Studies in Platonic Chronology* (Helsinki: Societas Scientiarum Fennica, 1982). Important studies since 1981 include Gerald R. Ledger, *Re-Counting Plato: A Computer Analysis of Plato's Style* (Oxford: Oxford University Press, 1989); Leonard Brandwood, *The Chronology of Plato's Dialogues* (Cambridge: Cambridge University Press, 1990); and Charles Kahn, "On Platonic Chronology," in Julia Annas and Christopher Rowe (eds.), *New Perspectives on Plato: Modern and Ancient* (Cambridge, MA: Harvard University Press, 2003), ch. 4.

22. Holger Thesleff, *Studies in Platonic Chronology*, and "Platonic Chronology," *Phronesis* 34 (1989): 1–26, were watershed studies in criticizing the stylometric method of dating and arguing that many of the dialogues underwent revision, thereby rendering dates of composition less relevant. Thesleff's critical posture towards the whole chronological project has been embraced and further developed by Jacob Howland, "Re-reading Plato: The Problem of Platonic Chronology," *Phoenix* 45 (1991): 189–214; Debra Nails, *Agora, Academy, and the Conduct of Philosophy* (Dordrecht: Kluwer, 1995), 53–135. See also Charles Griswold's comments following Kahn's "On Platonic Chronology" in Annas and Rowe, *New Perspectives on Plato.*
23. Joseph Cropsey, *Plato's World: Man's Place in the Cosmos* (Chicago: University of Chicago Press, 1995). Catherine Zuckert, *Plato's Philosophers: The Coherence of the Dialogues* (Chicago: University of Chicago Press, 2009). Charles Griswold also offers a dramatic dating of the dialogues in "Irony in the Platonic Dialogues," in *The Sovereignty of Construction: Studies in the Thought of David Lachterman*, ed. D.W. Conway and P. Kerszberg (Amsterdam: Rodopi, 1996).
24. The Tübingen School, which grounds itself on Plato's reservations about writing expressed in the *Seventh Letter* (342c–d) and the *Phaedrus* (274–276) and maintains that Plato's serious doctrines were unwritten, was pioneered by Konrad Gaiser, *Platons ungeschriebene Lehre* (Stuttgart: Klett, 1959). Its most prominent figure today is Thomas Szlezák. See his *Platon lessen* (Stuttgart: Verlag frommann-holzboog, 1993), republished as *Reading Plato*, trans. Graham Zanker (London: Routledge, 1996). In Italy the approach is espoused by Giovanni Reale, *Per una nuava interpretatzione di Platone: Rilettura della metafisica dei grandi dialoghi alla luce delle "Dottrine non scritte"* (Milan: Vita e Pensiero, 1987).
25. One cannot be exhaustive, but some prominent recent examples

include Mary Nichols, *Socrates on Friendship and Community: Reflections on Plato's Symposium, Phaedrus, and Lysis* (Cambridge: Cambridge University Press, 2009); C.J. Rowe, *Plato and the Art of Philosophical Writing* (Cambridge: Cambridge University Press, 2007); Blondell, *Play of Character*; Kenneth Sayre, *Plato's Literary Garden: How to Read a Platonic Dialogue* (Notre Dame, IL: University of Notre Dame Press, 2002); Jill Gordon, *Turning Toward Philosophy: Literary Device and Dramatic Structure in Plato's Dialogues* (University Park: Pennsylvania State University Press, 1999); and Jacob Howland, *The Paradox of Political Philosophy* (Lanham, MD: Rowman & Littlefield, 1998).

26. Press, "The State of the Question," 516.
27. A notable exception is Marina McCoy, *Plato on the Rhetoric of Philosophers and Sophists*, which is an exemplary study focusing on the *Apology, Protagoras, Gorgias, Republic, Sophist*, and *Phaedrus*. Arguing that Plato separates Socrates from the sophists and rhetoricians less in terms of method than in terms of moral orientation, McCoy offers a rich look at the interplay of dramatic and philosophical aspects of the dialogues she considers. Though we differ in our understanding of what a sophist is (McCoy does not draw a sharp line between sophist and rhetorician, as I argue Plato does) McCoy's method and the conclusions she reaches pave the way for future studies including my own. Other exceptions include Ruby Blondell, *Play of Characters*, ch. 3 on the *Hippias Minor*; Thomas Chance, *Plato's* Euthydemus; and Patrick Coby, *Socrates and the Sophistic Enlightenment: A Commentary on Plato's* Protagoras (Lewisburg: Bucknell University Press, 1987).
28. This is the case with Kerferd, *The Sophistic Movement*; and also Irwin's "Plato's Objections to the Sophists," which remains invaluable nevertheless insofar as it marshals evidence from Plato's dialogues with thoroughness and sound judgment and is thereby able to refute much nonsense that has passed for truth about the sophists in Plato.

CHAPTER 2. DEFINING THE PLATONIC SOPHISTS

1. I have much more to say about this in the chapters ahead. But for now consider the way Plato's Socrates defends the sophists

against "the many" and their elite representatives (Anytus, for example) in such passages as *Meno* 92c; *Rep.* 492a; *Euthyd* 272d. When Socrates does criticize the sophists it is not so obviously as their enemy. This point has been well made by T.H. Irwin, "Plato's Objections to the Sophists," in C.A. Powell, ed., *The Greek World* (London: Routledge, 1995), 568–587.

2. Along with a handful of others. See especially, C.J. Rowe, "Plato on the Sophists as Teachers of Virtue," *History of Political Thought* IV (1983): 409–427; see also M. Pohlenz, *Aus Platons Werdezeit* (Berlin: Weidmann, 1913), 195 ff.; Hans Raeder, "Platon und die Sophisten," *Proceedings of the Royal Danish Academy* (1938), 1–36; and E.R. Dodds, *Plato: Gorgias* (Oxford: Oxford University Press, 1959), 7.
3. C.C.W. Taylor, "Socrates the Sophist," in L. Judson and V. Karasmanis, eds., *Remembering Socrates* (Oxford: Oxford University Press, 2006), notices that Plato deliberately presents Socrates as sharing qualities with the sophists. But Taylor's contention is that Plato does this in order to remove Socrates from Plato's own claim to philosophy. Compared to Plato, Socrates was but a "very noble sophist" (168).
4. Cf. Marina McCoy, *Plato on the Rhetoric of Philosophers and Sophists* (Cambridge: Cambridge University Press, 2008), 12: "Rather than simply stating how philosophy is different from sophistry, Socrates often uses sophistry . . . as a kind of foil for philosophy in order to explore the value of philosophy."
5. The pre-Platonic history of the word has been well surveyed by a number of modern authors. The seminal treatment by George Grote, *History of Greece*, vol. VIII (London: John Murray, 1850), 479ff., is still worth reading though it is overly hostile toward Plato. See also, G.B. Kerferd, "The First Greek Sophists," *Classical Review* 64 (1950): 8–10; W.K.C. Guthrie, *The Sophists* (Cambridge: Cambridge University Press, 1971), 27–33; Joseph Moreau, "Qu'est-ce Qu'un Sophiste?" in *Platon devant les sophistes* (Paris: Librairie Philosophique J. Vrin, 1987), 7–17; Edward Schiappa, *Protagoras and Logos* (Columbia: University of South Carolina Press, 1991), 3–4; and Edward Schiappa, *The Beginnings of Rhetorical Theory in Classical Greece* (New Haven: Yale University Press, 1999), 48–56.
6. Fifth Isthmian Ode, lines 24–29.
7. See Diogenes Laertius I.12; and Plato *Protagoras*, 316d–317a.

8. Xenophon may have had Pythagoras and his followers in mind, conjectures Guthrie, *The Sophists*, 31.
9. *Antidosis*, 268.
10. Kerferd, "The First Sophists," 8.
11. Isocrates, *Antidosis* 235, cf. 312; Aristotle fr. 5, in Jonathan Barnes, ed., *The Complete Works of Aristotle*, vol. 2 (Princeton: Princeton University Press, 1984), 2390. See also Plutarch *Moralia*, 96a. The seven sages were teachers who flourished in the sixth century, including Solon of Athens, Bias of Priene, Chilon of Sparta, Cleobulus of Lindus, Periander of Corinth, Pittacus of Mytilene, and Thales of Miletus.
12. Herodotus I.29; Isocrates *Antidosis*, 235, 312–314.
13. Damastes was a younger contemporary of Herodotus. His work, *Concerning Poets and Sophists*, is thought to be the first serious attempt to write a history of Greek literature.
14. Guthrie, *The Sophists*, 30; Kerferd, "First Greek Sophists," 8.
15. Trans., George Norlin, *Isocrates with an English Translation* (Cambridge: Harvard University Press, 1980), except that Norlin translates *sophistai* as "sages."
16. See Marina McCoy, "Alcidamas, Isocrates, and Plato on Speech, Writing, and Philosophical Rhetoric," *Ancient Philosophy* 29 (2009), 51–52.
17. Grote, *History*, vol. VIII, 483, wrote that Plato "stole the name [sophist] out of general circulation . . . [and] connected it with express discreditable attributes, which formed no part of its primitive and recognized meaning, and were altogether distinct from, though grafted upon, the vague sentiment of dislike associated with it." Similarly, Karl Popper, *The Open Society and its Enemies*, vol. I, *The Spell of Plato* (Princeton: Princeton University press, 1966), 263, n. 52: "We must not forget that Plato . . . is the man who by his attacks on the 'Sophists' created the bad associations connected with that word." The influential essay by Joseph Moreau, *Platon devont les sophistes* (Paris: Librairie Philosophique J. Vrin, 1987), 7, similarly asserts: "C'est Platon, cependant, qui a définitivement attaché au nom de sophiste une signification infâmante." More recent statements along these lines include Robert W. Wallace, "Plato's Sophists: Intellectual History after 450, and Sokrates" in L.J. Samons II, ed., *Cambridge Companion to the Age of Pericles* (Cambridge: Cambridge University Press, 2009), 216–218,

233–234; and Håken Tell, *Plato's Counterfeit Sophists* (Cambridge, MA: Center for Hellenic Studies, 2010), 2.

18. *Clouds* lines 331, 1111, 1307.
19. *Apology* 18a–e, 19c–e.
20. David L. Blank, "Socrates versus Sophists on Payment for Teaching," *Classical Antiquity* 4 (1985): 1–49, contends for this point, and I have benefited from his study. However, Blank has been criticized for finding sophists under every bush, even where they are not expressly mentioned. See Håken Tell, *Plato's Counterfeit Sophists*, 46–47. Blank's mistakes notwithstanding, it remains the case that the poets of Old Comedy ridiculed the sophists. This was correctly sensed by Eric Havelock, *The Liberal Temper in Greek Politics* (London: Cape, 1957), 158.
21. Translations mine. The fragments appear in Rudolph Kassel and Colin Austin, eds., *Poetae Comici Graeci*, 8 vols. (Berlin: Walter de Gruyter, 1983–). For English translations and a useful commentary, see Ian C. Storey, *Eupolis: Poet of Old Comedy* (Oxford: Oxford University Press, 2003).
22. "Social nuisance" is Christopher Carey's generalization of the attitude of Old Comedy toward the sophists in "Old Comedy and the Sophists," in David Harvey and John Wilkins, eds., *The Rivals of Aristophanes: Studies in Athenian Old Comedy* (London: Duckworth and the Classical Press of Whales, 2000), 430.
23. Aeschylus in the *Prometheus Bound* (944–946; cf. 61–62) has Hermes call out to Prometheus when he is chained to the rock: "Hey you! *Sophistēs*, bitter beyond all bitterness; you have sinned against the gods!" But this is not quite an insult in itself; for Zeus in the same play is also called a sophist—an even shrewder sophist than Prometheus—and the word simply means something like deviser or contriver. So, too, in Euripides' *Children of Hercules* (993–995), where Eurystheus describes himself as a "*sophistēs* of many pains." Again, "deviser" is a suitable translation, though here the term is somewhat colored by the wickedness of Eurystheus' character.
24. In addition to the plays just mentioned, consider also Plato's *Protagoras* (set in or around 433/2), esp. 314d; and *Republic* 600c.
25. To ensure accuracy, I ran a search on the stem "σοφιστ -" in the Thesaurus Linguae Graecae (TLG) and studied all results in the genuine, or possibly genuine, dialogues (so, for example, omitting

results from the *Theages*, *Minos*, and *Definitiones*). Though this is not a flawless method (Plato sometimes discusses the sophists without actually employing the term), it is a good place to begin. In the analysis below, I supplement the TLG results with other relevant passages and considerations.

26. Terrence Irwin has recognized the importance of categorizing the various statements made of the sophists in Plato. Though he does not separate out the evidence that I present in Category 3, he reaches strikingly similar conclusions. See Irwin, "Plato's Objections to the Sophists." As I did not know of Irwin's study until after I conducted my own, I take it as an independent verification of my results.
27. This problem is well discussed in Gerald A. Press, ed., *Who Speaks for Plato: Studies in Platonic Anonymity* (Lanham: Rowman & Littlefield, 2000).
28. This is not to say there were only nine sophists in Athens. As I noted earlier, Athens was likely overrun with them. Socrates thus refers in the *Republic* (600c) to "a good many others," but he does not name them.
29. Plato *Republic* 337a1, 337a8, 339e5.
30. Aristotle mentions him several times, but never as a sophist; hence C. Joachim Classen, "Aristotle's Picture of the Sophists," in G.B. Kerferd, ed., *The Sophists and Their Legacy* (Wiesbaden: Franz Steiner Verlag, 1981), 21, observes rightly that in Aristotle, there is absolutely no "indication of a connection between him [Thrasymachus] and the sophists." As we move to much later sources, the issue becomes blurred. In the third century AD, Atheneus describes Thrasymachus as a sophist (without explanation) in the *Deipnosophistae*; yet Philostratus, (*Lives* I.14) denies that he was a sophist on the grounds that he was nothing but a lawyer. In the tenth century, the Greek lexicon-encyclopedia called the *Suda*, referred to Thrasymachus as a sophist, perhaps relying on Atheneus.
31. I discuss the relevant passages in ch. 8.
32. I elaborate on this in ch. 6.
33. E.g., Guthrie, *The Sophists*, 31.
34. Hence Stanley Lombardo's translation, "competent instructor," in *Plato: Complete Works*, ed. J.M. Cooper (Indianapolis: Hackett, 1997), 688, is quite reasonable.
35. He seems, from Plato's point of view, to warrant occasional mention,

but nothing more. In the *Phaedrus* (267a) he is mentioned in connection with some rhetorical devices he may have invented, and in the *Phaedo* (60c–61c) he is said to have prompted the question that Cebes put to Socrates concerning Socrates' sudden musical turn.

36. Håken Tell, *Plato's Counterfeit Sophists*, 31, n. 49 notices the difference between being labeled a sophist by others and declaring oneself a sophist.
37. *Meno* 90b–e; see further Wilhelm Nestle, *Vom Mythos zum Logos: Die Selbstentfaltung des griechischen Denkens von Homer bis auf die Sophistik und Sokrates* (Stuttgart: A. Kroner, 1942), 259, n. 36; and C.A. Forbes, *Teachers' Pay in Ancient Greece*, University of Nebraska Studies in the Humanities, vol. 2 (Lincoln: University of Nebraska Press, 1942).
38. *Meno* 92e–93a; see further David D. Corey, "The Case against Teaching Virtue for Pay: Socrates and the Sophists," *History of Political Thought* 23 (2002), 190–191.
39. No occasion arises in the *Protagoras* for Prodicus to affirm the title, sophist; and Prodicus is never treated in a dialogue of his own. So we must make do here with what we have.
40. The "Choice of Hercules," alluded to in the *Symposium* (177b) and discussed further in ch. 5. That Prodicus was fundamentally a moral educator was recognized by E. Dupréel, *Les sophistes, Protagoras, Gorgias, Prodicus, Hippias* (Neuchâtel: Du Griffon, 1948), 18.
41. The point is reiterated in the same dialogue at 284a. Regarding their (considerably high) fees see, for Prodicus, *Cratylus* 384a–c; and for Hippias, *Hippias Major* 282d–e; see further, Corey, "The Case against Teaching Virtue for Pay," 207–208.
42. That Euthydemus and Dionysodorus charged fees for teaching virtue can be inferred from the fact that they did so for their earlier, less exalted subjects (see *Euthyedemus* 272a). Plato's presentation of these sophists seems to catch them at the very inception of their sophistic practice, when they were still willing to offer a demonstration (at least for Socrates) without charging a fee. Thus Socrates' rather playful remark at 304b: "if you must have an audience, then let no one come unless he gives you money."
43. Socrates' elaborate comparison of mass culture to sophistry turns on the premise that sophists are in the business of imparting moral beliefs and dispositions.
44. The *Sophist* is most remarkable in this regard, because its ostensible

purpose is to reach a definition of sophistry. Of the seven major sophistic types described in that dialogue, five are directly related to teaching *aretē*. The two that are not can be explained by the fact that one is evidently a description of Socrates, while the other (final definition) is deliberately false, at least as I read it (see, ch. 8). This prompts a further question: If the *Sophist* is Plato's effort to define sophistry, then why does that dialogue not end with a clear statement of the definition I have been advancing? The answer is contained in the faulty premise: The *Sophist* is not essentially, or not simply, "Plato's effort to define sophistry." We must ask, for example, what the significance is of Plato's assigning the lead role in that dialogue to the Eleatic Stranger. Let me merely say here that while the *Sophist* does not culminate in a definition of the sophists as paid teachers of aretē, it nevertheless corroborates that definition by showing how consistently it applies.

45. Consider, for example, *Euthydemus* 305b–c; *Sophist* 222d, 225b; and *Gorgias* 464b–466a.
46. The fee is a necessary but not sufficient condition, according to Plato's most precise use of *sophistēs*, while for many ancient observers, the fee was all that mattered. Socrates seems to be speaking colloquially here—using the term in a way he knows his audience will accept. Later figures in the Platonic tradition seem to have fastened on pay as a sufficient criterion. See Håken Tell's interesting treatment of the fourth-century AD philosopher Themistius in *Plato's Counterfeit Sophists*, 43–44.
47. Contrast those passages in which Socrates asks the sophists about their art (*Protagoras* 349a, *Hippias Major* 281d, and *Euthydemus* 271b–c, 277e).
48. This was noticed by George Grote, *Plato and the Other Companions of Sokrates* (London: J. Murray, 1868–1870), 521: "If the line could be clearly drawn between rhetors and sophists, Gorgias ought rather to be ranked with the former." See also Hans Raeder, "Platon und die Sophisten," *Proceedings of the Royal Danish Academy* (1938), 11, and "Platon und die Rhetoren," ibid., (1956), 4. E.R. Dodds followed the lead of Grote and Raeder in his revised version of the Greek text, *Plato: Gorgias* (Oxford: Clarendon Press, 1959), 6–10: "What then was Gorgias?" asks Dodds (p. 8), "If we can believe Plato, the answer is clear: he was simply *deinos legein* [clever at speaking] (*Symposium* 198c), a man who could alter the

appearance of things *dia rhōmēn* logou (*Phaedrus* 267a), and whose only profession was to make others *deinous legein* (*Meno* 95c)." Terrence Irwin, "Plato's Objection to the Sophists," 588, n. 2, similarly argues, "I do not believe there is sufficient evidence to suggest that Gorgias was a Sophist." Against their view stands E.L. Harrison, who claims that Gorgias *was* a sophist; see his influential essay, "Was Gorgias a Sophist?" *Phoenix* 18 (1964): 183–192. And Harrison's view has been recently adopted by John M. Dillon and Tania Gergel, *The Greek Sophists* (New York: Penguin, 2003), 43 ff. For my own part, I find Harrison's argument unconvincing, because it places too much emphasis on "pay" as a sufficient definitional criterion, fails to discriminate among the types of witnesses Plato presents and the audiences to whom they speak, and cannot explain the contempt that Gorgias' followers express toward the sophists in Plato's *Gorgias*. In this book I make a methodological move that Harrison does not make, which is to place a premium on what Gorgias himself says (in Plato) over what is said of him in passing by others (in Plato).

49. This is no less true for the fact that in the *Gorgias* (460a, cf. 461b) Socrates shames the rhetorician into admitting that he pays at least some attention to virtue. If a pupil were to arrive with absolutely no knowledge of justice or injustice, then (Gorgias concedes reluctantly), "he will learn these things from me too." The point is that Gorgias' curriculum did not contain any provisions for such instruction. He was a teacher of rhetoric, not a moral mentor.
50. The basic distinction between immoralist rhetoricians and moralist sophists has been previously marked by A.W.H. Adkins in *Merit and Responsibility* (Oxford: Clarendon Press, 1960); Terrence Irwin, *Plato's Moral Theory* (Oxford: Oxford University Press, 1979), 35; and C.J. Rowe, *Plato: Poets, Orators, Sophists* (Brighton: Harvester, 1984), 145 and 147. My own evidence for the moral qualities of the sophists is developed in the subsequent chapters.
51. This is not to deny the possibility of good forms of rhetoric and good rhetoricians. Marina McCoy, *Plato on the Rhetoric of Philosophers and Sophists*, helps to reveal Plato's ambivalence toward rhetoric as an art, since philosophy necessarily makes use of it, too.
52. For example, Aristophanes and other comic poets did not.
53. This is why Plato sometimes mentions the sophists alongside the rhetoricians when the question concerns rhetorical innovations

(e.g., *Phaedrus* 267a–d). The fact that the sophists and rhetoricians both taught rhetoric leads Dillon and Gergel, *The Sophists*, to conclude (rashly) that any distinction between these camps "seems an unreal one" (p. xviii).

54. See, further, Guthrie, *The Sophists*, 45; and Irwin, *Plato's Moral Theory*, 27.
55. Consider, for example, *Meno* 71b–72a and 80a. In Aristotle's *Politics* (1260a25 ff.) Gorgias is described, for example, as having maintained that there were different kinds of virtues for different kinds of people.
56. The similarities themselves become thematic in the *Gorgias*. When Socrates wants to vex the lovers of rhetoric with whom he is speaking, he draws attention to their close but unwelcome relationship to the sophists. See, for example, 462e–466a.
57. Corey, "The Case Against Teaching Virtue for Pay: Socrates and the Sophists."
58. Thus Socrates' remarks in the *Laches* (185e, 186c): "The question whether any of us is expert in the care of the soul and is capable of caring for it well, and has had good teachers is the one we ought to investigate. . . . I am the first to say concerning myself that I have had no teacher in this subject. And yet I have desired it from youth on. But I did not have any money to give the sophists, who were the only ones who professed to be able to make me noble and good; and I myself, on the other hand am unable to discover the art even now." Consider also Socrates' provocative remark to Meno (*Meno* 71a): "You must think I am singularly fortunate to know whether virtue can be taught or how it is acquired. The fact is that far from knowing whether it can be taught, I have no idea what virtue itself is."
59. Something like this is suggested by Edward Schiappa, *Protagoras and Logos: A Study in Greek Philosophy and Rhetoric* (Columbia: University of South Carolina Press, 1991), 5–7. In Schiappa's view, Plato was engaged in an elaborate act of "dissociation," separating Socratic philosophy from sophistry by redefining terms. This view is also endorsed by Håken Tell, *Plato's Counterfeit Sophists*, 2.
60. See, for example, Isocrates, *Against the Sophists* (2–3), and the *Dissoi Logoi* VI (=Diels and Kranz [hereafter DK] 90).
61. Rosamond Kent Sprague, *The Older Sophists* (Columbia: University of South Carolina Press, 1972), 279, describes the *Dissoi Logoi*

as "an anonymous sophistic treatise written in literary Doric at some time subsequent to the end of the Peloponnesian War." For more information about the text, see, T.M. Robinson, *Contrasting Arguments: An Edition of the Dissoi Logoi* (Salem, MA: Ayer, 1979), 1–93.

62. Cf. C.J. Rowe, *Plato: Poets, Orators, Sophists*, 157: the sophists "are thus a group of special interest to Plato [since] they lay claim to that knowledge which he and Socrates regard as the most important."
63. Again, consider *Republic* VI.492a ff. in this light: The sophist "educates in nothing other than the convictions of the many."
64. *Meno* 80a–81e: "Socrates, before I even met you," says Meno, "I used to hear that you are always in a state of perplexity and that you bring others to the same state, and now I think you are bewitching and beguiling me, simply putting me under a spell, so that I am quite perplexed. . . . I have made speeches about virtue before large audiences on a thousand occasions, very good speeches as I thought, but now I cannot even say what it is" (trans., Grube).

CHAPTER 3. THE "GREAT SPEECH" IN PLATO'S *PROTAGORAS*

1. Plato indicates his critical view of Protagoras in many ways, for instance by stressing the sophist's agonistic tendencies as opposed to Socrates' cooperativeness. See Malcolm Schofield, "Socrates versus Protagoras," in Barry S. Gower and Michael C. Stokes, eds., *Socratic Questions: New Essays on the Philosophy of Socrates* (London: Routledge, 1992), 122–123. He also casts suspicion on the sophist by having him appear in the company of some of Athens' most notorious citizens. See D. Wolfsdorf, "The Historical Reader of Plato's *Protagoras*," *Classical Quarterly* 48 (1998): 126–133.
2. Michael Gagarin, "The Purpose of Plato's *Protagoras*," *Transactions and Proceedings of the American Philological Association* 100 (1969): 133–164 advances an argument similar to mine, maintaining that the dialogue is meant to highlight the remarkable similarities between Protagoras and Socrates along with certain differences. Although the main thrust of Gagarin's case seems to me sound, his method of analysis prevents a full appreciation of the extent of the comparison, which the dialogue makes possible. Gagarin, for instance, does not devote much attention to the Great Speech (pp. 142–144).

3. G.B. Kerferd treats the challenge narrowly in this way. See Kerferd, "Protagoras' Doctrine of Justice and Virtue in the *Protagoras* of Plato," *Journal of Hellenic Studies* 73 (1953): 42–45. Kerferd's approach is followed by Gagarin.
4. This is recognized also by Scott R. Hemmenway, "Sophistry Exposed: Socrates on the Unity of Virtue in the *Protagoras*," *Ancient Philosophy* 16 (1996): 1–23.
5. Jacqueline de Romily analyzes only the initial myth without considering its context. See, *The Great Sophists in Periclean Athens* (Oxford: Oxford University Press, 1992), 162–166. Edward Schiappa, *Protagoras and Logos: A Study of Greek Philosophy and Rhetoric* (Columbia: University of South Carolina Press, 2003), also analyzes various parts and pieces of the Great Speech as though its context within the dialogue were irrelevant (see, e.g., 31, 146–148, 170, and 180). He does so because he accepts the view that the speech is a genuine artifact of the historical Protagoras rather than a Platonic creation (see 146ff. with notes). If this is so, which I doubt, one must notice that Plato has so masterfully woven the Great Speech into the dialogue as a whole that its function *in Plato* can be understood in no other way than contextually.
6. See Alfredo Ferrarin, "Homo Faber, Homo Sapiens, or Homo Politicus? Protagoras and the Myth of Prometheus," *Review of Metaphysics* 54 (2000): 289–319; and Patrick J. Deneen, *Democratic Faith* (Princeton: Princeton University Press, 2005), 119–139.
7. Evidence for this familiarity is supplied by *Prt.* 325e4–326a4; see also H.I. Marrou, *A History of Education in Antiquity*, trans. George Lamb (New York: Sheed and Ward, 1956), 10, 41–43.
8. DK 80 A30.
9. DK 80 A25; the source is the Gnomologium Vaticanum, a collection of ancient Greek sayings discovered in 1888; the author of this saying is not known.
10. Consider also his critical tone toward the poets at *Prt.* 317a and 317b. This should be compared to the deceptively pious attitude he takes toward the poets at 325e–326a (a passage that is discussed in context later). Consider also his critique of the poet Simonides on the theme of aretē (*Prt.* 339a–e).
11. *Rep.* 607b. There were other major voices—Xenophanes chief among them; see DK21 B1.21–24; and DK21 B11.
12. The scene is well treated by Robert Bartlett, "Political Philosophy

and Sophistry: An Introduction to Plato's *Protagoras*," *American Journal of Political Science* 47 (1981): 612–644, reprinted in Robert C. Bartlett, trans., *Plato: "Protagoras and Meno*," (Ithaca: Cornell University Press), 67–89. See also Wolfsdorf, "The Historical Reader of Plato's *Protagoras*."

13. See Malcolm Schofield, "*Euboulia* in the *Iliad*," in Schofield, *Saving the City: Philosopher-Kings and Other Classical Paradigms* (Cambridge: Cambridge University Press, 1999), 3–30.
14. Thus, for example, the paradigmatic education of Achilles by Phoenix described at *Iliad* 9.440 is centered on "words and deeds" as the pathways to preeminence.
15. Those who present Protagoras as a democratic theorist fail to account for this line. See Adolf Menzel, "Protagoras, der äelteste Theoretiker der Demokratie," *Zeitschrift fuer Politik* 3 (1910): 205–238; Eric Havelock, *The Liberal Temper in Greek Politics* (New Haven: Yale University Press, 1957); Cynthia Farrar, *The Origins of Democratic Thinking: The Invention of Politics in Classical Athens* (New York: Cambridge University Press, 1988); William J. Prior, "Protagoras' Great Speech and Plato's Defense of Athenian Democracy," in Victor Caston and Daniel Graham, eds., *Presocratic Philosophy: Essays in Honour of Alexander Mourelatos* (Burlington, Vermont: Ashgate, 2002), 313–326; and Patrick J. Deneen, *Democratic Faith*, 122.
16. Socrates denies he educates people and thus contrasts himself with the sophists in the *Apology* 19d–20c. But Socrates' denial did not work. See Gagarin, "Purpose of Plato's Protagoras," 140.
17. See Plato *Apology* 23c ff.
18. For whatever reason, this is not remarked by Marina McCoy, *Plato on the Rhetoric of Philosophers and Sophists* (Cambridge: Cambridge University Press, 2008), though it is the kind of thing in which she is interested. Instead, her chapter on the *Protagoras* focuses on Socrates' art of questioning.
19. Patrick Coby, "The Education of a Sophist: Aspects of Plato's *Protagoras*," *Interpretation* 10 (1982): 139–158, esp. 143–144; A.W.H. Adkins, "*Aretē*, *Technē*, Democracy and Sophists: *Protagoras* 316b–328d," *Journal of Hellenic Studies* 93 (1973): 3–12, esp. 10–11.
20. Hemmenway, "Sophistry Exposed," 7, also considers the importance of Protagoras' audience but places more stress than I do on the presence of Alcibiades, Charmides, and Critias in the audience.

On Hemmenway's reading—which presents Protagoras as a covert instructor of injustice—these are precisely the kind of students to whom this sophist caters. On this reading, Protagoras differs from villains like Callicles only in his higher degree of discretion.

21. Adkins, "*Aretē*, *Technē*, Democracy and Sophists." For a more detailed discussion of competitive and cooperative excellences, see his *Merit and Responsibility* (Oxford: Oxford University Press, 1960).
22. A.E. Taylor thought the myth, and the Great Speech generally, was "a complete *ignoratio elenchi*." See Taylor *Plato: The Man and His Work* (London: University Paperbacks, [1926] 1966), 243.
23. See Aristotle *Rhetoric* I.1 (24–30); Quintilian *Institutes* III 1, 12 (=DK 90 B6) lists Protagoras as among the first thinkers to discuss the emotions.
24. Adkins makes the point well: "warlike *aretē* was traditionally the prerogative of the wealthier members of society who could purchase their own hoplite-armour, those, that is, who were socially, politically, and militarily *agathoi*, in contrast to with the mass of the *kakoi*." See Adkins, "*Aretē*, *Technē*, Democracy and Sophists," 11.
25. On the distribution of *aidōs* and *dikē* to man, not animals, in Hesiod, see *Works and Days* 275–285, 192–193. There is also a striking verbal resemblance between *Works and Days* 134–137 and the Platonic version of the myth. Aeschylus' play, *Prometheus Bound* also presents an account of Prometheus that differs markedly from Hesiod's. Aeschylus' hero, like that of Protagoras, is a benefactor for men, and the play similarly contains no Pandora. But Aeschylus' myth differs substantially from the one Plato ascribes to Protagoras. For a comparison, see Patrick Deneen, *Democratic Faith*, 130–136. In what follows, I focus on the comparison between the versions in Hesiod and Plato.
26. Nemesis is the feeling of righteous indignation aroused by the sight of wicked people faring well.
27. See Ferrarin, "Homo Faber, Homo Sapiens or Homo Politicus," 309–310.
28. This is closely related to the problem expressed (with Hesiod, among others in mind) in *Republic* II.
29. For a helpful study of the role of *aidōs* (and *aischunē*, a closely related word for shame/respect) in a healthy polity, see Christina H. Tarnopolsky, *Prudes, Perverts and Tyrants: Plato's Gorgias and the Politics of Shame* (Princeton: Princeton University Press, 2010).

30. The way punishment is handled in Protagoras' myth resonates with a report about him in Plutarch's *Pericles*, 36: a javelin thrower in some games accidentally struck and killed a fellow competitor with his javelin, and Pericles is said to have spent the entire day with Protagoras trying to decide whether, in the strictest sense (*kata ton orthotaton logon*), it would be necessary to blamc the javelin for the mishap, its thrower, or the game's organizers. Protagoras seems to have been interested in the different types of causation that affect ethical and legal culpability, and the problem of choosing the proper perspective. Giuseppe Rensi first pointed out that, to a doctor, the cause of death might be viewed as the javelin, while to a judge or an overseer of the games it might be viewed as the athlete or the game's organizers respectively (*Introduzione alla sceptsi etica* [Firenze: F. Perrella, 1921], 118; quoted in Mario Untersteiner, *The Sophists*, trans., Kathleen Freeman [Oxford: Basil Blackwell, 1954], 31).
31. *Works and Days* 11–16; see the appendix for a more detailed discussion.
32. 322c–d; note that this is the principle that Plato's Socrates employs in *Republic* II to begin his own reworking of Hesiod. Hesiod offers a cosmos in which all gods and men compete for the same scarce goods; Plato's Protagoras and Socrates alike respond to this by positing a cosmos in which each person does (or should do) one thing well.
33. Cf. Homer *Iliad* 13.835–854, where the Trojan counselor Polydamus tells Hector: "Won't you listen to reason? Just because some god exalts you in battle you think you can beat the rest in tactics too. How can you hope to garner all the gifts at once? One man is a splendid fighter—a god has made him so—one's a dancer, another skilled at lyre and song, and deep in the next man's chest farseeing Zeus plants the gift of judgment, good clear sense. And many reap the benefits of that treasure: troops of men he saves, as he himself knows best. So now I will tell you what seems best to me . . ." Protagoras may be drawing on Homer as he reworks Hesiod.
34. Mentioned in passing in Diogenes Laertius IX.52.
35. As Plato presents him in the *Theaetetus*, Protagoras had a way of making alternate appearances emerge for someone who's view was partial (incomplete and biased). This was Protagoras' powerful "art of contradiction" (*antilogikē*) and the subject of his two-volume book, *Antilogiōn* (*Contradictory Arguments*, DK 80 B5).

36. Protagoras' revisions are not perfect. His gods commit errors, and even crimes. Consider, however, Patrick Deneen's musing that Prometheus may have committed his error "intentionally," so that the results would turn out the way they did. On this reading, at least Prometheus (whose name is "foresight") and Zeus would have been free from error. See Deneen, *Democratic Faith*, 135–136.
37. G.B. Kerferd poses this question and answers that the section constitutes an "explanation and application of the myth." See Kerferd, "Protagoras' Doctrine of Justice and Virtue," 42.
38. See Aristotle *Rhetoric*. Deducing arguments from common opinion is typical of this genre, as are a number of other argumentative techniques that Protagoras here demonstrates, most noticeably the "*tekmērion*," or "fixed proof."
39. *dei dia dikaiosunēs pasan ienai kai sōphrosunēs* (323a1)
40. The phrase, "and the rest," is deliberately vague.
41. Here the surface similarity between Protagoras and Socrates is clear. Socrates in Plato's *Apology* (24 c–d, 29d–30b) also insists that virtue requires deliberate care.
42. Many commentators have appreciated how theoretically advanced this theory is. See T.J. Saunders, *Plato's Penal Code* (Oxford: Oxford University Press, 1991), 133–136 and 162–164; Saunders, "Protagoras and Plato on Punishment," in G.B. Kerferd, ed., *The Sophists and Their* Legacy (Weisbaden: Franz Steiner Verlag, 1981), 129–141; M.M. Mackenzie, *Plato on Punishment* (Berkeley: 1981), 188–192; Gregory Vlastos, *Socrates* (Cambridge: Cambridge University Press, 1991), 179–199. For a useful challenge to some of the assertions put forth by scholars who try to attribute this passage to the "historical" Protagoras, see R.F. Stalley, "Punishment in Plato's 'Protagoras,'" *Phronesis* 40 (1995): 1–19.
43. I am heartened to find this thesis corroborated by a study that analyzes the Great Speech from an historical-institutional approach. According to C. Fred Alford, "A Note on the Institutional Context of Plato's 'Protagoras,'" *The Classical World* 81 (1988): 167–176, "Protagoras can be seen as emphasizing those aspects of leadership that most [citizens] might have learned, and downplaying those aspects that required special training. In other words Protagoras' argument is . . . designed perhaps especially to appeal to the ideological self-understanding of the democrats."
44. See Adkins, "*Aretē*, *Technē*, Democracy and Sophists."

45. And because commentators frequently fail to see how deep and yet equivocal the similarities are, they have tended to mistake the differences. Gagarin "Plato's *Protagoras*" notices the basic similarity: Protagoras and Socrates both treat the "nature and teachability of *aretē*" as "the crucial problem in life" (133). This is not the only similarity, nor is it true without qualification. The sophist who appears in Plato does not treat the quest for an understanding of the nature (*physis*) of *aretē* as the crucial problem of life. He assumes he already knows what aretē is. On this point, see also, Terrance Irwin, "Plato's Objections to the Sophists," in Anton Powell, ed., *The Greek World* (New York: Routledge, 1995), 568–590.
46. Noticed by Ferrarin, "Protagoras and the Myth of Prometheus," 304.
47. This is not to deny the crucial differences between Protagoras' and Socrates' accounts of civic origins. War, for instance, is not handled in the same way. But I stress (a) that the accounts are basically similar—in other words, their similarity should strike commentators more than it has; and (b) only on the basis of the similarities can we home in on the differences. Socrates is not original (according to Plato's presentation) in offering a fresh account of the origins of cities. In this, he follows Protagoras. He is original in the specifics of his account.
48. For example, we might consider the way Socrates presents justice in the *Crito*, as if it were synonymous with obedience to the laws, when we know that Socrates allowed for the possibility of civil disobedience under some conditions. He obscures his full understanding in the *Crito* because his interlocutor shows insufficient concern for civic justice and is thus unprepared to hear of its limits. This is an example of the pedagogical use of artful speech, equivalent to Protagoras' encouraging all citizens to be (civically) just, moderate, and pious.
49. That Protagoras sensed this tension is evident from his remark about forethought (316c) just prior to his speech.
50. The theme of forethought runs through the entire dialogue, and careful attention to it illuminates many passages. Socrates' understanding of forethought is apparent in his initial exchange with Hippocrates (310d–314b), and again in the dialogue's closing lines. Protagoras' understanding is stated at 316d–317c, and is exemplified by the Great Speech.

51. Similarly, see Stalley, "Punishment in Plato's "Protagoras," 18; and Irwin, "Plato's Objections to the Sophists."

CHAPTER 4. PRODICUS

1. (Baton Rouge: Louisiana State University Press, 1957), 271.
2. The report about Xenophon in Boeotia comes from the third-century A.D. chronicler of the sophists, Philostratus (*Lives of the Sophists*, I.12). According to other sources, Prodicus also instructed Isocrates, Euripides, and Thucydides (see DK 84 A7–9). For an ambitious (though sometimes dubious) attempt to detect Prodicus' influence in numerous concrete passages of Sophocles, Euripides, Herodotus, Thucydides, and a host of other figures, see H. Mayer, *Prodikos von Keos und die Anfänge der Synonymik bei den Griechen* (Paderborn: Ferdinand Schöningh, 1913); for his likely influence on Thucydides in particular see also W.K.C. Guthrie, *The Sophists* (Cambridge: Cambridge University Press, 1969), 223–224.
3. *Prt.* 315c–316a, 337a–c, 339e-342a, 357e, 358a–e; see also *Apol.* 19e; *Charm.* 163d; *Crat.* 384b; *Lach.* 197d; *Meno* 75e, 96d; *Euthyd.* 277e, 305c; *Hipp. Maj.* 282c; *Phdr.* 256b; *Symp.* 177b; *Rep.* 600c; and *Tht.* 151b. He is also discussed in the pseudo-Platonic *Axiochus*; *Eryxias*, and *Theages*.
4. Contrast D.J. Stewart's remark in his introduction to "Prodicus" in R.K. Sprague, ed., *The Older Sophists* (Columbia: University of South Carolina Press, 1972), 70: "it is undeniable that Plato's general estimation of [Prodicus] was very negative: Plato is particularly insistent upon Prodicus' avid pursuit of both pleasure and the financial means to achieve it, and upon his monomania for overly precise definitions." I hope to show that this generalization fails to reflect Plato's nuanced treatment of Prodicus.
5. R.C. Bartlett, *Plato: Protagoras and Meno* (Ithaca: Cornell University Press, 2004), 70.
6. To these passages one may add a passage from the pseudo-Platonic *Axiochus* (366c): as he is attempting to explain to Axiochus that death is preferable to life, Socrates states, "These things I have been saying are just chance echoes from the words of Prodicus, which I purchased from time to time for a half-drachma, or two drachmas, or even four." The *Axiochus* contains well-known Stoic

and Epicurean arguments that suggest that the text was composed sometime between 100 BC and 50 AD. I thus do not rely on it for any essential points, even though the author likely had more access to information about Prodicus' life and teachings than we currently possess.

7. Guthrie's cautionary remark (*Sophists*, 276) is very much on my mind. He, too, was intrigued by the "close personal relations" between Socrates and Prodicus, but he thought it practically impossible "to extract from the nuances of Plato's literary portraits a prosaic and agreed account of the relations between the two men"—or, if not impossible, then "at least very much at the mercy of subjective impressions." I agree that the matter is not one that can be settled. However, many students of Plato will not be aware of the close connection between Socrates and Prodicus at all, and thus an honest examination of the evidence can only be helpful.
8. I am referring to the setting in Xenophon, but the speech had another setting as well, which is unfortunately lost to us. It was, according to a number of ancient sources, part of Prodicus' book called the *Horai*, or *Seasons*. That the speech appeared in written form is not at all incompatible with Prodicus' having recited it—books (and parts of books) were often read out loud to live audiences. For some conjectures about the possible contents and purposes of the *Horai*, see W. Nestle, "Die Horen des Prodikos," *Hermes* 71 (1936): 151–170. The discussion in M. Untersteiner, *The Sophists*, trans. K. Freeman (Oxford: Basil Blackwell, 1954), 206–216, is also of interest, though more speculative than Nestle's study and somewhat too prone to present conjecture as fact.
9. A follower of Socrates (cf. *Phd.* 59c) known for teaching that the goal of human action ought to be pleasure and that present pleasures should not be deferred for the sake of future ones. As such, his outlook was the extreme opposite of that articulated by Prodicus in the *Choice of Hercules*. Aristippus (or possibility his grandson) would go on to found the Cyrene school of hedonistic philosophy, named after his birthplace in Africa.
10. Xenophon (*Mem.* II.i.34) has Socrates vouch for the content of the speech, but not the style; "Prodicus," he says, "has clothed the thoughts in even finer phrases than I have done now."
11. All translations from the *Memorabilia* are my own.
12. Ibid., 29; the historical Prodicus was famous for making distinctions

such as this (see below), and we might thus reasonably suppose that some element of Prodicus' own language is preserved in this speech.

13. Prodicus' fable was a commonplace in art and literature from the sixteenth century through the late nineteenth century. There were paintings made by Veronese, Poussin, Rubens, Caracci, and Ricci. In England, it was a favorite of the third Earl of Shaftesbury, who in 1713 commissioned another painting by Matteis; it was also popularized through a translation (from Xenophon) by Joseph Addison in *The Tatler* (November 22, 1709). Then came a number of musical settings: Bach's "Hercules auf dem Scheideweg," (BWV213), first performed in Leipzig in 1733; and Handel's "The Choice of Hercules" (HWV69), first performed at Covenant Garden in 1751. There were also poetic settings too numerous to detail, and the story was widely anthologized, so that by 1850 the historian George Grote, *History of Greece*, vol. 8 (London: John Murray), 511, could write that it was available "in every book professing to collect impressive illustrations of elementary morality." The waning of the speech's popularity, on the other hand, seems to have accompanied the critique of Victorian moralizing that began in the twentieth century. Guthrie, *The Sophists*, 278, for example, remarks with notable disdain that "if all sophistic teaching were like this it would confirm the view expressed by Plato in the *Republic* (493a) that the so-called wisdom of the sophists boils down to a rehash of the conventional opinions of the crowd." What is hard to explain is how the love of Prodicus' speech prior to the twentieth century could have been reconciled with the general view that the sophists were villains; as far as I can tell, Grote was the first to notice the incongruity.
14. That Plato did indeed know of the speech is suggested by another reference to it at *Symposium* 177b.
15. I would not go as far as E. Dupréel, *Les Sophistes* (Neuchatel: Éditions du Griffon, 1948), 18: "because Prodicus was above all else a moralist; it is necessary to see him as the moralist *par excellence* of his time." This is a *non sequitur*.
16. In the *Works and Days*, there are two kinds of divine strife, one that is cruel and warlike, another that is more wholesome and kind. Perses—the pupil of the poem—is to keep company with wholesome strife (striving jealously to work harder than one's neighbors)

while steering clear of cruel strife (striving to seize another's goods). Yet Hesiod's advice to Perses is not advice for man *qua* man, but for man *qua* poor and weak man (*WD* 214). Once Perses has produced enough stock of his own to keep him strong, then he too might "raise disputes and strive to get another's goods" (ibid., 11–34). The equivocation in Hesiod's case for justice is illustrated in the famous fable of the hawk and nightingale (ibid., 201–212), which teaches that power places its possessor above the moral constraints of the weak and the poor. Zeus, who sees crooked judgments and unjust minds, *may* punish the wicked for their folly (ibid., 1–10, 248–266), but this is hardly a ringing endorsement of justice. The problem with the moral universe as Hesiod conceives it is traceable ultimately back to the nature of the gods themselves. Zeus's rule is the rule of power.

17. 317d10–e2; Alcibiades' beauty is stressed in the opening lines of the dialogue, 309a–b.
18. In this vein Henry Sidgwick, "The Sophists," *Journal of Philology* (1873), 68, chided the "refined barbarity with which Plato . . . satirized the poor invalid professor shivering under his sheepskins."
19. *The Sophists*, 247.
20. The earliest evidence for Prodicus' theory comes from a treatise (*On Piety*) by an Epicurean poet and philosopher of the first century BC named Philodemus, who himself appears to be relying on the testimony of a minor Stoic writer named Persaeus (ca. 306–243 BC) as well as the philosopher Epicurus (341–270 BC). None of this gets us quite to the fifth century BC; but there is so much independent testimony about Prodicus' theory that its existence is hard to doubt. For the references in Philodemus (most of which are not in DK), see A. Henrichs, "Two Doxographical Notes: Democritus and Prodicus on Religion," *Harvard Studies in Classical Philology*, vol. 79 (1975): 93–123; and further, D. Obbink, *Philodemus On Piety Part I: Critical Text with Commentary* (Oxford: Oxford University Press, 1996), esp. 13, 143, and 352–357. For the other ancient sources see the list in Guthrie, *Sophists*, 238–239 (updating DK, but failing to capture the full range of references in Philodemus).
21. *Herculaneum Papyrus* 1428, fragment 19, on which, see the indispensable philological analysis of A. Henrichs, "The Atheism of Prodicus," *Cronache Ercolanesi* 6 (1976): 15–21.
22. *On Piety* I.519–530 in Obbink, *Philodemus*, 143. To date, Obbink

has only come out with Part I of *On Piety*, which is why the previous note refers to the papyrus itself, even though this is a later part of the same treatise.

23. On the possible connotations of the term and its abuses in fifth-century discourse, see Obbink, ibid., 1–23 with references.
24. For a discussion of various elements of this interpretation, see Guthrie, *Sophists*, 40; and A. Henrichs, "The Sophists and Hellenistic Religion: Prodicus as the Spiritual Father of the ISIS Aretalogies," *Harvard Studies in Classical Philology* 88 (1984): 139–158, esp. 144–145 (both of whom shy away from it in favor of a more thoroughgoing atheism). As for other commentators, I am unable to determine whether it is this option (1) or rather option (3) being attributed to Prodicus by L. Versényi, *Socratic Humanism* (Yale: Yale University Press, 1963), 59–60; and by E.R. Dodds, *Euripides Bacchae* (Oxford: Clarendon Press, 1960), 104, on the basis of a striking similarity between Prodicus' doctrines and the words of the blind seer Teiresias at *Bacchae* 274ff.
25. I state this emphatically because A. Henrichs, whose work on Prodicus is in so many ways superb, seems to exaggerate (in "Two Doxographical Notes," 109) the extent to which *Herculaneum Papyrus* 1428, fr. 19, "provides clear proof of Prodicus' own confession of radical atheism." It does nothing of the sort. It merely states Philodemus' view (the accuracy of which we do not know) that Prodicus denied the *traditional* gods. If he did so, he would certainly have been radical (though not original); but his radicalism in this case should not be conflated with complete atheism, especially not when we are dealing with a thinker like Prodicus whose business it was to make careful distinctions; cf. the brief but quite sound-minded comments on this matter by J. de Romilly, *The Great Sophists in Periclean Athens*, trans., J. Lloyd (Oxford: Clarendon Press, 1992), 107 and 142.
26. Trans., anonymous, in W. Oates and E. O'Neill Jr., ed., *Complete Greek Drama*, vol. 2 (New York: Random House, 1938), 762.
27. *Prt.* 337a–c, 339e–342a, 358a–e; *Charm.* 163d; *Crat.* 384b; *Lach.* 197d; *Meno* 75e, 96d; and *Euthyd.* 277e, 305c.
28. See further C.J. Classen, "The Study of Language amongst Socrates' Contemporaries," *Proceedings of the African Classical Associations* (1959), 33–49; reprinted in Classen, ed. *Sophistik* (Darmstadt:

Wissenschaftliche Buchgesellschaft, 1976), 215–247, to which all subsequent references are made.

29. Trans., R. Bartlett, *Plato: Protagoras and Meno* (Ithaca: Cornell University Press, 2004), 35–36.
30. So Alexander of Aphrodisias suggests in his *Commentary on Aristotle's Topics*, 181.2 (= DK 84 A19); see n. 40 below.
31. See Meyer, *Prodikos von Keos*, 78; and Romilly, *The Great Sophists*, 75. There are other passages, too, in Thucydides where Prodicean-style *diairesis* appears; perhaps the most striking is the speech by Pericles at II.62.4, which distinguishes between fighting with "spirit" and with "disdain," and between "hope" and "judgment." See further, Guthrie, *The Sophists*, 224, who gathers some of these references up and offers a brief discussion.
32. That Prodicus would have used *diairesis* in his work as a diplomat has not been adequately noticed in the literature on this sophist; Classen considers only various philosophical applications of the art in "The Study of Language amongst Socrates' Contemporaries," 231–238.
33. Trans., R.K. Sprague in *Plato's Complete Works* (Indianapolis: Hackett, 1997), 682.
34. The number of names invoked makes this a delightfully complex interlude in the *Protagoras*. To recapitulate, a conversation between Socrates and Protagoras about *aretē* gives way to Protagoras' monologue about Simonides, in which he accuses the poet of self-contradiction. The supposed contradiction occurs at the point where Simonides refers to the views of the earlier poet, Pittacus, on aretē. After Protagoras finishes his display, Socrates reenters the conversation, invoking Prodicus' art of diairesis, to show that Protagoras has failed to notice a subtle distinction, which Simonides likely did notice. Reinterpreting Simonides' poem with this distinction in mind, Socrates shows that the supposed contradiction is spurious.
35. See the witty and interesting analysis by Anne Carson, "How Not to Read a Poem: Unmixing Simonides from *Protagoras*," *Classical Philology* 87 (1992): 110–130; see also, Dorothea Frede, "The Impossibility of Perfection: Socrates' Criticism of Simonides' Poem in the *Protagoras*," *Review of Metaphysics* 39 (1986): 713–753; Marina Berzins McCoy, "Socrates on Simonides: The Uses of Poetry in Socratic and Platonic Rhetoric," *Philosophy and Rhetoric*

32 (1999): 349–367; and Franco V. Trivigno, "Childish Nonesense? The Value of Interpretation in Plato's *Protagoras*," *Journal of the History of Philosophy* 51 (2013): 509–543.

36. I am reminded of William James' rule of thumb in his lecture, "What Pragmatism Means" that "whenever you meet a contradiction you must make a distinction," *William James: Pragmatism and Other Essays* (New York: Penguin, 2000), 24.
37. *Abusus non tollit usum.*
38. Trans., R.K. Sprague, *Complete Works of Plato*, 715.
39. Trans., A. Bloom, *The Republic of Plato* (New York: Basic Books, 1968), 132.
40. Aristotle (*Topics* II.6) warns against "taking something to be a different thing because it has a different name, as Prodicus used to divide pleasures into joy and delight and good cheer; for all these are names of the same thing, to wit, pleasure." And Alexander of Aphrodisias writes in his *Commentary on the Topics* (181.2 = DK 84 A19) that "this is the sort of thing said by men who love to lay down trivial laws, but have not care to say anything sensible."
41. The only commentator I can find who even mentions this passage is Dupréel, *Les Sophistes*, 128; but far from perceiving this as a criticism of Prodicus, Dupréel concludes simply that Prodicus "really was one of the commentators on Simonides." This is not the point.
42. Trans., Sprague, *Complete Works of Plato*, 715.
43. Extremely useful, but also limited: this characterization of *diairesis* comports with Socrates' proposal in the *Phaedrus* that *two* arts are necessary for philosophical clarity: one that "consists in seeing together [συνορῶντα] things that scattered about everywhere and collecting them into one kind," another that consists in "cutting up [διατέμνειν] each kind according to its species along its natural joints, and trying not to splinter any part, as a bad butcher might do" (265c–266a).

Chapter 5. The Sophist Hippias and the Problem of *Polytropia*

1. Aristotle, *Ethics* 1140b, trans. Martin Ostwald, *Aristotle: Nicomachean Ethics* (Indianapolis: Library of the Liberal Arts, 1962).
2. See Charles Kahn, "The Beautiful and the Genuine," *Oxford Studies in Ancient Philosophy* 3 (1985): 267–273, with references.

3. For discussion of some of Hippias' chief traits, see W.K.C. Guthrie, *The Sophists* (Cambridge: Cambridge University Press, 1971), 280 ff.; and G.B. Kerferd, *The Sophistic Movement* (Cambridge: Cambridge University Press, 1981), ch. 5.
4. *Odyssey* I.1; see also *Odyssey* 10.330.
5. The importance of *polytropia* for understanding Socrates' encounter with Hippias has been noticed by Laurence Lampert, "Socrates' Defense of Polytropic Odysseus: Lying and Wrong-Doing in Plato's *Lesser Hippias*, *Review of Politics* 64 (2002): 231–259. Though I admire what Lampert accomplishes in his study, I offer an interpretation that differs in crucial respects. The Socrates I present is less knowing, more searching; and his *polytropia* is a pedagogical and philosophical tool, not a political tool for veiling his wisdom from the masses.
6. For the chronological link, see *Hipp. Maj.* 286a–c. Hippias' speech, on the subject of fine (or noble) practices, which a young man must take up if he wants to become esteemed, stands in the background of both dialogues. Plato does not allow us to hear the speech, but he has Hippias summarize its content as involving the heroic character, Nestor, propounding a "great many very noble customs" to the son of Achilles, Neoptolemus, in order to teach him how to earn respect (*Hipp. Maj.* 286a–b).
7. *Hipp. Min.* 363b–c. Unless otherwise noted, I use the translation by James Leake in Thomas Pangle, ed., *The Roots of Political Philosophy: Ten Forgotten Socratic Dialogues* (Ithaca: Cornell University Press, 1987).
8. Apemantus' view was probably conventional wisdom. Odysseus tended to be vilified in fifth-century Athenian literature.
9. The dialogue offers further delights in this vein: Hippias claims to have an expert memory but Socrates has to remind him about details from the *Iliad* that bear on the issue at hand. More fundamentally, Socrates has to remind Hippias of the various things he has assented to over the course of the conversation in order to show him that he has contradicted himself.
10. Thus Wilamowitz, *Platon* (Berlin: Weidmann, 1919), band I, p. 139, described it as an exquisitely humorous little work with no moral content but the sole purpose of satirizing Hippias.
11. For a good discussion of the fallacies, see for example, John Beversluis, *Cross-Examining Socrates: A Defense of the Interlocutors in*

Plato's Early Dialogues (Cambridge: Cambridge Univesity Press, 2000), 94–110.

12. In other words, we must wrestle with the problem brought out by Otto Apelt, *Platonische Aufsaetze* (Leipzig, 1912), who referred to the *Hippias Minor* as "a kind of apologia for sin" and spoke of its "reversal of all moral ideas." Horrified by such apparent immorality, Apelt rejected the dialogue as spurious. If we, by contrast, are to accept the dialogue as authentic (as is now standard, because Aristotle seems to reference it at *Metaph.* 1025a6), it is incumbent on us to explain the purpose of the traits that Apelt found so abhorrent.
13. In his notes (p. 284), James Leake tracks the alterations: "In verse 310 [Hippias] changes our text of Homer from 'as I think' to 'as I am going to do,' and in verse 314 he changes 'as it seems to me to be best' to 'as it is also going to be fulfilled,' apparently to underline Achilles' certainty."
14. An illuminating treatment of Socratic irony is Alexander Nehamas, "Socratic Irony: Character and Interlocutors," in *The Art of Living* (Berkeley: University of California Press, 1998), 46–98, which serves as a useful corrective to Gregory Vlastos, "Socratic Irony," in *Socrates: Ironist and Moral Philosopher* (Cambridge: Cambridge University Press, 1991), 21–44.
15. Consider, for example, *Republic* 337a, *Symposium* 216e, and *Apology* 37e–38a. Lampert, "Socrates' Defense of Polytropic Odysseus," 234–235 and 255–259, fruitfully compares Socrates' polytropism to that of his unscrupulous pupil, Alcibiades.
16. *Kalon* is, according to Hippias, a fine girl, gold, burying one's parents, the appropriate, the able and useful, the beneficial, and/or aesthetic pleasure.
17. Roslyn Weiss, "*Ho Agathos* as *Ho Dunatos* in the *Hippias Minor*," *Classical Quarterly* 31 (1981): 287–304; and *The Socratic Paradox and Its Enemies* (Chicago: University of Chicago Press, 1998), 122–129, points out that this argument (as well as Socrates' subsequent arguments in the dialogue) can be read in a way that avoids fallacy. In the present case, one need only read the argument as saying: the man who is *able* to lie is the same as the man who is *able* to speak the truth; then the fallacy vanishes. This is true, but Socrates intentionally implies more than this. He implies that the liar and the truth teller are the same *simpliciter*, not merely in their potential

ability to lie but in their whole self; and it is this that makes Hippias uncomfortable. Throughout the dialogue, then, Socrates makes arguments that are technically valid from the vantage point of *dunamis* (ability), but fallacious insofar as that vantage point is too narrow. For analysis of some of the fallacies that result when the arguments are read broadly as Plato invites them to be read, see (in addition to my remarks here) Ruby Blondell, *Play of Character in Plato's Dialogues* (Cambridge: Cambridge University Press, 2002), 137–138; Charles H. Kahn, *Plato and the Socratic Dialogue: The Philosophical Use of a Literary Form* (Cambridge: Cambridge University Press, 1996), 113–124; and Rosamond Kent Sprague, *Plato's Use of Fallacy* (London: Routledge, 1962).

18. "The same man is a liar and truthful" (367c, 367d). In context, Socrates may mean this in a non-fallacious sense: liars and truth tellers are the same with respect to specific characteristics, but the statement is ambiguous and intended to be so. The alternate meaning—that is, truth tellers and liars are identical—is implied from the start, and this meaning becomes dominant at 369b: "Now then, do you perceive that the same man has come to light as being both truthful and a liar, . . . and these men are not different from one another or opposite but alike [*homoioi*]." See also, Beversluis, *Cross-Examining Socrates,* 100.

19. *Antilogikē* was the subject of Protagoras' two-volume book, *Antilogiôn* (*Contradictory Arguments*, DK 80 B5) and probably several other books as well, such as *On Truth* and *The Art of Debating*. I discuss the technique in detail in, "The Sophist Protagoras in Plato's *Theaetetus*," a paper presented to the American Political Science Association, Washington DC, September 2005. As I understand it, *antilogikē* was designed to have a certain effect on a specific type of interlocutor, the type who is too quick to accept initial appearances as true. It consisted in manipulating mental impressions so that opposite appearances would emerge, with the result that the interlocutor would either have to admit self-contradiction, or abandon the belief that his first impression should count simply as true. Socrates illustrates the technique in the *Theaetetus* (*Tht.* 154c–d): if one examines a group of six dice next to a group of four dice, the group of six will appear to be "more." They *are* more (we are inclined to say). But if we now swap out the group of four for a

group of twelve, the six will suddenly appear "less." Are they less? If we affirm that they are, then Protagoras will accuse us of contradicting ourselves, for we have just a second ago affirmed them to be "more," and yet the six dice have not changed or altered in any way. If we deny they are less, however, we not only defy common sense, we also beg the question of how (on our own assumptions) something that "appears" less will not *be* less.

20. Mary Whitlock Blundell, "Character and Meaning in Plato's *Hippias Minor*," *Oxford Studies in Ancient Philosophy* (Supplementary Volume, 1992): 131–172, offers a thoughtful analysis of the many ways in which Hippias' character determines Socrates' pedagogical strategies.
21. Earlier in the dialogue, (*Hipp Min* 365d) Socrates had advised Hippias: "Well, let us leave Homer aside, since it is impossible to ask him what he was thinking when he composed these verses anyway." Compare Socrates' remarks in the *Protagoras* (347c–348a) about "setting the poets aside and conducting the conversation on the basis of our own ideas."
22. See esp. *Hipp. Min.* 372a: "How, Socrates, can those who are voluntarily unjust, who have voluntarily plotted and done evil, be better than those who do so involuntarily, when for the latter there seems to be much forgiveness—when someone unknowingly acts unjustly or lies or does some other evil? And the laws, surely, are much more harsh toward those who do evil voluntarily and lie than toward those who do so involuntarily."
23. I am sympathetic to the move that Lampert makes at this point ("Socrates' Defense of Polytropic Odysseus," 249, 253), but I take a different tack. Lampert argues that nothing has gone wrong in Socrates' argument. Socrates means to say that from the vantage point of the many, the actions of the philosopher (the truly good man) will be *regarded* as harmful, unjust, deceptive, and wrong. The philosopher commits these acts voluntarily, knowing them to be just from a higher point of view; but they seem criminal to most men. Lampert is not specific about what these acts might be, but he suggests that lying in order to preserve a place for philosophy in civic life might be one of them.
24. As, for example, in Thucydides' account of the two-day debate over Mytilene (III.36–50). Also, Plato's *Crito* is a sustained meditation

on the tension: the character Crito feels the extreme pressure to live up to certain standards of competence and power, even as he acknowledges Socrates' arguments about the importance of being just.

25. *Hipp. Maj.* 304a–b.
26. Here I agree with Weiss, "If There Be Such a Man," in *Socratic Paradox*, 146. "The justice that the conventional Hippias associates with guilelessness and innocence is clearly no *technē*. But Hippias, qua teacher of *aretē*, feels constrained to call justice a *technē*."
27. According to the *Apology* (21b–22e), Socrates was well known for interrogating high-profile figures with a reputation for wisdom. Politicians, poets, and manual artisans were especially interesting to him, and it is striking to consider the extent to which Hippias fits such categories—not one, but all. Politician: He served his native city of Elis as a diplomat, perhaps the chief diplomat, during the intense years of the Peloponnesian War (*Hipp. Maj.* 281a–c). Poet: Hippias regularly lists poetry (epic, tragic, and dithyrambic) among his areas of expertise (see *Hipp. Min.* 368c–d; cf. 363c), and we read in Pausanius *Description of Greece* V.25.4, that he was indeed a poet of some note, one of his elegies having been inscribed on a set of bronze statues at Olympia. Craftsman: *Hipp. Min.* 368b–e rather humorously relates a time when Hippias showed up in the city of Olympia bearing nothing but articles of his own making: a girdle more fine than the most expensive ones from Persia, a cloak, a tunic, sandals, a ring with an intricately engraved seal, an oil flask, and a strigil. Blondell, *Play of Character*, 139, also senses the connection between Socrates' conduct in his dialogue and his elenctic mission described at *Ap.* 21c.
28. "The Meaning of 'Ethical Neutrality' in Sociology and Economics," in Edward Shils and Henry Finch, trans., *Max Weber on the Methodology of the Social Sciences* (Glencoe: Free Press, 1949), 19: "The social sciences, which are strictly empirical sciences, are the least fitted to presume to save the individual the difficulty of making a choice, and they should therefore not create the impression that they can do so."
29. *The Human Condition* (Chicago: University of Chicago Press, 1958), 3. "The question is only whether we wish to *use* our new scientific and technical knowledge . . . , and this is a question that

cannot be decided by scientific means; it is a political question of the first order and therefore can hardly be left to the decision of professional scientists or professional politicians."

30. Blondell, *Play of Character*, 146–147, likewise sees a pedagogical strategy behind Socrates' refutations in this dialogue, one based on Hippias' inability to distinguish (as Blondell puts it) between "capacity" and "disposition."
31. Cf. Kahn, *Plato and the Socratic Dialogue*, 124: Socrates is engaged in "a *reductio* of the moralizing or 'allegorical' interpretation of Homer. If this is possible in Homeric exegesis, anything is possible. Philosophers concerned with moral truth should busy themselves with something else." For a quite different interpretation, see Lampert, "Socrates' Defense of Polytropic Odysseus," who claims that Socrates' ostensible doubts about knowing Homer's meaning are themselves polytropic. Socrates thinks it *is* possible to know what Homer thought. Like Socrates, Homer thought that polytropic Odysseus was the best man—one who knew when to lie, when to be "unjust" (by conventional standards). However, it was necessary for Homer to veil his endorsement of Odysseus because such an endorsement would not be salutary as a political teaching for the masses.
32. So, too, Blundell, "Character and Meaning," 170–171: "The purpose is not to mislead Hippias, but to provoke him into thinking for himself," and so on.
33. "The Irony of Liberalism," in *Soliloquies in England and Later Soliloquies* (New York: Charles Scribner's Sons, 1922), 181. Santayana was criticizing modern liberalism in particular for its moral oppressiveness, but he recognizes early on in this powerful soliloquy (178) that the ancients had it even worse.
34. Weber (op. cit., 18) is extremely perceptive and quite Socratic on this point: "The shallowness of our routinized daily existence . . . consists indeed in the fact that the persons who are caught up in it do not become aware, and above all do not wish to become aware, of this partly psychologically, part pragmatically conditioned motley of irreconcilably antagonistic values. . . . The fruit of the tree of knowledge, which is distasteful to the complacent but which is, nonetheless, inescapable, consists in the insight that every single important activity and ultimately life as a whole, if it is not to be permitted to run on as an event in nature but is instead to be

consciously guided, is a series of ultimate decisions through which the soul—as in Plato—chooses its own fate, i.e., the meaning of its activity and existence."

35. Blondell, *Play of Character*, 121–124, discusses the competitive aspects of Socratic refutation and goes on in the end to argue that Socrates subordinates the competitive side of *aretē* to the moral side; her interpretation thus moves beyond the tension I present as the upshot the dialogue.

Chapter 6. Brother Sophists

1. *I Sophisti*, 2. edizione riveduta e notevolmente ampliata, con un'appendice su le origini sociali della sofistica (Milano: Lampugnani Nigri, 1967); also in English as *The Sophists*, trans. Kathleen Freedman (Oxford: Basil Blackwell, 1954).
2. *History of Greek Philosophy*, vol. III, part I (Cambridge: Cambridge University Press, 1969).
3. *The Great Sophists in Periclean Athens*, trans. Janet Lloyd (Oxford: Oxford University Press, 1992), 2.
4. As recognized rightly by Rosamond Kent Sprague, who has done more than anyone else to bring these important sophists to light. In the English translation of *Die Fragmente der Vorsokratiker* over which she presided, *The Older Sophists* (Columbia: University of South Carolina Press, 1972), Euthydemus and Dionysodorus are included as an appendix; Sprague has also offered multiple studies of Plato's *Euthydemus* over the course of her productive career. Her recognition of the brothers' importance is followed by G.B. Kerferd, *The Sophistic Movement* (Cambridge: Cambridge University Press, 1981).
5. Skepticism about their historical existence was laid to rest some time ago by Karl Praechter, "Platon und Euthydemos," *Philologus* 87 (1932): 121–135. Aristotle mentions Euthydemus twice (*Soph. Ref.* 177b12ff. and *Rhet.* 1401a26ff.), and cites him for a sophism that is not among those described in Plato's *Euthydemus*; Aristotle thus knows of him independently of the Platonic dialogue. Xenophon treats Dionysodorus in the *Memorabilia* (III.1) in a way that comports with, but clearly does not derive from, Plato's description of him.

6. 268c–d, translation F.M. Cornford in Edith Hamilton and Huntington Cairnes, eds., *The Collected Dialogues of Plato*, 7th ed. (Princeton: Princeton University Press, 2005).
7. See for example, Paul Natorp, *Platos Edeenlehre* (Leipzig: Verlag von Felix Meiner, 1921), 119–122, who presents it as "eine Art Satyrspiel" and little more than an appendix to the *Theaetetus*. In English, see A.E. Taylor, *Plato: The Man and His Work*, (London: Methuen, [1926] 1960), 89–90; and Benjamin Jowett, *The Dialogues of Plato*, Vol. I (Oxford: Oxford University Press, 1953), 194.
8. The *Euthydemus* is now well treated in a number of book-length studies: Herman Keulen, *Untersuchungen zu Platons "Euthydem"* (Wiesbaden: Otto Harrassowitz, 1971); Michael Narcy, *Le philosophe et son double. Un commentaire de l'Euthydème de Platon* (Paris, Librairie Philosophique J. Vrin, 1984); Monique Canto, *L'intrigue philosophique. Essai sur l'Euthydème de Platon* (Paris: Société d'Édition "Les Belles Lettres," 1987); and Thomas Chance, *Plato's Euthydemus: Analysis of What Is and Is Not Philsophy* (Berkeley: University of California Press, 1992). Also helpful is R.S.W. Hawtrey, *Commentary on Plato's Euthydemus* (Philadelphia: American Philological Society, 1981); and Thomas M. Robinson and Luc Brisson, *Plato: Euthydemus, Lysis, Charmides: Proceedings of the Fifth Symposium Platonicum* (Sankt Augustin: Academia Verlag, 2000), 3–153. Especially noteworthy among shorter studies are David Roochnik, "The Serious Play of Plato's *Euthydemus*," *Interpretation* 18, no. 2, (Winter 1990): 211–232; and Francisco J. Gonzalez, *Dialectic and Dialogue: Plato's Practice of Philosophical Inquiry* (Evanston: Northwestern University Press, 1998), 94–128.
9. The *Euthydemus* is one of the most structurally pleasing of all Plato's dialogues. Employing the technique of ring composition, it begins with a two-part prologue (the opening frame with Crito, and an introduction by Socrates) and ends with a two-part epilogue (Socrates' conclusion, and the closing frame with Crito) in between, which appear five alternating eristic and protreptic scenes. The structure is thus A B [C D C D C] B A. Thomas Chance's otherwise very fine discussion of the dialogue's structure (*Plato's Euthydemus*, 13–15, 211) fails to mention the ring technique, the significance of which is that the rings of the same letter (as I have represented them here) contain similar thematic material and thus cross-illuminate each other in important ways (cf. Hawtrey,

Commentary, 33). This is why, for example, it is not only possible but also *necessary* for me to consider material from the closing frame in my discussion of the opening frame, and vice versa.

10. As, for example, he does with Hippocrates in the *Protagoras* (313a–c). The difference will be explained by Crito's age and his unique pedagogical needs.
11. Unless otherwise noted, translations of the *Euthydemus* are those of Rosamond Kent Sprague in John M. Cooper and D.S. Hutchinson, eds., *Plato: Complete Works* (Indianapolis: Hackett, 1997).
12. See Narcy, *Le philosophe et son double*, 35–57.
13. One may be tempted to explain Socrates' irony thus: just as the sophists possess a merely apparent excellence in speaking, Socrates grants them his merely apparent praise. But this does not explain why Socrates would also allow Crito to be confused about the sophists' value. Whatever lies behind Socrates' irony, it must extend to his interaction with Crito.
14. I am aware of only seven appearances in all of Plato.
15. Socrates' mention of the "third wave" at *Euthydemus* 293a combined with the references to the lover of hearing (304c, 274c) effectively links the dialogue to *Rep.* V. I am convinced that these dialogues in general should be used to illuminate each other.
16. The lover of sights is consistently paired with the *philēkoos* in *Rep.* V.
17. This is evident also in the way Crito is portrayed in the *Crito* and the *Phaedo*.
18. This becomes especially clear at the end of the dialogue (304d–305b, 305e, 306d–307a).
19. For example, Leo Strauss, "On the Euthydemus," *Interpretation* 1 (1970), 1.
20. It is described as a sickness in *Rep.* V (476e2).
21. See ch. 5, n. 19 earlier.
22. The frequent repetition of the verb *akouō* at pivotal places in the dialogue (twenty-three instances in all) helps corroborate the connection between Crito and the lover of hearing in *Rep.* V. I point to some of the more important appearances of the verb as I come upon them; but see the short passage that runs 304c6–305a8 as an example.
23. See, for example, Chance, *Plato's Euthydemus*, 23–26; Hawtrey, *Commentary*, 54.

24. Setting the *Euthydemus* aside, Socrates uses the word only three times in all the genuine dialogues and never in its pedagogical connotation (*Ap.* 31d; *Prt.* 328d, 348c). Socrates does claim to *exhort* Athenians (see, e.g., *Ap.* 29d ff.); and his conversations in general can certainly be *described* as protreptic, as I describe them in this book and as they are also described by Clitophon in the dialogue that bears his name (408c, 410b); see also Ruby Blondell, *The Play of Character in Plato's Dialogues* (Cambridge: Cambridge University Press, 2002), 115. On the absence of explicit Socratic protreptic, see further Ann N. Michelini, "Socrates Plays the Buffoon: Cautionary Protreptic in *Euthydemus*," *American Journal of Philology* 121 (2000), 510–513; S.R. Slings, *Plato: Clitophon* (Cambridge: Cambridge University Press, 1999), 59–164; and Konrad Gaiser, *Protreptik und Paränese bei Platon: Untersuchengen zur Form des platonischen Dialogus* (Stuttgart: W. Kohlhammer Verlag, 1959).
25. Diongenes Laeretius II.121, attributes a number of dialogues to Crito, of which one is entitled, *That Men Are Not Made Good By Teaching*. Still, this should not be used as decisive evidence, because scholars generally agree that Crito is unlikely to have authored the dialogues in question; see Debora Nails, *The People of Plato: A Prosopography of Plato and Other Socratics* (Indianapolis: Hackett, 2002), 115–116; for the opposite view, however, see, for example, Rudolph Hirzel, *Der Dialog. Ein literarhistorischer Versuch*, vol. I (Leipzig: S. Hirzel, 1895), 107, who not only regards the dialogues as genuine, but also finds that their mostly practical subjects comport with Crito's character. The entry for Crito in *Paulys Realencyclopädie der Classischen Altertumswissenschaft* (Stuttgart: Alfred Druckenmüller Verlag, 1957) leans toward accepting them as well, pointing out that the dialogues could have been written "without philosophical depth—somewhat like Xenophon does."
26. For paradigmatic examples of these dangers consider Socrates' exchanges with Hippocrates (*Prt.* 313a–c) and Anytus (*Meno* 92a–c); his reply to Anytus' contemptuous dismissal of the sophists is especially pertinent to our central thesis: "How . . . can you know whether there is something good or useless in this matter when you are completely without experience of it?"
27. There is humor here: Dionysodorus, master of troop formation and military command, fails to position himself well and leaves his regiment to take their positions according to chance. In the

Memorabilia (III.1), Xenophon's Socrates conveys a similarly dim view of Dionysodorus' ability to practice and teach generalship.

28. The danger of "misology"; see *Phd.* 89c–90d, a passage that is, intriguingly, connected to the *Euthydemus* by the myth of Hercules, Iolaus, and the Hydra, on which, more later.
29. On Socrates' powerful role as narrator, see Anne-Marie Schultz, *Plato's Socrates as Narrator: A Philosophical Muse* (Lanham: Lexington Press, 2013). In her chapter on the *Euthydemus*, Schultz illuminates many features of this dialogue's narrative frame, as well as Socrates' role as narrator in the body of the dialogue itself.
30. Some superior being is τις τῶν κρειττόνων. Hawtrey (*Commentary*, 130–131) is certainly right that Socrates is alluding to something divine, while Crito assumes him to be alluding to himself; but either way, we are dealing here with considerable dramatic license.
31. Because Crito saw it occur (though he did not hear it), and its eristic quality is attested by the anonymous critic in the final frame.
32. Too fond, see *Rep.* 539b (this turns out to be a danger that Ctesippus does not escape); too frustrated, see *Phd.* 89c–90d (a danger that Socrates blocks for Clinias).
33. See n. 45 earlier, with the obvious foreshadowing of Socrates' trial.
34. The brothers' sophisms span a wide array of topics and are carefully catalogued in Herman Bonitz, *Platonische Studien* (Hildesheim: Georg Olms Verlagsbuchhandlung, [1886] 1968); a useful adumbration appears in Chance, *Plato's Euthydemus*, Appendix II.
35. Double twist (*dipla estrephe*) is Socrates' locution at 276d; if one compares the word for twist (*strephō*) to the stem of *protreptic* (*trepō*) one gleans an important insight: instead of turning their pupil towards wisdom, the sophists twist him around in circles.
36. They thus, in effect, practice *apotreptic* instead of protreptic, as Chance, *Plato's Euthydemus*, points out (see p. 14 with p. 226, n. 56.)
37. For a similar demystification of this sophism, see *Tht.* 199a. More generally, Socrates similarly proposes in *Rep.* V (454a ff.) that the confusion that eristic engenders can be removed by making proper distinctions, separating things out into their forms.
38. This helps explain why Socratic elenchus seems so different in the *Euthydemus*. Its gentleness struck Gregory Vlastos as a "strange departure" from earlier dialogues and led him to assert that the otherwise ubiquitous Socratic method had here been "jettisoned" by a profoundly changed Plato: *Socrates: Ironist and Moral*

Philosopher (Cambridge: Cambridge University Press, 1991), 117; see also Vlastos, "The Demise of the Elenchus in the *Euthydemus*, *Lysis* and *Hippias Major*," in Miles Burnyeat, ed., *Socratic Studies* (Cambridge: Cambridge University Press, 1994), 29–30. I regard this as a mistake (see also, Gonzalez, *Dialectic and Dialogue*, p. 94, n. 1, who does, too), and I highlight later the ways Socrates in fact refutes Clinias (multiple times) over the course of their discussion. That the views Socrates refutes originate with him rather than Clinias is explained by the need to build Clinias up.

39. Hawtrey refers to this as the "*ad hominem*" quality (in a good sense) of Socratic protreptic (*Commentary*, 76 and 91).
40. *Eu prattein*, used interchangeably with *eudaimones einai* in this protreptic, cf. 282a.
41. There is no agreement among commentators on this point; Roochnik ("Serious Play," 219–220) reads the digression as an attempt to highlight certain features of *technē.*
42. Cf. *Meno* 75c–d, where Socrates differentiates his own approach from eristic on two grounds: its comparative gentleness and its concern that the interlocutor understand the terms of the argument.
43. Rightness is *to orthōs*, but the word for "knowledge" changes throughout the passage because (as we later learn) it is not clear what sort of knowledge would be required: *epistēmē, phronēsis, sophia.*
44. For a provocative discussion of the implications of this passage for Socrates' ethical theory, see further, Christopher Gill, "Protreptic and Dialectic in Plato's *Euthydemus*," in Robinson and Brisson, eds., *Plato*, 133–143.
45. Notice that the protreptic begins and ends with Socrates describing what *he* desires and delights to hear (278d4–5, 282d4).
46. In the *Crito*, Crito proposes to use his wealth and that of others in a way Socrates regards as harmful (45a–b, 48c).
47. See 303d with 304d; 305a–b.
48. On the important idea that there is no shame in associating with people so long as one's quest for wisdom may be advanced, cf. *Symp*. 184c–d.
49. This is why Socrates ironically addresses them as though they were gods (*hosper theō prosagoreuō*), begging them to be propitious (*hileō*) and to forgive his mistake (273e). If they do indeed possess the knowledge they claim to possess, then they have discovered what Socrates cannot.

50. Cf. *Republic* 504d–505b, a crucial turning point in the argument, where it is revealed that the cardinal virtues defined in Book IV are of no advantage whatsoever without knowledge of the Good.
51. See, for example, Gonzalez, *Dialectic and Dialogue*, 102–104; Chance, *Plato's Euthydemus*, 67: "Socrates, too, can juggle ambiguous terms and even equivocate if he determines the situation warrants it.); Roochnik, "Serious Play," 217–222; Sprague, *Plato's Use of Fallacy* (London: Routledge and Kegan Paul, 1962); and M.A. Stewart, "Plato's Sophistry," *The Aristotelian Society*, Supplementary Volume LI (1977): 21–44.
52. Gonzalez, *Dialectic and Dialogue*, 102.
53. Gonzalez, ibid., 103, neatly catalogues the four major fallacies he detects in the passage.
54. That Socrates knows this argument to be lacking is suggested by the aside he offers as he reaches the conclusion. He tells Crito (280b1): "We finally agreed (*I don't know quite how*)."
55. Gonzalez, *Dialectic and Dialogue*, 104; cf. Richard Kraut, *Socrates and the State* (Princeton: Princeton University Press, 1984), 263ff. and 294ff.
56. As I have suggested there may be two ends in view here: Clinias' learning that he must be willing to reconsider and revise his views, and Crito's learning that he may be paying too much attention to fortune. Thus, although I agree with Gonzalez's general view that the fallaciousness is irrelevant to Socrates' purpose (p. 104, n. 17), I do not think that the fact of its irrelevance is the *only* lesson here; Gonzalez does not look far enough for what Clinias and Crito might learn even from fallacious arguments.
57. See Chance, *Plato's Euthydemus*, 97–100, for a thorough analysis of the fallacies.
58. Socrates recognizes the argument that "it is impossible to contradict" to be piece of leftover wisdom from the followers of Protagoras (286c), and he proceeds to demolish it by a line of attack similar to one he uses against Protagoras himself at *Tht.* 161c–e and *Crat.* 385e–386e.
59. Here is an interesting angle on the difference between Socrates and these sophists: the latter are forced to live in an ongoing intellectual present because nothing they say can be taken seriously enough to repeat or compare to anything else they say (cf. Hawtrey, *Commentary*, 35: "there is no need for any conclusion to be respected in later argument"). Meanwhile, Socrates seeks a knowledge that

accounts for and combines (and thus transcends) past, present, and future. Socrates thus uses memory and notoriously reintroduces interlocutors' earlier remarks back into the stream of conversation.

60. Ctesippus' anger at the sophists' *words* would have been more aptly directed toward Socrates' deeds, if he could only see what was happening.
61. This is an odd step in the argument designed, perhaps, to facilitate the removal of speechwriting and statesmanship as the consummate arts (see later). That the desired knowledge must entail knowledge of right use is a given, but why must it also include a *productive* capacity of its own (cf. *Charm.* 165e–166c)? Why should it not stand as the ethical knowledge that governs the productive capacity of the other arts? This latter possibility is suggested only briefly in the dialogue when, in describing the missing art, Socrates paraphrases a line from Aeschylus (291c–d): "the art we are looking for . . . alone sits at the helm of the state, governing all things, ruling all things, and making all things *useful*" (i.e., not making all things). For a fruitful exploration of this possibility, consider Rosamond Kent Sprague, *Plato's Philosopher King* (Columbia: University of South Carolina Press, 1976), 55 ff., who distinguishes helpfully between "first-order" and "second-order" *technai*.
62. Clinias has miraculously intuited the role of dialectic in the upper portion of the "divided line" (*Rep.* VI, 511b–c).
63. See Hawtrey, *Commentary*, 129–130.
64. Hearing continues to play an important role in the text. At this point, Socrates tells Crtio: "you will form an opinion yourself if you wish to hear (*ean boulē akouein*) what happened to us next" (291d5). Crito is hooked.
65. A wonderful metaphor for philosophy: childlike enjoyment of the chase, pursuing something beautiful and exotic, which, however, cannot be fully captured, and yet we continue to enjoy the attempt. As for looking utterly ridiculous (*panu geloioi*, 291b1), that is a matter of perspective; Plato is anticipating the end of the dialogue where the anonymous critic calls philosophy a valueless waste of time.
66. Clinias had earlier mentioned statesmanship, and Socrates here incorporates it into the discussion. But perhaps the simple equation of statesmanship with the more philosophically pregnant *basilikē* is part of the problem, which leads to the labyrinth to come.

It is precisely the "paradoxical" issue of a philosophical *basilikē* that leads to the "third wave" argument in *Rep.* V (see esp. 473c–e).

67. Roochnik is certainly right to locate the significance, in part, in the problematic analogy to art (*technē*): "The epistemological lesson . . . is this: Knowledge of *aretē* cannot be completely analogous to an ordinary *technē* " ("Serious Play," 227; cf. Hawtrey, 132–133). But this does not exhaust the potential insights one can glean from the *aporia*. There is also the problem of trying to construe the ground of all ethical knowledge along the lines of statesmanship in particular; and, more fundamentally, there is the problem that the knowledge in question may be ineffable and ultimately beyond our grasp; in this latter sense, it really does not matter *what* the specifics of the labyrinth are, which Socrates describes, so long as they convey to Crito the elusive quality of ultimate knowledge. I should note that in opposition to this last interpretation will be those who find a solution to Socrates' *aporia* in an esoteric wisdom, which he possesses but will not always state: this is the view, for example, of Thomas Szlezák, "Socrates' Spott über Geheimhaltung: Zum Bild des φιλόσοφος in Platons 'Euthydemos,' *Antike und Abendland* 26 (1980): 75–89, who discovers the missing knowledge in the philosophical rhetoric of the *Phaedrus*.
68. An appropriate image in a number of ways: the Dioscuri are not simply saviors of those in peril at sea, they are also twin brothers (Castor and Polydeuces, see *Iliad* 3.237ff; Pindar, *Nem.* 10.80); and *humans* who possess a tenuously divine status, forced (as Pindar has it) to share immortality between them (hence, Socrates' remark at 296e that Euthydemus cannot help Socrates unless his brother lends a helping hand).
69. The sophists' fallacy at this point also seems to epitomize the "technician's" approach to politics even today: rather than confronting his ultimate ignorance about the grounds of ethical action, the technician proceeds as if he already knows what he does not know—fooling himself, somehow, into believing that if he knows many things, he must also know what he is doing. The sophists' *secundum quid* thus apes the logic of some of the most disastrous political activities of the twentieth century.
70. Cf. *Gorgias* 458a–b.
71. This may be what lies behind Dionysodorus' blushing at 297a—not just that he has botched the argument, but also that in order to

make it right he must state explicitly what he would wish to leave unsaid, that eristic arguments facilitate the practice of injustice with a completely clear conscience; on Dionysodorus' *libido dominandi* and desire to refabricate the world according to his whims, consider his remark at 301b6.

72. Or, literally, "he would do the opposite." Minor debate has been ongoing over the identity of Iolaus as Ctesippus, but I have found no persuasive case against it and much evidence for it; on the debate and an able defense of the Ctesippus view, see Robin Jackson, "Socrates' Iolaos: Myth and Eristic in Plato's *Euthydemus*," *Classical Quarterly* 40 (1990): 378–395.
73. According to Socrates in the *Republic* (VII, 539a–c), it is necessary to take great precautions not to let students "taste of arguments" while they are too young, lest they "misuse them as though it were play, always using them to contradict." Socrates goes on to worry that by "imitating those men by whom they are refuted, they themselves will refute others, like puppies enjoying pulling and tearing with argument at those who happen to be near."
74. Euthydemus had argued that if it is good to be armed in battle (*secundum quid*) then it must be good to be absolutely armed—we should each be weighed down by as many swords and shields as possible. Ctesippus elicits an admission from Euthydemus that he himself would prefer one sword and one shield, and then the fallacy can be run in the opposite direction (*a dicto simpliciter ad dictum secundum quid*): "and so you would also arm Geryon and Briareus in this fashion?" Geryon and Briareus are proverbial many-limbed monsters. Ctesippus' point is that if it is better for Euthydemus to have one sword, then it must be better *simpliciter*, and yet this is refuted by the case of many-limbed monsters.
75. Recall that one of the sophists' boasts is that they can teach quickly.
76. Translators do not usually capture the seriousness of this epithet: Ctesippus has become villainous, ready to do *anything and everything* wicked. Cf. Callicles in the *Gorgias*, who is πανοῦργος, according to Socrates (499b–c).
77. According to Socrates (300d), Ctesippus went on to become something of an eristic himself. Likewise in the *Lysis* (211b–c) it is suggested that Ctesippus was (and taught others to be) *eristikos*.
78. The arguments themselves are no more or less sound than any of the sophists' arguments; for a full account of them, see Chance,

Plato's Euthydemus, 175–193. The attack on the forms has been thought to have some interesting implications for understanding the development of Plato's philosophical views; these are well treated by Rosamond Kent Sprague, "The *Euthydemus* Revisited," in Robinson and Brisson, ed., *Plato*, 3–19.

79. The earlier reversal (that philosophy is aporetic with respect to its end) was crafted for Clinias and Crito by Plato's Socrates. This one is crafted by Plato for his readers. It is thus crucial to the overall interpretation of the dialogue, but separate from the inner dynamics of Crito's education that has occupied me so far.
80. But we must remember that the arguments themselves are not always the problem. Socrates (as we saw) is willing to refute people with arguments like these.
81. This is the line that allowed me to determine that Crito is a lover of hearing and thus to construct this interpretation of the dialogue. That the line comes at the end rather than the beginning is no surprise. It is typical of works dealing with intellectual and spiritual ascent, especially those like the *Euthydemus*, which employ ring composition, to offer insights at the end that are essential to the interpretation of the work as a whole. As Robert McMahon says in his insightful study of the genre, *Understanding the Medieval Meditative Ascent: Augustine, Anselm, Boethius and Dante* (Washington, DC: Catholic University Press, 2006), we read forward, but we understand backward.
82. Notice that Crito still refers to the sophists as one, rather than two. He did the same at 293b. At no point in the dialogue does he acknowledge that they are double.
83. 303e–304a; their art can be so quickly acquired that anyone can master it in a very short time.
84. Commentators generally assume him to be Isocrates; see Hawtrey, *Commentary*, 190. My own view is that the identity of the critic is quite irrelevant. If Plato wanted to name him, he could have done so. In fact, the persistent desire to know the "*who*" of the critic betrays something of the lover of hearing himself. (Notice Crito's first word in the dialogue and the final reproach Socrates gives him at the end.)
85. See Chance's excellent discussion of the "trigger words," which the sophists seize on (*Plato's Euthydemus*, 43–47).
86. Cf. *Tht.* 151b, *Prt.* 339e ff.

87. Cf. *Crito* 44b–c.
88. For an interesting parallel, compare Alcidamas' negative appraisal of speech writers in *On Those Who Write Written Speeches*, discussed in Marina McCoy, "Alcidama, Isocrates, and Plato on Speech, Writing, and Philosophical Rhetoric," *Ancient Philosophy* 29 (2009): 45–66.
89. Socrates does make weaker arguments stronger, as, for instance, when he argues that fortune is not a good (279c–280b), or that it is better to possess and do as little as possible (281b–c); for an even more disconcerting weak argument made strong, recall Socrates' conclusion in the *Hippias Minor* that it is better to do wrong voluntarily than involuntarily.
90. Catherine Zuckert offers an interpretation along these lines in "Socrates v. the Sophists?" a paper presented at the annual meeting of the American Political Science Association, 2004.
91. Hawtrey references scores of these and remarks in his Preface: "I find it hard to believe that Plato did not often have the *Clouds* in mind as he wrote the *Euthydemus*—I have sometimes felt that he must have known the play by heart, or that he had it open beside him as he wrote" (*Commentary*, viii).
92. Not to mention the theme of father beating (*Euthyd.* 298e); cf. Zuckert, "Socrates v. the Sophists?" 3–5.
93. Zuckert, ibid., 1.
94. It may well have been numerically close; Thomas G. West and Grace Starry West, *Four Texts on Socrates* (Ithaca: Cornell University Press, 1984), 89, n. 65, put the votes at 280 to 220.
95. Crito was Socrates' fellow demesman. I stress the element of chance deliberately here, with Socrates' earlier argument about chance in mind. Crito is insecure as a defender of Socrates precisely because his affection rests on chance, not on reason.

Chapter 7. Protagorean Sophistry in Plato's *Theaetetus*

1. For a similar line of interpretation, see "Reading A" in Myles Burnyeat, *The Theaetetus of Plato* (Indianapolis: Hackett, 1990), 8–10.
2. This is the vexing challenge that Socrates confronted when he met Parmenides as a young man and shared with the great sage his ideas about the forms. Parmenides' challenge to Socrates was that

he had a disjointed view of Being. Socrates could not explain how the material world participated in the Forms. What was their connection? Again wisdom requires knowledge of the parts of being, but also the principles of connection. Cf. Catherine Zuckert, *Plato's Philosophers* (Chicago: Chicago University Press, 2009), 599, who refers to "the fundamental philosophical problem that runs through Plato's entire corpus, that is, the problem of relating the ever-changing character of sensible existence to stable, hence intelligible, types of being."

3. Not a boaster (145c), not a coward (142b–c), not unjust (163a2).
4. See *Rep.* VI, 485d–487a. Cf. Catherine Zuckert, *Plato's Philosophers*, 601. Seth Benardete, *Plato's Theaetetus* (Chicago: University of Chicago Press, 1986), 90, emphasizes one missing trait: musicality.
5. Malcolm Brown presents a lengthy analysis of what has come down to us of the historical Theaetetus' mathematics in "Theaetetus: Knowledge as Continued Learning," *Journal of the History of Philosophy*, 7 (1969): 359–379. See also Martin Andic and Malcolm Brown, "False Statement in the *Sophist* and *Theaetetus'* Mathematics," *Phoenix* 27 (1973): 26–34.
6. That Theaetetus is familiar with Socrates' questions involving analogy to the arts is revealed at 148e.
7. A good discussion is Scott Hemmenway, "Philosophical Apology in the *Theaetetus*," *Interpretation* 17 (1990): 323–346.
8. Unless otherwise noted, all quotations from the *Theaetetus* are from Benardete, *Plato's Theaetetus.*
9. Readers do not have to suppose that Socrates anticipates already that the conversation will turn to an analysis of Protagoras. Perhaps he does. But then again we may be dealing here with an example of Plato's brilliant way of inviting readers to read holistically. Plato, who *does* know which way the conversation will turn, plants a seed early on (the midwife analogy), which bears fruit only after we come to reflect on it in light of Protagorean theory.
10. At 152a, Theaetetus confesses that he has read Protagoras' book *On Truth* "many times."
11. I refer to the opening line of *On Truth* in the conventional manner as the "man-measure doctrine." It should be understood however that man (*anthrōpos*) refers generically to a human being, not only to a male. For a discussion of this and other philological points, see Edward Schiappa, *Protagoras and Logos* (Columbia: University

of South Carolina Press, 2003), 118–121, who prefers the locution, "human-measure" doctrine.

12. The meaning of the man-measure dictum is disputed in the secondary literature. That it refers to a form of relativism is the majority view espoused by Gregory Vlastos, *Introduction to Plato's Protagoras* (Indianapolis: Bobbs-Merrill, 1956); John McDowell, *Plato: Theaetetus* (Oxford: Clarendon, 1973); and David Bostock, *Plato's Theaetetus* (Oxford: Clarendon, 1988); and Burnyeat, *Theaetetus*. Gale Fine reads the dictum rather as a statement of infalliblism. See Gale Fine, "Plato's Refutation of Protagoras in the *Theaetetus*," *Apeiron* 31 (1998): 201–234.
13. For a helpful discussion of the depths to which Protagoras' relativism may or may not have gone, see Richard Bett, "The Sophists and Relativism," *Phronesis* 34 (1989): 139–169, esp. 166–168.
14. Protagoras may have appealed to Theodorus and Theaetetus in part because his relativism declares man a "measurer," which must sound about right to someone who specializes in numbers.
15. 152c, 159d–e. The suggestion that Protagoras was an esotericist does not comport with the sophist's own claim in the *Protagoras* (317a–c) to have rejected esotericism in favor of frankness; however, the slyness involved in that claim is revealed (as I have shown) in the speech that follows it. Protagoras's "Great Speech" unmistakably communicates radically different teachings to different listeners at one and the same time. He was an expert esotericist as Plato presents him. On the other hand, Socrates may simply be making up the connection between Heraclitean ontology and Protagoras' man-measure doctrine for strategic reasons. See Burnyeat, *Theaetetus*, 12.
16. *Theaetetus* 152d, 156a–157b.
17. See further, John McDowell, *Plato Theaetetus* (Oxford: Clarendon Press, 1973), 134–137.
18. For example, Theaetetus is said to be ugly, but not as ugly as Socrates; when he is placed next to Socrates, he is no longer ugly; conclusion: Theaetetus is ugly and not ugly. Again, Theaetetus is said (by Theodorus) to be intellectually excellent; but when he can't answer Socrates' questions (see, e.g., 148b–c) he appears not excellent; conclusion: Theaetetus is intellectually excellent and not so; and Theodorus turns out to have been both right and wrong about the lad.

19. On the importance of wonder in the *Theaetetus*, see further, David Roochnik, "Self-Recognition in Plato's *Theaetetus*," *Ancient Philosophy* 22 (2002): 37–52.
20. Cf. Jacob Howland, *The Paradox of Political Philosophy* (Lanham: Rowman & Littlefield, 1998), 159.
21. Cf., *Crito* 48d–e; and *Gorgias* 473b, "what is true is never refuted."
22. This is what Prodicus did through his art of distinction making; see ch. 4. More impressively, it is what Aristotle did in his *Sophistical Refutations*.
23. Protagoras did not think one could know the truth about the gods, and Socrates here (162d–e) alludes to the opening line of his book *On the Gods*: "Concerning the gods, I have no means of knowing whether they exist or not or of what sort they may be, because of the obscurity of the subject, and the brevity of human life" (DK 80 B4).
24. Cf. Aristotle *Sophistical Refutations*, 165b.
25. This lesson may be intended not only for Theaetetus, but also for Euclides—the Megarian philosopher to whom Socrates recited this conversation and who, in the opening frame of the dialogue, arranges for it to be read out loud. According to Diogenes Laertius (II, 106–108), Euclides made a practice of arguing against others by showing that absurd conclusions followed from their premises (rather than examining the premises on their own terms).
26. I supply *hexis* in the Greek to invite comparison between the position articulated here and that of Aristotle in the *Nicomachean Ethics*. Aristotle's general definition of virtue is a "*hexis* involving choice" (1106b36), and he appears to take Protagorean relativity with the utmost seriousness, even while he insists that we can speak of the truth and falsity of perceptions. Consider his discussion of "wish" in *EN* III.4: What does a person wish for? He wishes for what is good (*agathos*) for him, and some things really *are* good for him, whether he realizes it or not. The difficulty, Aristotle recognizes, is that what is attractive (*kala*) and pleasant for an individual "differs with different *hexeis*" (1113a31), so that each individual ends up wishing for "whatever *appears* (*phainomenon*) good to him" (1113a24). What is the solution to this? With respect to the body, we must accept that a person whose constitution is healthy, judges such matters "correctly," and with respect to ethical matters, a person whose standards are high, the *spoudaios*, judges

correctly, too, so that in each case what is "truly good will appear good to him" (1113a30). In such questions, the person with the best *hexis* serves as the "measure" (*metron*, 1113a33). Aristotle's framework is unmistakably Protagorean, and even Aristotle's conclusion about the role of the *spoudaios* in supplying a standard for evaluation seems to retain an element of the Protagorean *sophos anêr*, the "wise man." Aristotle designates the *hexis* of the well-functioning man as "true" in a way that carries more normative weight than anything we find in Protagoras. For Aristotle there is such a thing as judging correctly (*orthôs*) and with truth.

27. Burnyeat, *Theaetetus*, 24, mentions some modern advocates of this view, including F.C.S. Schiller, John Burnet, and G.B. Kerferd. McCoy, "Argument against Protagoras," 28, remarks that Socrates-as-Protagoras' position is "a sensible stance for a rhetorician to take, for then rhetoric and not philosophy, is then the most powerful form of wisdom."
28. Cf. *Gorgias*. On Protagoras' theory, though, the question of "valid criteria" can be avoided by maintaining that whatever appears valid for any patient (e.g., whatever seems to him "better") is valid, as long as it seems so. For this interpretation and a rival objectivist way of reading the speech, see Burnyeat, *Theaetetus*, 26–27.
29. Cf. *Prt.* 335a, where Protagoras unmistakably reveals that he views conversations as competitions.
30. Cynthia Farrar, *The Origins of Democratic Thinking* (Cambridge: Cambridge University Press, 1988), 50 ff., uses the name "Platagoras," to refer to Protagoras in the *Theaetetus*, because she sees that the sophist's ideas here have been manipulated.
31. See also Joseph P. Maguire, "Protagoras . . . or Plato?" *Phronesis* 18 (1973): 115–138.
32. Throughout the third test, Socrates references Theodorus' expertise at measuring. The old geometer should be offended by Protagoras' claim that everyman is the measure of all things.
33. Scholars debate whether Protagoras' relativism is self-refuting. See, for example, McCoy, "The Argument against Protagoras," 30; with Burnyeat, *Theaetetus*, 181. McCoy places weight on the fact that Socrates himself says that Protagoras would not be convinced of his theory's refutation. Socrates, for McCoy (p. 32), "suggests that Protagoras' theory is internally consistent, and he holds out the possibility that Protagoras could be right."

34. In the preface to *Humanism: Philosophical Essays* (London and New York: Macmillan, 1903), p. xvii, F.C.S. Schiller proclaimed Protagoras' doctrine "the truest and most important thing that any thinker ever has propounded"; see also Schiller's extensive treatment of Protagoras in *Studies in Humanism* (London: Macmillan, 1907); for more on the contemporary appropriation of Protagoras' man-measure doctrine, see Steven Mailloux, ed., *Rhetoric, Sophistry, Pragmatism* (Cambridge: Cambridge University Press, 1995), 1–31.
35. My interpretation of the digression differs from both possible interpretations sketched out by Burnyeat, *Theaetetus*, 35–37. In general, Burnyeat's alternatives render the digression less vital to the meaning of the *Theaetetus* as a whole, though the second of his options carries more philosophical weight and is at least compatible with what I offer here.
36. I can only remark in passing on the astonishing artistry with which Plato has composed the digression. The "bigger argument," which Socrates will resume after the digression, is the insight that the future contains information that can reshape what we previously thought. Not just perception, but also *reflection* over time is essential to knowledge; and Protagoras fails to account for this. Remarkably, Plato constructs the digression in such a way that it demonstrates this. The digression impacts first-time readers exactly like a present perception. But the digression is radically misleading unless and until it is reinterpreted in light of facts that are revealed later on in the dialogue. For example, the digression begins with what appears to be a nonsequitur; yet the sequence of Socrates' thought makes perfect sense once we learn from the dialogue's final passage that Socrates is on his way to the porch of the king. Several other aspects of the digression invite similar reinterpretation in light of the dialogue as a whole, chief among them the characterization of philosophy.
37. The philosopher is described at 173e as one who "geometricizes," and "star gazes." At 174e–175b he is one who regards 10,000 acres of land as a small number and who "calculates" that everyone has countless thousands of ancestors.
38. Socrates does allow (177b) that in private conversations, when he presses people to give a coherent account of themselves, their inability to do so leads them to be dissatisfied in a potentially healthy way. The advantages of private conversation over public

persuasion are similarly emphasized in the *Gorgias* (474a–b, 455a, 476a) and the *Sophist* (230a).

39. I prefer "flowing ones" to Benardete's "streamers," because the word "flow" links this section of the dialogue to the opening frame (more details later).
40. All three of these associations are pointed out by Benardete, *Plato's Theaetetus*, 188, n. 59.
41. Not all Platonic dialogues are set up in this way—with Socrates narrating (or having narrated in the past) a story to a specific auditor. Those that do—*Protagoras, Euthydemus* and *Theaetetus*—all involve Socrates describing the way he intervened to help an Athenian youth navigate the perils (and possibilities) of sophistic education. The *Theaetetus*, then, is linked to the *Protagoras* and *Euthydemus* both in form and content.
42. This establishes the date of the frame as either 390–87 BC or 369 BC, the two possible occasions on which an Athenian would be fighting in Corinth.
43. Euclides and Terpsion are both present at Socrates' death as described in Plato's *Phaedo* (59c).
44. See Anne-Marie Schultz, *Plato's Socrates as Narrator* (Lanham: Lexington Press, 2013), 1.
45. Cf. 144b, where Theodorus describes the young Theaetetus as someone who learns as smoothly as a stream of olive oil flows (*rheontos*) without a sound.
46. Diogenes Laertius, II, 106–108. Euclides . . . devoted himself to the study of the writings of Parmenides; and his successors were called the philosophers of the Megaric school. Diogenes goes on to attribute six dialogues to Euclides: the *Lamprias*, the *Aeschines*, the *Phoenix*, the *Crito*, the *Alcibiades*, and the *Amatory Dialogue*.
47. Cf. *Republic* VII (537b): "fatigue and sleep are the enemies of learning."
48. Would it not be shocking if Socrates on the brink of death had nothing important to communicate *about* his conversation on the meaning of wisdom and knowledge? Notice what Euclides says (and fails to observe) in the opening frame about the context of Socrates' narrative. He says, "My impression is that Socrates met [Theaetetus] shortly before his [Socrates'] death" (142c). He fails to recall what we later learn from the written record, that Socrates

was on his way to receive his indictment. He therefore fails to appreciate the heightened importance of Socrates' reflections in this dialogue.

49. John Stuart Mill, *On Liberty* (Boston: Ticknor and Fields, 1862), 72, puts "ninety-nine in a hundred of what are called educated men," in this condition.
50. On the other hand, it can be politically explosive when coupled with a desire to make politics conform to the absolute.
51. Socrates says (151a–b) that his art of midwifery is able to arouse labor pains as well as put them to rest. And at 150d–151a, he describes what happens to people who leave his care too early.
52. When an innocent bystander is accidently killed in battle (to choose a somewhat random example), he and his loved ones have been done an injustice, even if the forces that killed him were engaged in an effort to serve justice at a broader level. From one perspective we see justice, from another, injustice. For an example from Protagoras' own teaching, consider the episode of the javelin thrower who accidently struck and killed a competitor with his javelin (Plutarch *Pericles*, 36). According to Plutarch, Pericles spent an entire day with Protagoras considering whether one ought to regard the cause of the accident the javelin, the man who threw it, or the directors of the games.
53. Diogenes Laertius (IX.8) credits Protagoras with composing an *Art of Debating* and a two-volume book called *Contradictory Arguments*. He also credits him with being the first to (1) to claim that on every question there are two opposing sides, and using these in his arguments; (2) conduct formal debates and teach disputants the "tricks of argument."
54. I base this not only on Socrates' "defense of Protagoras" in the *Theaetetus* but also on the fact that Protagoras crafted a constitution for the Pan-Hellenic colony of Thurii.
55. Diogenes Laertius (IX.53) reports that Protagoras appropriated the argument of Antisthenes that "contradiction is impossible." Diogenes bases this on *Euthydemus* 286c.
56. Jill Gordon, *Turning Toward Philosophy: Literary Device and Dramatic Structure in Plato's Dialogues* (University Park: Pennsylvania State University Press, 1999), 22–28, offers an insightful analysis of the role of shame in Socratic dialectic that supports this point.

CHAPTER 8. PLATO'S CRITIQUE OF THE SOPHISTS?

1. "The Study of Texts," in *Giants and Dwarfs: Essays 1960–1990* (New York: Simon & Schuster, 1990), 307.
2. G.B. Kerferd, *The Sophistic Movement* (Cambridge: Cambridge University Press, 1981), 1; John Dillon and Tania Gergel, *The Greek Sophists* (New York: Penguin Books, 2003), xix.
3. Kerferd, *Sophistic Movement*, 5 with n. 2.
4. Terrence Irwin, "Plato's Objections to the Sophists," in Anton Powell, ed., *The Greek World* (New York: Routledge, 1995), 568–590, is an excellent study for debunking common beliefs about Plato's critique of the sophists. The supposed critiques are simply hard to find in Plato, he shows. I agree, but try to show also how attention to the difference between generalities and particulars helps explain some of the misunderstandings. This also leads me to reject as invalid, a criticism that Irwin takes to be Plato's real point. See my discussion of *Republic* 492a later.
5. "The Case Against Teaching Virtue for Pay: Socrates and the Sophists," *History of Political Thought* 23 (2002): 189–210.
6. Commentators often interpret Anytus' outburst as an expression of Plato's own hostility toward the sophists; see, for example, John Poulakos, *Sophistical Rhetoric in Classical Greece* (Columbia: University of South Carolina Press, 1995), 80–81, 91.
7. This is the view of Paul Woodruff, *Plato's Hippias Major* (Indianapolis: Hackett, 1982), 114.
8. In the present context of the *Republic*, this danger is associated not with sophistry, but with dialectic. However, the emphasis on the refutational power of dialectic is a trait shared by the sophistic practices of eristic and *antilogikē*.
9. Translation from the Republic in this chapter are from Allan Bloom, *The Republic of Plato* (New York: Basic Books, 1968).
10. Among those who take the passage at face value are W.K.C. Guthrie, *The Sophists* (Cambridge: Cambridge University Press, 1971), 21; Poulakos, *Sophistical Rhetoric in Classical Greece*, 92–93; and Irwin, "Plato's Objection to the Sophists," 577–582.
11. So Protagoras refers to the "envy, ill will and hostile plots" that arise against sophists (*Prt.* 316d), and he assures his listeners that what he teaches is much the same as what parents, schoolmasters, and the laws teach; he simply teaches more effectively (*Prt.* 328a–b).

12. That rhetoricians following Gorgias tended to denounce sophistry themselves, makes Socrates' task all the easier. If Socrates can show Polus that rhetoric and sophistry have much in common, then Polus must concede that rhetoric is not simply praiseworthy in every respect. For the rhetoricians' attack on sophistry, see Chapter 2 earlier. Gorgias was famous for ridiculing the sophists' promise to teach virtue (*Men* 95c); see also *Grg*. 520a, where Callicles denounces the sophists.
13. By referring to "care of the soul" as politics, Socrates gestures toward the city-soul analogy that becomes thematic in the *Republic* and suggests that the job of caring for souls involves the ordering of diverse classes or elements into a harmonious whole.
14. All translations from the Gorgias in this chapter are from James H. Nichols, *Plato: Gorgias* (Ithaca: Cornell University Press, 1998).
15. An example of the common tendency to interpret it as such is Kerferd, *Sophistic Movement*, 4.
16. See, for example, E.L. Harrison, "Was Gorgias a Sophist?" *Phoenix* 18 (1964): 183–192, with notes.
17. Cf. *Timeaeus* 19e; *Statesman* 291c, 303c.
18. For an excellent discussion of this, see David Roochnik, *Of Art and Wisdom: Plato's Understanding of Technē* (University Park: Pennsylvania State University Press, 1996). Roochnik, too, challenges the grand scheme, which Socrates presents to Polus in the *Gorgias* (182–192), as well as Socrates' claim that he practices the true art of politics (192).
19. Cf. Roochnik, *Of Art and Wisdom*, 194, commenting on the *Gorgias*: "Plato wrote dialogues. As a drama, that is an imitation of characters both speaking and acting, a dialogue is infused with irremediable particularity. Socrates does not, for example, offer a straight theoretical refutation of rhetoric. Instead, he argues against Gorgias at a very specific time and place, and when doing so he assumes rhetoric is a *technē*. When shifting to Polus, a different strategy is required. Because the dialogue is written thus, the reader can never extract any single argument Socrates makes and then declare it 'Platonic.' The argument may well be tailored to meet the dialogical needs generated by the particular context in which it is spoken."
20. Kerferd, *Sophistic Movement*, 4–5. Kerferd, like most commentators, treats the Eleatic Stranger as a mouthpiece for Plato and assumes

that the purpose of the dialogue is simply to criticize the sophists. Cf. Harold Barrett, *The Sophists: Rhetoric, Democracy and Plato's Idea of Sophistry* (Novato: Chandler & Sharp, 1987), 45–46; and John Poulakos, *Sophistical Rhetoric in Classical Greece*, 82, 84.

21. All translations from the *Sophist* in this chapter are from Seth Benardete, *The Being of the Beautiful: Plato's Theaetetus, Sophist and Statesman* (Chicago: University of Chicago Press, 1984).
22. For a recent treatment of this issue, see Francisco Gonzalez, "The Eleatic Stranger: His Master's Voice?" in Gerald A. Press, ed., *Who Speaks for Plato: Studies in Platonic Anonymity* (Lanham: Rowman & Littlefield, 2000), 161–162. Gonzalez points to difficulties similar to the ones I identify later and concludes that neither the Stranger nor Socrates is Plato's mouthpiece, but that both offer perspectives from which the other can be critically viewed.
23. The word *region* seems intentionally ambiguous. Does it refer to a geographical or an intellectual area? The ambiguity is noted by Seth Benardete, *The Being of the Beautiful*, II.72–73.
24. Benardete, ibid., 76–77.
25. Theaetetus' decision to ascribe "art" to the angler determines to a surprising degree the course of the entire dialogue. For an illuminating discussion of this crucial moment, see Martin Heidegger's lectures on the dialogue, published posthumously as *Plato's Sophist*, trans. Richard Rojcewicz and Andre Schuwer (Bloomington: Indiana University Press, 1997), 182–186.
26. Indeed, it bears some resemblance to the method of *diairesis* credited to Prodicus (see Chapter 4); and Plato's Socrates famously speaks of division as an essential part of philosophy in the *Phaedrus* (265c–266a). Friedländer, *Plato*, vol. III, 248–249 points to antecedents in the *Republic* and *Gorgias*, but is less concerned than I am to mark the significant differences.
27. This same dogmatic quality is reflected in the Stranger's "having heard" the answer to the question at hand. Unlike Socrates, for whom conversations are inductive and conclusions always tentative, the Stranger treats knowledge as information. This makes him similar to his friend Theodorus the mathematician and may shed light on the latter's admiration for him.
28. The accounts of sophistry reached by the Stranger and Theaetetus are numerous and divergent, not to say incompatible; they thus effectively refute each other, though the Stranger does not

point this out. That his purpose may be subtly to refute or at least complicate various ways of defining the sophists is suggested by Socrates' prophetic remark at the beginning of the dialogue (*Soph.* 216b) that the Stranger is perhaps a "spirit of refutation" (*theos elengtikos*). Theodorus' reply—namely, that the Stranger's way is "morc measured than those devoted to contentiousness"—leaves open the possibility that he does refute in a gentle way.

29. See n. 32 below.
30. Not exhaustive because it does not capture the public side of their art (the delivery of *epideixeis*); in fact, the Stranger's sharp distinction at this point (222d) between public and private persuasion seems artificial and suggests a propensity to distort reality by drawing distinctions where they do not naturally occur.
31. Cf. *Prt.* 309a, where Socrates is described as just returning from a hunt after Alcibiades; see also *Phdr.* 253c–257d, *Lysis* 206a, and, further, Benardete, *The Being of the Beautiful*, part II, 86–87; and Friedländer, *Plato*, vol. III, 252–253. Interestingly, the Stranger also refers to himself as a hunter (e.g., *Sph.* 218d, 235a–c, 241b).
32. Compare the summary of their search at 231d–e, which does not match the number of sophists actually sighted. Nor does the Stranger capture all the possible permutations, which must, logically, appear in the genus of exchange. See further Catherine H. Zuckert, "Who's a Philosopher? Who's a Sophist? The Stranger *v.* Socrates" *Review of Metaphysics* 54 (2000): 71–72 with n. 16. That the number of possible sophistic types is so unclear corroborates our sense that the Stranger's method is not up to the task of penetrating to the essence of sophistry.
33. This claim was made in different ways: Protagoras evidently promised his students they would be able to dispute on any subject whatsoever (*Soph.* 232e); Euthydemus and Dionysodorus made a related, but even more daring claim, that their students would "know everything" (*Euthyd.* 293b ff.); and Hippias was *in fact* polymathic and polytechnic, and taught his students to be the same (*Prt.* 318e; *Hipp. Maj.* 385b–e; *Hipp. Min.* 366c–368e).
34. Cf. *Prt.* 335a, where the great sophist tells Socrates, that he has fought many a contest (*agōna*) of words and that this accounts for his reputation all over Greece.
35. Cf. *Hipp. Min.* 369b–c; *Hipp. Maj.* 304a–b.
36. See, for example, *Prt.* 334e–335a; *Euthyd.* 272a.

37. The use of the plural raises questions; see the classic exchange between G.B. Kerferd, "Plato's Noble Art of Sophistry: *Sophist* 226a–231b" *Classical Quarterly*, n. s. IV (1954): 84–90; and J.R. Trevaskis, "The Sophistry of Noble Lineage," *Phronesis* I (1955/56): 36–49. If my own understanding of Protagorean *antilogikē* is correct (see Chapter 5, n. 19), then he, too, can be categorized as someone who uses refutation to purify his students' souls (consider especially *Theaetetus* 166d–167d; cf. Kerferd, "Plato's Noble Art of Sophistry" 89).
38. I have made minor stylistic alterations to Benardete's translation.
39. Notice the absence of any reference to money in the description of Sophist VI; money was the only basis by which the Stranger was able to distinguish Socrates from the sophists in the earlier accounts; money is empirically observable and value-neutral (in ethical terms). It can thus be recognized by the Stranger's method while Socrates' ethical singularity cannot.
40. The Stranger certainly has Protagoras in mind here, because explicit mention is made of his work (232e). Euthydemus and Dionysodorus would also fit the bill. That the Stranger also has Socrates in mind, however, may be suggested by his formulation at 233c, which is similar to Socrates' comment in the *Apology* (23a): "for those present on each occasion suppose I myself am wise in the things about which I refute someone else." In Greek, cf. *Soph.*, 233c, Δοκοῦσι γὰρ οἶμαι πρὸς ταῦτα ἐπιστημόνως ἔχειν αὐτοὶ πρὸς ἅπερ ἀντιλέγουσιν; and *Apol.*, 23a, οἴονται γάρ με ἑκάστοτε οἱ παρόντες ταῦτα αὐτὸν εἶναι σοφὸν ἃ ἂν ἄλλον ἐξελέγξω. The term, ἐξελέγξω is the specific form of contradiction unique to Socrates. The passage from the *Sophist* may be said, then, to include Socrates while also including other sophists.
41. For a good discussion, see Zuckert, "Who is a Sophist?" 79–90.
42. Modifying the Benardete translation here for readability; it is a humorously difficult sentence in any language.
43. Cf. C.J. Rowe, *Plato* (Brighton: Harvester Press, 1984), 160, who notices that the final description of the dialogue "fits Euthydemus and Dionysodorus perfectly, but hardly fits a Protagoras or a Hippias."
44. See further, Jacob Howland, *The Paradox of Political Philosophy: Socrates' Philosophic Trial* (Lanham: Rowman & Littlefield, 1998), 220.

45. Zuckert, "Who's a Philosopher? Who's a Sophist?"
46. Howland, *The Paradox of Political Philosophy*, ch. 6.
47. Contrast the recent interpretation by Noburu Notomi, *The Unity of Plato's Sophist: Between the Sophist and the Philosopher* (Cambridge: Cambridge University Press, 1999).
48. Eric Voegelin, *The New Science of Politicsi* (Chicago: University of Chicago Press, 1952), 20.

Appendix

1. I have benefited in the following analysis from Jenny Strauss Clay, *Hesiod's Cosmos* (Cambridge: Cambridge University Press, 2003).
2. Perhaps the settlement according to which gods and men became separated for the first time; the settlement would have consisted of the terms of separation.
3. Epimetheus functions in the poem as a mortal.
4. This is a question that became existentially pressing in the fifth century. It animates Aristophanes' *Clouds* as well as Plato's *Rep*. II. Protagoras and Plato are both interested in reworking the Hesiodic foundations.

BIBLIOGRAPHY

Adkins, A.W.H. "*Aretê*, *Technê*, Democracy and the Sophists: *Protagoras* 316b–328d." *Journal of Hellenic Studies* 93 (1973): 3–12.

Adkins, A.W.H. *Merit and Responsibility*. Oxford: Oxford University Press, 1960.

Alford, C. Fred. "A Note on the Institutional Context of Plato's 'Protagoras.'" *Classical World* 81 (1988): 167–176.

Andic, Martin, and Malcolm Brown. "False Statement in the *Sophist* and Theaetetus' Mathematics." *Phoenix* 27 (1973): 26–34.

Annas, Julia, and Christopher Rowe, eds. *New Perspectives on Plato: Modern and Ancient*. Cambridge, MA: Harvard University Press, 2003.

Apelt, Otto. *Platonische Aufsaetze*. Leipzig: Teubner, 1912.

Arendt, Hannah. *The Human Condition*. Chicago: University of Chicago Press, 1958.

Barnes, Jonathan, ed. *The Complete Works of Aristotle*. 2 vols. Princeton: Princeton University Press, 1984.

Barrett, Harold. *The Sophists: Rhetoric, Democracy, and Plato's Idea of Sophistry*. Novato: Chandler & Sharp, 1987.

Bartlett, Robert C. *Plato: "Protagoras and Meno."* Ithaca: Cornell University Press, 2004.

Bartlett, Robert C. "Political Philosophy and Sophistry: An Introduction to Plato's *Protagoras*." *American Journal of Political Science* 47 (1981): 612–644.

Beck, Frederick. *Greek Education: 450–350 B.C.* New York: Teachers' Press, 1964.

Benardete, Seth. *The Being of the Beautiful: Plato's Theaetetus, Sophist and Statesman*. Chicago: University of Chicago Press, 1984.

Benardete, Seth. *Plato's Theaetetus*. Chicago: University of Chicago Press, 1986.

Bett, Richard. "The Sophists and Relativism." *Phronesis* 34 (1989): 139–169.

Beversluis, John. *Cross-Examining Socrates: A Defense of the Interlocutors in Plato's Early Dialogues*. Cambridge: Cambridge University Press, 2000.

Blanchard, Kenneth. "The Enemies of Socrates: Piety and Sophism in the Socratic Drama." *Review of Politics* 62 (2000): 421–449.

Blank, David. "Socrates *versus* Sophists on Payment for Teaching." *Classical Antiquity* 4 (1985): 1–49.

Blondell, Ruby. *The Play of Character in Plato's Dialogues*. Cambridge: Cambridge University Press, 2002.

Bloom, Allan. *The Republic of Plato*. New York: Basic Books, 1968.

Bloom, Allan. "The Study of Texts." In *Giants and Dwarfs: Essays 1960–1990*. New York: Simon & Schuster, 1990.

Blundell, Mary Whitlock. "Character and Meaning in Plato's *Hippias Minor*." *Oxford Studies in Ancient Philosophy* (Supplementary Volume, 1992): 131–172.

Blundell, Mary Whitlock. "Self-Censorship in Plato's *Republic*." In Terrence Irwin and Martha Nussbaum, eds. *Virtue, Love and Form: Essays in Memory of Gregory Vlastos*. Edmonton: Academic, 1994.

Bonazzi, Mauro. *I Sofisti*. Roma: Carocci Editore, 2010.

Bonitz, Herman. *Platonische Studien*. Hildesheim: Georg Olms Verlagsbuchhandlung, [1886] 1968.

Bostock, David. *Plato's Theaetetus*. Oxford: Clarendon Press, 1988.

Brandwood, Leonard. *The Chronology of Plato's Dialogues*. Cambridge: Cambridge University Press, 1990.

Brown, Malcolm. "Theaetetus: Knoweldge as Continuted Learning." *Journal of the History of Philosophy* 7 (1969): 359–379.

Burnyeat, Miles. *The Theaetetus of Plato*. Indianapolis: Hackett, 1990.

Burnyeat, Miles, ed. *Socratic Studies*. Cambridge: Cambridge University Press, 1994.

Byrd, Miriam. "The Summoner Approach: A New Method of Plato

Interpretation." *Journal of the History of Philosophy* 45 (2007): 365–381.

Canto, Monique. *L'intrigue philosophique. Essai sur l'Euthydème de Platon*. Paris: Société d'Édition "Les Belles Lettres," 1987.

Carey, Christopher. "Old Comedy and the Sophists." In David Harvey and John Wilkins, eds. *The Rivals of Aristophanes: Studies in Athenian Old Comedy*. London: Duckworth and the Classical Press of Whales, 2000.

Carson, Anne. "How Not to Read a Poem: Unmixing Simonides from *Protagoras*." *Classical Philology* 87 (1992): 110–130.

Cassin, Barbara. *L'effet sophistique*. Paris: Gallimard, NRF Essais, 1995.

Cassin, Barbara. "Qui a peur de la sophistique? Contre l'ethical correctness." *Le Débat* 72 (1991): 52–64.

Cassin, Barbara. "Who's Afraid of the Sophists? Against Ethical Correctness." Translated by Charles Wolfe. *Hypatia* 15 (Fall 2000): 102–120.

Caston, Victor, and Daniel Graham, eds. *Presocratic Philosophy: Essays in Honour of Alexander Mourelatos*. Burlington, VT: Ashgate, 2002.

Chance, Thomas. *Plato's* Euthydemus*: Analysis of What Is and Is Not Philosophy*. Berkeley: University of California Press, 1992.

Classen, C. Joachim. "Aristotle's Picture of the Sophists." In G. B. Kerferd, ed. *The Sophists and their Legacy*. Wiesbaden: Franz Steiner Verlag, 1981.

Classen, C. Joachim. "The Study of language amongst Socrates' Contemporaries." *Proceedings of the African Classical Association* 2 (1959): 33–49.

Classen, C. J., ed. *Sophistik*. Darmstadt: Wissenschaftliche Buchgesellschaft, 1976.

Coby, Patrick. "The Education of a Sophist: Aspects of Plato's *Protagoras*." *Interpretation* 10 (1982): 139–158.

Coby, Patrick. *Socrates and the Sophistic Enlightenment: A Commentary on Plato's* Protagoras. Lewisburg: Bucknell University Press, 1987.

Cooper, John M., ed. *Plato: The Complete Works*. Indianapolis: Hackett, 1997.

Corey, David D. "The Case against Teaching Virtue for Pay: Socrates and the Sophists." *History of Political Thought* 23 (2002): 189–210.

Cornford, F. M., trans. *Sophist*. In Edith Hamilton and Huntington Cairnes, eds. *The Collected Dialogues of Plato*, 7th ed. Princeton: Princeton University Press, 2005.

Cropsey, Joseph. *Plato's World: Man's Place in the Cosmos*. Chicago: University of Chicago Press, 1995.

Deneen, Patrick J. *Democratic Faith*. Princeton: Princeton University Press, 2005.

Diels, Hermann, and Walther Kranz. *Die Fragmente der Vorsokratiker*. 3 vols. Berlin: Weidmann, 1951–1952.

Dillon, John, and Tania Gergel. *The Greek Sophists*. New York: Penguin, 2003.

Dodds, E. R. *Euripides Bacchae*. Oxford: Clarendon Press, 1960.

Dodds, E. R. *Plato: Gorgias*. Oxford: Clarendon Press, 1959.

Dupréel, E. *Les sophistes, Protagoras, Gorgias, Prodicus, Hippias*. Neuchâtel: Éditions Du Griffon, 1948.

Farrar, Cynthia. *The Origins of Democratic Thinking: The Invention of Politics in Classical Athens*. Cambridge: Cambridge University Press, 1988.

Ferranin, Alfredo. "Homo Faber, Homo Sapiens, or Homo Politicus? Protagoras and the Myth of Prometheus." *Review of Metaphysics* 54 (2000): 289–319.

Fine, Gail. "Plato's Refutation of Protagoras in the *Theaetetus*." *Apeiron* 31, no. 3 (1998): 201–234.

Forbes, C. A. *Teachers' Pay in Ancient Greece. University of Nebraska Studies in the Humanities*. Vol. 2. Lincoln: University of Nebraska Press, 1942.

Frede, Dorothea. "The Impossibility of Perfection: Socrates' Criticism of Simonides' Poem in the *Protagoras*." *Review of Metaphysics* 39 (1986): 713–753.

Friedlander, Paul. *Plato*. Vol. 3, *The Dialogues: Second and Third Periods*. Translated by Hans Meyerhoff. Princeton: Princeton University Press, 1969.

Gagarin, Michael. "The Purpose of Plato's *Protagoras*." *Transactions and Proceedings of the American Philological Association* 100 (1969): 133–164.

Gaiser, Konrad. *Platons ungeschriebene Lehre*. Stuttgart: Klett, 1959.

Gaiser, Konrad. *Protreptik und Paränese bei Platon: Untersuchengen zur Form des platonischen Dialogus*. Stuttgart: W. Kohlhammer Verlag, 1959.

Gerson, Lloyd P. "Plato *absconditus*." In Gerald Press, ed. *Who Speaks for Plato? Studies in Platonic Anonymity*. Lanham, MD: Rowman & Littlefield, 2000.

Gill, Christopher. "Protreptic and Dialectic in Plato's *Euthydemus*." In Thomas M. Robinson, and Luc Brisson, eds. *Plato: Euthydemus, Lysis, Charmides: Proceedings of the Fifth Symposium Platonicum*. Sankt Augustin: Academia Verlag, 2000.

Gonzalez, Francisco. *Dialectic and Dialogue: Plato's Practice of Philosophical Inquiry*. Evanston, IL: Northwestern University Press, 1998.

Gordon, Jill. *Turning Toward Philosophy: Literary Device and Dramatic Structure in Plato's Dialogues*. University Park: Pennsylvania State University Press, 1999.

Gould, J. *The Development of Plato's Ethics*. New York: Russell & Russell, 1972.

Gower, Barry S., and Michael C. Stokes, eds. *Socratic Questions: New Essays on the Philosophy of Socrates and its Significance*. London and New York: Routledge, 1992.

Griswold, Charles. "Irony in the Platonic Dialogues." In D. W. Conway and P. Kerszberg, eds. *The Sovereignty of Construction: Studies in the Thought of David Lachterman*. Amsterdam: Rodopi, 1996.

Grote, George. *History of Greece*. Vol. 8. London: J. Murray, 1850.

Grote, George. *Plato and the Other Companions of Sokrates*. London: J. Murray, 1868–1870.

Guthrie, W.K.C. *History of Greek Philosophy*. 3 vols. Cambridge: Cambridge University Press, 1969.

Guthrie, W.K.C. *The Sophists*. Cambridge: Cambridge University Press, 1971.

Hamilton, Edith, and Huntington Cairns, eds. *The Collected Dialogues of Plato*. Princeton: Princeton University Press, 1961.

Harrison, E. L. "Was Gorgias a Sophist?" *Phoenix* 18 (1964): 183–192.

Harvey, David, and John Wilkins, eds. *The Rivals of Aristophanes: Studies in Athenian Old Comedy*. London: Duckworth and the Classical Press of Whales, 2000.

Havelock, Eric. *The Liberal Temper in Greek Politics*. New Haven: Yale University Press, 1957.

Hawtrey, R.S.W. *Commentary on Plato's Euthydemus*. Philadelphia: American Philological Society, 1981.

Heath, Thomas. *A History of Greek Mathematics*. Oxford: Oxford University Press, 1921.

Heidegger, Martin. *Plato's Sophist*. Translated by Richard Rojcewicz and Andre Schuwer. Bloomington: Indiana University Press, 1997.

Hemmenway, Scott. "Philosophical Apology in the *Theaetetus.*" *Interpretation* 17, no. 3 (1990): 323–346.

Hemmenway, Scott. "Sophistry Exposed: Socrates on the Unity of Virtue in the *Protagoras.*" *Ancient Philosophy* 16 (1996): 1–23.

Henrichs, A. "The Atheism of Prodicus." *Cronache Ercolanesi* 6 (1976): 15–21.

Henrichs, A. "The Sophists and Hellenistic Religion: Prodicus as the Spiritual Father of the ISIS Aretalogies." *Harvard Studies in Classical Philology* 88 (1984): 139–158.

Henrichs, A. "Two Doxographical Notes: Democritus and Prodicus on Religion." *Harvard Studies in Classical Philology*, vol. 79 (1975): 93–123.

Hermann, Karl Friedrich. *Geschichte und System der platonischen Philosophie*. Heidelberg: Winter, 1839.

Hirzel, Rudolph. *Der Dialog. Ein literarhistorischer Versuch*, vol. I. Leipzig: S. Hirzel, 1895.

Howland, Jacob. *The Paradox of Political Philosophy*. Lanham, MD: Rowman & Littlefield, 1998.

Howland, Jacob. "Re-reading Plato: The Problem of Platonic Chronology." *Phoenix* 45 (1991): 189–214.

Irwin, Terence. *Plato's Ethics*. Oxford: Oxford University Press, 1995.

Irwin, Terence. *Plato's Moral Theory: The Early and Middle Dialogues*. Oxford: Oxford University Press, 1977.

Irwin, Terrence. "Plato's Objections to the Sophists." In C. A. Powell, ed. *The Greek World*. London: Routledge, 1995.

Irwin, Terrence, and Martha Nussbaum, eds. *Virtue, Love and Form: Essays in Memory of Gregory Vlastos*. Edmonton: Academic, 1994.

Jaeger, Werner. *Paideia: The Ideals of Greek Culture*. Vol. 1. Translated by Gilbert Highet. New York: Oxford University Press, 1945.

James, William. "What Pragmatism Means." In *William James: Pragmatism and Other Essays*. New York: Penguin, 2000.

Jowett, Benjamin. *The Dialogues of Plato*. Vol. I. Oxford: Oxford University Press, 1953.

Judson, L., and Karasmanis V., eds. *Remembering Socrates*. Oxford: Oxford University Press, 2006.

Kahn, Charles H. "The Beautiful and the Genuine." *Oxford Studies in Ancient Philosophy* 3 (1985): 267–273.

Kahn, Charles H. "On Platonic Chronology." In Julia Annas and

Christopher Rowe, eds. *New Perspectives on Plato: Modern and Ancient.* Cambridge, MA: Harvard University Press, 2003.

Kahn, Charles H. *Plato and the Socratic Dialogue: The Philosophical Use of a Literary Form.* Cambridge: Cambridge University Press, 1996.

Kassel, Rudolph, and Colin Austin, eds. *Poetae Comici Graeci*, 8 vols. Berlin: Walter de Gruyter, 1983–.

Kerferd, G. B. "The First Greek Sophists." *Classical Review* 64 (1950): 8–10.

Kerferd, G. B. "Future Direction of Sophistic Studies." In G. B. Kerferd, ed. *The Sophists and their Legacy.* Wiesbaden: Franz Steiner Verlag, 1981.

Kerferd, G. B. "Plato's Noble Art of Sophistry: *Sophist* 226a–231b." *Classical Quarterly*, n. s. IV (1954): 84–90.

Kerferd, G. B. "Protagoras' Doctrine of Justice and Virtue in the *Protagoras* of Plato." *Journal of Hellenic Studies* 73 (1953): 42–45.

Kerferd, G. B. *The Sophistic Movement.* Cambridge: Cambridge University Press, 1981.

Kerferd, G. B. "Sophists." In Paul Edwards, ed. *The Encyclopedia of Philosophy.* Vol. 7. New York: Macmillan, 1967.

Kerferd, G. B., ed. *The Sophists and their Legacy.* Wiesbaden: Franz Steiner Verlag, 1981.

Keulen, Herman. *Untersuchungen zu Platons* "Euthydem." Wiesbaden: Otto Harrassowitz, 1971.

Klosko, George. *The Development of Plato's Political Theory.* New York: Metheun, 1986.

Kraut, Richard. *Socrates and the State.* Princeton: Princeton University Press, 1984.

Lampert, Laurence. "Socrates' Defense of Polytropic Odysseus: Lying and Wrong-Doing in Plato's *Lesser Hippias.*" *Review of Politics* 64 (2002): 231–259.

Leake, James. "Hippias Minor." In Thomas Pangle, ed. *The Roots of Political Philosophy: Ten Forgotten Socratic Dialogues.* Ithaca: Cornell University Press, 1987.

Ledger, G. R. *Re-counting Plato.* Oxford: Oxford University Press, 1989.

MacIntyre, Alasdair. *After Virtue: A Study in Moral Theory.* Notre Dame: University of Notre Dame Press, 1981.

Mackenzie, M. M. *Plato on Punishment.* Berkeley: 1981.

Maguire, Joseph P. "Protagoras—or Plato?" *Phronesis* 18 (1973): 115–138.

Mailloux, Steven, ed. *Rhetoric, Sophistry, Pragmatism*. Cambridge: Cambridge University Press, 1995.

Marrou, H. I. *A History of Greek Education in Antiquity*. Translated by George Lamb. New York: Mentor Books, 1956.

Mayer, Herman. *Prodikos von Keos und die Angänge der Synonymik bei den Griechen*. Paderborn: Ferdinand Schöningh, 1913.

McCoy, Marina. "Alcidamas, Isocrates, and Plato on Speech, Writing, and Philosophical Rhetoric." *Ancient Philosophy* 29 (2009): 45–66.

McCoy, Marina. *Plato on the Rhetoric of Philosophers and Sophists*. Cambridge: Cambridge University Press, 2008.

McCoy, Marina. "Reason and Dialectic in the Argument against Protagoras in the *Theaetetus*." *International Philosophical Quarterly* 45, no. 1 (2005): 22–39.

McCoy, Marina. "Socrates on Simonides: The Uses of Poetry in Socratic and Platonic Rhetoric." *Philosophy and Rhetoric* 32 (1999): 349–367.

McDowell, John. *Plato: Theaetetus*. Oxford: Clarendon Press, 1973.

McMahon, Robert. *Understanding the Medieval Meditative Ascent: Augustine, Anselm, Boethius and Dante*. Washington, DC: Catholic University Press, 2006.

Menzel, Adolf. "Protagoras, der älteste Theoretiker der Demokratie." *Zeitschrift für Politik* 3 (1910): 205–238.

Michelini, Ann N. "Socrates Plays the Buffoon: Cautionary Protreptic in *Euthydemus*." *American Journal of Philology* 121 (2000): 509–535.

Mill, John Stuart. *On Liberty*. Boston: Ticknor and Fields, 1862.

Momigliano, Arnaldo D. "Podico di Ceo e le Dottrine del Linguaggio da Democrito ai Cinici." *Atti della Accedemia delle Scienze di Torino, Classe di Scienza Morali, Storiche e Filologiche* 65 (1929–30): 95–107.

Moreau, Joseph. *Platon devant les sophists*. Paris: J. Vrin, 1987.

Mulhern, J. J. "Two Interpretive Fallacies." *Systematics* 9 (1971): 168–172.

Nails, Debra. *Agora, Academy, and the Conduct of Philosophy*. Dordrecht: Kluwer, 1995.

Nails, Debra. *The People of Plato: A Prosopography of Plato and Other Socratics*. Indianapolis: Hackett, 2002.

Narcy, Michael. *Le philosophe et son double. Un commentaire de l'Euthydème de Platon*. Paris, Librairie Philosophique J. Vrin, 1984.

Natorp, Paul. *Platos Edeenlehre*. Leipzig: Verlag von Felix Meiner, 1921.

Nehamas, Alexander. *The Art of Living*. Berkeley: University of California Press, 1998.

Nestle, Wilhelm. "Die Horen des Prodikos." *Hermes* 71 (1936): 151–170.

Nestle, Wilhelm. *Vom Mythos zum Logos: Die Selbstentfaltung des griechischen Denkens von Homer bis auf die Sophistik und Sokrates*. Stuttgart: Kroner, 1942.

Nichols, James H., Jr. *Plato: Gorgias*. Ithaca: Cornell University Press, 1998.

Nichols, Mary. *Socrates on Friendship and Community: Reflections on Plato's* Symposium, Phaedrus, *and* Lysis. Cambridge: Cambridge University Press, 2009.

Norlin, George. *Isocrates with an English Translation*. Cambridge: Harvard University Press, 1980.

Notomi, Noburu. *The Unity of Plato's* Sophist*: Between the Sophist and the Philosopher*. Cambridge: Cambridge University Press, 1999.

Oates, W., and E. O'Neill, Jr., ed. *Complete Greek Drama*, vol. 2. New York: Random House, 1938.

Obbink, D. *Philodemus On Piety Part I: Critical Text with Commentary*. Oxford: Oxford University Press, 1996.

Ostwald, Martin. *Aristotle: Nicomachean Ethics*. New Jersey: Library of Liberal Arts, 1962.

Pangle, Thomas. *The Roots of Political Philosophy: Ten Forgotten Dialogues*. Ithaca: Cornell University Press, 1987.

Pohlenz, M. *Aus Platons Werdezeit*. Berlin: Weidmann, 1913.

Popper, Karl. *The Open Society and Its Enemies*. Vol. 1, *The Spell of Plato*. Princeton University Press, 1966.

Poulakos, John. *Sophistical Rhetoric in Classical Greece*. Columbia: University of South Carolina Press, 1995.

Powell, C. A., ed. *The Greek World*. London: Routledge, 1995.

Praechter, Karl. "Platon und Euthydemos." *Philologus* 87 (1932): 121–135.

Press, Gerald A. "The State of the Question in the Study of Plato." *Southern Journal of Philosophy* 34 (1996): 507–522.

Press, Gerald A., ed. *Who Speaks for Plato? Studies in Platonic Anonymity*. Lanham, MD: Rowman & Littlefield, 2000.

Prior, William J. "Protagoras' Great Speech and Plato's Defense of Athenian Democracy." In Victor Caston and Daniel Graham, ed.

Presocratic Philosophy: Essays in Honour of Alexander Mourelatos. Burlington, VT: Ashgate, 2002.

Prior, William J. *Unity and Development in Plato's Metaphysics*. LaSalle, IL: Open Court, 1985.

Raeder, Hans. "Platon und die Rhetoren." *Proceedings of the Royal Danish Academy* (1956).

Raeder, Hans. "Platon und die Sophisten." *Proceedings of the Royal Danish Academy* (1938).

Raven, J. E. *Plato's Thought in the Making: A Study of the Development of his Metaphysics*. Cambridge: Cambridge University Press, 1965.

Reale, Giovanni. *Per una nuava interpretatzione di Platone: Rilettura della metafisica dei grandi dialoghi alla luce delle "Dottrine non scritte."* Milan: Vita e Pensiero, 1987.

Rensi, Giuseppe. *Introduzione alla sceptsi etica*. Firenze: F. Perrella, 1921.

Robinson, Richard. *Plato's Earlier Dialectic*, 2nd ed. Oxford: Clarendon Press, 1984.

Robinson, Thomas M. *Contrasting Arguments: An Edition of the Dissoi Logoi*. Salem: Ayer, 1984.

Robinson, Thomas M., and Luc Brisson, eds. *Plato: Euthydemus, Lysis, Charmides: Proceedings of the Fifth Symposium Platonicum*. Sankt Augustin: Academia Verlag, 2000.

Romilly, Jacqueline De. *The Great Sophists in Periclean Athens*. Translated by Janet Lloyd. Oxford: Clarendon Press, 1992.

Roochnik, David. *Of Art and Wisdom: Plato's Understanding of Technē*. University Park: Pennsylvania State University Press, 1996.

Roochnik, David. "Self-Recognition in Plato's *Theaetetus*." *Ancient Philosophy* 22, no. 1 (2002): 37–52.

Roochnik, David. "The Serious Play of Plato's *Euthydemus*." *Interpretation* 18 (1991): 211–232.

Rowe, C. J. *Plato and the Art of Philosophical Writing*. Cambridge: Cambridge University Press, 2007.

Rowe, C. J. "Plato on the Sophists as Teachers of Virtue." *History of Political Thought* 4 (1983): 409–427.

Rowe, C. J. *Plato: Poets, Orators, Sophists*. Brighton: Harvester, 1984.

Samons, L. J. II, ed. *Cambridge Companion to the Age of Pericles*. Cambridge: Cambridge University Press, 2009.

Santayana, George. "The Irony of Liberalism." In George Santayana,

Soliloquies in England and Later Soliloquies. New York: Charles Scribner's Sons, 1922.
Saunders, T. J. *Plato's Penal Code*. Oxford: Oxford University Press, 1991.
Sayre, Kenneth. *Plato's Literary Garden: How to Read a Platonic Dialogue*. Notre Dame, IL: University of Notre Dame Press, 2002
Schiappa, Edward. *Protagoras and Logos: A Study in Greek Philosophy and Rhetoric*. Columbia: University of South Carolina Press, 1991.
Schiller, F.C.S. *Humanism: Philosophical Essays*. London and New York: Macmillan, 1903.
Schiller, F.C.S. *Studies in Humanism*. London: Macmillan, 1907.
Schofield, Malcolm. *Saving the City: Philosopher-Kings and Other Classical Paradigms*. Cambridge: Cambridge University Press, 1999.
Schofield, Malcolm. "Socrates versus Protagoras." In Barry S. Gower and Michael C. Stokes, eds. *Socratic Questions: New Essays on the Philosophy of Socrates and its Significance*. London and New York: Routledge, 1992.
Schram, J. M. "Prodicus' Fifty-drachma Show Lecture." *Antioch Review* 25 (1965): 105–130.
Schultz, Anne-Marie. *Plato's Socrates as Narrator: A Philosophical Muse*. Lanham: Lexington Books, 2013.
Sidgwick, Henry. *Lectures on the Philosophy of Kant and Other Philosophical Lectures and Essays*. London: Macmillan, 1905.
Sidgwick, Henry. "The Sophists." *Journal of Philology* 4 (1872): 288–307.
Slings, S. R. *Plato: Clitophon*. Cambridge: Cambridge University Press, 1999.
Sprague, Rosamond Kent. "The *Euthydemus* Revisited." In Thomas M. Robinson and Luc Brisson, eds. *Plato: Euthydemus, Lysis, Charmides: Proceedings of the Fifth Symposium Platonicum*. Sankt Augustin: Academia Verlag, 2000.
Sprague, Rosamond Kent. *Plato's Philosopher King*. Columbia: University of South Carolina Press, 1976.
Sprague, Rosamond Kent. "Plato's Sophistry." *Supplementary Volume of the Aristotelian Society* 51 (1977): 45–61.
Sprague, Rosamond Kent. *Plato's Use of Fallacy: A Study of the* Euthydemus *and Some other Dialogues*. London: Routledge, 1962.
Sprague, Rosamond Kent, ed. *The Older Sophists*. Columbia: University of South Carolina Press, 1972.

Stalley, R. F. "Punishment in Plato's 'Protagoras'" *Phronesis* 40 (1995): 1–19.

Stewart, D. J. "Prodicus." In R. K. Sprague, ed. *The Older Sophists*. Columbia: University of South Carolina Press, 1972.

Stewart, M. A. "Plato's Sophistry." *The Aristotelian Society*, Supplementary Volume LI (1977): 21–44.

Storey, Ian C. *Eupolis: Poet of Old Comedy*. Oxford: Oxford University Press, 2003.

Strauss, Leo. *City and Man*. Chicago: University of Chicago Press, 1964.

Strauss, Leo. "On the Euthydemus." *Interpretation* 1 (1970): 1–20.

Szlezák, Thomas. *Platon lesen*. Stuttgart: Verlag frommann-holzboog, 1993.

Szlezák, Thomas. *Reading Plato*. Translated by Graham Zanker. London: Routledge, 1996.

Szlezák, Thomas. "Socrates' Spott über Geheimhaltung: Zum Bild des φιλόσοφος in Platons 'Euthydemos.'" *Antike und Abendland* 26 (1980): 75–89.

Tarnopolsky, Christina H. *Prudes, Perverts and Tyrants: Plato's Gorgias and the Politics of Shame*. Princeton: Princeton University Press, 2010.

Taylor, A. E. *Plato: The Man and his Work*. London: University Paperbacks, 1960.

Taylor, C.C.W. *Plato: Protagoras*. Oxford: Clarendon Press, 1991.

Taylor, C.C.W. "Socrates the Sophist." In L. Judson and V. Karasmanis, eds. *Remembering Socrates*. Oxford: Oxford University Press, 2006.

Thesleff, Holger. "Platonic Chronology." *Phronesis* 34 (1989): 1–26.

Thesleff, Holger. *Studies in Platonic Chronology*. Helsinki: Societas Scientiarum Fennica, 1982.

Tigerstedt, E. N. *Interpreting Plato*. Stockholm: Almqvist and Wiksell, 1977.

Trevaskis, J. R. "The Sophistry of Noble Lineage." *Phronesis* I (1955/56): 36–49.

Trivigno, Franco V. "Childish Nonesense? The Value of Interpretation in Plato's Protagoras." *Journal of the History of Philosophy* 51 (2013): 509–543.

Untersteiner, Mario. *The Sophists*. Translated by Kathleen Freeman. Oxford: Basil Blackwell, 1954.

Versényi, L. *Socratic Humanism*. Yale: Yale University Press, 1963.

Vlastos, Gregory. "The Demise of the Elenchus in the *Euthydemus*, *Lysis* and *Hippias Major*." In Miles Burnyeat, ed. *Socratic Studies*. Cambridge: Cambridge University Press, 1994.

Vlastos, Gregory. *Socrates: Ironist and Moral Philosopher*. Cambridge: Cambridge University Press, 1991.

Voegelin, Eric. *The New Science of Politics*. Chicago: University of Chicago Press, 1952.

Voegelin, Eric. *Order and History*. Vol. 2, *The World of the Polis*. Baton Rouge: Louisiana State University Press, 1957.

Voegelin, Eric. *Order and History*. Vol. 3, *Plato and Aristotle*. Baton Rouge: Louisiana State University, 1957.

Wallace, Robert W. "Plato's Sophists, Intellectual History after 450, and Socrates." In L. J. Samons II, *Cambridge Companion to the Age of Pericles*. Cambridge: Cambridge University Press, 2009.

Waterfield, Robin. *The First Philosophers: The Presocratics and Sophists*. Oxford: Oxford University Press, 2000.

Weber, Max. "The Meaning of 'Ethical Neutrality' in Sociology and Economics." In Edward Shils and Henry Finch, trans. *Max Weber on the Methodology of the Social Sciences*. Glencoe: Free Press, 1949.

Weiss, Roslyn. "*Ho Agathos* as *Ho Dunatos* in the *Hippias Minor*." *Classical Quarterly* 31 (1981): 287–304.

Weiss, Roslyn. *The Socratic Paradox and Its Enemies*. Chicago: University of Chicago Press, 1998.

West, Thomas G., and Grace Starry West. *Four Texts on Socrates: Plato's* Euthyphro, Apology, *and* Crito *and Aristophanes'* Clouds. Ithaca: Cornell University Press, 1998.

Wilamowitz-Moellendorff, Enno Friedrich Wichard Ulrich von. *Platon*. Berlin: Weidmann, 1919.

Wolfsdorf, D. "The Historical Reader of Plato's *Protagoras*." *Classical Quarterly* 48 (1998): 126–133.

Woodruff, Paul. *Plato: Hippias Major*. Indianapolis: Hackett, 1982.

Zuckert, Catherine H. *Plato's Philosophers: The Coherence of the Dialogues*. Chicago: University of Chicago Press, 2009.

Zuckert, Catherine, H. "Socrates v. the Sophists?" Paper presented at the annual meeting of the American Political Science Association, 2004.

Zuckert, Catherine, H. "Who's a Philosopher? Who's a Sophist? The Stranger v. Socrates." *Review of Metaphysics* 54 (2000): 65–97.

INDEX